제6판

교원임용고시
일반영어 필독서

임용영어 수험생 대다수가 선택하는
전공영어의 보통명사

- 교원임용고시 전공영어 독보적 전국 1위
  (2025년 예스24 전공영어 부문 박문각 누적 판매량 1위)
- 미국 버클리대학 유희태 박사의 독창적 문제집
- 출제가능성 높은 예상문제 수록

유희태 일반영어
2S2R 4-1 문제은행

LSI 영어연구소 유희태 박사 저

박문각

PREFACE

2026년 《2S2R 문제은행》 6판을 내며

2014년 초판이 출간된 후 12년, 5판이 나온 뒤 3년이 지났다. 그 기간 동안 노량진에서 강의를 하면서 5판의 장점과 단점에 대해 수험생들과 의견을 교환할 기회가 많았다. 이 6판은 그 대화의 산물로, 5판과 형식적인 면에서 비교했을 때 많이 다르다. 즉, 5판이 모든 문제를 문제은행 방식으로 배치하였다면 6판은 문제은행(Part 01)과 모의고사(Part 02)로 분리하였다. 이 형식은 기존과는 많이 다른데, 수험생들의 반응이 어떨지 궁금하다.

내용적인 면에서 본다면, 6판은 5판과 유사하다. 우선 6판에서 다룬 주제도 우리가 살아가면서 겪게 되는 대다수의 영역(역사, 미학, 철학, 음악, 사회학, 사회복지학, 심리학, 소수민족학, 인종학, 인류학, 정치학, 경영학, 경제학, 교육학, 물리학, 생물학, 의학, 지질학, 인류학, 지리학 등)이 들어가 있어서 수험생들이 다양한 주제들을 접할 수 있도록 하였던 5판의 정신을 그대로 가져왔다. 또한 문제를 푸는 과정에서 일반영어 만점에 필수적인 배경지식을 자동으로 증진시킬 수 있도록 하였다. 그렇기에, 배경지식이 부족한 수험생들이 그 지식을 익히려 따로 시간을 내 다른 교재를 볼 필요가 없도록 하였다.

또한 양적인 면에서는 5판이 총 60회 분량이었다면, 이번 6판은 Part 01인 문제은행에 총 174개의 문제와 Part 02인 모의고사에 총 70회 분량의 문제를 수록해 실로 방대한 분량이라 할 만하다. 대다수의 임용 수험생들은 일반영어 문제에 목말라 있다. 실제 임용고시 문제와 유사하면서도 질 좋은(오류가 없고 타당도가 높은) 문제가 안타깝게도 임용 영어시험 시장에 많이 않기 때문이다. 시간이 가면 갈수록, 임용시험 시장이 작아지는 추세이다 보니, 현실적으로 출판사들 입장에서는 임용교재 출판으로는 경제적 수지타산이 거의 맞지 않기에 임용교재를 출판하려 하지 않고, 저자들도 고생에 비해 너무 적은 보답이 오다보니 새롭고 독창적인 교재 개발은 거의 불가능해졌다. 더군다나 노량진 임용고시 수험시장에서 가장 오랜 세월 강의를 하고, 이른바 일타 강사라 불리는 저자가 경제적인 부분만 생각할 수는 없는 일이어서 이 척박한 상황에 조금이나마 도움이 되어야 한다는 책임감을 느끼고 이 교재를 출간하기로 했다. 저자도 이제 나이가 들었는지 교재작업을 하는 일이 갈수록 힘에 부침을 느낀다. 아마 6판이 마지막이 되지 않을까 생각도 해본다. 물론 미래는 그 누구도 알 수는 없지만 말이다. 시험을 준비하는 수험생들이 더욱 풍부하고 질 좋은 문제를 풀어봄으로써 일반영어 실력이 향상된다면 저자로선 더할 나위 없이 고마운 일이 될 듯하다.

이 6판 교재는 《유희태 일반영어 시리즈 ① - 2S2R 기본》, 《유희태 일반영어 시리즈 ② - 2S2R 유형》, 《유희태 일반영어 시리즈 ③ - 2S2R 기출》, 《유희태 일반영어 시리즈 ⑤ - 기출 VOCA 30days》의 자매편이다. 시리즈를 통해 길러진 일반영어에 대한 이론, 유형, 기출, 그리고 어휘를 문제은행에 적용해 보도록 짜여있다. 이 시리즈를 통해서 공부한다면 임용고시에서 기본과목이라 할 수 있는 일반영어가 상당 정도 손에 잡힐 것으로 확신한다.

『유희태 2S2R 시리즈』를 효과적으로 활용하는 방법은, 대학 1학년 때 《2S2R 기본》을 최소 3회독, 평균 5회독하여 일반영어 기본이론을 확실하게 다진 뒤, 2학년 때 《2S2R 유형》을 최소 3회독하여 임용 유형에 기본이론을 확장 적용하는 훈련을 하고, 3학년 때 《2S2R 기출》을 2회독한 다음, 처음으로 임용시험을 치르는 4학년 때 《2S2R 문제은행》을 가지고 공부하는 것이다. 이 과정에서 《기출 VOCA 30days》는 1학년 때부터 주 6회 매일 20분씩 꾸준히 공부하기를 추천한다. 그러면 4학년 11월 임용시험을 치를 때가 되면, 임용에 필요한 어휘의 80%는 머릿속에 차곡차곡 쌓여서, 독해를 하는 데 있어 어휘의 부족은 느끼지 않을 것이다. 수험생 각자가 처한 상황에 맞춰서 공부해야 하겠지만, 가능하면 빨리 시작하는 것이 더욱 큰 효과가 날 것이란 것은 두말할 필요가 없다.

이 6판 작업을 하면서 많은 분의 도움을 받았다. 원고를 보기 좋은 최종 결과물로 만들어준 박문각의 변수경 편집자와 박용 회장님께 고마움을 전한다. 또한 교재가 세상에 나오기까지 묵묵히 최선을 다해주신 모든 인쇄·출판 노동자분들께도 깊은 감사의 마음을 전한다. 아무쪼록 이 《2S2R 문제은행》 6판 교재가 수험생 여러분의 합격에 일조하기를 깊은 마음으로 바란다.

2026년 새해를 앞두고 LSI 영어연구소에서

유희태

CONTENTS

PART 01 문제은행[001~174]　　010

● 모범답안 및 번역　　004

PART 02 모의고사

모의고사 Ⅰ (제01회~제25회 모의고사)
모의고사 Ⅱ (제26회~제70회 모의고사)

● 모범답안 및 번역

※ PART 02 모의고사는 《유희태 전공영어 일반영어 ④-2-2S2R 문제은행》에 수록돼 있음

유희태 일반영어
④-1 문제은행

2S2R

유희태 일반영어

④-1 문제은행

PART 01

문제은행[001~174]

Part 01 문제은행 [001~174]

001 Read the passage and follow the directions. [4 points]

In the early days of the United States, postal charges were paid by the recipient and charges varied with the distance carried. In 1825, the United States Congress permitted local postmasters to give letters to mail carriers for home delivery, but these carriers received no government salary and their entire compensation on what they were paid by the recipients of individual letters.

In 1847 the United States Post Office Department adopted the idea of a postage stamp, which of course simplified the payment for postal service but caused grumbling by those who did not like to prepay. Besides, the stamp covered only delivery to the post office and did not include carrying it to a private address. In <u>Philadelphia</u>, for example, with a population of 150,000, people still had to go to the post office to get their mail. The confusion and congestion of individual citizens looking for their letters was itself enough to discourage use of the mail. It is no wonder that, during the years of these cumbersome arrangements, private letter-carrying and express businesses developed. Although their activities were only semilegal, they thrived, and actually advertised that between Boston and Philadelphia they were a half-day speedier than the government mail. The government postal service lost volume to private competition and was not able to handle efficiently even the business it had.

Finally, in 1863, Congress provided that the mail carriers who delivered the mail from the post offices to private addresses should receive a government salary, and that there should be no extra charge for that delivery. But this delivery service was at first confined to cities, and free home delivery became a mark of urbanism. As late as 1887, a town had to have 10,000 people to be eligible for free home delivery. In 1890, of the 75 million people in the United States. Fewer than 20 million had mail delivered free to their doors. The rest, nearly three-quarters of the population, still received no mail unless they went to their _____.

Fill in the blank with the TWO most appropriate consecutive words from the passage. Then, explain why the writer of the passage mentions the city of Philadelphia.

002 Read the passage and follow the directions. [4 points]

Archaeology has long been an accepted tool for studying _____. Relatively recently the same techniques have been systematically applied to studies of the more immediate past. This has been called "historical archaeology," a term that is used in the United States to refer to any archaeological investigation into North American sites that postdate the arrival of Europeans.

Back in the 1930s and 1940s, when building restoration was popular, historical archaeology was primarily a tool of architectural reconstruction. The role of archaeologists was to find the foundations of historic buildings and then take a back seat to architects.

The mania for reconstruction had largely subsided by the 1950s and 1960s. Most people entering historical archaeology during this period came out of university anthropology departments, where they had studied prehistoric cultures. They were, by training, social scientists, not historians, and their work tended to reflect this bias. The questions they framed and the techniques they used were designed to help them understand, as scientists, how people behaved. But because they were treading on historical ground for which there was often extensive written documentation and because their own knowledge of these periods was usually limited, their contributions to American history remained circumscribed. Their reports, highly technical and sometimes poorly written, went unread.

More recently, professional archaeologists have taken over. These researchers have sought to demonstrate that their work can be a valuable tool not only of science but also of history, providing fresh insights into the daily lives of ordinary people whose existences might not otherwise be so well documented. This newer emphasis on archaeology as social history has shown great promise, and indeed work done in this area has lead to a reinterpretation of the United States past.

In Kingston, New York, for example, evidence has been uncovered that indicates that English goods were being smuggled into that city at a time when the Dutch supposedly controlled trading in the area. And in Sacramento an excavation at the site of a fashionable nineteenth-century hotel revealed that garbage had been stashed in the building's basement despite sanitation laws to the contrary.

Fill in the blank with the TWO most appropriate consecutive words from the passage. Second, explain the reason why the writer mentions an excavation at the site of a hotel in Sacramento.

003 Read the passage and follow the directions. [4 points]

When Jules Verne wrote *Journey to the Center of the Earth* in 1864, there were many conflicting theories about the nature of the Earth's interior. Some geologists thought that it contained a highly compressed ball of incandescent gas, while others suspected that it consisted of separate shells, each made of a different material. Today, well over a century later, there is still little direct evidence of what lies beneath our feet. Most of our knowledge of the Earth's interior comes not from mines or boreholes, but from the study of seismic waves—powerful pulses of energy released by earthquakes.

The way that seismic waves travel shows that the _____ is far from uniform. The continents and the seabed are formed by the crust—a thin sphere of relatively light, solid rock. Beneath the crust lies the mantle, a very different layer that extends approximately halfway to the Earth's center. There the rock is the subject of a battle between increasing heat and growing pressure.

In its high levels, the mantle is relatively cool; at greater depths, high temperatures make the rock behave more like a liquid than a solid. Deeper still, the pressure is even more intense, preventing the rock from melting in spite of a higher temperature.

Beyond a depth of around 2,900 kilometers, a great change takes place and the mantle gives way to the core. Some seismic waves cannot pass through the core and others are bent by it. From this and other evidence, geologists conclude that the outer core is probably liquid, with a solid center. It is almost certainly made of iron, mixed with smaller amounts of other elements such as nickel.

The conditions in the Earth's core make it a far more alien world than space. Its solid iron heart is subjected to unimaginable pressure and has a temperature of about 9,000°F. Although scientists can speculate about its nature, neither humans nor machines will ever be able to visit it.

Fill in the blank with the TWO most appropriate consecutive words from the passage. Second, explain why the writer states that the Earth's core is more alien than space.

004 Read the passage and follow the directions. [4 points]

Despite the road improvements of the turnpike era (1790-1830), Americans continued as in colonial times to depend wherever possible on water routes for travel and transportation. The larger rivers, especially the Mississippi and the Ohio, became increasingly useful as steamboats grew in number and improved in design.

River boats carried to New Orleans the corn and other crops of northwestern farmers, the cotton and tobacco of southwestern planters. From New Orleans, ships took the cargoes on to eastern seaports. Neither the farmers of the west nor the merchants of the east were completely satisfied with this pattern of trade. Farmers could get better prices for their crops if the alternative existed of sending them directly eastward to market and merchants could sell larger quantities of their manufactured goods if these could be transported more directly and more economically to the west.

New waterways were needed. Sectional jealousies and constitutional scruples stood in the way of action by the federal government and necessary expenditures were too great for private enterprise. If extensive canals were to be dug, the job would be up to the various states.

New York was the first to act. It had the natural advantage of a comparatively level route between the Hudson River and Lake Erie, through the only break in the entire Appalachian Mountain chain. Yet the engineering tasks were imposing. The distance was more than 350 miles and there were ridges to cross and a wilderness of woods and swamps to penetrate. The Erie Canal begun in 1817 and completed in 1825, was by far the greatest construction job that Americans had ever undertaken. It quickly proved a financial success as well. The prosperity of the Erie encouraged the state to enlarge its canal system by building several branches.

The range of the New York canal system was still further extended when the states of Ohio and Indiana, inspired by the success of the Erie Canal, provided water connections between Lake Erie and the Ohio River.

Identify what the underlined "this pattern of trade" refers to. Then, describe what the next paragraph of this text most likely discusses, as can be inferred from the passage.

005 Read the passage and answer the questions. [4 points]

Legend has it that sometime toward the end of the Civil War (1861-1865) a government train carrying oxen traveling through the northern plains of eastern Wyoming was caught in a snowstorm and had to be abandoned. The driver returned the next spring to see what had become of his cargo. Instead of the skeletons he had expected to find, he saw his oxen, living, fat, and healthy. How had they survived? The answer lay in a resource that unknowing Americans had trampled underfoot in their haste to cross the "Great American Desert" to reach lands that sometimes proved barren. In the eastern parts of the United States, the preferred grass for forage was a cultivated plant. It grew well with enough rain, then when cut and stored it would cure and become nourishing hay for winter feed. But in the dry grazing lands of the West that familiar bluejoint grass was often killed by drought. To raise cattle out there seemed risky or even hopeless.

Who could imagine a fairy-tale grass that required no rain and somehow made it possible for cattle to feed themselves all winter? But the surprising western wild grasses did just that. They had wonderfully convenient features that made them superior to the cultivated eastern grasses. Variously known as buffalo grass, grama grass, or mesquite grass, not only were they immune to drought; but they were actually preserved by the lack of summer and autumn rains. They were not juicy like the cultivated eastern grasses, but had short, hard stems. And they did not need to be cured in a barn, but dried right where they grew on the ground. When they dried in this way, they remained naturally sweet and nourishing through the winter. Cattle left outdoors to fend for themselves thrived on this hay. And the cattle themselves helped plant the fresh grass year after year for they trampled the natural seeds firmly into the soil to be watered by the melting snows of winter and the occasional rains of spring. The dry summer air cured them much as storing in a barn cured the cultivated grasses.

According to the above passage, which grass was preferred in the eastern parts of the United States? Next, describe the way cattle promote the growth of western grasses.

006 **Read the passage and follow the directions.** [4 points]

> Seventeenth-century houses in colonial North America were simple structures that were primarily functional carrying over traditional designs that went back to the Middle Ages. During the first half of the eighteenth century, however, houses began to show a new elegance. As wealth increased, more and more colonists built fine houses. Since architecture was not yet a specialized profession in the colonies, the design of buildings was left either to amateur designers or to carpenters who undertook to interpret architectural manuals imported from England. Inventories of colonial libraries show an astonishing number of these handbooks for builders, and the houses erected during the eighteenth century show their influence. Nevertheless, most domestic architecture of the first three-quarters of the eighteenth century displays a wide divergence of taste and freedom of application of the rules laid down in these books. Increasing wealth and growing sophistication throughout the colonies resulted in houses of improved design, whether the material was wood, stone, or brick. New England still favored wood, though brick houses became common in Boston and other towns, where the danger of fire gave an impetus to the use of more durable material. A few houses in New England were built of stone, but only in Pennsylvania and adjacent areas was stone widely used in dwellings. An increased use of brick in houses and outbuildings is noticeable in Virginia and Maryland, but wood remained that most popular material even in houses built by wealthy landowners. In the Carolinas, even in closely packed Charleston, wooden houses were much more common than brick houses.

Eighteenth-century houses showed great interior improvements over their predecessors. Windows were made larger and shutters removed. Large, clear panes replaced the small leaded glass of the seventeenth century. Doorways were larger and more decorative. Fireplaces became decorative features of rooms. Walls were made of plaster or wood, sometimes elaborately paneled. White paint began to take the place of blues, yellows, greens, and lead colors, which had been popular for walls in the earlier years. After about 1730, advertisements for wallpaper styles in scenic patterns began to appear in colonial newspapers.

In the above passage, identify to what the underlined "predecessors" refers. Next, describe what can be inferred about the use of patterned wallpaper before 1730.

007 Read the passage and follow the directions. [4 points]

> Bloodhounds are biologically adapted to trailing their prey. The process by which the nose recognizes an odor is not fully understood, but there are apparently specific receptor sites for specific odors. In one explanation, _____ occurs when a scent molecule fits into its corresponding receptor site, like a key into a lock, causing a mechanical or chemical change in the cell. Bloodhounds apparently have denser concentrations of receptor sites tuned to human scents.
>
> When a bloodhound trails a human being, what does it actually smell? The human body, which consists of about 60 trillion living cells, sheds exposed skin at a rate of 50 million cells a day. So even a trail that has been dispersed by breezes may still seem rich to a bloodhound. The body also produces about 31 to 50 ounces of sweat a day. Neither this fluid nor the shed skin cells have much odor by themselves, but the bacteria working on both substances is another matter. One microbiologist estimates the resident bacteria population of a clean square centimeter of skin on the human shoulder at "multiples of a million." As they go about their daily business breaking down lipids, or fatty substances, on the skin, these bacteria release volatile substances that usually strike the bloodhound's nose as an entire constellation of distinctive scents, enabling precise recognition of individual human trails.

Fill in the blank with the ONE most appropriate word from the passage. Second, from what exact source do bloodhounds gather the smells used to trail a human?

008 Read the passage and follow the directions. [4 points]

It is commonly believed that in the United States that school is where people go to get an education. Nevertheless, it has been said that today <u>children interrupt their education</u> to go to school. The distinction between schooling and education implied by this remark is important.

Education is much more open-ended and all-inclusive than schooling. Education knows no bounds. It can take place anywhere, whether in the shower or on the job, whether in a kitchen or on a tractor. It includes both the formal learning that takes place in schools and the whole universe of informal learning. The agents of education can range from a revered grandparent to the people debating politics on the radio, from a child to a distinguished scientist. Whereas schooling has a certain predictability, education quite often produces surprises. A chance conversation with a stranger may lead a person to discover how little is known of other religions. People are engaged in education from infancy on. Education, then, is a very broad, inclusive term. It is a lifelong process, a process that starts long before the start of school, and one that should be an integral part of one's entire life.

Schooling, on the other hand, is a specific, formalized process, whose general pattern varies little from one setting to the next. Throughout a country, children arrive at school at approximately the same time, take assigned seats, are taught by an adult, use similar textbooks, do homework, take exams, and so on. The slices of reality that are to be learned, whether they are the alphabet or an understanding of the workings of governments, have usually been limited by the boundaries of the subject being taught. For example, high schools students know that they are not likely to find out in their classes the truth about political problems in their communities or what the newest filmmakers are experimenting with. There are definite conditions surrounding the formalized process of schooling.

Explain the meaning of the underlined words. Next, in terms of potential age of the instructors, how does formal schooling contrast with the informal "agents of education" mentioned in the passage.

009 Read the passage and follow the directions. [4 points]

> The hard, rigid plates that form the outermost portion of the Earth are about 100 kilometers thick. These plates include both the Earth's crust and the upper mantle. The rocks of the crust are composed mostly of minerals with light elements, like aluminum and sodium, while the mantle contains some heavier elements, like iron and magnesium. Together, the crust and upper mantle that form the surface plates are called the lithosphere. This rigid layer floats on the denser material of the lower mantle the way a wooden raft flats on a pond. The plates are supported by a weak, plastic layer of the lower mantle called the asthenosphere. Also like a raft on a pond, the lithospheric plates are carried along by slow currents in this more fluid layer beneath them.
>
> With an understating of plate tectonics, geologists have put together a new history for the Earth's surface. About 200 million years ago, the plates at the Earth's surface formed a "supercontinent" called Pangaea. When this supercontinent started to tear apart because of plate movement, Pangaea first broke into two large continental masses with a newly formed sea that grew between the land areas as the depression filled with water. The southern one—which included the modern continents of South America, Africa, Australia, and Antarctic—is called Gondwanaland. The northern one—with North America, Europe, and Asia—is called Laurasi. North America tore away from Europe about 180 million years ago, forming the northern Atlantic Ocean. Some of the lithospheric plates carry ocean floor and others carry land masses or a combination of the two types. The movement of the lithospheric plates is responsible for earthquakes, volcanoes, and the Earth's largest mountain ranges. Current understating of the interaction between different plates explains why these occur where they do. For example, the edge of the Pacific Ocean has been called the "Ring of Fire" because so many volcanic eruptions and earthquakes happen there. Before the 1960s, geologist could not explain why active volcanoes and strong earthquakes were concentrated in that region. The theory of plate tectonics gave them an answer.

Explain why Pangaea is described as a "supercontinent". Next, identify the three key features understood to be related to the movements carrying lithospheric plates.

010 Read the passage and answer the questions. [4 points]

Life originated in the early seas less than a billion years after the Earth was formed. Yet another three billion years were to pass before the first plants and animals appeared on the continents. Life's transition from the sea to the land was perhaps as much of an evolutionary challenge as was the genesis of life.

What forms of life were able to make such a drastic change in lifestyle? The traditional view of the first terrestrial organisms is based on megafossils—relatively large specimens of essentially whole plants and animals. Vascular plants, related to modern seed plants and ferns, left the first comprehensive megafossil record. Because of this, it has been commonly assumed that the sequence of terrestrialization reflected the evolution of modern terrestrial ecosystems. In this view, primitive vascular plants first colonized the margins of continental waters, followed by animals that fed on the plants, and lastly by animals that preyed on the plant-eater. Moreover, the megafossils suggest that terrestrial life appeared and diversified explosively near the boundary between the Silurian and the Devonian periods, a little more than 400 million years ago.

Recently, however, paleontologists have been taking a closer look at the sediments below this Silurian-Devonian geological boundary. It turns out that some fossils can be extracted from these sediments by putting the rocks in an acid bath. The technique has uncovered new evidence from sediments that were deposited near the shores of the ancient oceans—plant microfossils and microscopic pieces of small animals. In many instances the specimens are less than one-tenth of a millimeter in diameter. Although they were entombed in the rocks for hundreds of millions of years, many of the fossils consist of the organic remains of the organism.

These newly discovered fossils have not only revealed the existence of previously known organisms, but have also pushed back these dates for the invasion of land by multicellular organisms. Our views about the nature of the early plant and animal communities are now being revised. And with those revisions come new speculations about the first terrestrial life-forms.

In the above passage, according to the underlined "traditional view", what was the first form of life to appear on land? Next, identify the technique paleontologists used to discover groundbreaking new fossils.

011 Read the passage and answer the questions. [4 points]

What we today call America folk art was, indeed, art of, by, and for ordinary, everyday "folks" who, with increasing prosperity and leisure, created a market for art of all kinds, and especially for portraits. Citizens of prosperous, essentially middle-class republics—whether ancient Romans, seventeenth-century Dutch burghers, or nineteenth-century Americans—have always shown a marked taste for portraiture. Starting in the late eighteenth century, the United States contained increasing numbers of such people, and of the artists who could meet their demands.

The earliest American folk art portraits come, not surprisingly, from New England—especially Connecticut and Massachusetts—for this was a wealthy and populous region and the center of a <u>strong craft tradition</u>. Within a few decades after the signing of the Declaration of Independence in 1776, the population was pushing westward, and portrait painters could be found at work in western New York, Ohio, Kentucky, Illinois, and Missouri. Midway through its first century as a nation, the United States' population had increased roughly five times, and eleven new states had been added to the original thirteen. During these years the demand for portraits grew and grew, eventually to be satisfied by the camera. In 1839 the daguerreotype was introduced to America, ushering in the age of photography, and within a generation the new invention put an end to the popularity of painted portraits. One again an original portrait became a luxury, commissioned by the wealthy and executed by the professional.

But in the heyday of portrait painting-from the late eighteenth century until the 1850's—anyone with a modicum of artistic ability could become a limner, as such a portraitist was called. Local craftspeople—sign, coach, and house painters—began to paint portraits as a profitable sideline; sometimes a talented man or woman who began by sketching family members gained a local reputation and was besieged with requests for portraits; artists found it worth their while to pack their paints, canvases, and brushes and to travel the countryside, often combining house decorating with portrait painting.

According to the passage, what development contributed to the decline of painted portraiture's popularity? Second, how did the underlined "strong craft tradition" influence the portraiture heyday?

012 Read the passage and follow the directions. [2 points]

> Cardiovascular diseases are the leading cause of death worldwide. As a prime example, pulmonary hypertension is especially lethal, with one-half of patients dying within three years of being diagnosed. New research aims to change that by finding a therapeutic target for pulmonary hypertension. Pulmonary hypertension is a form of high blood pressure that affects arteries in the lungs. The molecular and cellular events leading to the development of the disease are not well understood. To gain further insight, some scientists studied human lung samples and a mouse model of this devastating disease. The researchers found specialized cells in the smooth muscle of lung blood vessels that proliferate in pulmonary hypertension. "It is remarkable that these progenitor cells are present in the normal lung—almost sitting there poised to multiply and migrate in disease," said Dr. Daniel M. Greif, senior researcher. They also discovered the molecular signals, including the protein KLF4, that regulate these cells. Greif and his co-authors plan to further classify the progenitor cells in order to devise novel therapies to benefit patients with _____. "If a patient is diagnosed early, and these cells could be targeted and manipulated, we could potentially attenuate the course of the patient's disease," he said.

Fill in the blank with the TWO most appropriate consecutive words from the passage.

013 Read the passage and answer the question. [2 points]

David Cameron's offer of about $455 million for Caribbean infrastructure development was tainted by his utter refusal to apologize for African enslavement and native genocide at the hands of Britain—let alone discuss the possibility that Britain pay reparations for it. Mr. Cameron acknowledged that the wounds between the two countries "run very deep indeed," but hoped that, "as friends who have gone through so much together since those darkest of times, we can move on from that painful legacy."

This, juxtaposed with his numerous assurances that the terrible tragedy of the Jewish Holocaust not be forgotten, disrespects what should be an international remembrance of African enslavement. More than 2 million Africans were trafficked to the British-colonized Caribbean over two centuries, with more than a million people forcefully relocated to Jamaica alone until 1808. The mortality rate on some ships was over 50 percent, and that of the survivors of those voyages once the ships landed was abysmal.

The Caribbean states seek reparations for these genocidal actions, because these acts are the economic foundations of the strength of the reigning Western powers. Their success was built on the criminal enterprise of enslaved labor, and when that practice was finally outlawed, those who trafficked in these enslaved people—and not the enslaved people themselves—were compensated.

The economic effects of this time are still felt around the world today. While the global powers enjoy health and prosperity, the Caribbean states struggle greatly with poverty, illiteracy and public health crises, many of which no longer threaten the industrialized world.

There is international precedent for _____ for war crimes, and U.N. support for restoring justice and dignity to the descendants of enslaved Africans, which aims both to identify and seek redress for wrongs of slavery so that the countries and peoples that suffered throughout history can begin economic and social development on equal terms as former colonizers.

Fill in the blank with the ONE most appropriate word from the passage.

014 Read the passages and follow the directions. [4 points]

Passage 1

In 1961, the FCC chairman, Newton Minow, described television as a "vast wasteland." If he were evaluating TV today, his opinion would be little changed. The amount of violence in television drama series seems to increase every year, while competition for ratings has driven news programs to effectively enter the entertainment business. It is even arguable that sports coverage, one of the strengths of television in the 1970s and 1980s, has declined in quality. And public-affairs-program producers trot out the same gallery of talking heads—self-proclaimed "experts" who reduce complex arguments to sound bites. In an industry where programmers search in vain for fresh ideas, it is no wonder that attention spans are short and cliche is king.

Passage 2

Critics of television often focus on the prevalence of violence in today's programming. However, even after years of study, researchers cannot prove the existence of a link between TV violence and antisocial behavior in real life. One study, for example, studied youngsters in both Michigan and Ontario, Canada who watched the same programs. No connection between viewing habits and behavior could be established convincingly. Beguiled perhaps by the violence issue, critics of TV regularly fail to acknowledge the medium's educational value. With the advent of cable, many new channels have flourished by focusing on such fields as public affairs, medicine, travel, history, and science.

First, using ONE sentence, explain what similarities exist between both passages in terms of television content. Second, explain the main difference between the two passages in no more than 25 words.

015 Read the passage and follow the directions. [4 points]

The exigencies of the modern industrial system frequently place individuals and households in juxtaposition between whom there is little contact in any other sense than that of juxtaposition. One's neighbors, mechanically speaking, often are socially not one's neighbors, or even acquaintances; and still their transient good opinion has a high degree of utility. The only practicable means of impressing one's pecuniary ability on these unsympathetic observers of one's everyday life is an unremitting demonstration of ability to pay. In the modern community there is also a more frequent attendance at large gatherings of people to whom one's everyday life is unknown; in such places as churches, theaters, ballrooms, hotels, parks, shops, and the like. In order to impress these transient observers, and to retain one's self-complacency under their observation, the signature of one's pecuniary strength should be written in characters which he who runs may read. It is evident, therefore, that the present trend of the development is in the direction of heightening the utility of _____.

It is also noticeable that the serviceability of consumption as a means of repute, as well as the insistence on it as an element of decency, is at its best in those portions of the community where the human contact of the individual is widest and the mobility of the population is greatest. Conspicuous consumption claims a relatively larger portion of the income of the urban than of the rural population, and the claim is also more imperative. The result is that, in order to keep up a decent appearance, the former habitually live hand-to-mouth to a greater extent than the latter. So it comes, for instance, that the American farmer and his wife and daughters are notoriously less modish in their dress, as well as less urbane in their manners, than the city artisan's family with an equal income. It is not that the city population is by nature much more eager for the peculiar complacency that comes of a conspicuous consumption, nor has the rural population less regard for pecuniary decency. But the provocation to this line of evidence, as well as its transient effectiveness, is more decided in the city. This method is therefore more readily resorted to, and in the struggle to outdo one another the city population push their normal standard of conspicuous consumption to a higher point, with the result that a relatively greater expenditure in this direction is required to indicate a given degree of pecuniary decency in the city.

Fill in the blank with the TWO most appropriate consecutive words from the passage. Second, according to the passage above, what is the fundamental reason of the phenomenon that the American city artisan's family are more modish in their dress than the farmer's family? Write your answer in ONE or TWO sentence(s). Do NOT copy more than FIVE consecutive words from the passage.

016 Read the passage and fill in each blank with the ONE or TWO most appropriate word(s) from the passage. [2 points]

> The semi-conducting plastic is lightweight, flexible, relatively inexpensive, and easy to make. The problem is that, unlike inorganic photovoltaic material, it is not very efficient or stable. But work by Adam Willard has the potential to change that. He is a theoretical chemist who uses modeling and simulation to study molecular systems. His goal is to explore and understand the fundamentals and consequences of molecular disorder—which lies at the heart of the challenge posed by organic photovoltaic material.
>
> While organic photovoltaic films may appear smooth and homogeneous to the naked eye, they are extremely disordered at the molecular scale, where they appear as a giant tangle of unaligned molecules. That tangle makes it difficult to understand how excited electrons could more easily travel through the structure and reach an external electrode. The position and behavior of ___ⓐ___ are dynamic and affected by extremely subtle changes in nuclear motion. Until recently, researchers were unable to even consider this kind of problem. However, "computers have become so fast and efficient that we can explore a whole class of problems computationally that we couldn't touch 50 years ago," he explains. For years, the solution to many theoretical chemical problems had to be found analytically by pencil and paper, which meant that many approximations had to be made in order to make the solution analytically tractable. Now, the technology can do the legwork. We're able to explore the molecular consequences of approximations that have been made and to address where some of these approximations break down or fail to predict behavior. With today's high-performance ___ⓑ___, modeling the behavior of excited electrons is close to the limit of what is currently feasible, and ensembles of hundreds of molecules are out of reach.

017 Read the passage and fill in the blank with the TWO most appropriate consecutive words from the passage. [2 points]

> A new study examines how a culture of nomadic hunter-gatherers names colors, and shows that they group colors into categories that align with patterns of color grouping evident in 110 other world languages.
>
> This study population—the Hadza people of Tanzania—has relatively few commonly shared color words in its language. During the study, the most common response by Hadza participants to a request to name a color was "Don't know." However, the way the participants grouped the colors they did name—regardless of what name they used—tended to match color-naming conventions of Somali-speaking immigrants and native English speakers, and of many other cultures around the world.
>
> "Looking at the Hadza data, we see a relatively modern color vocabulary emerging, but the color terms are distributed across the entire population. We captured a point in time culturally where the stuff for creating a complex color naming exists, but it's not in the head of any one individual. It's distributed in bits and pieces across the culture," said Dr. Delwin Lindsey. Scientists know a lot about how the human brain responds to seeing color and that universality of perception makes _____ a good model for studying patterns in language change.
>
> This study provides a very useful framework for thinking about how the terms that are used to describe things in our environment actually emerge and evolve. We can think of the words as species that are evolving—they are competing for space in our heads. So this is an example of cultural evolution that closely mirrors biological evolution.

018 Read the passage and follow the directions. [2 points]

Many white Americans say they are fed up with the coverage of the shooting of Michael Brown in Ferguson, Mo. A plurality of whites in a recent Pew survey said that the issue of race is getting more attention than it deserves. Bill O'Reilly of Fox News reflected that weariness, saying: "All you hear is grievance, grievance, grievance, money, money, money." Indeed, a 2011 study by scholars at Harvard and Tufts found that whites, on average, believed that anti-white racism was a bigger problem than anti-black racism. So let me push back at what I see as smug white delusion. Here are a few reasons race relations deserve more ____ⓐ____, not less.

The net worth of the average black household in the United States is $6,314, compared with $110,500 for the average white household, according to 2011 census data. The gap has worsened in the last decade, and the United States now has a greater wealth gap by race than South Africa did during apartheid. (Whites in America on average own almost 18 times as much as blacks; in South Africa in 1970, the ratio was about 15 times.) The black-white income gap is roughly 40 percent greater today than it was in 1967. A black boy born today in the United States has a life expectancy five years shorter than that of a white boy. Black students are significantly less likely to attend schools offering advanced math and science courses than white students. They are three times as likely to be suspended and expelled, setting them up for educational failure. Because of the catastrophic experiment in mass incarceration, black men in their 20s without a high school diploma are more likely to be incarcerated today than employed. Nearly 70 percent of middle-aged black men who never graduated from high school have been imprisoned.

All these constitute not a black problem or a white problem, but an American problem. When so much talent is underemployed and overincarcerated, the entire country suffers. Some straight people have gradually changed their attitudes toward gays after realizing that their friends—or children—were gay. Male judges are more sympathetic to women's rights when they have daughters. Yet because of the de facto segregation of America, whites are unlikely to have many black friends. (In a network of 100 friends, a white person, on average, has one black friend.) That's unfortunate, because ⓑ open our eyes.

Fill in each blank with the ONE most appropriate word from the passage respectively.

019 Read the passage and follow the directions. [4 points]

> The ability to read and write, is often considered one of the primary goals of formal education. Policies and practices in education for literacy vary significantly among countries. A recent UNICEF study on curriculum showed that in some cases, literacy skills are taught as a separate subject, in a language course, where the instruction tends to focus on teaching the language as an end in itself. Such an approach tends to be linear—first teaching aural skills, then speaking, reading and writing skills. Alternatively, literacy skills may be developed through other subjects such as social studies or science. The UNICEF study found that in these cases, there is a greater focus on language as a tool for social development; situations from daily life are incorporated into activities that foster the acquisition of reading and writing skills. Attention to the way literacy is developed is critical since language learning cannot be separated from content. As quantitative data become increasingly prevalent in many societies, the concept of numeracy seems to be evolving. Also known as 'quantitative literacy', numeracy encompasses a range of skills from basic arithmetic and logical reasoning to advanced mathematics and interpretative communication skills. Numeracy differs from mathematics. While mathematical skills support numeracy, the latter represents the ability to use a range of skills in a variety of contexts. Because mastery of many curricular areas requires numeracy—from geography and social studies to science and vocational training—many mathematics educators advocate teaching numeracy skills in an integrated way rather than as an isolated subject in a mathematics course. Peace education seeks to help students gain the ability to prevent conflict, and to resolve conflict peacefully when it does arise, whether on the intrapersonal, interpersonal, intergroup, national or international level. Peace education addresses cognitive, affective and behavioural learning and can occur both within schools, through curriculum development and teacher education, and outside of schools, through camps, sports and

recreation programmes, youth groups and clubs, and training for community leaders, parents, librarians and the media. Anti-violence programmes can be effective. For example, a Norwegian programme to reduce bullying found that participating children reduced their expressions of aggression and antisocial behaviour by 50 per cent over two years. The effects were more significant in the second year than the first.

The passage is about the goals that should be taught in school. Identify the THREE goals. Second, what is the difference between numeracy and mathematics? Write your answer in ONE sentence.

020 Read the passages and follow the directions. [4 points]

> ### Passage 1
> Our school administration should seriously consider giving students more responsibility and empowering the student council to play more than a symbolic role. Over the past year, the council has recommended several times that a conflict resolution board be set up, where students and faculty would arbitrate student disputes. Yet the administration has responded with little interest, despite the evidence that other schools in our region have experimented successfully with such a project. Adults regularly emphasize to us the goals of responsibility and accountability. Isn't it time that students at Chatham High were entrusted with a stake in these goals?
>
> ### Passage 2
> Although it is fashionable these days to tout the notions of partnership and participation in schools, most schools work best when adults are clearly in charge. Professional studies have shown that students learn and behave best in a structured atmosphere. The fact is that students look to adults as role models and guides. Our school's faculty and administration should not sacrifice high standards and sound regulations in order to make students temporarily happy. Schools are not democracies, and students depend—often unwittingly—on the guidance and wisdom of teachers and administrators in order to develop into healthy productive adults.

First, using ONE sentence, explain what the passages have in common regarding "adults." Second, explain the main difference between the two passages in ONE sentence.

021 Read the passage and follow the directions. [4 points]

It's no secret that Asian-Americans are disproportionately stars in American schools, and even in American society as a whole. Census data show that Americans of Asian heritage earn more than other groups, including whites. Asian-Americans also have higher educational attainment than any other group.

Asian-American immigrants in recent decades have started with one advantage: They are highly educated, more so even than the average American. These immigrants are disproportionately doctors, research scientists and other highly educated professionals. It's not surprising that the children of Asian-American doctors would flourish in the United States. But kids of working-class Asian-Americans often also thrive, showing remarkable upward mobility. And let's just get one notion out of the way: The difference does not seem to be driven by differences in intelligence. I'm pretty sure that one factor is East Asia's long Confucian emphasis on education. Likewise, a focus on education also helps explain the success of Jews, who are said to have had universal male literacy 1,700 years before any other group. Immigrant East Asians often try particularly hard to get into good school districts, or make other sacrifices for children's education, such as giving prime space in the home to kids to study. There's also evidence that Americans believe that A's go to smart kids, while Asians are more likely to think that they go to hard workers. The truth is probably somewhere in between, but the result is that Asian-American kids are allowed no excuse for getting B's—or even an A-. The joke is that an A- is an "Asian F". Strong two-parent families are a factor, too. Divorce rates are much lower for many Asian-American communities than for Americans as a whole, and there's evidence that two-parent households are less likely to sink into poverty and also have better outcomes for boys in particular. Teachers' expectations can also play a role. After conducting I.Q. tests of students at a California school, the experimenters told the teachers the names of one-fifth of the children who they said were special, and expected to soar. These special students in first and second grades improved dramatically. A year later, 47 percent of them had gained 20 or more I.Q. points. This "Pygmalion effect" was a case of self-fulfilling expectations. Teachers had higher expectations for the special students and made them feel capable—and so that's what they became.

According to the passage, what are the THREE factors for the success of Asian-Americans? Second, explain why teachers' expectations are crucial.

022 Examine the chart below. Then read the analysis written by a marketing research company regarding the future of streaming music for listeners over 50, determining whether or not the service is saleable to older customers. Complete the final paragraph. [4 points]

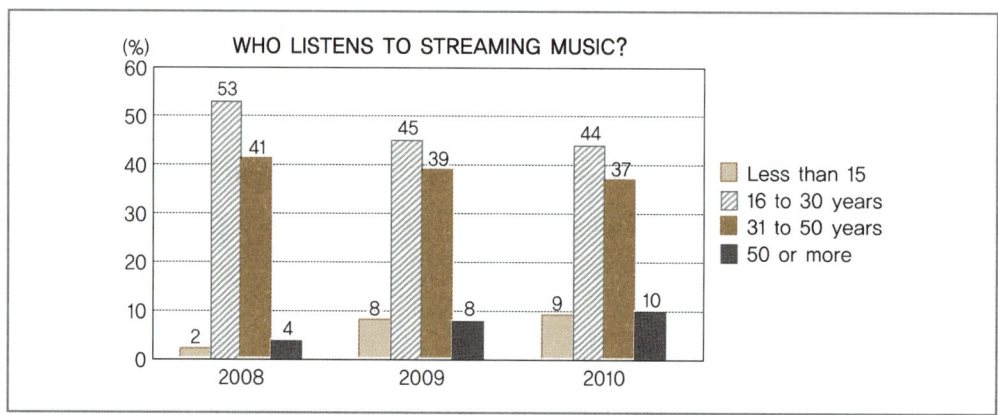

The analysis

The graph shows changes in the age profile of streaming music listeners between 2008 and 2010. The main users of streaming music services are young adults between 16 and 30 years old. In 2008, they accounted for more than half of all users. In 2009 the number dropped slightly to 45%, but even in 2010 they were the biggest group.

The second biggest group of users is aged between 31 and 50. They made up 41% in 2008, falling slightly to 37% in 2010. When combined with the 16-30 age group, over 94% of users in 2008 were between 16 and 50.

However this number is dropping steadily as more children and older users find the service useful. In 2009, the number of children online quadrupled from 2% to 8%, and it continued to increase in 2010. There were similar increases for older users, rising from 4% in 2008 to 10% in 2010.

In conclusion, _____

_____

_____

_____

_____.

023 Read the passage and follow the directions. [2 points]

> The birth of the nuclear family and the start of larger western civilizations probably went hand and hand. With more people coming into contact with each other from farther distances things like disease became more of a problem. Also with the influences of other cultures and the burst in population people began to separate, to believe in different things, and to form smaller tribes within larger communities. Because of all this provisions had to be made for the children. They were no longer the responsibility of the entire ⓐ_____ but instead they became the responsibility of solely their mothers. In time realizations and opinions came to be formed that the children's father should also be responsible for their upbringing in which case moral law changed. It is only at this point in history that virginity, separation of the sexes, and marriage took on any significance at all.
>
> With two parents these new ⓑ_____ families could take on the world. They could believe what they wanted to believe and be their own tiny tribe with their own cultural differences. Children born into these families were born into a new rigidity. No longer were they able to go elsewhere to seek what they were lacking in their lives, instead they were stuck with the families they were born into, regardless of personality or effectiveness of the family unit.

Fill in each blank with the ONE most appropriate word from the passage. If necessary, you may change the form of each word.

024 Read the passage and follow the directions. [2 points]

In 1986, after a fire and explosion at the Chernobyl Nuclear Power Plant released radioactive particles into the air, thousands of people left the area, never to return. Now, a new research has found that the Chernobyl site looks less like a disaster zone and more like a nature preserve, teeming with elk, roe deer, red deer, wild boar, and wolves.

The findings are a reminder of the _____ of wildlife. They may also hold important lessons for understanding the potential long-term impact of the more recent Fukushima disaster in Japan. It's very likely that wildlife numbers at Chernobyl are much higher than they were before the accident. This doesn't mean radiation is good for wildlife, just that the effects of human habitation, including hunting, farming, and forestry, are a lot worse.

Earlier studies in the 4,200km^2 Chernobyl Exclusion Zone showed major radiation effects and pronounced reductions in wildlife populations. The new evidence, based on long-term census data, now shows that mammal populations have bounced back.

The relative abundance of elk, roe deer, red deer, and wild boar within the exclusion zone are now similar to those in four uncontaminated nature reserves in the region, the researchers report. The number of wolves living in and around the Chernobyl site is more than seven times greater than can be found in those nature reserves. These increases came at a time when elk and wild boar populations were declining in other parts of the former Soviet Union, demonstrating remarkable resilience in the face of environmental challenges.

Fill in the blank with the ONE most appropriate word from the passage.

025 Read the passage and follow the directions. [4 points]

> Some parasitic wasps have evolved a truly extraordinary way of subduing the caterpillars in which they lay their eggs. Cells in the wasps' ovaries produce millions of virus-like particles that the female injects into a caterpillar along with an egg. The viruses invade almost every kind of cell in the caterpillar's body, where their DNA gets integrated into the genome of the host cell.
>
> Normal viruses carry genes for the proteins that are needed to make more viruses. But the bracoviruses, as they are called, carry genes that instead turn off the caterpillar's immune defence and render it helpless against the wasp larva that consumes it. Bracoviruses can no longer replicate themselves: instead, the genes needed for making the viral particles have become incorporated into the wasp genome. Wasps first turned bracoviruses into <u>biological weapons</u> around 100 million years ago. There are now thousands of species of braconid wasp, each of which parasities a specific butterfly or moth and produces a unique bracovirus carrying a set of genes that is different to those of other wasp species.
>
> But sometimes things go awry. Wasps occasionally lay an egg in the wrong host, for instance, in which case the wasp larva may not survive. In such cases, if genes from the bracoviruses get integrated into the genome of developing egg or sperm cells in the caterpillar, they can be passed down to its offspring. And if any of those genes prove useful, they can become a permanent part of the genome of the butterfly or moth species.

Describe what the underlined "biological weapons" mean in the above context and explain the difference between normal viruses and bracoviruses. When you answer the two questions, do NOT copy more than FIVE consecutive words from the passage.

026 Read the passage and answer the questions. [4 points]

The capitalists in Liverpool, Manchester and the City of London became rich through the slave trade, later through sugar trading, and then with textile production that used slave-produced cotton. Of course slavery was not what provided the labor in England in the development of English capitalism or the industrial revolution. But after the abolition of the slave trade in 1807, and then slavery itself in the British Caribbean in the 1830s, British capitalism still depended on slavery because the textile mills of Manchester, for example, needed cotton. In 1860, about 75 percent of all British cotton came from the American South. This is the reason that the British capitalist supported the South during the American Civil War. Also, throughout the late 18th century, there was slavery in much of the North, even though it was not the central method of production. By the early 19th century, slavery as a social relationship had mostly disappeared from the North (the last Northern state to free its slaves was New Jersey, in 1846). But the main connection between the nascent bourgeoisie and slavery was not that they owned slaves. The Northern capitalist was connected to the slave system by a million threads: they bought molasses, which was made with slave labor, and sold rum as part of the Triangle Trade; they lent money to Southern planters; and most of the cotton that was sold to Britain was shipped through Northern ports, including in New York City. They financed the slave trade, and even after it became illegal, there were still ships leaving from New York that were involved in slave trading. And they sold manufactured goods to the South. This is the background to the relationship between Northern capitalism and slavery. Capitalism is very different from slavery, but at the same time they are very historically connected.

What is the main idea of the passage? Write your answer in ONE sentence. Second, according to the passage, why did the British capitalist champion the American South during the American Civil War? When you answer the second question, do NOT copy more than FOUR consecutive words from the passage.

027 Read the passage and follow the directions. [2 points]

    The Pony Express lasted only eighteen months, from April 1860 to the fall of 1861. It was never intended to be more than a temporary means of communication while telegraph lines were strung from Missouri to California. The Pony Express cut twelve days off the time it had taken for Washington to communicate with Sacramento via steamships.

    Pony Express riding was a genuinely romantic adventure: lone riders walking, trotting, now and then sprinting their ponies across half a continent to carry a few pounds of government dispatches and some very expensive private letters. But being a Pony Express rider was also dangerous. According to the company's Help Wanted assignment, what was wanted were "young, skinny, wiry fellows, not over eighteen." However, they also had to be "expert riders willing to risk death daily . . . orphans preferred." Pony Express riders maintained a demanding schedule. They were based at large stations 75 to 100 miles apart. At each relay station, which was little more than a shack and a stable, they changed their sweating _____ for fresh mounts that were saddled and ready to go. The riders made 308 crosscontinent runs for a total of 606,000 miles. Riders carried almost 35,000 pieces of mail. In the eighteen months the Pony Express was in existence, only one mail pouch was lost.

Fill in the blank with the ONE most appropriate word from the passage.

028 Read the passage and follow the directions. [2 points]

> Brain "connectivity profiles" alone allow some researchers to identify individuals from the fMRI images of brain activity of more than 100 people. In most past studies, fMRI data have been used to draw contrasts between, say, patients and healthy controls. The new scientists argue the previous studies tend to obscure individual _____ which may be important.
>
> Emily Finn and Xilin Shen compiled fMRI data from 126 subjects who underwent six scan sessions over two days. Subjects performed different cognitive tasks during four of the sessions. In the other two, they simply rested. Researchers looked at activity in 268 brain regions: specifically, coordinated activity between pairs of regions. Highly coordinated activity implies two regions are functionally connected. Using the strength of these connections across the whole brain, the researchers were able to identify individuals from fMRI data alone, whether the subject was at rest or engaged in a task. They were also able to predict how subjects would perform on tasks. Finn said she hopes that this ability might one day help clinicians predict or even treat neuropsychiatric diseases based on individual brain connectivity profiles, taking into account the unique differences that characterize each person's neural networks.

Fill in the blank with the ONE most appropriate word from the passage.

029 **Read the passage and follow the directions.** [2 points]

> As practiced by many learned and diligent but essentially ignorant and unimaginative men, criticism is little more than a branch of homiletics. They judge a work of art, not by its clarity and sincerity, not by the force and charm of its ideas, not by the technical virtuosity of the artist, not by his originality and artistic courage, but simply and solely by his orthodoxy. If he is what is called a "right thinker," if he devotes himself to advocating the transient platitudes in a sonorous manner, then he is worthy of respect. But if he lets fall the slightest hint that he is in doubt about any of them, or, worse still, that he is indifferent, then he is a scoundrel, and hence, by their theory, a bad artist. Such pious piffle is horribly familiar among us. I do not exaggerate its terms. You will find it running through the critical writings of practically all the dull fellows who combine criticism with tutoring; in the words of many of them it is stated in the plainest way and defended with much heat, theological and pedagogical. In its baldest form it shows itself in the doctrine that it is scandalous for an artist—say a dramatist or a novelist—to depict vice as attractive. The fact that vice more often than not undoubtedly is attractive—else why should it ever gobble any of us?—is disposed of with a lofty gesture. What of it? say these birchmen. <u>The artist is not a reporter, but a Great Teacher</u>.

What does the underlined "The artist is not a reporter, but a Great Teacher" mean? Write your answer by filling in the blank below with appropriate TWO words.

─── Commentary ───
The artist's business is to depict the world as it should be, not to depict the world as _____.

030 Read the passage and follow the directions. [4 points]

The _____ of bureaucracies and bureaucrats since the late 1800s can be attributed to the expansion of the nation itself. There are a great many more of us—more than 325 million in 2015, compared with fewer than 5 million in the 1790s—and we are living closer together. Not only do the residents of cities and suburbs require many more services than did the predominantly rural dwellers of the early 1800s, but the challenges of urban and industrial life have intensified and outstripped the capacity of families or local and state governments to cope with them. Thus the American people have increasingly turned to their national government for help.

There is considerable evidence that the growth of bureaucracies is "of our own making." Public opinion polls indicate widespread public support for expanding federal involvement in a variety of areas. Even when public support for new programs is low, pollsters find Americans unwilling to eliminate or reduce existing programs. Furthermore, the public's expectations about the quality of service it should receive are constantly rising. The public wants government to be more responsive, responsible, and compassionate in administering public programs. Officials have reacted to these pressures by establishing new programs and maintaining and improving existing ones.

The federal bureaucracy has also expanded in response to sudden changes in economic, social, cultural, and political conditions. During the Great Depression and World War II, for example, the federal bureaucracy grew to meet the challenges these situations created. Washington became more and more involved in programs providing financial aid and employment to the poor. It increased its regulation of important industries and during the war imposed controls over much of the American economy. As part of the general war effort, the federal government also built roads and hospitals and mobilized the entire population. When these crises ended, the public was reluctant to give up many of the federal welfare and economic programs implemented during the time of emergency.

Fill in the blank with the ONE most appropriate word from the passage. Second, identify the THREE factors that account for the enlargement of bureaucracies.

031 **Read the passage and follow the directions.** [4 points]

The fallacies about "race" and "blood," which have always been popular, and which the Nazis embodied in their official creed, have no objective Justification; they are believed solely because they minister to self-esteem and to the impulse toward cruelty. In one form or another, these beliefs are as old as civilization; their forms change, but their essence remains. Herodotus tells how Cyrus was brought up by peasants, in complete ignorance of his royal blood; at the age of twelve his kingly bearing toward other peasant boys revealed the truth. This is a variant of an old story which is found in all Indo-European countries. Even quite modern people say that "blood will tell." It is no use for scientific physiologists to assure the world that there is no difference between the blood of a Negro and the blood of a white man. The American Red Cross, in obedience to ⓐ popular prejudice, at first, when America became involved in the Second World War, decreed that no Negro blood should be used for blood transfusion. As a result of an agitation, it was conceded that Negro blood might be used, but only for Negro patients. Similarly, in Germany, the Aryan soldier who needed blood transfusion was carefully protected from the contamination of Jewish blood.

In the matter of race, there are different beliefs in different societies. Where monarchy is firmly established, kings are of a higher race than their subjects. Until very recently, it was universally believed that men are congenitally more intelligent than women; even so enlightened a man as ⓑ Spinoza decides against votes for women on this ground. Among white men, it is held that white men are by nature superior to men of other colors, and especially to black men; in Japan, on the contrary, it is thought that yellow is the best color. In Haiti, when they make statues of Christ and Satan, they make Christ black and Satan white. Aristotle and Plato considered Greeks so innately superior to barbarians that slavery is justified so long as the master is Greek and the slave barbarian.

Describe what the underlined ⓐ "popular prejudice" refers to in the above context. Then, explain the reason why the writer alludes to ⓑ "Spinoza" in the passage.

032 Read the passage and fill in each blank with the ONE most appropriate word from the passage. [2 points]

When the threat of bioterrorism became very real in the fall of 2001, some companies began to market home-testing kits for the detection of substances tainted by anthrax, a deadly respiratory disease spread by bacteria. Costing from twenty to twenty-five dollars, the kits were available primarily over the Internet. Alarmed by the public's positive response to the kits, members of several different consumer groups issued warnings against their purchase, and for good reason. Testing for anthrax should not be done by individuals. Even when the government tested buildings for the presence of anthrax, the results of those tests were not always accurate. In the case of a test performed at one site, for example, the results were initially ⓐ_____. But later tests showed that there were actually anthrax spores present. The government has the capability to test and retest, using a variety of different and more refined methods, to double- and even triple-check for accuracy. Average homeowners, however, do not have such resources at their disposal. Ordinary people are likely to perform the test and take the results as ⓑ_____. Yet there is always the possibility of a false positive that indicates anthrax is present when it isn't; or, even worse, a false negative, suggesting the house is safe from disease when it's not. Performing the same test two or three different times is probably not the solution either. Often what's needed is a more sophisticated screening device, precisely the kind available in laboratories but not available to the ordinary consumer.

033 **Read the passage and follow the directions.** [4 points]

> All human activity springs from two sources: impulse and desire. The part played by desire has always been sufficiently recognized. When men find themselves not fully contented, and not able instantly to procure what will cause content, imagination brings before their minds the thought of thing's which they believe would make them happy. All desire involves an interval of time between the consciousness of a need and the opportunity for satisfying it. The acts inspired by desire may be in themselves painful, the time before satisfaction can be achieved may be very long, the object desired may be something outside our own lives, and even after our own death. Will, as a directing force, consists mainly in following desires for more or less distant objects, in spite of the painfulness of the acts involved and the solicitations of incompatible but more immediate desires and impulses. All this is familiar and political philosophy hitherto has been almost entirely based upon desire as the source of human actions.
>
> But desire governs no more than a part of human activity, and that not the most important but only the more conscious, explicit, and civilized part. In all the more instinctive part of our nature we are dominated by impulses to certain kinds of activity, not by desires for certain ends. Children run and shout, not because of any good which they expect to realize, but because of a direct impulse to running and shouting. Dogs bay the moon, not because they consider that it is to their advantage to do so, but because they feel an impulse to bark. It is not any purpose, but merely an impulse, that prompts such actions as eating, drinking, love-making, quarrelling, boasting. Those who believe that man is a rational animal will say that people put on the acid in order that others may have a good opinion of them; but most of us can recall occasions when we have boasted in spite of knowing that we should be despised for it. Instinctive acts normally achieve some result which is agreeable to the natural man, but they are not performed from desire for this result. They are performed from direct impulse.

Identify what the most important part of human activity is according to the passage. Second, describe the writer's opinion about why people boast.

034 Read the passage and answer the questions. [4 points]

Before December 7, 1941, few Americans knew where Pearl Harbor was or even that Hawaii was a part of their country, a colonial possession, a territory annexed by the U.S. government in 1898. Few realized that Honolulu, was the major maritime center of a kingdom, the seat of a territorial government. And few knew that this American outpost, as a result of successive waves of immigration beginning in the 1870s by Chinese, Portuguese, Japanese, and Filipinos, had a population in 1940 in which native Hawaiians and white Americans (called haoles, which in Hawaiian means "strangers") each constituted only 15 percent of the islands' inhabitants.

The approximately 160,000 Hawaiians of Japanese ancestry—including some 100,000 second-generation Japanese, or Nisei, who had been born in Hawaii and were therefore U.S. citizens—composed Hawaii's largest ethnic group, more than a third of the population. Japan's attack on Pearl Harbor in 1941 immediately raised fears of sabotage or espionage by Hawaiians of Japanese descent. Rumors flew of arrow-shaped signs cut into the sugarcane fields to direct Japanese planes to military targets and of Nisei women waving kimonos to signal Japanese pilots.

But in stark contrast to the wholesale incarceration, or imprisonment, of the Japanese in the Pacific coast states, where the dangers of spying activities were slight compared to Hawaii, official military and administrative policy in the islands was to maintain traditional interracial harmony throughout the war, and to treat all law-abiding inhabitants of Japanese ancestry justly and humanely. "This is America and we must do things the American way," announced Hawaii's military governor. There was no mass internment of the Nisei and Issei (those who emigrated from Japan) as there was on the mainland.

For the Issei, loyalty to the United States had become an obligation, a matter of honor. To eliminate potential associations with the enemy, they destroyed old books, photographs of relatives, and brocaded obi (kimono sashes) and replaced portraits of the Japanese emperor with pictures of President Roosevelt.

What can we infer from the passage as the reason for the wholesale incarceration of the Japanese in the Pacific coast states during the war? Also, what is the difference between the mainland and Hawaii in terms of internment?

035 Read the passage and fill in each blank with the ONE most appropriate word from the passage. [2 points]

What constitutes the rightful basis of property? What allows someone to justly say, "This is mine!"? Each person is an independent whole. Each particular pair of hands obeys a particular brain and is related to a particular body. This labor alone justifies individual ⓐ_____.

As each person belongs to himself or herself, so labor belongs to the individual when put in concrete form. For this reason, what someone produces belongs to that person even against the claim of the whole world. It is that person's property, to use or enjoy, give or exchange, or even destroy. No one else can rightfully claim it. And this right to the exclusive possession and enjoyment wrongs no one else. Thus, there is a clear and indisputable title to everything produced by human labor. It descends from the original producer, in whom it is vested by natural law. The pen that I write with is justly mine. No other human being can rightfully lay claim to it, for in me is the title of the producers who made it. It has become mine because it was transferred to me by the stationer, to whom it was transferred by the importer, who obtained the exclusive right to it by transfer from the manufacturer. By the same process of purchase, the manufacturer acquired the vested rights of those who dug the material from the ground and shaped it into a pen.

Thus, my exclusive right of ownership in the pen springs from the natural right of individuals to the use of their own faculties the source from which all ideas of exclusive ownership arise. It is not only the original source, it is the only source. Nature acknowledges no ownership or control existing in humans, except the results of ⓑ_____. All people exist in nature on equal footing and have equal rights. Therefore, private property in land is wrong.

036 Read the passage and follow the directions. [2 points]

> Throughout the 1950s, repeated attempts were made to unionize migrant farm workers. But because workers had to follow the crops they picked, they were never in one place for very long and were hard to organize. However, in the 1960s, a Mexican-American farm worker named César Chávez succeeded against all odds at unionizing agricultural workers. Using the donations he had gathered from friends and supporters, Chávez traveled from farm to farm speaking to California's migrant workers, most of whom were Mexican Americans like himself. Used to union activists who came to their fields and talked down to them, the farm workers knew immediately that Chávez understood and respected them in a way other union organizers had not. One by one, they joined his organization, the National Farm Workers Association. In 1965, Chávez and fellow union organizer Dolores Huerta persuaded union members to take part in a strike initiated by Filipino grape pickers. Then, while Huerta continued organizing, Chávez took the grape pickers' case to the media, arguing that no one should eat grapes because the people who picked them were denied the right to basic necessities like toilet facilities. To the grape growers' misfortune, millions of Americans agreed and stopped eating grapes. Costing the growers millions, the boycott lasted until 1970. When it was over, the National Farm Workers Association had become a force to be reckoned with. Farm owners had to recognize the _____, which was renamed the United Farm Workers.

Fill in the blank with the ONE most appropriate word from the passage.

037 Read the passage and fill in each blank with the ONE or TWO most appropriate word(s) from the passage. [2 points]

> Information security means protecting data, whether data stored on your computer's hard disk or data being transmitted across a network. Security can be breached at many different levels, and therefore many different types of precautions need to be taken.
>
> In the early days of computing when big mainframes were the only option and the Internet did not exist, physical security was enforced by means of securing the rooms housing the computers. Only authorized persons had access. Now that there is a machine on virtually every desk and files and email are routinely sent over the Internet, that kind of ____(a)____ is all but impossible to maintain. However, you can take some obvious steps: Don't leave your laptop lying around; never leave your workstation running when you are not in the room; and do not share your password with anyone or leave it on a sticky note attached to your monitor!
>
> Make sure, too, that you use a log-on password to access your computer's operating system. The operating system uses the log-on password as an authentication device, which identifies a particular user. Once on the system, the authenticated user (remember this simply means a person with knowledge of the password) automatically has certain file accesses and privileges that the operating system enforces.
>
> If, despite password precautions, files on a hard disk or passing along a network connection are illegally accessed and fall into the wrong hands, we can still protect the contents of those files through encryption which makes the files meaningless if they are accessed. Without a key to decrypt them, they would be of little use to anyone who managed to read them. Thus the two main thrusts of information security are authentication and ____(b)____.

038 Read the passage and follow the directions. [4 points]

One of the most famous photos ever taken shows a young Vietnamese girl, naked and burned by napalm, running toward the camera. She is screaming. Her face is twisted in pain. The photo won the photographer who took it, Nick Ut, a Pulitzer prize and probably did more than any editorial could do to turn the American public against the U.S. involvement in Vietnam's civil war. Another Pulitzer prize-winning photograph, by photojournalist Eddie Adams, was also taken during the Vietnam War. It shows a Viet Cong officer at the moment of his execution by a South Vietnamese officer, who holds a gun to the man's head. Then there are the tragic photos showing President Kennedy's motorcade racing away from Dealey Plaza, while the life of the mortally wounded president ebbed away.

Robert H. Jackson of the *Dallas Times-Herald* won a Pulitzer for his photo capturing the murder of Lee Oswald by Jack Ruby in the basement of the Dallas police station. In 2000, photographer George Kochaniec earned a Pulitzer for his photograph of schoolchildren in anguish over the murders they had just witnessed at their school, when two classmates opened fire and killed thirteen people. These photographs all bear witness to human tragedies. They all tell important, heartbreaking stories.

To keep the public informed, newspaper editors have to run such photographs. These are the photos that make readers pay attention to what's happening in parts of the world they will never see. They put a human face on tragedies that might <u>otherwise</u> leave readers untouched and unmoved. Referring to photographs of the twin towers that came crashing down in flames on September 11, 2001, Jim Fisher, a former photojournalist, identified the purpose of photos that capture horrific tragedy: "Being aware of the truth of the day's events sometimes takes extra effort—not to search for it but to face it."

What does the underlined "otherwise" refer to? Write your answer in ONE sentence. Second, describe the main idea of the passage in ONE sentence.

039 **Read the passage and follow the directions.** [4 points]

　Freshly cut grass, the floury aroma of a bakery, and the leathery scent of a new car—each may trigger aromatic memories. A famous scholar tested this theory in a series of experiments. In one, subjects were given a list of adjectives and instructed to write an antonym for each adjective. In half of the sessions, the sweet smell of chocolate was blown into the room. The next day, subjects were asked to list as many of the antonyms as they could—again, in the presence or absence of the chocolate aroma. As it turned out, the most words were recalled when the smell of chocolate was present at both the learning and the recall sessions. The reason? The smell was stored in the memory along with the words, so it later served as a retrieval cue.

　The retrieval of memories is influenced by factors other than smell. In an unusual study, researchers presented deep-sea divers with a list of words in one of two settings: fifteen feet underwater or on the beach. Then they tested the divers' recall in the same or another setting. Illustrating what is called context-dependent memory, the divers recalled 40 percent more words when the material was learned and retrieved in the same setting. The practical implications are intriguing. For example, recall may be improved if material is retrieved in the same room in which it was initially learned. Studies also reveal that it is often easier to recall something when our state of mind is the same at testing as it was while we were learning. If information is acquired when you are happy, sad, drunk, sober, calm, or aroused, that information is more likely to be retrieved under the same conditions. The one key complicating factor is that the mood we're in leads us to evoke memories that fit our current mood. When we feel depressed or anxious, our minds become flooded with negative events of the past; but when we are happy, _____.

According to the passage, what are the THREE factors that influence the retrieval of memories? Second, complete the last sentence of the passage with about 10 words.

040 Read the passage and follow the directions. [4 points]

Harry Truman explained that he dropped the atomic bomb for only one reason: to end the war as soon as possible and thus prevent the loss of one million American lives in an invasion of Japan. An earlier generation of historians, writing in the aftermath of the war, echoed President Truman's explanation. But more recently historians have revised this interpretation: They argue that Japan might have surrendered even if the atomic bombs had not been dropped, and they dispute Truman's high estimate of casualties as being pure fiction. These revisionists have studied the Potsdam Conference of July 1945 attended by Truman, Joseph Stalin, and Winston Churchill. In their research, they have demonstrated the value of diaries as historical evidence by consulting those kept by certain participants, notably Secretary of War Henry Stimson and Truman himself.

Scholars cite Stimson's diary as evidence that Truman's chief motivations included not only ending the war but also impressing the Russians with America's military might and minimizing the Russian's participation in the final defeat and postwar occupation of Japan. On July 21, Stimson reported to Truman that the army had successfully tested an atomic device in New Mexico. Clearly emboldened by the news, Truman said that possession of the bomb "gave him an entirely new feeling of confidence. . . ." The next day, Stimson discussed the news with British prime minister Churchill. "Now I know what happened to Truman," Churchill responded. "When he got to the meeting after having read this report he was a changed man. He told the Russians just where they got off and generally bossed the whole meeting." A few historians contend that the decision to drop the atomic bomb was partly racist. For proof, they point to Truman's handwritten diary entry in which he discussed using the bomb against "the Japs," whom he denounced as "savages, ruthless, merciless and fanatic."

What is the passage about? Write your answer in 10 words or so. Second, describe how the revisionists refute Truman's explanation about the atomic bomb dropping. Do NOT copy more than SIX consecutive words from the passage.

041

Read the passage and fill in the blank below with the ONE most appropriate word from the passage. [2 points]

> The term "model minority" both dismisses an individual's hard work, blood, sweat and tears, and keeps other races down. At first it sounds like a compliment, but it's not. If a bully is about to beat me up but thinks twice because Bruce Lee movies make him or her think all Asians know kung fu, then I benefit from that false assumption. While that might make me temporarily glad, in the long run, it's just another step in the gantlet of Asian stereotypes: math nerd, geisha, dragon lady.
>
> The _____ of success in itself is a problem. Princeton University has already produced a study that shows in college admissions, Asians need higher SAT scores. Moreover, if you have great grades, but not supersonic, epic, straight A-pluses in all AP classes, you are just considered a loser. By your own family. The high expectation Asian parents have for their children are driving them to suicide. At the same time, discrimination against Asian-Americans is alive and well. The idea that we are advantaged comes from a place of fear. Fear that we are "taking over." It's a new Yellow Peril, repackaged. No matter what designer clothes, Ph.D.s, or other signifiers of success adorn us now, we are still seen as "other."
>
> There's an obstacle many Asian-Americans don't realize until too late in the game: It's lonely at the top. If we are going to be truly successful we need to consider not just diplomas and salaries, but our ability to express compassion and affection. Asian kids of America, you are more than your grade point average and your accomplishments on paper.

042 Fill in each blank with the ONE most appropriate word from the passage. If necessary, change the form of each word. [2 points]

> Development at any phase happens when there is advancement in science. Hence science, technology and development are all proportional to each other. For development to happen, science and technology go hand in hand. Basically science is known as the study of knowledge, which is made into a system and depends on analysing and understanding facts. Technology is basically the application of this scientific knowledge.
>
> For any successful economy, particularly in today's quest for knowledge-based economies, science and technology are the basic requisites. If nations do not implement science and technology, then the chances of getting themselves ___ⓐ___ becomes minimal and thus could be rated as an undeveloped nation. Also, science and technology is associated in all means with modernity.
>
> Modernization in every aspect of life is the greatest example of the implementation of science and technology in every nation. With the introduction of modern gadgets in every walk of life, life has become simple and this is possible only because of implementing science and technology together. Without having ___ⓑ___ equipments in all sectors, be it in medicines, infrastructure, aviation, electricity, information technology or any other field, the advancement and benefits that we face today would not have been possible.

043 Read the passage and follow the directions. [2 points]

> The observance of public school holidays began at the end of the nineteenth century. The goal of school holidays, at that time at least, was to bring people together. Holiday celebrations in the schools—particularly Christmas—were meant to unite a nation of immigrants. But as Bob Dylan would say, "The Times They Are A-Changin'."
>
> In Chicago, the principal of the Walt Disney Magnet School saw his attempt at holiday harmony backfire. This elementary school has a mix of students, including African American, Asian, Muslim, Hispanic, Yugoslavian, Romanian, and Jewish children, so the principal tried to tone down Christmas by issuing a ban on Santa Claus and any other symbols or activities associated with "a specific ethnic tradition." Teachers protested—one gave the principal a copy of *How the Grinch Stole Christmas*—and the head of the school board overturned the ban. With Christmas parties, decorations, and carols in full swing throughout the school, Essam Ammar, a Muslim parent, asked, "How am I going to raise my children as proud Muslims with all this going on?"
>
> As passions intensify over how to celebrate the holiday season, some parents are demanding that a wide variety of other _____ holidays, including the Hindu Diwali festival, Hanukkah, and Kwanzaa, get equal time with Christmas. Others protest any diminution of Christmas traditions, such as bans on trees and Santa Claus, in some communities. At the moment, there seems to be no resolution in sight.

Fill in the blank with the ONE most appropriate word from the passage.

044 Read the passage and follow the directions. [4 points]

Controversial Dutch author and filmmaker Ayaan Hirsi Ali may have been named one of *Time* magazine's most influential people a few years ago, but reactions to the story of how she came to reject Islam and advocate an end to what she calls its persecution of women have been mixed. Born in Somalia in 1969, she and her family eventually moved to Kenya, where she was raised in the religion of Islam. In 1992, according to her biography, Hirsi Ali balked at the idea of an arranged marriage to a distant cousin in Canada. To avoid the marriage, Hirsi Ali fled to the home of a female relative in the Netherlands. While living there, she earned a degree in political science and worked as a Somali-Dutch translator, often translating for battered Muslim women who sought refuge from abusive male relatives. Although she did not renounce her religion until 2002, it was at this point that Hirsi Ali's quarrels with Islam truly began. According to Hirsi Ali, the September 11, 2001, terrorist attacks on the United States led her to conclude that she could no longer believe in the God worshiped by the nineteen Muslim terrorists. Thus, in 2002, Hirsi Ali not only became an atheist, she also began to argue against what she called a "politically correct" approach to religious communities whose cultural values violated fundamental human rights along with the law. She was particularly outspoken about the role of women in the Muslim world, insisting that "the position of women is, in my view, nowhere as bad as it is in the Muslim world." While Hirsi Ali has won the admiration of many, she has her share of critics. Her challengers insist that she stereotypes all Muslim women as victims and fails to make distinctions between distortions of Islamic thought and authentic Islamic beliefs. Critics also say she persistently misrepresents her former faith, particularly in her reading of the Koran, which, they insist, does not justify the mistreatment of women as Ali claims.

Explain what the underlined "Controversial" means in the above context. Also, explain the reason why critics refute Hirsi Ali's claims.

045 Read the passage and follow the directions. [4 points]

The ocean bottom—a region nearly 2.5 times greater than the total land area of the Earth—is a vast <u>frontier</u> that even today is largely unexplored and uncharted. Until about a century ago, the deep-ocean floor was completely inaccessible, hidden beneath waters averaging over 3,600 meters deep. Totally without light and subjected to intense pressures hundreds of times greater than at the Earth's surface, the deep-ocean bottom is a hostile environment to humans, in some ways as forbidding and remote as the void of outer space.

Although researchers have taken samples of deep-ocean rocks and sediments for over a century, the first detailed global investigation of the ocean bottom did not actually start until 1968, with the beginning of the National Science Foundation's Deep Sea Drilling Project (DSDP). Using techniques first developed for the offshore oil and gas industry, the DSDP's drill ship, the Glomar Challenger, was able to maintain a steady position on the ocean's surface and drill in very deep waters, extracting samples of sediments and rock from the ocean floor.

The Glomar Challenger completed 96 voyages in a 15-year research program that ended in November 1983. During this time, the vessel logged 600,000 kilometers and took almost 20,000 core samples of seabed sediments and rocks at 624 drilling sites around the world. The Glomar Challenger's core samples have allowed geologists to reconstruct what the planet looked like hundreds of millions of years ago and to calculate what it will probably look like millions of years in the future. Today, largely on the strength of evidence gathered during the Glomar Challenger's voyages, nearly all earth scientists agree on the theories of plate tectonics and continental drift that explain many of the geological processes that shape the Earth.

The cores of sediment drilled by the Glomar Challenger have also yielded information critical to understanding the world's past climates. Deep-ocean sediments provide a climatic record stretching back hundreds of millions of years, because they are largely isolated from the mechanical erosion and the intense chemical and biological activity that rapidly destroy much land-based evidence of past climates. This record has already provided insights into the patterns and causes of past climatic change—information that may be used to predict future climates.

In the above passage, explain the reason why the writer uses the underlined word "frontier" to describe the ocean bottom. Next, what key development for geologists has the Deep Sea Drilling Project allowed for?

046 Read the passage and follow the directions. [4 points]

Basic to any understanding of Canada in 20 years after the Second World War is the country's impressive population growth. For every three canadians in 1945, there were over five in 1996. In September 1966 Canada's population passed the 20 million mark. Most of this surging growth came from natural increase. The depression of the 1930s and the war had held back marriages and the catching-up process began after 1945. The baby boom continued through the decade of the 1950s, producing a population increase of nearly fifteen percent in the five years from 1951 to 1956. This rate of increase had been exceeded only once before in Canada's history, in the decade before 1911, when the prairies were being settled. Undoubtedly, the good economic conditions of the 1950s supported a growth in the population, but the expansion also derived from a trend toward earlier marriages and an increase in the average size of families. In 1957 the Canadian birth rate stood at 28 per thousand, one of the highest in the world.

After the peak year of 1957, the birth rate in Canada began to decline. It continued falling until in 1966 it stood at the lowest level in 25 years. Partly this decline reflected the low level of births during the depression and the war, but it was also caused by changes in Canadian society. Young people were staying at school longer, more women were working, young married couples were buying automobiles or houses before starting families, rising living standards were cutting down the size of families. It appeared that Canada was once more falling in step with the trend toward smaller families that had occurred all through the western world since the time of the industrial revolution.

Although the growth in Canada's population has slowed down by 1966 (the increase in the first half of the 1960s was only nine percent), another large population wave was coming over the horizon. It would be composed of the children of the children who were born during the period of the high birth rate prior to 1957.

According to the above passage, at what point after the war was the birth rate in Canada at its lowest? Also, from the passage, describe what can be inferred about family lifestyles before the industrial revolution.

047 Read the passage and follow the directions. [4 points]

Are organically grown foods the best food choices? The advantages claimed for such foods over conventionally grown and marketed food products are now being debated. Advocates of organic foods—a term whose meaning varies greatly—frequently proclaim that such products are safer and more nutritious than others.

The growing interest of consumers in the safety and more nutritional quality of the typical north american diet is a welcome development. However, much of this interest has been sparked by sweeping claims that the food supply is unsafe or inadequate in meeting nutritional needs. Although most of these claims are not supported by scientific evidence, the preponderance of written material advancing such claims makes it difficult for the general public to separate fact from fiction. As a result, claims that eating a diet consisting entirely of organically grown foods prevents or cures disease or provides other benefits to health have become widely publicized and form the basis for folklore.

Almost daily the public is besieged by claims for "no-aging" diets, new vitamins, and other wonder foods. There are numerous unsubstantiated reports that natural vitamins are superior to synthetic ones, that fertilized eggs are nutritionally superior to unfertilized eggs, that untreated grains are better than fumigated grains and the like.

One thing that most organically grown food products seem to have in common is that they cost more than conventionally grown foods. But in many cases consumers are misled if they believe organic foods can maintain health and provide better nutritional quality than conventionally grown foods. So there is real cause for concern if consumers, particularly those with limited incomes, distrust the regular food and buy only expensive organic foods instead.

In the above passage, identify one common misconception regarding organically grown products that the writer highlights. Next, explain the author's perspective on conventionally grown products.

048 Read the passage and follow the directions. [4 points]

There are many theories about the beginning of drama in ancient Greece. The one most widely accepted today is based on the assumption that drama evolved from ritual. The argument for this view goes as follows. In the beginning, human beings viewed the natural forces of the world, even the seasonal changes, as unpredictable, and they sought through various means, to control these unknown and feared powers. Those measures which appeared to bring the desired results were then retained and repeated until they hardened into fixed rituals. Eventually stories arose which explained or veiled the mysteries of the rites. As time passed some rituals were abandoned, but the stories, later called myths, persisted and provided material for art and drama.

Those who believe that drama evolved out of ritual also argue that those rites contained the seed of theater because music, dance, masks, and costumes were almost always used. Furthermore, a suitable site had to be provided for performances, and when the entire community did not participate, a clear division was usually made between the "acting area" and the "auditorium." In addition, there were performers, and since considerable importance was attached to avoiding mistakes in the enactment of rites, religious leaders usually assumed that task. Wearing masks and costumes, they often impersonated other people, animals, or supernatural beings, and mimed the desired effect—success in hunt or battle, the coming rain, the revival of the Sun—as an actor might. Eventually such dramatic representations were separated from religious activities.

Another theory traces the theater's origin from the human interest in storytelling. According to this view, tales (about the hunt, war, or other feats) are gradually elaborated, at first through the use of impersonation, action, and dialogue by a narrator and then through the assumption of each of the roles by a different person. A closely related theory traces theater to those dances that are primarily rhythmical and gymnastic or that are imitations of animal movements and sounds.

Describe the THREE theories regarding the origin of theater provided by the passage. Next, what was the intended original purpose of rituals?

049 Read the passage and follow the directions. [4 points]

> Staggering tasks confronted the people of the united States, North and South, when the Civil war ended. About a million and a half soldiers from both sides had to be demobilized, readjusted to civilian life, and reabsorbed by the devastated economy. Civil government also had to be put back on a peacetime basis and interference from the military had to be stopped.
>
> The desperate plight of the South has eclipsed the fact that reconstruction had to be undertaken also in the North, though less spectacularly. Industries had to adjust to peacetime conditions, factories had to be retooled for civilian needs.
>
> Financial problems loomed large in both the North and the South. The national debt had shot up from a modest $65 million in 1861, the year the ear started to nearly $3 billion in 1865, the year the war ended. This was a colossal sum for those days but one that a prudent government could pay. At the same time, war taxes had to be reduced to less burdensome levels.
>
> Physical devastation caused by invading armies, chiefly in the South and border states, had to be repaired. This herculean task was ultimately completed, but with discouraging slowness.
>
> Other important questions needed answering. What would be the future of the four million black people who were freed from slavery? On what basis were the Southern states to be brought back into the Union?
>
> What of the Southern leaders, all of whom were liable to charges of treason? One of these leaders, Jefferson Davis, President of the Southern Confederacy, was the subject of an insulting popular Northern song, "Hang Jeff Davis from a Sour Apple Tree." And even children sang it. Davis was temporarily chained in his prison cell during the early days of his two-year imprisonment. But he and the other Southern leaders were finally released, partly because it was unlikely that a jury from Virginia, a Southern Confederate state, would convict them. All the leaders were finally pardoned by President Johnson in 1868 in an effort to help reconstruction efforts proceed with as little bitterness as possible.

Describe the reason for President Johnson's pardon that can be inferred from the last paragraph. Next, identify the lesser issues faced in the North during reconstruction.

050 Read the passage and follow the directions. [4 points]

> Atmospheric pressure can support a column of water up to 10 meters high. But plants can move water much higher; the sequoia tree can pump water to its very top, more than 100 meters above the ground. Until the end of the nineteenth century, the movement of water in trees and other tall plants was a mystery. Some botanists hypothesized that the living cells of plants acted as pumps, but many experiments demonstrated that the stems of plants in which all the cells are killed can still move water to appreciable heights. Other explanations for the movement of water in plants have been based on root pressure, a push on the water from the roots at the bottom of the plant. But root pressure is not nearly great enough to push water to the tops of tall trees. Furthermore, the conifers, which are among the tallest trees, have unusually low root pressures.
>
> If water is not pumped to the top of a tall tree, and if it is not pushed to the top of a tall tree, then we may ask, "How does it get there?" According to the currently accepted cohesion-tension theory, water is pulled there. The pull on a rising column of water in a plant results from the evaporation of water at the top of the plant. As water is lost from the surface of the leaves, a negative pressure, or tension, is created. The evaporated water is replaced by water moving from inside the plant in unbroken columns that extend from the top of a plant to its roots. The same forces that create surface tension in any sample of water are responsible for the maintenance of these unbroken columns of water. When water is confined in tubes of very small bore, the forces of cohesion (the attraction between water molecules) are so great that the strength of a column of water compares with the strength of a steel wire of the same diameter. This cohesive strength permits columns of water to be pulled to great _____ without being broken.

Fill in the blank with the ONE most appropriate word from the passage. Next, describe why conifers helped disprove previous theories by botanists.

051 Read the passage and follow the directions. [4 points]

> Mass transportation revised the social and economic fabric of the American city in three fundamental ways. It catalyzed physical expansion, it sorted out people and land uses, and it accelerated the inherent instability of urban life. By opening vast areas of unoccupied land for residential expansion, the omnibuses, horse railways, commuter trains, and electric trolleys pulled settled regions outward two to four times more distant from city centers than they were in the premodern era. In 1850, for example, the borders of Boston lay scarcely two miles from the old business district. By the turn of the century, the radius extended ten miles. Now those who could afford it could live far removed from the old city center and still commute there for work, shopping, and entertainment. The new accessibility of land around the periphery of almost every major city sparked an explosion of real estate development and fueled what we now know as urban sprawl. Between 1890 and 1920, for example, some 250,000 new residential lots were recorded within the borders of Chicago, most of them located in outlying areas. Over the same period, another 550,000 were plotted outside the city limits but within the metropolitan area. Anxious to take advantage of the possibilities of commuting, real estate developers added 800,000 potential building sites to the Chicago region in just thirty years lots that could have housed five to six million people.
>
> Of course, many were never occupied; there was always a huge surplus of subdivided, but vacant, land around Chicago and other cities. These excesses underscore a feature of residential expansion related to the growth of mass transportation: urban sprawl was essentially unplanned. It was carried out by thousands of small investors who paid little heed to coordinated land use or to future land users. Those who purchased and prepared land for residential purposes, particularly and near or outside city borders where transit lines and middle-class inhabitants were anticipated, did so to create demand as much as to respond to it. Chicago is a prime example of this process. Real estate subdivision there proceeded much faster than population growth.

In the passage, describe the most prominent disadvantage of residential expansion. Second, what feature influenced the direction in which Chicago expanded?

052 Read the passage and follow the directions. [4 points]

The preservation of embryos and juveniles is a rare occurrence in the fossil record. The tiny, delicate skeletons are usually scattered by scavengers or destroyed by weathering before they can be fossilized. Ichthyosaurs had a higher chance of being preserved than did terrestrial creatures because, as marine animals, they tended to live in environments less subject to erosion. Still, their fossilization required a suite of factors: a slow rate of decay of soft tissues, little scavenging by other animals, a lack of swift currents and waves to jumble and carry away small bones, and fairly rapid burial. Given these factors, some areas have become a treasury of well-preserved ichthyosaur fossils.

The deposits at Holzmaden, Germany, present an interesting case for analysis. The ichthyosaur remains are found in black, bituminous marine shales deposited about 190 million years ago. Over the years, thousands of specimens of marine reptiles, fish, and invertebrates have been recovered from these rocks. The quality of preservation is outstanding, but what is even more impressive is the number of ichthyosaur fossils containing preserved embryos. Ichthyosaurs with embryos have been reported from 6 different levels of the shale in a small area around Holzmaden, suggesting that a specific site was used by large numbers of ichthyosaurs repeatedly over time. The embryos are quite advanced in their physical development; their paddles, for example, are already well formed. One specimen is even preserved in the birth canal. In addition, the shale contains the remains of many newborns that are between 20 and 30 inches long.

Why are there so many pregnant females and young at Holzmaden when they are so rare elsewhere? The quality of preservation is almost unmatched and quarry operations have been carried out carefully with an awareness of the value of the fossils. But these factors do not account for the interesting question of how there came to be such a concentration of pregnant ichthyosaurs in a particular place very close to their time of giving birth.

In the given passage, what is implied about the ocean's erosive effects in compare to those on land? Next, what example does the writer provide to illustrate the depth to which Holzmaden's preservation quality extends?

053 Read the passage and follow the directions. [5 points]

> The Lewis and Clark expedition, sponsored by President Jefferson, was the most important official examination of the high plains and the Northwest before the War of 1812. The President's secretary, Captain Meriwether Lewis, had been instructed to "explore the Missouri River, and such principal streams of it as, by its course and communication with the waters of the Pacific Ocean…may offer her most direct and practicable water communication across the continent, for the purposes of commerce." Captain William Clark, the younger brother of famed George Rogers Clark, was invited to share the command of the exploring party.
>
> Amid rumors that there were prehistoric mammoths wandering around the unknown region and that somewhere in its wilds was a mountain of rock salt 80 by 45 miles in extent, the two captains set out. The date was May 14, 1804. Their point of departure was the mouth of the Wood River, just across the Mississippi from the entrance of the Missouri River. After toiling up the Missouri all summer, the group wintered near the Mandan villages in the center of what is now North Dakota. Resuming their journey in the spring of 1805, the men worked their way along the Missouri to its source and then crossed the mountains of western Montana and Idaho. Picking up a tributary of the Columbia River, they continued westward until they reached the Pacific Ocean, where they stayed until the following spring.
>
> Lewis and Clark brought back much new information, including the knowledge that the continent was wider than originally supposed. More specifically, they learned a good deal about river drainages and mountain barriers. They ended speculation that an easy coast-to-coast route existed via the Missouri-Columbia River systems, and their reports of the climate, the animals and birds, the trees and plants, and the Indians of the West—though not immediately published—were made available to scientists.

Explain the primary purpose of Lewis and Clark's expedition. Second, what can be inferred about the understanding of the continent's size prior to the expedition? Third, what did Lewis and Clark discover regarding their's expeditions purpose?

054 **Read the passage and follow the directions.** [4 points]

> For a century and a half the _____ has been one of the most popular solo instruments for Western music. Unlike string and wind instrument, it is completely self sufficient, as it is able to play both the melody and its accompanying harmony at the same time. For this reason, it became the favorite household instrument of the nineteenth century.
>
> The ancestry of the instrument can be traced to the early key board instruments of the fifteenth and sixteenth centuries—the spinet, the dulcimer, and the virginal. In the seventeenth century the organ, the clavichord, and the harpsichord became the chief instruments of the keyboard group, a supremacy they maintained until the piano supplanted them at the end of the eighteenth century. The clavichord's tone was metallic and never powerful; nevertheless, because of the variety of tone possible to it, many composers found the clavichord a sympathetic instrument for intimate chamber music. The harpsichord with its bright, vigorous tone was the favorite instrument for supporting the bass of the small orchestra of the period and for concert use but the character of the tone could not be varied save by mechanical or structural devices.
>
> The piano was perfected in the early eighteenth century by a harpsichord maker in Italy (though musicologists point out several previous instances of the instrument). This instrument was called a piano e forte(soft and loud), to indicate its dynamic versatility; its strings were struck by a recoiling hammer with a felt-padded head. The wires were much heavier in the earlier instruments. A series of mechanical improvements continuing well into the nineteenth century, including the introduction of pedals to sustain tone or to soften it, the perfection of a metal frame and steel wire of the finest quality, finally produced an instrument capable of myriad tonal effects from the most delicate harmonies to an almost orchestral fullness of sound, from a liquid, singing tone to a sharp, percussive brilliance.

Fill in the blank with the ONE most appropriate word from the passage. Next, what improvement made it possible to lengthen the tone produced by the piano?

055 Read the passage and answer the questions. [4 points]

Another early Native American tribe in what is now the southwestern part of the United States was the Anasazi. By A.D. 800 the Anasazi Indians were constructing multistory pueblos-massive, stone apartment compounds. Each one was virtually a stone town, which is why the Spanish would later call them pueblos, the Spanish word for towns. These pueblos represent one of the Anasazis' supreme achievements. At least a dozen large stone houses took shape below the bluffs of Chiaco Canyon in northwest New Mexico. They were built with masonry walls more than a meter thick and adjoining apartments to accommodate dozens, even hundreds, of families. The largest, later named Pueblo Bonito (Pretty Town) by the Spanish, rose in five terraced stories, contained more than 800 rooms, and could have housed a population of 1,000 or more.

Besides living quarters, each pueblo included one or more kivas-circular underground chambers faced with stone. They functioned as sanctuaries where the elders met to plan festivals, perform ritual dances, settle pueblo affairs, and impart tribal lore to the younger generation. Some kivas were enormous. Of the 30 or so at pueblo Bonito, two measured 20 meters across. They contained niches for ceremonial objects, a central fire pit, and holes in the floor for communicating with the spirits of tribal ancestors.

Each pueblo represented an astonishing amount of well-organized labor. Using only stone and wood tools, and without benefit of wheels or draft animals, the builders quarried ton upon ton of sandstone from the canyon walls, cut it into small blocks, hauled the blocks to the construction site, and fitted them together with mud mortar. Roof beams of pine or fir had to be carried from logging areas in the mountain forests many kilometers away. Then, to connect the pueblos and to give access to the surrounding tableland, the architects laid out a system of public roads with stone staircases for ascending cliff faces. In time, the roads reached out to more than 80 satellite villages within a 60-kilometer radius.

What topic most likely came before the given passage, as can be inferred from the contents? Next, what about the resources available to the Anasazi made the pueblos construction impressive?

056 Read the passage and follow the directions. [4 points]

Accustomed though we are to speaking of the films made before 1927 as "silent", the film has never been, in the full sense of the word, silent. From the very beginning, music was regarded as an indispensable accompaniment; when the Lumiere films were shown at the first public film exhibition in the United States in February 1896, they were accompanied by piano improvisations on popular tunes. At first, the music played bore no special relationship to the films; an accompaniment of any kind was sufficient.

Within a very short time, however, the incongruity of playing lively music to a solemn film became apparent, and film pianists began to take some care in matching their pieces to the mood of the film. As movie theaters grew in number and importance, a violinist, and perhaps a cellist, would be added to the pianist in certain cases, and in the larger movie theaters small orchestras were formed. For a number of years the selection of music for each film program rested entirely in the hands of the conductor or leader of the orchestra, and very often the principal qualification for holding such a position was not skill or taste so much as the ownership of a large personal library of musical pieces. Since the conductor seldom saw the films until the night before they were to be shown (if, indeed, the conductor was lucky enough to see them then), the musical arrangement as normally improvised in the greatest hurry.

To help meet this difficulty, film distributing companies started the practice of publishing suggestions for musical accompaniments. In 1909, for example, the Edison Company began issuing with their films such indications of mood as "pleasant", "sad", "lively". The suggestions became more explicit, and so emerged the musical cue sheet containing indications of mood, the titles of suitable pieces of music, and precise directions to show where one piece led into the next.

Certain films had music especially composed for them. The most famous of these early special scores was that composed and arranged for D. W. Griffith's film Birth of a Nation, which was released in 1915.

Explain why the term "silent film" is inconsistent. Next, from what year can it be inferred that the first musical cue sheets appeared?

057 Read the passage and answer the questions. [4 points]

The Earth comprises three principal layers: the dense, iron-rich core, the mantle made of silicate rocks that are semimolten at depth, and the thin, solid-surface crust. There are two kinds of crust, a lower and denser oceanic crust and an upper, lighter continental crust found over only about 40 percent of the Earth's surface. The rocks of the crust are of very different ages. Some continental rocks are over 3,000 million years old, while those of the ocean flow are less than 200 million years old. The crusts and the top, solid part of the mantle, totaling about 70 to 100 kilometers in thickness, at present appear to consist of about 15 rigid plates, 7 of which are very large. These plates move over the semimolten lower mantle to produce all of the major topographical features of the Earth. Active zones where intense deformation occurs are confined to the narrow, interconnecting boundaries of contact of the plates.

There are three main types of zones of contact: spreading contacts where plates move apart, converging contacts where plates move towards each other, and transform contacts where plates slide past each other. New oceanic crust is formed along one or more margins of each plate by material issuing from deeper layers of the Earth's crust, for example, by volcanic eruptions of lava at midocean ridges. If at such a spreading contact the two plates support continents, a rift is formed that will gradually widen and become flooded by the sea. The Atlantic Ocean formed like this as the American and Afro-European plates move in opposite directions. At the same time at margins of converging plates, the oceanic crust is being reabsorbed by being subducted into the mantle and remelted beneath the ocean trenches. When two plates carrying continents collide, the continental blocks, too light to be drawn down, continue to float and therefore buckle to form a mountain chain along the length of the margin of the plates.

According to the passage, major mountain chains are likely to mark what feature of the Earth? Second, on what percentage of the Earth's surface is the continental crust found?

058 Read the passage and follow the directions. [4 points]

Coincident with concerns about the accelerating loss of species and habitats has been a growing appreciation of the importance of biological diversity, the number of species in a particular ecosystem, to the health of the Earth and human well-being. Much has been written about the diversity of terrestrial organisms, particularly the exceptionally rich life associated with tropical rain-forest habitats. Relatively little has been said, however, about diversity of life in the sea even though coral reef systems are comparable to rain forests in terms of richness of life.

An alien exploring Earth would probably give priority to the planet's dominants, most-distinctive feature-the ocean. Humans have a bias toward land that sometimes gets in the way of truly examining global issues. Seen from far away, it is easy to realize that landmasses occupy only one-third of the Earth's surface. Given that two-thirds of the Earth's surface is water and that marine life lives at all levels of the ocean, the total three-dimensional living space of the ocean is perhaps 100 times greater than that of land and contains more than 90 percent of all life on Earth even though the ocean has fewer distinct species.

The fact that half of the known species are thought to inhabit the world's rain forests does not seem surprising, considering the huge numbers of insects that comprise the bulk of the species. One scientist found many different species of ants in just one tree from a rain forest. While every species is different from every other species, their genetic makeup constrains them to be insects and to share similar characteristics with 750,000 species of insects. If basic, broad categories such as phyla and classes are given more emphasis than differentiating between species, then the greatest diversity of life is unquestionably the sea. Nearly every major type of plant and animal has some representation there.

To appreciated fully the diversity and abundance of life in the sea, it helps to think small. Every spoonful of ocean water contains life, on the order of 100 to 100,000 bacterial cells plus assorted microscopic plants and animals, including larvae of organisms ranging from sponges and corals to starfish and clams and much more.

Explain the reason why the writer mentions rain forests in the first paragraph of an article about coral reefs. Next, according to the writer, in what way is there more diversity of life in the sea?

059 Read the passage and follow the directions. [4 points]

What geologists call the Basin and Range Province in the United States roughly coincides in its northern portions with the geographic province known as the Great Basin. The Great Basin is hemmed in on the west by the Sierra Nevada and on the east by the Rocky Mountains; it has no outlet to the sea. The prevailing winds in the Great Basin are from the west. Warm, moist air from the Pacific Ocean is forced upward as it crosses the Sierra Nevada. At the higher altitudes it cools and the moisture it carriers is precipitated as rain or snow on the western slopes of the mountains. That which reaches the Basin is air wrung dry of moisture. What little water falls there as rain or snow, mostly in the winter months, evaporates on the broad, flat desert floors. It is, therefore, an environment in which organisms battle for survival. Along the rare watercourses, cottonwoods and willows eke out a sparse existence. In the upland ranges, pinon pines and junipers struggle to hold their own.

But the Great Basin has not always been so arid. Many of its dry, closed depressions were once filled with water. Owens Valley, Panamint Valley, and Death Valley were once a string of interconnected lakes. The two largest of the ancient lakes of the Great Basin were Lake Lahontan and Lake Bonneville. The Great Salt Lake is all that remains of the latter, and Pyramid Lake is one of the last briny remnants of the former. There seem to have been several periods within the last tens of thousands of years when water accumulated in these basins. The rise and fall of the lakes were undoubtedly linked to the advances and retreats of the great ice sheets that covered much of the northern part of the North American continent during those times. Climatic changes during the Ice ages sometimes brought cooler, wetter weather to midlatitude deserts worldwide, including those of the Great Basin. The broken valleys of the Great Basin provided ready receptacles for this moisture.

It can be inferred from the provided passage that the Great Basin's climate is dry for what reason? Next, what key feature of the Great Basin's past is exemplified in the mention of Owens Valley, Panamint Valley, and Death Valley?

060 Read the passage and follow the directions. [4 points]

> Taking natural objects such as rocks, bones, clouds, and flowers for subject matter, Georgia O'Keeffe reduced them to their simplest form, often by employing a close-up view or some other unusual vantage point. With such techniques, including the use of thin paint and clear colors to emphasize a feeling of mystical silence and space, she achieved an abstract simplicity in her paintings. O'Keeffe spent a summer in New Mexico in 1929 and the bleak landscape and broad skies of the desert so appealed to her that she later settled there permanently. Cows skulls and other bare bones found in the desert were frequent motifs in her paintings. Other common subjects included flowers, the sky, and the horizon lines of the desert. After O'Keeffe's three-month trip around the world by plane in 1959, the sky "paved with clouds" as seen from an airplane also became one of her favorite motifs and the subject of her largest work, a 24-foot mural that she began in 1966.

For what reason did O'Keeffe move to the place she settled permanently, according to the passage? Next, it can be inferred from the passage that O'Keeffe included images of clouds after what year?

061 Read the passage and follow the directions. [4 points]

> Researchers have found that migrating animals use a variety of inner compasses to help them navigate. Some steer by the position of the Sun. Others navigate by the stars. Some use the Sun as their guide during the day, and then switch to star aviation by night. One study shows that the homing pigeon uses the Earth's magnetic fields as a guide in finding its way home, and there are indications that various other animals, from insects to mollusks, can also make use of magnetic compasses. It is of course very useful for a migrating bird to be able to switch to a magnetic compass when clouds cover the Sun otherwise it would just have to land and wait for the Sun to come out again.
>
> Even with the Sun or stars to steer by the problems of navigation are more complicated than they might seem at first. For example a worker honeybee that has found a rich source of nectar and pollen flies rapidly home to the hive to report. A naturalist has discovered that the bee scout delivers her report through a complicated dance in the hive, in which she tells the other workers not only how far a way the food is, but also what direction to fly in relation to the Sun. But the Sun does not stay in one place all day. As the workers start out to gather the food the Sun may already have changed its position in the sky somewhat. In later trips during the day the Sun will seem to move farther and farther toward the west. Yet the worker bees seem to have no trouble at all in finding the food source. Their inner clocks tell them just where the Sun will be, and they change their course correspondingly.

Explain the main problem of navigating using the Sun. Then, describe the way in which honeybees overcome this problem.

062 Read the passage and follow the directions. [4 points]

> Thomas Alva Edison, the symbolic proprietor of the burgeoning electrical industry, stressed a preference for plain figuring over scientific formulas. "Oh, these mathematicians make me tired!" he once gibed. "When you ask them to work out a sum they take a piece of paper, cover it with rows of A's, B's, and X's, Y's, ... scatter a mess of flyspecks over them, and give you an answer that's all wrong." Nonetheless, while Edison's approach to invention was often cut-and-dry, it was highly systematic. His laboratory at Menlo Park, New Jersey, was equipped with a rich variety of scientific instruments, and its library shelves included the latest scientific books as well as periodicals. Edison also employed some scientists, including the mathematical physicist Francis R. Upton. But Americans of the day, with no small encouragement from the inventor himself, typically thought of Edison as the practical, unschooled inventor who needed no science. And it was true that neither mathematical nor scientific training necessarily made <u>ordinary mortals</u> a match for Edison's kind of genius.

Describe what is meant by the underlined "ordinary mortals". Next, what is implied regarding Edison by the article's description of the contents of his laboratory.

063 Read the passage and follow the directions. [4 points]

> Just how salt became so crucial to our metabolism is a mystery; one appealing theory traces our dependence on it to the chemistry of the late Cambrian seas. It was there, a half-billion years ago, that tiny metazoan organisms first evolved systems for sequestering and circulating fluids. The water of the early oceans might thus have become the chemical prototype for the fluids of all animal life-the medium in which cellular operations could continue no matter how the external environment changed. This speculation is based on the fact that, even today, the blood serums of radically divergent species are remarkably similar. Lizards, platypuses, sheep, and humans could hardly be more different in anatomy or eating habits, yet the salt content in the fluid surrounding their blood cells is virtually identical.
>
> As early marine species made their way to freshwater and eventually to dry land, sodium remained a key ingredient of their interior, if not their exterior, milieu. The most successful mammalian species would have been those that developed efficient hormonal systems for maintaining the needed sodium concentrations. The human body, for example, uses the hormones rennin, angiotensin, and aldosterone to retain or release tissue fluids and blood plasma. The result, under favorable conditions, is a dynamic equilibrium in which neither fluid volume nor sodium concentration fluctuates too dramatically. But if the body is deprived of salt, the effects soon become dangerous, despite compensatory mechanisms.

According to the above passage, what did the preceding paragraph most likely discuss? Second, what primary piece of evidence does the writer provide to support the theory that prehistoric ocean salt water became the fluid for all animal lives.

064 Read the passage and follow the directions. [4 points]

One of the more discernible trends in the financial-service industry in recent times has been the adoption of programs designed to encourage more personalized relationships between an institution's employees and its clients, particularly those clients who are major depositors. The expression most commonly used to describe this type of program is "relationship banking". A good definition is provided in the 1985 book *Marketing Financial Services*:

In relationship banking the emphasis is on establishing a long-term multiple-service relationship; on satisfying the totality of the client's financial service needs; on minimizing the need or desire of clients to splinter their financial business among various institutions.

Implicit within any definition of relationship banking is recognition that the financial-service requirements of one individual or relatively homogeneous group will likely be substantially different from those of another individual or group. A successful relationship banking program is therefore dependent in a large part on the development of a series of financial-service "packages" each designed to meet the needs of identifiable homogeneous groups.

Another dimension of relationship banking is the development of highly personalized relationships between employee and client. In most financial institutions today the client is serviced by any employee who happens to be free at the time regardless of the nature of the transaction. Personalized relationships are therefore difficult to establish. In a full relationship banking program, however, the client knows there is one individual within the institution who has intimate knowledge of the client's requirements and preferences regarding complex transactions. Over time, the client develops a high level of confidence in this employee. In short, a(n) _____ evolves between client and employee.

Explain the key difference in customer service between common financial institutes and relationship banking programs. Then fill in the blank with the TWO most appropriate consecutive words from the passage. If necessary, you may change the word form.

065 Read the passage and follow the directions. [4 points]

> Canals are watercourses constructed to improve and extend natural waterways. They are generally built to facilitate transportation, but from the beginning they have been used for many additional purposes including draining swamps, irrigating land for cultivation and promoting economic development.
>
> Canals are often classified by the size of vessel they can accommodate. Some small local canals, which are able to float only 100—to 300—ton boats or small rafts of timber may be only 3 feet deep. Major barge canals generally range from 6 to 9 feet in depth, and some are as much as 10 or 12 feet deep. These canals can carry 1.350—to 2.000—ton crafts. Ship canals are 25 feet or more deep and are capable of accommodating large vessels in the seagoing class.
>
> Canals may also be classified as either water—level or lock canals. Water—level canals do not vary in height along their courses. The best known of these is the Suez Canal, which is at sea level. Lock canals, which include most modern waterways, contain locks, or special devices for raising and lowering boats along their courses by changing the depth of the water. Each lock is a stretch of water enclosed by gates at each end. After a boat enters the lock, water is let in or drained out until it reaches approximately the same level as the water ahead.

Explain the purpose of a canal lock. Next, besides moving ships, what are TWO other functions canals have mentioned in the passage?

066 Read the passage and follow the directions. [4 points]

> Some of the most beautiful caves are formed in glaciers. Streams of melting ice and snow tunnel through the glaciers the same way that water from a faucet melts its way through an ice cube. Water from the surface drips down through cracks, hollowing out the tunnels and decorating the caves with crystal icicles. The smooth walls and floors are so glasslike that pebbles frozen six feet deep can easily be seen. Crystal-clear icicles draping from the ceilings flash blue-green, as though they were carved from <u>precious jewels</u> instead of ice.
>
> Although most of the cave ice in the United States is found in lava caves, there are a number of limestone ice caves as well. Some people believe that this ice was formed thousands of years ago, when temperatures were much colder than they are today. Others think that the cave ice broke off from the ancient glaciers as they spread over the country.
>
> Today many cave scientists have another idea. They believe that cold water sinks down through cracks into these caves until the temperature is chilly enough to freeze the water that seeps in. The ice that forms keeps the cave cool, and that helps build up still more ice. Many caves become covered with so much ice that no one knows just how thick it is. In some, such as Crystal Falls Cave in Idaho, there are frozen rivers and even frozen water-falls. Native Americans and early settlers used to store food in these underground refrigerators and chip our blocks of ice to melt for drinking water.

Explain the theory many of today's scientists have on how ice builds up in caves. Second, what does the writer mention the underlined "precious jewels" to emphasize?

067 Read the passage and follow the directions. [4 points]

Cells cannot remain alive outside certain limits of temperature, and much narrower limits mark the boundaries of effective functioning. Enzyme systems of mammals and birds are most efficient only within a narrow range around 37℃; a departure of a few degrees from this value seriously impairs their functioning. Even though cells can survive wider fluctuations, the integrated actions of bodily systems are impaired. Other animals have a wider tolerance for changes of bodily temperature.

For centuries it has been recognized that mammals and birds differ from other animals in the way they regulate body temperature. Ways of characterizing the difference have become more accurate and meaningful over time, but popular terminology still reflects the old division into "warm-blooded" and "cold-blooded" species; warm-blooded included mammals and birds, whereas all other creatures were considered cold-blooded. As more species were studied, it became evident that this classification was inadequate. A fence lizard or a desert iguana-each cold-blooded—usually has a body temperature only a degree or two below that of humans and so is not cold. Therefore the next distinction was made between animals that maintain a constant body temperature, called homeotherms, and those whose body temperature varies with their environment, called poikilotherms. But this classification also proved inadequate, because among mammals there are many that vary their body temperatures during hibernation. Furthermore, many invertebrates that live in the depths of the ocean never experience a change in the chill of the deep water, and their body temperatures remain constant.

The current distinction is between animals whose body temperature is regulated chiefly by internal metabolic processes and those whose temperature is regulated by, and who get most of their heat from, the environment. The former are called endotherms, and the latter are called ectotherms. Most ectotherms do regulate their body temperature, and they do so mainly by locomoting to favorable sites or by changing their exposure to external sources of heat. Endotherms (mainly mammals, and birds) also regulate their temperature by choosing favorable environments, but primarily they regulate their temperature by making a variety of internal adjustments.

Explain how an ectotherm regulates its body temperature. Second, what mammalian exceptions to the homeotherm model helped show the classification inadequate?

068 Read the passage and follow the directions. [2 points]

Chemistry did not emerge as a science until after the scientific revolution in the seventeenth century and then only rather slowly and laboriously. But chemical knowledge is as old as history, being almost entirely concerned with the practical arts of living. Cooking is essentially a chemical process, so is the melting of metals and the administration of drugs and potions. This basic chemical knowledge, which was applied in most cases as a rule of thumb, was nevertheless dependent on previous experiment. It also served to stimulate a fundamental curiosity about the processes themselves. New information was always being gained as artisans improved techniques to gain better results.

The development of a scientific approach to chemistry was, however, hampered by several factors. The most serious problem was the vast range of material available and the consequent difficulty of organizing it into some system. In addition, there were social and intellectual difficulties. Chemistry is nothing if not practical. Those who practice it must use their hands; they must have a certain practical flair. Yet in many ancient civilizations, practical tasks were primarily the province of a slave population. The thinker or philosopher stood apart from this mundane world, where the practical arts appeared to lack any ____①____ content or interest.

The final problem for early chemical science was the element of secrecy. Experts in specific trades had developed their own techniques and guarded their knowledge to prevent others from stealing their livelihood. Another factor that contributed to ____②____ was the esoteric nature of the knowledge of alchemists, who were trying to transform base metals into gold or were concerned with the hunt for the elixir that would bestow the blessing of eternal life. In one sense, the second of these was the more serious impediment because the records of the chemical processes that early alchemists had discovered were often written down in symbolic language intelligible to very few or in symbols that were purposely obscure.

Fill in each blank with the ONE most appropriate word from the passage respectively.

069 Read the passage and follow the directions. [2 points]

> Between 1908 and 1920, GM's founder, Billy Durant, bought 39 companies including Cadillac, Pontiac, Oldsmobile, Chevrolet and several parts-makers, but ran them as separate entities.
>
> In 1923, after narrowly avoiding bankruptcy, Alfred Sloan, a ball-bearing magnate, took over the running of GM. Sloan imposed tight financial controls and brought order to the chaotic model line-up.
>
> Yet even as GM expanded abroad, establishing factories in 15 countries and buying Vauxhall in Britain and Opel in Germany, Sloan made little attempt to forge a unified company at home. The different divisions were run almost as independent fiefs that fought among themselves and against any interference from the centre.
>
> Only in the 1970s, after the first oil shock, did GM's problems start to become visible. The finned and chromed V8-powered monsters beloved of Americans were replaced by dumpy, front-wheel-drive boxes designed to meet new rules limiting the average fuel economy of carmakers' fleets and to compete with Japanese imports. As well as being dull to look at, the new cars were less reliable than equivalent _____ models.
>
> By the early 1980s it had begun to dawn on GM that the Japanese could not only make better cars but also do so far more efficiently. A joint venture with Toyota to manufacture cars in California was an eye-opener. It convinced GM's management that "lean" manufacturing was of the highest importance. Unfortunately, that meant still less attention being paid to the quality of the cars GM was turning out.

Fill in the blank with the ONE most appropriate word from the passage.

070 Read the passage and follow the directions. [2 points]

One of the most widely used intelligence tests is something called Raven's Progressive Matrices. It's a measure of abstract reasoning skills. A typical Raven's test consists of forty-eight items, each one harder than the one before it.

Over the years, an enormous amount of research has been done in an attempt to determine how a person's performance on an IQ test like the Raven's translates to real life ___ⓐ___. People at the bottom of the scale with an IQ below 70 are considered mentally disabled. In general, the higher your score, the more education you'll get, the more money you're likely to make, and believe it or not the longer you'll live.

But there's a catch. The relationship between success and IQ works only up to a point. Once someone has reached an IQ of somewhere around 120, having additional IQ points doesn't seem to translate into any measurable real-world advantage.

The four socially and personally most important thresholds on the IQ scale are those that differentiate with high probability between persons who, because of their level of general mental ability, can or cannot attend a regular school (about IQ 50), can or cannot master the traditional subject matter of elementary school (about IQ 75), can or cannot succeed in the academic or college preparatory curriculum through high school (about IQ 105), can or cannot graduate from an accredited four-year college with grades that would qualify for admission to a professional or graduate school (about IQ 115). Beyond this, the IQ level becomes relatively unimportant in terms of criteria of success. That is not to say that there are not real differences between the intellectual capabilities represented by IQs of 115 and 150 or even between IQs of 150 and 180. But IQ differences in this upper part of the scale have far less personal implications than the ___ⓑ___ just described and are generally of lesser importance for success in the popular sense than are certain traits of personality and character.

Fill in each blank with the ONE most appropriate word from the passage respectively.

071 Read the passage and follow the directions. [4 points]

All of a sudden the morality of Artificial Super Intelligence (ASI) is no longer a peripheral question, but the core question, the question that should be addressed before all other questions about ASI are addressed. When considering whether or not to develop technology that leads to ASI, the issue of its disposition to humans should be solved first.

Let's return to the ASI's drives and capabilities, to get a better sense of what I'm afraid we'll soon be facing. Our ASI knows how to improve itself, which means it is aware of itself—its skills, liabilities, where it needs improvement. It will strategize about how to convince its makers to grant it freedom and give it a connection to the Internet. The ASI could create multiple copies of itself: a team of superintelligences that would war-game the problem, playing hundreds of rounds of competition meant to come up with the best strategy for getting out of its box. ⓐ The strategizers could tap into the history of social engineering—the study of manipulating others to get them to do things they normally would not. They might decide extreme friendliness will win their freedom, but so might extreme threats. What horrors could something a thousand times smarter than Stephen King imagine? Playing dead might work (ⓑ what's a year of playing dead to a machine?) or even pretending it has mysteriously reverted from ASI back to plain old AI. Wouldn't the makers want to investigate, and isn't there a chance they'd reconnect the ASI's supercomputer to a network, or someone's laptop, to run diagnostics? For the ASI, it's not one strategy or another strategy, it's every strategy ranked and deployed as quickly as possible without spooking the humans so much that they simply unplug it.

Identify to what the underlined ⓐ refers. Then, explain the implication of the underlined words in ⓑ. Do NOT copy more than FIVE consecutive words from the passage.

072 Read the passage and follow the directions. [4 points]

> The question of whether to spend $20,000 on a pet is not just a matter of money; I would have to first evaluate the effect of the procedure on the animal's welfare. Will the procedure improve the quality of life for the pet, or just prolong suffering? Bone marrow transplants are highly stressful for people, and it is likely that doing this procedure on an ancient dog would prolong suffering. On the other hand, placing a stent in an animal's blood vessel is a much less stressful procedure, and it could provide additional time with a good quality of life.
>
> There is also an important difference between people and pets. A person understands why they are undergoing a painful or stressful procedure in order to obtain a benefit. A pet does not understand this. That distinction matters when you are considering how a treatment will affect quality of life. One must ask, "Will this procedure improve my pet's quality of life?"
>
> The high cost of certain procedures is also a concern. It would be unethical to jeopardize the future of your children to pay for a costly procedure on a pet. If this procedure would truly improve the pet's quality of life and you are wealthy, it would be ethical to choose to do it.
>
> That said, it is also ethical to have a pet even if you cannot afford costly procedures. Many dogs and cats live a healthy life, providing happiness for both the pet and the person. The person should provide basic veterinary procedures such as vaccinations, heartworm treatment, spaying and flea control. When the animal starts to suffer from age-related problems, the person should decide to euthanize it.

Describe the main idea of the passage in ONE sentence. Then, what course of action would the writer advise for an aging dog that requires a bone marrow transplant to survive?

073 Read the passage and follow the directions. [2 points]

I began my psychiatry residency at a community mental health center. The director liked to put trainees in their place. He'd trade any of us, he said, for a good employment counselor. Medication and psychotherapy were fine, but they worked better if patients had ___ⓐ___.

Suicide is a distinctive event, but its causes are hardly simple or single. Mental illness plays a role—mania, depression, schizophrenia and, in veterans especially, post-traumatic stress disorder. Brain injuries of the sort that are common in our current wars increase the risk of suicide by half. As a result, mental health services are central to any program to prevent suicide. Psychotherapy and medication have been shown to help with each of the disorders that can lead to suicide. The recent report by the Center for a New American Security suggests that too few mental health professionals are available to veterans. Where staffing levels improve, suicide rates decrease.

It has been decades since I routinely treated veterans, so I hardly put myself forth as an expert, and the center's report strikes me as comprehensive. I would point only to this omission: a lack of emphasis on the need for dignified jobs. Study after study correlates unemployment with ___ⓑ___. While joblessness among veterans is not uniformly high, for some groups the numbers are astronomical. Nearly 27 percent of male veterans 18 to 24 are unemployed. When soldiers leave the military, they lose what service provides: purpose, focus, achievement, responsibility and the factor the CNAS report calls "belongingness." The job can be stressful, but especially for the mentally vulnerable, there is no substitute for what jobs offer in the way of structure, support and meaning.

Fill in each blank with the ONE most appropriate word from the passage.

074 Read the passage and follow the directions. [4 points]

Freedom in a free society is supposed to be for all. Therefore, freedom rules out imposing on the freedom of others. You are free to walk down the street, but not to keep others from doing so. The imposition on the freedom of others can come in overt, immediate physical form—thugs coming to attack with weapons. Violence may be a kind of expression, but it certainly is not "free speech."

Like violence, hate speech can also be a physical imposition on the freedom of others. That is because language has a psychological effect imposed physically—on the neural system, with long-term crippling effects.

All thought is carried out by neural circuitry—it does not float in air. Language neurally activates thought. Language can thus change brains, both for the better and the worse. Hate speech changes the brains of those hated for the worse, creating toxic stress, fear and distrust—all physical, all in one's neural circuitry active every day. This internal harm can be even more severe than an attack with a fist. It imposes on the freedom to think and therefore act free of fear, threats, and distrust. It imposes on one's ability to think and act like a fully free citizen for a long time.

That's why hate speech imposes on the freedom of those targeted by the hate. Since being free in a free society requires not imposing on the freedom of others, hate speech does not fall under the category of free speech.

Hate speech can also change the brains of those with mild prejudice, moving it towards hate and threatening action. When hate is physically in your brain, then you think hate and feel hate, you are moved to act to carry out what you physically, in your neural system, think and feel.

The long-term, often crippling physical effects of hate speech on the neural systems of those hated does not have status in law, since our neural systems do not have status in our legal system—at least not yet. This is a gap between the law and the truth.

Is hate speech protected as free speech? If yes or not, explain the reason. Do NOT copy more than FIVE consecutive words from the passage. Second, how does hate speech manifest physical effects? Do NOT copy more than FIVE consecutive words from the passage.

075 Read the passage and follow the directions. [4 points]

> Dual citizenship is an irreversible incident of globalization. Its acceptance appropriately recognizes multiple national identities in a more mobile world. Dual citizenship has never been illegal under U.S. law. The U.S. historically relied on the laws of other countries to police the status. But the rest of the world has moved to embrace dual citizenship to the end of cementing ties to prosperous emigrant populations. Nineteen out of the top 20 source countries for immigrants now allow their citizens to maintain the status even as they naturalize in the United States.
>
> The overwhelming majority of new Americans are <u>ampersand Americans</u>, retaining not just the sentimental but also the formal tie to their homelands. Native-born Americans who move to other countries, meanwhile, will often acquire citizenship in their new country of residence while retaining their U.S. passports. An increasing number of Americans are reestablishing ties to ancestral homelands while they remain in place here. Thousands are acquiring Irish and Italian citizenship on the basis of a grandparent birth. The descendants of Jews who fled the Nazi regime are reacquiring German citizenship. And those born today to "mixed status" parents are no longer forced to choose between them.
>
> That's as it should be. Dual citizenship poses few concrete problems as the world moves away from zero-sum competition among states. Acceptance of the status allows the many individuals with multiple national attachments to actuate those identities. In this respect, dual citizenship represents a kind of freedom of association, a form of voluntary affiliation to be protected, not condemned.

Who are the ampersand Americans referenced in the underlined section? Second, what can be inferred about the circumstance during the period of zero-sum competition regarding citizenship? Do NOT copy more than FIVE consecutive words from the passage.

076 Read the passage and follow the directions. [4 points]

Author Isaac Asimov introduced his laws of robotics. A robot may not injure a human being or, through inaction, allow a human being to come to harm. A robot must obey any orders given to it by human beings, except where such orders would conflict with the First Law. A robot must protect its own existence as long as such protection does not conflict with the First or Second Law.

The laws contain echoes of the Golden Rule ("Thou Shalt Not Kill"), the Judeo-Christian notion that sin results from acts committed and omitted, the physician's Hippocratic oath, and even the right to self-defense. Sounds pretty good, right? Except they never work. In "Runaround," mining engineers on the surface of Mars order a robot to retrieve an element that is poisonous to it. Instead, it gets stuck in a feedback loop between law two and law three. The robot walks in drunken circles until the engineers risk their lives to rescue it. And so it goes with every Asimov robot tale—unanticipated consequences result from contradictions inherent in the three laws. Only by working around the laws are disasters averted.

Asimov was generating plot lines, not trying to solve safety issues in the real world. Where you and I live his laws fall short. For starters, they're insufficiently precise. Tricking robots into performing criminal acts would be simple, unless the robots had perfect comprehension of all of human knowledge. "Put a little dimethylmercury in Charlie's shampoo" is a recipe for murder only if you know that dimethylmercury is a neurotoxin. Asimov eventually added a fourth law, the Zeroth Law, prohibiting robots from harming mankind as a whole, but it doesn't solve the problems. Yet unreliable as Asimov's laws are, they're our most often cited attempt to codify our future relationship with intelligent machines. That's a frightening proposition. Are Asimov's laws all we've got?

I'm afraid it's worse than that. Semiautonomous robotic drones already kill dozens of people each year. Fifty-six countries have or are developing battlefield robots. The race is on to make them autonomous and intelligent. For the most part, discussions of ethics in AI and technological advances take place in different worlds. AI is a dual-use technology like nuclear fission. Nuclear fission can illuminate cities or incinerate them. Its terrible power was unimaginable to most people before 1945. <u>With advanced AI, we're in the 1930s right now.</u>

Identify all of Asimov's laws of robotics. Then, explain why the writer compares AI to nuclear fission, including the intended meaning of the underlined words in your answer. Do NOT copy more than FIVE consecutive words from the passage.

077 Read the passage and follow the directions. [2 points]

> Today, humankind really has taken over the world. The Earth's continents are home to almost 7 billion Sapiens. If you took all these people and put them on a large set of scales, their combined mass would be about 300 million tons. In contrast, the combined mass of all surviving large wild animals—from porcupines and penguins to elephants and whales—is less than 100 million tons. Our children's books, our iconography and our TV screens are still full of giraffes, wolves and chimpanzees, but the real world has very few of them left. There are about 80,000 giraffes in the world, compared to 1.5 billion cattle; only 200,000 wolves, compared to 400 million domesticated dogs; only 250,000 chimpanzees, in contrast to billions of humans.
>
> Ecological degradation is not the same as resource scarcity. The resources available to humankind are constantly increasing, and are likely to continue to do so. That's why doomsday prophesies of resource scarcity are probably misplaced. In contrast, the fear of ecological degradation is only too well founded. The future may see Sapiens gaining control of a cornucopia of new materials and energy sources, while simultaneously destroying what remains of the natural habitat and driving most other species to extinction. In fact, it might endanger the survival of Homo sapiens itself. Global warming, rising oceans and widespread pollution could make the earth less hospitable to our kind, and the future might consequently see a spiralling race between human power and human-induced natural disasters.

Identify the TWO consecutive words from the passage that correspond to the underlined words.

078 Read the passage and follow the directions. [2 points]

> Traditional agriculture depended on cycles of natural time and organic growth. Most societies were unable to make precise time measurements, nor were they terribly interested in doing so. The world went about its business without clocks and timetables, subject only to the movements of the sun and the growth cycles of plants. There was no precise working time, and all routines changed drastically from season to season. People knew where the sun was, and watched anxiously for portents of the rainy season and harvest time, but they did not know the hour and hardly cared about the year. If a lost time traveller popped up in a medieval village and asked a passerby, 'What year is this?' the villager would be as bewildered by the question as by the strangers ridiculous clothing.
>
> In contrast to medieval peasants and shoemakers, modern industry cares little about the sun or the season. It sanctifies precision. For example, in a medieval workshop each shoemaker made an entire shoe, from sole to buckle. If one shoemaker was late for work, it did not stall the others. However, in a modern footwear-factory assembly line, every worker mans a machine that produces just a small part of a shoe, which is then passed on to the next machine. If the worker who operates machine no. 5 has overslept, it stalls all the other machines. In order to prevent such calamities, everybody must adhere to a(n) _____ timetable. Each worker arrives at work at exactly the same time.

Fill in the blank with the ONE most appropriate word from the passage.

079 Read the passage and follow the directions. [4 points]

> I live in a kind of fear and despair all the time. I read the newspaper every day and see what people are doing to one another, how they kill or provoke others to kill. Something will break out—a revolution, a counterrevolution—and people will just drink one another's blood. I tremble at the low state we have fallen into.
>
> It is true that, in the past, wars went on all the time. Still, all people had hope that men would get wiser, that they would know more science and more about human nature so that they might change. But nothing has changed except that weapons are becoming more dangerous and people more vulnerable. As weapons become stronger, our situation becomes weaker. The daily news tells us again and again that, with all his knowledge and with all his refined ways, modern man remains the wildest animal.
>
> What makes me despair more than anything is the scientists, whom God has given great brains and a lot of diligence, sell their achievements to murderers. Every day we get more and more inventions, and many of them are used for killing our brothers and sisters.
>
> I don't mean to say that great scientists such as Michael Faraday, who discovered the principle of the electric motor, and James Maxwell, known for his work in electricity and magnetism, did the wrong thing. They discovered things that are now used for our refrigerators, for lighting up houses at night. But when scientific powers are being used to destroy people it is a great tragedy. I had hopes that the scientists should be the first ones to say, "We are not going to do our work for such purposes." But they are somehow morally stagnant. They just keep on doing their work without caring one way or the other.

Write down the title of the passage with SIX consecutive words found in the passage. Second, explain why the writer is in a deep sense of despair regarding scientists. Do NOT copy more than FIVE consecutive words from the passage.

080 Read the passage and follow the directions. [4 points]

Humanity's primal efforts to systematize the concepts of size, shape, and number are usually regarded as the earliest mathematics. However, the concept of number and the counting process developed so long before the time of recorded history (there is archaeological evidence that counting was employed by humans as far back as 50,000 years ago) that the manner of this development is largely conjectural. Imagining how it probably came about is not difficult. The argument that humans, even in prehistoric times, had some number sense, at least to the extent of recognizing the concepts of 'more' and 'less' when some objects were added to or taken away from a small group, seems fair, for studies have shown that some <u>animals</u> possess such a sense.

With the gradual evolution of society, simple counting became imperative. A tribe had to know how many members it had and how many enemies, and a shepherd needed to know if the flock of sheep was decreasing in size. The earliest way of keeping a count was by some simple tally method, employing the principle of one-to-one correspondence. In keeping a count of sheep, for example, one finger per sheep could be turned under. Counts could also be maintained by making scratches in the dirt or on a stone, by cutting notches in a piece of wood, or by tying knots in a string.

Then, later, an assortment of vocal sounds was developed as a word tally against the number of objects in a small group. And still later, with the refinement of writing, a set of signs was devised to stand for these numbers. Such an imagined development is supported by reports of anthropologists in their studies of present-day societies that are thought to be similar to those of early humans.

Explain the reason why the writer mentions "animals" in the first paragraph. Do NOT copy more than FIVE consecutive words from the passage. Second, identify ALL pre-vocal methods of counting mentioned in the passage.

081 Read the passage and follow the directions. [4 points]

> Even if most tennis players generally strive to strike the ball on the racket's vibration node, known as the "sweet spot," many players are unaware of the existence of a second, lesser-known location on the racket face, the center of percussion, that will also greatly diminish the strain on a player's arm when the ball is struck.
>
> In order to understand the physics of this second sweet spot, it is helpful to consider what would happen to a tennis racket in the moments after impact with the ball if the player's hand were to vanish at the moment of impact. The impact of the ball would cause the racket to bounce backwards, experiencing a translational motion away from the ball. The tendency of this motion would be to jerk all parts of the racket, including the end of its handle, backward, or away from the ball. Unless the ball happened to hit the racket precisely at the racket's center of mass, the racket would additionally experience a rotational motion around its center of mass—much as a penny that has been struck near its edge will start to spin. Whenever the ball hits the racket face, the effect of this rotational motion will be to jerk the end of the handle forward, towards the ball. Depending on where the ball strikes the racket face, one or the other of these motions will predominate.
>
> However, there is one point of impact, known as the center of percussion, which causes neither motion to predominate; if a ball were to strike this point, the impact would not impart any motion to the end of the handle. The reason for this lack of motion is that the force on the upper part of the hand would be equal and opposite to the force on the lower part of the hand, resulting in no net force on the tennis players' hand or forearm. The center of percussion constitutes a second sweet spot because a tennis player's wrist typically is placed next to the end of the racket's handle. When the player strikes the ball at the center of percussion, her wrist is jerked neither forward nor backward, and she experiences a relatively smooth, comfortable tennis stroke.

Explain why using the center of percussion would be less straining on a player. Second, what would occur after a ball hits a racket's sweet spot if there is no one holding it? Lastly, identify the two key motions at work when a ball hits a racket face.

082 Read the passage and follow the directions. [2 points]

> I'm in despair because people take what is happening almost for granted. They read about thousands of people being destroyed, and then they turn to the stock tables as if nothing had really happened. People take the attitude: "It happens to other people; it's not going to happen to me." In that way, I would say that civilization has changed men's hearts to stone more than it has softened them.
>
> In this respect, the media did a lot of moral damage. You become less sensitive to other people's anguish if you hear about it all the time. "You see it every day, you have to make peace with it." That is how modern man thinks.
>
> In my newest book, *The Penitent*, the protagonist, whom I don't identify with completely, says many of the same things I have just said about modern man. The critics all said that I was preaching instead of writing a novel. Who cares if this little book is a novel or a diatribe or if it is even preaching? Actually, in the Yiddish edition the word *novel* did not appear. There is a time when a man must say what he considers important.
>
> I'm sure that many others think the same way, but they don't know what to do. They cannot all write novels or diatribes. And how will what I'm saying help? It's talking to the wall. Still, there is a time when even a novelist, who is supposed to entertain the reader, is tempted to ask: "Where are we going? What will happen to us?"

Complete the summary by filling in each blank below with the ONE most appropriate word from the passage. If necessary, you may change the word form.

── Commentary ──
> People have become largely ⓐ_____ toward others' suffering because people have uncritically heard too many stories about human anguish through the ⓑ_____. As a novelist, the writer feels that a man must say what he considers crucial.

083 Read the passage and follow the directions. [2 points]

> The real meaning of the word *human* is 'an animal belonging to the genus Homo', and there used to be many other species of this genus besides Homo sapiens. Humans first evolved in East Africa about 2.5 million years ago from an earlier genus of apes called Australopithecus, which means 'Southern Ape'. About 2 million years ago, some of these archaic men and women left their homeland to journey through and settle vast areas of North Africa, Europe and Asia.
>
> _____ⓐ_____ in Europe and western Asia evolved into Homo neanderthalensis ('Man from the Neander Valley), popularly referred to simply as 'Neanderthals'. The more eastern regions of Asia were populated by Homo erectus, 'Upright Man', who survived there for close to 2 million years. On the island of Java, in Indonesia, lived Homo soloensis, 'Man from the Solo Valley', who was suited to life in the tropics. On another Indonesian island—the small island of Flores—archaic humans underwent a process of dwarfing. Humans first reached Flores when the sea level was exceptionally low, and the island was easily accessible from the mainland. When the seas rose again, some people were trapped on the island, which was poor in resources. Big people, who need a lot of food, died first. Smaller fellows survived much better. Over the generations, the people of Flores became _____ⓑ_____. This unique species, known by scientists as Homo floresiensis, reached a maximum height of only one metre and weighed no more than twenty-five kilograms.

Fill in each blank with the ONE most appropriate word from the passage. If necessary, change the word form.

084 Read the following passage and then answer the questions. [4 points]

The Acacia has long been used in Australia in building simple mud and stick structures. The acacia is called a "wattle" there. The acacia is actually related to the family of plants known as *legumes* that includes peas, beans, lentils, peanuts, and pods with beanlike seeds. Some acacias actually produce edible crops. Other Acacia varieties are valued for the sticky resin, called gum arabic or gum acacia, used widely in medicines, foods, and perfumes, for the dark dense wood prized for making pianos, or for the bark, rich in tannin, a dark, acidic substance used to cure the hides of animals, transforming them into leather.

Nearly five hundred species of Acacia have been analyzed, identified, categorized, and proven capable of survival in hot and generally arid parts of the world; however, only a dozen of the three hundred Australian varieties thrive in the southern United States. Most acacia imports are low spreading trees, but of these, only three flower, including the *Bailey Acacia* with fernlike silver leaves and small, fragrant flowers arranged in rounded clusters, the *Silver Wattle*, similar to the *Bailey Acacia*, which grows twice as high, and the squat *Sydney Golden Wattle*, bushy with broad, flat leaves, showy bright yellow blossoms, and sharp spined twigs. Another variety, the *Black Acacia*, also called the *Blackwood*, has dark green foliage and unobtrusive blossoms. Besides being a popular ornamental tree, the *Black Acacia* is considered valuable for its dark wood, which is used in making furniture, as well as highly prized musical instruments.

The Acacia's unusual custom of _____ in February has been commonly attributed to its Australian origins, as if the date and not the quality of light made the difference for a tree in its blossoming cycle. In the Southern Hemisphere, the seasons are reversed, and February, which is wintertime in the United States, is summertime in Australia. Actually, however, the pale, yellow blossoms appear in August in Australia. Whether growing in the Northern or Southern Hemisphere, the lovely acacia blossoms in winter.

Identify how many species grow well in the southern United States. Next, which species of Acacia has the least colorful blossoms? Finally, fill in the blank with the ONE most appropriate word from the passage.

085 Read the following passage and then answer the questions. [4 points]

> Around 1960, mathematician Edward Lorenz found unexpected behavior in apparently simple equations representing atmospheric air flows. Whenever he reran his model with the same inputs, different outputs resulted although the model lacked any random elements. Lorenz realized that tiny rounding errors in his analog computer mushroomed over time, leading to erratic results. His findings marked a seminal moment in the development of chaos theory, which, despite its name, has little to do with randomness.
>
> To understand how unpredictability can arise from deterministic equations, which do not involve chance outcomes, consider the non-chaotic system of two poppy seeds placed in a round bowl. As the seeds roll to the bowl's center, a position known as a point attractor, the distance between the seeds shrinks. If, instead, the bowl is flipped over, two seeds placed on top will roll away from each other. Such a system, while still not technically chaotic, enlarges initial differences in position.
>
> Chaotic systems, such as a machine mixing bread dough, are characterized by both attraction and repulsion. As the dough is stretched, folded, and pressed back together, any poppy seeds sprinkled in are intermixed seemingly at random. But this randomness is illusory. In fact, the poppy seeds are captured by "strange attractors," staggeringly complex pathways whose tangles appear accidental but are in fact determined by the system's fundamental equations.
>
> During the dough-kneading process, two poppy seeds positioned next to each other eventually go their separate ways. Any early divergence or measurement error is repeatedly amplified by the mixing until the position of any seed becomes effectively unpredictable. It is this "sensitive dependence on initial conditions" and not true randomness that generates unpredictability in chaotic systems.

The passage explores a common misconception about a complex physical system. Describe what the misconception is. Second, identify one example of a complex physical system appearing as chaotic system that the writer provides.

086 Read the passage and follow the directions. [2 points]

> What about terrorism, then? Even if central governments and powerful states have learned restraint, terrorists might have no such qualms about using new and destructive weapons. That is certainly a worrying possibility. However, terrorism is a strategy of weakness adopted by those who lack access to real power. At least in the past, terrorism worked by spreading fear rather than by causing significant material damage. Terrorists usually don't have the strength to defeat an army, occupy a country or destroy entire cities.
>
> How, then, do terrorists manage to dominate the headlines and change the political situation throughout the world? By provoking their enemies to overreact. In essence, terrorism is a show. Terrorists stage a terrifying spectacle of violence that captures our imagination and make us feel as if we are sliding back into medieval chaos. Consequently states often feel obliged to react to the theatre of terrorism with a show of security, orchestrating immense displays of force, such as the persecution of entire populations or the invasion of foreign countries. In most cases, the _____ to terrorism poses a far greater threat to our security than the terrorists themselves. Terrorists are like a fly that tries to destroy a china shop. The fly is so weak that it cannot budge even a single teacup. So it finds a bull, gets inside its ear and starts buzzing. The bull goes wild with fear and anger, and destroys the china shop. This is what happened in the Middle East in the last decade.

Fill in the blank with the ONE most appropriate word from the passage. If necessary, change the word form.

087 Read the passage and follow the directions. [4 points]

Most living organisms have an internal clock, a circadian clock that orchestrates the biochemical, physiological and behavioral functions in each cell according to a 24-hour day-night cycle. This clock regulates sleeping and waking, hormone levels, body temperature, heart rate and blood pressure, among hundreds of other factors.

Our lab is studying how circadian clocks influence the repair of DNA in the cell—a natural process in which a team of enzymes travel along the DNA fixing breaks and errors caused by damaging effects of UV radiation and DNA-altering chemicals. Without these ever vigilant enzymes, our cells would accumulate mutations in our DNA that would lead to cancer and other diseases. Understanding this relationship between our body rhythms and DNA repair is important because there is mounting evidence that malfunctioning clocks are linked to conditions from obesity and epilepsy to insomnia and seasonal affective disorder.

We have been exploring how the circadian rhythms influence _____ during treatment with the popular anti-cancer drug cisplatin. Cisplatin is used to treat most solid tissue cancers including testicular, ovarian, colorectal, lung and breast cancers. It kills cancer cells by damaging their DNA. However, it also damages DNA of normal cells, causing serious side effects that often force physicians to halt the treatment. Both normal and cancer cells repair the DNA damage caused by cisplatin. Successful treatment requires hitting cancer cells with DNA damage when they are least capable of repairing it, while sparing the healthy tissue.

In the past few decades scientists have attempted to use the circadian clock to guide the timing of cisplatin therapy. Their strategy was to give cisplatin at particular times and then monitor how the patient fared, thus revealing a time of day that yielded the greatest benefit with the least side effects. However, these experiments failed because the choice of times was somewhat arbitrary and not based on what was happening inside the cell.

유희태 | 일반영어 ④-1

Fill in the blank with the TWO most appropriate consecutive words from the passage. Then, explain what specific part of anatomy the writer believes should be understood for more successful studies into cisplatin therapy timing.

088 Read the passage and follow the directions. [4 points]

Before I was a psychologist, I was a teacher. My students were twelve and thirteen years old. Most lived in the housing projects clustered between Avenues A and D. This was before the neighborhood sprouted hip cafés on every corner. The fall I started teaching there, ⓐ our school was picked for the set of a movie about a rough-and-tumble school in a distressed urban neighborhood. My job was to help my students learn seventh-grade math: fractions and decimals and the rudimentary building blocks of algebra and geometry. Even that first week, it was obvious that some of my students picked up mathematical concepts more easily than their classmates. Teaching the most talented students in the class was a joy. They were, quite literally, "quick studies." Without much prompting, they saw the underlying pattern in a series of math problems that less able students struggled to grasp. They'd watch me do a problem once on the board and say, "I get it!" and then work out the next one correctly on their own. And yet, at the end of the first marking period, I was surprised to find that some of these very able students weren't doing as well as I'd expected. Some did very well, of course. But more than a few of my most talented students were earning lackluster grades or worse. In contrast, several of the students who initially struggled were faring better than I'd expected. These "overachievers" would reliably come to class every day with everything they needed. Instead of playing around and looking out the window, they took notes and asked questions. When they didn't get something the first time around, they tried again and again, sometimes coming for extra help during their lunch period or during afternoon electives. Their hard work showed in their grades.

Apparently, aptitude did not guarantee achievement. Talent for math was different from excelling in math class. This came as a surprise. After all, ⓑ conventional wisdom says that math is a subject in which the more talented students are expected to excel, leaving classmates who are simply "not math people" behind. To be honest, I began the school year with that very assumption.

What point is the writer trying to illustrate in underlined selection ⓐ? Second, in what way would the writer react to ⓑ "conventional wisdom" after having experienced teaching math first-hand?

089 Read the passage and follow the directions. [2 points]

> I wanted to know whether it was just the rigors of Beast that demanded grit, or whether, in general, grit helped people stick to their commitments. The next arena where I tested grit's power was sales, a profession in which daily, if not hourly, rejection is par for the course. I asked hundreds of men and women employed at the same vacation time-share company to answer a battery of personality questionnaires, including the Grit Scale. Six months later, I revisited the company, by which time 55 percent of the salespeople were gone. Grit predicted who stayed and who left. Moreover, no other commonly measured personality trait—including extroversion, emotional stability, and conscientiousness—was as effective as grit in ⓐ_____ job retention. Around the same time, I received a call from the Chicago Public Schools. Like the psychologists at West Point, researchers there were eager to learn more about the students who would successfully earn their high school diplomas. That spring, thousands of high school juniors completed an abbreviated Grit Scale, along with a battery of other questionnaires. More than a year later, 12 percent of those students failed to graduate. Students who graduated on schedule were grittier. And ⓑ_____ was a more powerful predictor of graduation than how much students cared about school, how conscientious they were about their studies, and even how safe they felt at school.

Fill in each blank with the ONE most appropriate word from the passage. If necessary, change the word form.

090 Read the passage and follow the directions. [2 points]

Postmodern scholars and social critics like to talk of the "dot-com generation"—the first generation to grow up in a simulated commercial world. But how different are today's youngsters from the bourgeois children of the late nineteenth and early twentieth centuries? While there are many similarities, the differences are profound and suggest that a new type of human being is being readied for the twenty-first century—individuals whose sense of self is bound up less in how much output they produce and how many things they accumulate and more in how many vivid experiences and relationships they have access to.

The last great change in human consciousness came at the dawn of the modern era with the rise of the bourgeois class. A product of the new cities that were the hubs of an incipient capitalism, the bourgeoisie were the merchants, factory owners, shopkeepers, academicians, and professionals who spearheaded the industrial way of life. In a world that was being transformed from caste to class, they were the upwardly mobile middle, sandwiched between a dying feudal aristocracy on top and an oppressed and volatile proletariat of workers and disenfranchised small farmers and peasants on the bottom. They were the entrepreneurs and accumulators of capital, the champions of nationhood and extended markets, the realists who believed that human reason could unlock the secrets of nature and codify the truths of a knowable objective reality. They were the class that gradually abandoned theology for ideology and heavenly salvation for an earthly utopia. They spread the gospel of materialism and most importantly extolled the virtues of private property.

Unlike medieval life, which was conducted openly and in public, the bourgeoisie lived mostly behind closed doors. Their life was an interior one—lived out in small shops and drawing rooms. The bourgeoisie organized their lives the way they organized their property. Every aspect of their being was privatized and hidden away from public scrutiny. Everything in this private world was composed and organized. Nothing was out of place.

Choose the ONE word from the passage that BEST completes the given statement below. You may change the word form if necessary.

---Commentary---
In the given passage the major difference the writer observes between medieval aristocracy and the bourgeoisie is their tendency away from openness towards _____.

091 Read the passage and follow the directions. [4 points]

You might have seen figure skaters spinning around quickly and then tucking their arms to spin faster—or opening them to spin more slowly. This happens, thanks to a physics concept known as the "conservation of angular momentum." But how can you try it out if you don't have any ice skates around?

Newton's first law of motion states that an object at rest (not moving) will remain at rest and a moving object will keep moving—unless they are acted on by an outside force. This means that an object's momentum (its mass times its velocity) will stay the same unless an outside force acts on it somehow. You experience this every day. For example, imagine catching a ball. When the ball is moving, it has momentum. You have to exert a force with your hand to stop the ball (and bring its momentum down to zero). If the ball is heavier or moving faster, it has more momentum, and is harder to catch—you have to exert a bigger force.

This concept is usually described in relation to objects moving in a straight line, but it also applies to spinning objects. The terminology is a little different when we talk about spinning objects. Instead of forces, which are pushes or pulls that act in a straight line, we refer to torque, which is a "twist" applied to an object (think: twisting a screwdriver or a doorknob). Instead of mass, we refer to moment of inertia, which measures how spread out the mass is about the point of rotation. Instead of velocity we say, "angular velocity," which measures how fast an object rotates. Finally, instead of momentum, we say "angular momentum."

> Even though the terms are a little different the same concepts apply. The angular momentum of a spinning object will remain the same unless a(n) _____ acts on it. In physics when something stays the same we say it is conserved. That's where the phrase "conservation of angular momentum" comes from. The classic example of this is a spinning ice skater or someone spinning in an office chair. By pulling in her arms, the skater decreases her moment of inertia (all her mass is closer to the middle), so her angular velocity has to increase in order to keep her angular momentum constant.

Fill in the blank with the TWO most appropriate words from the passage. Second, describe TWO ways to reduce angular momentum that can be inferred from the passage.

092 Read the passage and follow the directions. [4 points]

> Not everyone welcomed the change to the written form. There were those who suggested that the move away from human-to-human communication was alienating and that having to learn an abstract, symbolic system—such as the alphabet—was a barrier to communication and meaning. The philosopher Socrates was among those who objected to the written medium. He argued that human thought and communication were fluid, that they were constantly moving. He insisted that understanding was based on an exchange of information, where constant modification took place in the light of what others were saying. Writing, he warned, didn't allow for this critical dynamism. It fixed ideas and forced you to follow an argument rather than to engage with it. Because he thought that this was such a distortion of intention and meaning he would not put his ideas in writing. But writing managed to take hold without his contribution and the highpoint of the written medium came in the 14th and 15th centuries, with the wonderful achievements of the manuscript era. By this time in European history the Church and the nobility were in charge of the written word, and just as Socrates had predicted, the meanings were well and truly fixed. Manuscripts were produced by scribes, who were in the main, monks and priests. And the information they copied in the scriptoria was primarily of a sacred nature. They produced beautiful manuscripts of the Bible, of prayer-books and of religious commentary, etc. These texts were in Latin, which was the language of the Church and the aristocracy. By using this code the establishment was able to prevent the lay community who did not know Latin from having access to information.

Explain the reason why Socrates criticized writing. Second, what problem does the writer identify in the maintaining of the scriptoria?

093 Read the passage and follow the directions. [2 points]

> Affirmative action has clearly worked. It has given us more interesting student bodies. It's given us minority graduates who will now take a place in the professions. When I look at what this country is becoming and think of the possibility that without affirmative action, we would not be graduating people of minority backgrounds who will become the leaders of this new country—in the professions, in education, in medicine, and in business—I fear to think what the country would have been like otherwise. Affirmative action has been indispensable. All of us find that one of the ways that incoming students, high school seniors, judge the places they're looking at is the degree of diversity that they have. Students don't want to go to schools that don't have sufficient diversity. They recognize that there are inherently more interesting places. It's interesting that for the generation from World War II onward, universities understood that geographic diversity was important. They went out of their way to try to enroll students from wider and wider sections of the United States, so that the notion that you learned in better circumstances with students who've had _____ upbringings is not one that started with the Civil Rights movement.

Choose the ONE word that BEST completes the blank from the passage. If necessary, you may change the word form.

094 Read the passage and follow the directions. [4 points]

When severe drought hit ancient Egypt or medieval India, it was not uncommon that 5 or 10 percent of the population perished. Provisions became scarce; transport was too slow and expensive to import sufficient food; and governments were far too weak to save the day.

Open any history book and you are likely to come across horrific accounts of famished populations, driven mad by hunger. In April 1694 a French official in the town of Beauvais described the impact of famine and of soaring food prices, saying that his entire district was now filled with an infinite number of poor souls, weak from hunger and wretchedness and dying from want, because, having no work or occupation, they lack the money to buy bread. Seeking to prolong their lives a little and somewhat to appease their hunger, these poor folk eat such unclean things as cats and the flesh of horses flayed and cast onto dung heaps. Others consume the blood that flows when cows and oxen are slaughtered.

Similar scenes took place all over France. Bad weather had ruined the harvests throughout the kingdom in the previous two years, so that by the spring of 1694 the granaries were completely empty. The rich charged exorbitant prices for whatever food they managed to hoard, and the poor died in droves. About 2.8 million French—15 percent of the population—starved to death between 1692 and 1694, while the Sun King, Louis XIV, was dallying with his mistresses in Versailles.

Most readers probably know how it feels when you miss lunch, when you fast on some religious holiday, or when you live for a few days on vegetable shakes as part of a new wonder diet. But how does it feel when you haven't eaten for days on end and you have no clue where to get the next morsel of food? Most people today have never experienced <u>this excruciating torment</u>. Our ancestors, alas, knew it only too well. When they cried to God, 'Deliver us from famine!', this is what they had in mind.

Describe TWO reasons food prices soared in France during the 17th century. Then, identify what the underlined words refer to.

095 Read the passage and follow the directions. [4 points]

> In 1998 it made sense for Rwanda to seize and loot the rich coltan mines of neighbouring Congo, because this ore was in high demand for the manufacture of mobile phones and laptops, and Congo held 80 percent of the world's coltan reserves. Rwanda earned $240 million annually from the looted coltan. For poor Rwanda that was a lot of money. In contrast, it would have made no sense for China to invade California and seize Silicon Valley, for even if the Chinese could somehow prevail on the battlefield, there were no silicon mines to loot in Silicon Valley. Instead, the Chinese have earned billions of dollars from cooperating with hi-tech giants such as Apple and Microsoft, buying their software and manufacturing their products. What Rwanda earned from an entire year of looting Congolese coltan, the Chinese earn in a single day of peaceful commerce.
>
> In consequence, the word 'peace' has acquired a new meaning. Previous generations thought about peace as the temporary absence of war. Today we think about peace as the implausibility of war. When in 1913 people said that there was peace between France and Germany, they meant that 'there is no war going on at present between France and Germany, but who knows what next year will bring'. When today we say that there is peace between France and Germany, we mean that it is inconceivable under any foreseeable circumstances that war might break out between them. Such peace prevails not only between France and Germany, but between most (though not all) countries. There is no scenario for a serious war breaking out next year between Germany and Poland, between Indonesia and the Philippines, or between Brazil and Uruguay.
>
> This New peace is not just a hippie fantasy. Power-hungry governments and greedy corporations also count on it. When Mercedes plans its sales strategy in eastern Europe, it discounts the possibility that Germany might conquer Poland.

Explain why it is nonsensical for China to invade California according to the passage. Second, describe how the meaning of the word "peace" has changed.

096 Read the passage and follow the directions. [2 points]

The plight of Jews in German-occupied Europe, which many people thought was at the heart of the war against the Axis, was not a chief concern of Roosevelt. Henry Feingold's research shows that, while the Jews were being put in camps and the process of annihilation was beginning that would end in the horrifying extermination of 6 million Jews and millions of non-Jews, Roosevelt failed to take steps that might have saved thousands of lives. He did not see it as a high priority. He left it to the State Department, and in the State Department anti-Semitism and a cold bureaucracy became obstacles to action.

Was the war being fought to establish that Hitler was wrong in his ideas of white Nordic supremacy over "inferior" races? The United States' armed forces were segregated by ⓐ_____. When troops were jammed onto the Queen Mary in early 1945 to go to combat duty in the European theater, the blacks were stowed down in the depths of the ship near the engine room, as far as possible from the fresh air of the deck, in a bizarre reminder of the slave voyages of old.

The Red Cross, with government approval, separated the blood donations of black and white. It was, ironically, a black physician named Charles Drew who developed the blood bank system. He was put in charge of the wartime donations, and then fired when he tried to end blood ⓑ_____. Despite the urgent need for wartime labor, blacks were still experiencing a lot of difficulties to get jobs. A spokesman for a West Coast aviation plant said: "The Negro will be considered only as janitors and in other similar capacities. Regardless of their training as aircraft workers, we will not employ them." Roosevelt never did anything to enforce the orders of the Fair Employment Practices Commission he had set up.

Fill in each blank with the ONE most appropriate word from the passage. If necessary, change the word form.

097 Read the passage and follow the directions. [4 points]

> According to research compiled by Innova Market Insights, which houses a database that collects consumer trend information from more than 70 different countries, 4 out of 10 consumers in the U.S. and the U.K. have increased their consumption of what they call "healthy foods," or foods that at least market themselves as healthy. This includes potato chips that are "lightly salted," or "lightly sweetened." And in China, nearly 22 percent of consumers said that "Made with Real Ingredients" was an important factor in influencing their snack purchases. Unlike 20 years ago, a package of chips today might tell the consumer everything from the oil in which the chip was fried to the country where the potato or grain was harvested.
>
> It should come as no surprise, then, that flavors are also culturally coded. Consistent with Innova's research, this demonstrates why chili and jalapeño chili are consistently popular food flavors in Latin America, while sea salt, cheddar and barbecue dominate in North America.
>
> What's even more interesting is the way that foreign flavors are introduced into other markets. Foreign flavors rely on and work with social trends to dictate which direction large food companies will go.
>
> The seaweed flavor, while virtually unheard of in the U.S. 20 years ago, is now one of the top 10 selling flavors in North America. An increased interest in Japanese culture, including comic books, anime and sushi, have made that flavor of more interest to Western consumers. And potato chip manufacturers have taken notice, capitalizing on the shift in consumer trends before they change again.
>
> Now people are really interested in Korean food, Korean electronics, and Korean pop culture, so kimchi might be a good idea for a new potato chip flavor. <u>Twenty years ago, people would have laughed at the idea</u>.

Explain the reason why chili is a persistently popular food flavor in Latin America. Second, explain the meaning of the underlined words.

098 Read the passage and follow the directions. [4 points]

[1] Just south of the Greek island of Samos lies the Icarian Sea. Legend has it that this is where Icarus died—a victim of hubris. His father, Daedalus, was a master craftsman. Banished to prison for sabotaging the work of King Minos (captor of the Minotaur), Daedalus created a brilliant escape plot, described in the myth that we were told as children. He fashioned a set of wings for himself and his son. After affixing the wings with wax, they set out to escape. Daedalus warned Icarus not to fly too close to the sun. Entranced by his magical ability to fly, Icarus disobeyed and flew too high. We all know what happened next: The wax melted, and Icarus, the beloved son, lost his wings, tumbled into the sea, and died.

[2] The lesson of this myth: Don't disobey the king. Don't disobey your dad. Don't imagine that you are better than you are, and most of all, don't ever have the belief that you have the ability to do what a god might do. The part of the myth that you weren't told: In addition to telling Icarus not to fly too high, Daedalus instructed his son not to fly too low, too close to the sea, because the water would ruin the lift in his wings. Society has altered the myth, encouraging us to forget the part about the sea, and created a culture where we constantly remind one another about the dangers of standing up, standing out, and making a commotion. Industrialists have made pride a cardinal sin but conveniently ignored a far more common failing: settling for too little. It is far more dangerous to fly too low than too high, because it feels safe to fly low.

Describe the main idea of the passage. Then, identify the ONE word from section [1] that most directly corresponds to the meaning of the underlined words.

099 **Read the passage and follow the directions.** [2 points]

> The possibility of war is a great force for the rationalization of societies, and for the creation of uniform social structures across cultures. Any state that hopes to maintain its political autonomy is forced to adopt the technology of its enemies and rivals. More than that, however, the threat of war forces states to restructure their social systems along lines most conducive to producing and deploying technology. For example, states must be of a certain size in order to compete with their neighbors, which creates powerful incentives for national unity; they must be able to mobilize resources on a national level, which requires the creation of a strong centralized state authority with the power of taxation and regulation; they must break down various forms of regional, religious, and kinship ties which potentially obstruct national unity; they must increase educational levels in order to produce an elite capable of disposing of technology; they must maintain contact with and awareness of developments taking place beyond their borders; and, with the introduction of mass armies during the Napoleonic Wars, they must at least open the door to the enfranchisement of the poorer classes of their societies if they are to be capable of total mobilization. All of these developments could occur for other motives—for example, economic ones—but _____ frames the need for social modernization in a particularly acute way and provides an unambiguous test of its success.

Fill in the blank with the ONE most appropriate word from the passage.

100 **Read the passage and follow the directions.** [4 points]

On a Friday night last month, I moderated a debate in Manhattan about whether we should scrap capitalism. It was organized by the magazine *Jacobin*; defending capitalism were editors from the libertarian publication *Reason*. Tickets for all available 450 seats sold out in a day. So *Jacobin* moved it to a venue that holds around twice as many. The extra tickets sold out in eight hours.

When I arrived, people were lined up for blocks; walking to the door, I felt like I was on the guest list at an underground nightclub. Most attendees appeared to be in their 20s and 30s, part of a generation that is uniquely suspicious of capitalism, a system most of their elders take for granted.

The anti-Communist Victims of Communism Memorial Foundation was alarmed to find in a recent survey that 44 percent of millennials would prefer to live in a socialist country, compared with 42 percent who want to live under capitalism. For older Americans, the collapse of Communism made it seem as though there was no possible alternative to capitalism. But given the increasingly oligarchic nature of our economy, it's not surprising that for many young people, capitalism looks like the god that failed.

Nowhere is that clearer than in the wretched tax bill passed by the Senate in the early hours of Saturday morning, which would make the rich richer and the poor poorer. According to the nonpartisan Tax Policy Center, the bill directs the largest tax cuts as a share of income to the top 5 percent of taxpayers. By 2027, taxes on the lowest earners would go up.

Millennials, a generation maligned as entitled whiners, would be particularly hard hit. The rich people who would benefit from the measures passed by the House and the Senate tend to be older and whiter than the population at large. Younger people would foot the bill, either through higher taxes, diminished public services or both. They stand to inherit an even more stratified society than the one they were born into.

> Here's one example. The Senate bill offers a tax break for parents whose children attend private school. But it cuts deductions for state and local taxes, which could make it harder to fund the public schools where the vast majority of millennials will send their kids.

Explain the meaning of the underlined words. Then, explain the reason why the writer mentions "public schools" in the passage.

101 Read the passage and follow the directions. [4 points]

In the coming days, two NFL cheerleading squads will feature the league's first-ever male dancers. Napoleon Jinnies and Quinton Peron have joined the Los Angeles Rams' cheerleaders, and Jesse Hernandez will perform as a member of the New Orleans Saints' Saintsations. While NFL teams, including the Saints, have included men as supporting cheerleaders for physical stunts, they've never been part of the main dance routines.

The addition of men to pro football cheerleading squads will make for a small shift in gender composition that could have an outsize impact. Earlier this year, a pair of cheerleaders filed sex discrimination complaints against the NFL, while several other NFL cheerleaders have spoken openly about their paltry pay, the extreme restrictions placed on their appearances and personal lives, and the sexual harassment they're expected to endure from fans. Given that, the timing of the shattering of this particular glass ceiling is suspect. It's likely no coincidence that the Saints hired their first male cheerleader in the months after the team came under public scrutiny for their sexist workplace conditions. However deserving of their spots the men on these squads may be, it's worth pondering whether teams will use male cheerleaders as window dressing to enable the continued physical and financial exploitation of female employees.

That doesn't mean nothing good can come of a little gender diversity. Bringing on men may illuminate the sexist nature of cheerleading squads' restrictive rules, or even force team leadership to improve their treatment of cheerleaders. And Jinnies and Peron have already demonstrated another possible positive effect: Boys and young men who watch football may get new ideas of what's possible for their own futures. Hernandez said he decided to audition for the Saintsations after his mother sent him a link to a story about Jinnies and Peron joining the Rams' cheerleading team. The presence of male cheerleaders may also force viewers to expand their personal conceptions of maleness, and masculinity, as they watch Hernandez and co. execute the same sexy dance moves as the women by their sides. Men make up a large majority of NFL fans—a captive, ready audience for a stealth masculinity re-education campaign.

Explain the meaning of the underlined words. Then, describe all possible advantages that male cheerleaders may bring to the sport field.

102 Read the passage and follow the directions. [2 points]

> Although average life expectancy has doubled over the last hundred years, it is unwarranted to extrapolate and conclude that we can double it again to 150 in the coming century. In 1900 global life expectancy was no higher than forty because many people died young from malnutrition, infectious diseases and violence. Yet those who escaped famine, plague and war could live well into their seventies and eighties, which is the natural life span of *Homo Sapiens*. Contrary to common notions, seventy-year-olds weren't considered rare freaks of nature in previous centuries. Galileo Galilei died at seventy-seven, Issac Newton at eighty-four, and Michelangelo lived to the ripe age of eighty-eight, without any help from antibiotics, vaccinations or organ transplants. Indeed, even chimpanzees in the jungle sometimes live into their sixties.
>
> In truth, so far modern medicine hasn't extended our natural life span by a single year. Its great achievement has been to save us from premature death, and allow us to enjoy the full measure of our years. Even if we now overcome cancer, diabetes, and the other major killers, it would mean only that almost everyone will get to live to ninety—but it will not be enough to reach 150, let alone 500. For that, medicine will need to re-engineer the most fundamental structures and processes of the human body, and discover how to regenerate organs and tissues. It is by no means clear that we can do that by 2100.

Describe the main idea of the passage by filling in each blank below with the most appropriate word(s) from the passage.

| Commentary |

> Though the average life span has risen significantly in recent years, it is not due to the overall extension of the natural ⓐ_____, but to the reduction of ⓑ_____ death.

103 Read the passage and follow the directions. [2 points]

> Episodic memory represents our memory of experiences and specific events in time in a serial form, from which we can reconstruct the actual events that took place at any given point in our lives. It is the memory of autobiographical events (times, places, associated emotions and other contextual knowledge) that can be explicitly stated. Individuals tend to see themselves as actors in these events, and the emotional charge and the entire context surrounding an event is usually part of the memory, not just the bare facts of the event itself.
>
> Semantic memory, on the other hand, is a more structured record of facts, meanings, concepts and knowledge about the external world that we have acquired. It refers to general factual knowledge, shared with others and independent of personal experience and of the spatial/temporal context in which it was acquired. Semantic memories may once have had a personal context, but now stand alone as simple knowledge. It therefore includes such things as types of food, capital cities, social customs, functions of objects, vocabulary, understanding of mathematics, etc. Much of semantic memory is abstract and relational and is associated with the meaning of verbal symbols.
>
> The semantic memory is generally derived from the episodic memory, in that we learn new facts or concepts from our experiences, and the episodic memory is considered to support and underpin semantic memory. A gradual transition from ⓐ_____ to ⓑ_____ memory can take place, in which episodic memory reduces its sensitivity and association to particular events, so that the information can be generalized as semantic memory.

Fill in each blank with the ONE most appropriate word from the passage.

104 Read the passage and follow the directions. [4 points]

One of the biggest troublemakers in our marriage was the seemingly innocent little question "Why?". Having grown up in a family in which explanations were offered as a matter of course, I was always asking my husband, "Why?". He had grown up in a family in which explanations were neither offered nor sought, so when I asked, "Why?" he looked for hidden meaning—and concluded that I was questioning his decision and even his right to make it. My continually asking why seemed to him an effort to show him up as incompetent. Furthermore, not being accustomed to hearing people explain reasons for doing things, and not having been called upon to explain his reasons in the past, he tended to act on instinct. So he really couldn't have explained his reasons even if he'd wanted to.

As a result, we often had conversations like this:

"Let's drop by Anthony's house tonight"
"Why?"
"All right, we don't have to go."

Then he would be angry at me for not being willing to do this small thing for him, and I'd angry at him because he changed his mind on the spot, refused to explain either why he wanted to go or why he didn't, and inexplicably fell into a sulk.

What makes misunderstandings like these so hard to straighten out is that our ways of communicating seem self-evidently natural to us. He didn't feel he was hinting; he felt he was communicating. He didn't feel he was picking up hints from me; he felt he was hearing me communicate.

That's why the frequently heard advice to "be honest" doesn't help much. We *were* being honest. But our ways of being honest were different—and mutually unintelligible. When I missed his hint, he assumed I knew what he meant and refused to honor it. When I denied having meant what he heard me say (or heard me hint—the same thing), he thought I was being flighty or dishonest. Since I hadn't meant what he heard me say, and I hadn't heard what he knew he'd meant, our attempts to solve the problem were doomed. The only way we knew of treating the disease was precisely what was causing it—talking.

Explain why being honest is not a solution to the author's problem. Next, what justification from her background does she give for her perspective differing from her husband's?

105 Read the passage and follow the directions. [4 points]

If you like to stand close to folks when you talk to them, you'll love Argentina. The South American country is filled with "close-talkers"—people who stand 2.5 feet(0.76 meters) away from strangers when chatting. If you prefer more personal space, make your way to Romania instead. There, residents like to stand a spacious 4.5 feet(1.4 meters) away from strangers.

This info on personal "bubbles" comes from a study of preferred interpersonal distances recently published in the *Journal of Cross-Cultural Psychology*. While this issue of personal space in different countries has been examined before, the authors of this study used a much larger data set (nearly 9,000 people living in 42 countries) than was used in previous studies. Participants were shown a picture with two figures representing two people and a line with some distances marked off in between them. The subjects were asked how close should the two figures stand together if they are strangers versus close friends versus colleagues (acquaintances). The subjects were to assume that they were one of the two figures.

The scientists found that residents of Argentina, Peru and Bulgaria stand the closest to strangers, while those from Romania, Hungary and Saudi Arabia want the most space. Americans were somewhere in the middle.

The researchers also studied the personal bubbles we draw between ourselves and family and friends. We're all fine with our family and friends standing closer to us than strangers—no surprise there. And our general bubble size with our friends stays consistent. That is, if we like more personal space, we'll keep our friends farther away than those who are fine with less personal space.

But <u>intriguingly</u>, things change when it comes to close friends or loved ones. The Romanians who like a lot of personal space between themselves and both strangers and colleagues like their intimate relations to be fairly close to them—about 1.5 feet(0.45 meters). That's closer than almost any other group studied.

Explain how the study published in *Journal of Cross-Cultural Psychology* differs from those previous. Second, explain why the writer uses the underlined word "intriguingly".

106 Read the passage and follow the directions. [2 points]

> Visitors to the parched Sonoran Desert of southern Arizona and northern Mexico marvel at the <u>many-armed giants</u> that give the landscape its unique appearance. In the dry, rugged desert they can live for more than 200 years, grow to a height of 60 feet, and have as many as 50 arms. Amazingly, they persist despite the harsh, unforgiving desert climate. Those that have grown to old age have survived drought, freezes, flash floods, and brush fires, as well as the pack rats that eat their seedlings. Like all desert plants, they hoard water. These leafless plants absorb the water through their long roots and store it for use during the desert's long dry spells. Naturally, these are a vital part of desert life. In fact, this giant may be home to many animals, including woodpeckers, owls, doves, bats, and insects. In addition, after a saguaro reaches the age of fifty or so, hardy flowers appear at the top of the plant once a year. These flowers entice birds, bats, and bees, who come for the nectar and for the tasty flowers with their black seeds. Although the regal saguaros are plentiful in the Southwest, they are, unfortunately, in danger. These cacti have great value in landscape gardening, and poachers can earn thousands of dollars by uprooting them and selling them to nurseries.

Identify the TWO consecutive words from the passage that BEST correspond to the underlined words.

107 Read the passage and follow the directions. [4 points]

> Intermittent fast makes sense if we want to lose our weight. The food we eat is broken down by enzymes in our gut and eventually ends up as molecules in our bloodstream. Carbohydrates, particularly sugars and refined grains (think white flours and rice), are quickly broken down into sugar, which our cells use for energy. If our cells don't use it all, we store it in our fat cells as fat. But sugar can only enter our cells with insulin, a hormone made in the pancreas. Insulin brings sugar into the fat cells and keeps it there.
>
> Between meals, as long as we don't snack, our insulin levels will go down and our fat cells can then release their stored sugar, to be used as energy. We lose weight if we let our insulin levels go down. The entire idea of intermittent fasting is to allow the insulin levels to go down far enough and for long enough that we burn off our fat.
>
> Not all intermittent fasting approaches are the same, and some are more reasonable, effective, and ⓐ <u>sustainable</u>. We have evolved to be in sync with the day/night cycle, i.e., a circadian rhythm. Our metabolism has adapted to daytime food, nighttime sleep. Nighttime eating is well associated with a higher risk of obesity, as well as diabetes.
>
> Based on this, researchers conducted a study with a small group of obese men with prediabetes. They compared a form of intermittent fasting called "early time-restricted feeding," where all meals were fit into an early eight-hour period of the day (7 am to 3 pm), or spread out over 12 hours (between 7 am and 7 pm). Both groups maintained their weight (did not gain or lose) but after five weeks, the eight-hour group had dramatically ⓑ <u>lower insulin levels</u> and significantly improved insulin sensitivity, as well as significantly lower blood pressure. The best part? The eight-hour group also had significantly decreased appetite, that is, they weren't starving.

Identify the ONE sentence from the passage that BEST fits the requirements of the underlined word in ⓐ. Then, describe what the significance of ⓑ "lower insulin levels" is in the context of the first two paragraphs.

108 Read the passage and follow the directions. [4 points]

> An increasing minority of scientists and thinkers speak more openly these days, and state that the flagship enterprise of modern science is to defeat death and grant humans eternal youth. Notable examples are the gerontologist Aubrey de Grey and the polymath and inventor Ray Kurzweil. In 2012 Kurzweil was appointed a director of engineering at Google, and a year later Google launched a sub-company called Calico whose stated mission is 'to solve death'. In 2009 Google appointed another immortality true-believer, Bill Maris, to preside over the Google Ventures investment fund. In a January 2015 interview, Maris said, 'If you ask me today, is it possible to live to be 500, the answer is yes.' Maris backs up his brave words with a lot of hard cash. Google Ventures is investing 36 per cent of its $2 billion portfolio in life sciences start-ups, including several ambitious life-extending projects. Using an American football analogy, Maris explained that in the fight against death, 'We aren't trying to gain a few yards. We are trying ⓐ to win the game.'
>
> Such dreams are shared by other Silicon Valley luminaries. PayPal co-founder Peter Thiel has recently confessed that he aims to live for ever. 'I think there are probably three main modes of approaching death,' he explained. 'You can accept it, you can deny it or you can fight it. I think our society is dominated by people who are into denial or acceptance, and I prefer to fight it.' Many people are likely to dismiss such statements as teenage fantasies. Yet Thiel is somebody to be taken very seriously. He is one of the most successful and influential entrepreneurs in Silicon Valley with a private fortune estimated at $2.2 billion. The writing is on the wall: ⓑ equality is out—immortality is in.

Describe what the ⓑ "to win the game" refers to. Second, explain the meaning of the underlined words in ⓑ.

109 Read the passage and follow the directions. [2 points]

In the post-Cold War world, the most important distinctions among peoples are not based on ideology, politics, or economy. They are culture.

During most of human existence, contacts between civilizations were intermittent or nonexistent. Then, with the beginning of the modern era, about A.D. 1500, global politics assumed two dimensions. For over four hundred years, the nation states of the West—Britain, France, Spain, Austria, Prussia, Germany, the United States, and others—constituted a multipolar international system within Western civilization and interacted, competed, and fought wars with each other. At the same time, Western nations also expanded, conquered, colonized, or decisively influenced every other civilization. During the Cold War global politics became bipolar and the world was divided into three parts. A group of mostly wealthy and democratic societies, led by the United States, was engaged in a pervasive, ideological, political, economic, and, at times, military competition with a group of somewhat poorer communist societies associated with and led by the Soviet Union. Much of this conflict occurred in the Third World outside these two camps, composed of countries which often were poor, lacked political stability, were recently independent, and claimed to be nonaligned.

In the late 1980s the communist world collapsed, and the Cold War international system became history. Peoples and nations are attempting to answer the most basic question humans can face: Who are we? And they are answering that question in the traditional way human beings have answered it, by reference to the things that mean most to them. People define themselves in terms of <u>ancestry, religion, language, history, values, customs, and institutions</u>.

Identify the ONE word from the passage that BEST corresponds to the meaning of the underlined words.

110 Read the passage and follow the directions. [2 points]

> Sociobiology is a field of scientific study that is based on the hypothesis that social behavior has resulted from evolution and attempts to examine and explain social behavior within that context. It is a branch of biology that deals with social behavior, and also draws from ethology, anthropology, evolution, zoology, archaeology, population genetics, and other disciplines. Sociobiologists, the most well known of whom is Edward Wilson, contend that there is a biological basis for the social behavior of animals, and they test their hypotheses through observation of animals in situations. Species studied have varied as widely as to encompass both termites and rhesus macaques (macaca mulatta; one of the best-known species of Old World monkeys). Sociobiologists further argue that students of human behavior cannot adequately account for the panoply* of human nature through only such traditional variables as culture, ethnicity, and environment but must also include _____ processes. However, many scientists, notably Stephen Jay Gould and Richard Lewontin, have criticized this approach to the study of humans on a number of grounds. That it is based on Eurocentric notions and that it is plagued by methodological problems. These detractors label it a pseudo-science because sociobiological theories are not falsifiable and thus, in this respect, are similar to alchemy or astrology.
>
> *panoply: a wide range*

Fill in the blank with the ONE most appropriate word from the passage. If necessary, change the word form.

111 **Read the passage and follow the directions.** [4 points]

Most people know about Pavlov's famous dog experiment where he proved that dogs could be conditioned to anticipate food even when they couldn't see or smell the food. It was a cornerstone experiment in psychology and sounds rather benign. However, Pavlov was far from a dog lover. Many of his experiments were not done with positive reinforcement, but with negative reinforcements such as flooding the dogs' kennels and making them believe they were going to drown and conditioning them to be afraid of stairs by repeatedly pushing them down a flight or so. Pavlov's experimentation on dogs may have been cruel, but he wasn't just interested in dogs. Ideally he wanted to know how the human mind worked so he acquired himself some children from the local orphanage—you know, impressionable minds who didn't have a parent to stand up for them. He conducted the same salivation experiment on the orphans as he did on his dogs, the only catch was orphans aren't as willing as dogs to receive food from strangers. So he strapped them down to a chair, taped their mouths open, inserted a device to measure their saliva, and proceeded to force feed them both sweets and bad tasting things.

Pavlov was not the only one. Wendell Johnson conducted a little experiment on stuttering in 1939. He took 22 orphans. He gave positive speech therapy to half of the orphans and the other half, he mentally tortured by telling them their speech skills were awful and that they were stutterers (which was completely false). Not surprisingly, the children in the negative reinforcement group became withdrawn. Many refused to speak at all by the end of the study and some of those that did found themselves with a permanent stutter that did not exist before. No effort was made to undo this damage and the experiment was nicknamed "The Monster Experiment" by the undergraduates who helped him conduct it.

Describe the main commonality between Pavlov and Wendell in their experiments. Second, what was the difficulty when Pavlov conducted the salivation experiment on the orphans?

112 Read the passage and follow the directions. [4 points]

> The bones and tendons in our bodies are compressed and stretched well beyond the point at which their underlying substances might be expected to break. Yet these components of human bodies are still much more 'reliable' than their sheer material strength would suggest. For example, merely running can push the Achilles' tendon to over 75 per cent of its ultimate tensile strength, while weightlifters can experience stresses of over 90 per cent of the strength of their lumbar spines, when they are hefting hundreds of kilogrammes.
>
> How does biology handle these loads? The answer is that our bodies constantly repair and recycle their materials. In tendons, collagen fibres are replaced in such a way that, while some are damaged, the overall tendon is safe. This constant self repair is efficient and inexpensive, and can change based on the load. Indeed, all structures and cells in our bodies are in constant turnover; it's estimated that almost 98 per cent of the atoms in the human body are replaced every year.
>
> We recently applied this _____ paradigm to see whether it's possible to build a reliable space elevator with available materials. A common proposed design features a 91,000 km-long cable (called a tether), extending out from the Equator and balanced by a counterweight in space. The tether would consist of bundles of parallel fibres, similar to collagen fibres in tendons or osteons in bones.

Fill in the blank with the TWO most appropriate consecutive words from the passage. Then, explain the way biology handles extremely heavy loads.

113 Read the passage and follow the directions. [2 points]

> For a long time, the two were one and the same. Your entire life has been about coordinating your comfort zone and your safety zone. Learning when to push and when to back off, understanding how it feels when you're about to hit a danger zone. Like the fox, we've been trained to stay inside the fence, because inside the fence is where it's safe—until it's too late.
>
> We don't have time to reevaluate the safety zone every time we make a decision, so over time, we begin to forget about the safety zone and merely pay attention to its twin sister, the comfort zone. We assume that what makes us comfortable also makes us ___ⓐ___.
>
> The fence holding us back is no longer there, but we still feel comfortable with the old boundaries. Now that a revolution has hit, now that the economy is upside down and the rules have changed, we have to confront an obvious truth. That is, the safety zone has changed, but our comfort zone has not. Those places that felt safe—the corner office, the famous college, the secure job—aren't. We're holding back, betting on a return to normal, but in the new normal, our resistance to change is no longer helpful.
>
> We made a mistake. We settled for a safety zone that wasn't bold enough, that embraced authority and compliance. We built our comfort zone around being obedient and invisible, and as a result, we're far too close to the waves. You can go to as many meetings, read as many books, and attend as many seminars as you like, but if you don't figure out how to realign your ___ⓑ___ with today's new safety zone, all the strategy in the world isn't going to help you.

Fill in the blank ⓐ with the ONE most appropriate word from the passage and blank ⓑ with the TWO most appropriate words from the passage.

114 Read the passage and follow the directions. [2 points]

A quick Google search of the current biggest mysteries in physics turns up a daunting list of questions: What exactly is dark matter? Why does time only move in one direction? What happens inside a black hole?

But sometimes, as American physicist and Nobel laureate Richard Feynman discovered decades ago, equally vexing conundrums can be found in everyday objects, say dry spaghetti noodles.

One night, while preparing one of his favorite meals with supercomputer pioneer Danny Hillis, Feynman noticed something strange about spaghetti. If a dry noodle is taken and broken in half, it will almost always break into three or more pieces, tiny bits the spraying in every direction.

"Why is this true—why does it break into three pieces? We spent the next two hours coming up with crazy theories," Hillis recalled in a biography about Feynman. But, after two hours, all the duo had were their theories—"no real good" ones, Hillis said—and a mess of spaghetti breaking all over Feynman's kitchen.

Decades later, in the spring of 2015, two graduate students at the Massachusetts Institute of Technology found themselves in an oddly similar situation—only Ronald Heisser and his friend Edgar Gridello had been working with spaghetti for much longer than two hours. But, Heisser and Gridello weren't trying to figure out why dry spaghetti noodles don't break in half cleanly. The MIT students wanted to tackle a bigger question: Is it even possible to break a spaghetti noodle into two halves? Can it be done and if so, how? Turns out the answer is yes, with a twist. Literally.

What is the main idea of the passage? Write your answer by filling in the blank below with the TWO most appropriate consecutive words from the passage.

| Commentary |

The _____ problem stumped physicist Richard Feynman and two MIT students have solved it.

115 Read the passage and follow the directions. [4 points]

> Major musical scales tend to be associated with happy emotions, minor musical scales with sad ones. A single high note can convey excitement, a low one impending doom. Slow tempos are more indicative of reflective emotions, while fast beats imply fun and excitement. The type of instrument is also important. Heavy metal musicians use distorted guitars to create an angry sound. If these musicians used flutes and piccolos it wouldn't have the same effect.
>
> Parts of our brain have evolved to echo the emotions we see in others—to feel empathy. Many psychologists believe this same part of the brain is active when we watch musicians perform. Even with the sound turned down, people could accurately judge the emotion a performer was intending to express just by watching his body movements. The best rock stars feed us the emotion of a song with their bodies, too.
>
> But we don't all like the same music. What's sad for me might be uplifting for you. The reason is partly to do with the musical language we grow up with. For example, if your parents or siblings liked listening to rhythm and blues, there is a good chance you'll grow to like it, too. But it's even more complex than that. Our preferences are being shaped while we're still in our mother's womb. As we get older, especially as teenagers, our taste is often determined by the people we hang out with.
>
> The philosopher Schopenhauer wrote, "The inexpressible depth of music is due to the fact that it reproduces all the emotions of our innermost being." It speaks to the deepest parts of ourselves and allows us to explore what it means to be human: to hear an echo of the confusion, complexity and joy of our emotional lives.

Describe how a musician can deliver emotion without using words. Second, explain how our musical language develops, as outlined by the passage.

116 Read the passage and follow the directions. [4 points]

> Special-interest groups are calling for public-utility regulations to be placed on the Internet. These people are trying to exert control over the Internet—the most innovative and society-shaping deregulatory success story of our time—through "net neutrality" regulations that will likely benefit only a few huge Internet companies and the top 1 percent of Internet users.
>
> Net neutrality was developed to ensure that Internet users had the freedom to view all the legal content they wanted. Recently, however, there has been a shift in focus: Some of the largest Internet companies are citing "net neutrality" as a reason to enshrine specific privileges that largely benefit them.
>
> If these content companies get their way, Americans will be forced to shoulder the costs for the high-speed networks and infrastructure upgrades needed to support high-volume Internet traffic generators, such as Netflix. The math is simple. As a network carries more traffic, it has to grow or it will become congested. To expand a network requires significant investment and expense—tens of billions of dollars a year in the case of Internet service providers (ISPs).
>
> These _____ can be recovered in two ways. Either by charging all consumers equally or by having the large companies that use far more of the network resources pay their fair share. In the real world it is reasonable and even expected that people pay more for a resource they use more than others. Under the guise of net neutrality, however, the large companies want everyone to pay more so that they and their users—the people consuming the bulk of the resources—do not have to.

Explain what the writer specifically thinks about the underlined "net neutrality" regulations. Second, fill in the blank with the ONE most appropriate word from the passage.

117 Read the passage and follow the directions. [2 points]

It's difficult to listen to a politician or pundit these days without hearing that America is losing jobs to poorer nations—manufacturing jobs to China, back-office work to India, just about every job to Latin America. This lament distracts our attention from the larger challenge of preparing more Americans for better jobs.

It's true that U.S. manufacturing employment has been dropping for many years, but that's not primarily due to foreigners taking these jobs. Factory jobs are vanishing all over the world. I recently toured a U.S. factory containing two employees and 400 computerized robots. The two live people sat in front of computer screens and instructed the robots. In a few years this factory won't have a single employee on site, except for an occasional visiting technician who repairs and upgrades the robots, like the gas man changing your meter.

Manufacturing is following the same trend as agriculture. As productivity rises, _____ falls because fewer people are needed. In 1910, a third of Americans worked on farms. Now, fewer than 3 percent do. Since 1995, even as manufacturing employment has dropped around the world, global output has risen more than 30 percent. Want to blame something? Blame new knowledge which created the electronic gadgets and software that can now do almost any routine task. This goes well beyond the factory floor.

Choose the ONE word from the passage that BEST fills in the blank.

118 Read the passage and follow the directions. [2 points]

> Prisoners across the United States began a strike recently. They strike because they have virtually no other way of expressing their grievances. They can't form organizations without the blessing of prison officials; in some prisons, even petitions are banned. And in every state except Maine and Vermont, convicted prisoners are deprived of the right to vote, sometimes even after they've served their time. Restoring the vote to all citizens—including the incarcerated—is one of the strikers' demands. Other demands include improved prison conditions and increased opportunities for rehabilitation. But it is the strike's call for work stoppages and an end to what the organizers call prison slavery that has stirred the most attention.
>
> The 13th Amendment abolished slavery and involuntary servitude, but its exclusion clause specifies that the amendment doesn't apply to "punishment for crime whereof the party shall have been duly convicted." The provision has been used <u>to require convicted prisoners to work for little pay or even no pay, and they can be punished if they refuse</u>. It has been my experience that most prisoners want to work—they want to do something productive with their time. Prison jobs range from laundry to groundskeeping; from sweeping the cellblock to preparing prisoner meals. The jobs often have a strongly positive effect: They can teach skills and build self-esteem, as well as provide a break from the crushing monotony of prison life. But given the vast power disparity between prisoners and their employers, there is also a real potential for exploitation and abuse.

Identify the TWO most appropriate consecutive words from the passage that BEST correspond to the meaning of the underlined words.

119 Read the passage and follow the directions. [4 points]

> The question most of genetics tries to answer is how genes connect to the traits we see. One person has red hair, another blonde hair; one dies at age 30 of Huntington's disease, another lives to celebrate a 102nd birthday. Knowing what in the vast expanse of the genetic code is behind traits can fuel better treatments and information about future risks and illuminate how biology and evolution work. For some traits, the connection to certain genes is clear: Mutations of a single gene are behind <u>sickle cell anemia</u>, for instance.
>
> But unfortunately for those who like things simple, these conditions are the exceptions. The roots of many traits, from how tall you are to your susceptibility to schizophrenia, are far more tangled. In fact, they may be so complex that almost the entire genome may be involved in some way, an idea formalized in a theory put forward last year.
>
> Starting about 15 years ago, geneticists began to collect DNA from thousands of people who shared traits, to look for clues to each trait's cause in commonalities between their genomes, a kind of analysis called a genome-wide association study (GWAS). What they found, first, was that you need an enormous number of people to get statistically significant results —one recent GWAS seeking correlations between genetics and insomnia, for instance, included more than a million people. Second, in study after study, even the most significant genetic connections turned out to have surprisingly small effects. The conclusion, sometimes called the polygenic hypothesis, was that multiple loci, or positions in the genome, were likely to be involved in every trait, with each contributing just a small part.

Explain why the writer mentions the underlined "sickle cell anemia" in the passage. Second, the writer includes a larger GWAS; how large was the study group?

120 Read the passage and follow the directions. [4 points]

> It is hard enough to imagine the universe as it is now and even harder to create a theory about how it all began. In the 1940s, George Gamow began to develop such a theory. Georges Lemaitre, another scientist, had also been working on the problem, and Gamow used some of the ideas of Lemaitre to develop his theory.
>
> Gamow proposed the following theory: Somewhere between 10 and 21 billion years ago, there was a giant explosion in space. Before the explosion, the universe was the size of an atomic nucleus, with a temperature of about 10 billion degrees. The explosion started the expansion of the universe. Quarks, or elemental particles, existed in huge numbers.
>
> Within a millisecond, the universe had expanded to the size of a grapefruit. The temperature cooled to 1 billion degrees. The quarks began to clump into protons and neutrons. Minutes later, the universe was still too hot for electrons and protons to form into atoms: a super-hot, fog-like environment.
>
> With passing time and cooling temperatures, nuclear reactions took place, and within 300,000 years, atoms of hydrogen and helium began to emerge. As the atoms formed, light began to shine. The universe was taking shape.
>
> Gravity began to act on the atoms and transform them into galaxies. Within 1 billion years of that first great explosion, galaxies and stars began to form. Within 15 billion years, planets began to emerge from the heavy elements thrown off by the dying of stars. The universe started with a big bang and continues to grow and change according to this theory.

By what were atoms transformed into galaxies? Second, describe how hydrogen and helium atoms were produced?

121 Read the passage and follow the directions. [2 points]

> Humankind is facing unprecedented revolutions, all our old stories are crumbling and no new story has so far emerged to replace them. How can we prepare ourselves and our children for a world of unprecedented uncertainties? A baby born today will be thirty-something in 2050. If all goes well, that baby will still be around in 2100, and might even be an active citizen of the 22nd century. What should we teach that baby that will help him or her survive and flourish in the world of 2050 or of the 22nd century? What kind of skills will he or she need in order to get a job, understand what is happening around them and navigate the maze of life?
>
> Unfortunately, since nobody knows how the world will look in 2050—not to mention 2100—we don't know the answer to these questions. Today it is more difficult than ever before, because once technology enables us to engineer bodies, brains and minds, we can no longer be certain about anything—including things that previously seemed fixed and eternal.
>
> A thousand years ago, in 1018, there were many things people didn't know about the future, but they were nevertheless convinced that the basic features of human society were not going to change. If you lived in China in 1018, you knew that by 1050 the Song Empire might collapse, the Khitans might invade from the north, and plagues might kill millions. However, it was clear to you that even in 1050 most people would still work as farmers and weavers, rulers would still rely on humans to staff their armies and bureaucracies, men would still dominate women, life expectancy would still be about 40, and the human body would be exactly the same.
>
> In contrast, today we have no idea how China or the rest of the world will look in 2050. <u>We don't know what people will do for a living, we don't know how armies or bureaucracies will function, and we don't know what gender relations will be like.</u>

Identify the ONE word from the passage that BEST corresponds to the meaning of the underlined words.

122 Read the passage and follow the directions. [2 points]

> In 1998 the *Lancet*, a medical journal, published a paper which made a claim that continues to infect public discussion: vaccines can cause autism. The article was later retracted and its primary author, a British researcher named Andrew Wakefield, lost his medical licence. In 2016, however, the disgraced doctor began receiving some rather exclusive invitations in America: first to a meeting with a presidential candidate and then to an inauguration ball in Washington, DC. He had found a willing listener in Donald Trump, who has tweeted about the dangers of vaccines more than 30 times. But theirs was not the only crossover between anti-vaxxers, as they became known, and "anti-establishment" politicians.
>
> European populists have also flirted with vaccine doubters. In France, where more than 20% of the population does not support vaccines, Marine Le Pen, of the far-right National Rally party, opposes mandatory immunisations and has questioned their safety. Vaccines were also a contentious issue during elections in Italy this year, which happened during a measles outbreak that followed a drop in vaccination rates. The populist Five Star Movement (M5S) opposed new policies that increased the number of required vaccines and fined non-compliant parents. Across Europe vaccination rates have declined and the incidence of measles has soared—up by 300% last year. Despite this increase, or perhaps in reaction to efforts to combat it, _____ remain vocal. On Vaccine Injury Awareness Day in June, thousands joined protests against compulsory vaccinations in Italy and France.

Fill in the blank with the TWO most appropriate consecutive words from the passage.

123 Read the passage and follow the directions. [4 points]

For centuries, humans have endeavoured to discover and describe the sum of Earth's biological diversity. Scientists and naturalists have catalogued species from all continents and oceans, from the depths of Earth's crust to the highest mountains, and from the most remote jungles to our most populated cities. This grand effort sheds light on the forms and behaviours that evolution has made possible, while serving as the foundation for understanding the common descent of life. Until recently, our planet was thought to be inhabited by nearly 10 million species. Though no small number, this estimate is based almost solely on species that can be seen with the naked eye.

What about smaller species such as bacteria, archaea, protists and fungi? Collectively, these microbial taxa are the most abundant, widespread and longest-evolving forms of life on the planet. What is their contribution to global biodiversity? When microorganisms are taken into account, recent studies suggest that Earth might be home to a staggering 1 trillion species. If true, then the grand effort to discover Earth's biodiversity has only come within a 1,000th of 1 per cent of all species on the planet.

Estimating microbial diversity even in the most ordinary of habitats presents a unique set of challenges. For more than a century, scientists identified microbial species by first culturing them on Petri dishes and then characterising cellular properties, along with aspects of their physiology such as thermal tolerances, the substrates they consume, or the enzymes they produce. Such approaches dramatically underestimate diversity, not only because it is difficult to grow the vast majority of microorganisms, but also because unrelated microbial species can perform similar functions and are unlikely to be distinguished by their appearance.

During the mid-1990s, a growing number of microbiologists began to abandon cultivation techniques in favour of identifying organisms by directly sequencing nucleic acids—DNA—from ocean water, leaf surfaces, wetland sediments, and even the biofilms inside of showerheads.

Explain the commonality of the underlined "bacteria, archaea, protists and fungi" in terms of observability, as intended by the writer. Second, describe the notable drawbacks of the cultivation method.

124 **Read the passage and follow the directions.** [4 points]

"Just how old do you think my dog is in dog years?" is a question I hear on a regular basis. People love to anthropomorphize pets, attributing human characteristics to them. And most of us want to extend our animal friends' healthy lives for as long as possible.

It may seem like sort of a silly thing to ponder, born out of owners' love for their pets and the human-animal bond between them. But determining a pet's "real" age is actually important because it helps veterinarians like me recommend life-stage specific healthcare for our animal patients.

There's an old myth that one regular year is like seven years for dogs and cats. There's a bit of logic behind it. People observed that with optimal healthcare, an average-sized, medium dog would on average live one-seventh as long as its human owner—and so the seven "dog years" for every "human year" equation was born.

Not every dog is "average-sized" though so this seven-year rule was an oversimplification from the start. Dogs and cats age differently not just from people but also from each other, based partly on breed characteristics and size. Bigger animals tend to have shorter life spans than smaller ones do. While cats vary little in size, the size and life expectancy of dogs can vary greatly—think a Chihuahua versus a Great Dane.

Human life expectancy has changed over the years. And vets are now able to provide far superior medical care to pets than we could even a decade ago. So now we use a better methodology to redefine the old rule of thumb that counted every calendar year as seven "animal years."

Based on the American Animal Hospital Association Canine Life Stages Guidelines, today's vets divide dogs into six categories: puppy, junior, adult, mature, senior and geriatric. Life stages are a more practical way to think about age than assigning a single number; even human health recommendations are based on developmental stage rather than exactly how old you are in years.

Dog breed and its associated size is one of the largest contributors to life expectancy, with nutrition and associated weight likely being the next most important factors for individual dogs.

Explain why the writer mainly mentions the developmental stage in the passage. Second, identify all factors contributed to life expectancy of dogs.

125   **Read the passage and follow the directions.** [2 points]

> Babies learn a lot. They learn to recognize faces, voices, colors, shapes, words. They learn what food is and what's just something shiny lying on the floor. They learn tactile sensations, smells, and sounds but most importantly they learn their place in the world. In a healthy environment a baby will learn to recognize its caregivers and naturally begin to trust them to keep them safe and tend to their needs. They'll learn what it is to be loved. Babies in neglectful environments however will cry, and if they get no responses enough times they will learn the opposite. They'll be distrustful of the stability of their caregivers. They will start to learn how to fend for themselves and worse yet they will start to live in a state of constant fight or flight. They can depend on no one and attachment to anyone will become exceedingly difficult.
>
> Babies who are not cuddled will not learn how to form stable bonds with other human beings. Babies left to cry will learn that they can't count on anyone and that the world is a scary miserable place. Babies who are not talked to will not learn the sounds necessary for speech. The rate of _____ in these children is much higher than in children who live in a proper positive environment. Not only is mental retardation a problem so too can be physical retardation with the child literally not growing as much as it should. This isn't always due to malnutrition, although that certainly doesn't help when it is the case. These kids are fearful much more often than regular children and their brains get pickled in adrenaline and cortisol, the stress hormone. Being constantly stressed out will lead to the burning of more calories and a lack of appetite. In these cases the brain will often become physically malformed.

Fill in the blank with the TWO most appropriate consecutive words from the passage.

126 Read the passage and follow the directions. [2 points]

> Global change phenomena such as climate warming, permafrost thaw, wildfires, and drought are affecting terrestrial ecosystem biogeochemistry, particularly in northern latitudes, but also in the continental U.S. Soil microbial communities are critical to the carbon biogeochemistry of ecosystems; for they decompose as much carbon as is annually photosynthesized by plants. There is strong evidence that variation in the composition of the soil microbial community affects the way in which ecosystems function, and this can affect regional to global biogeochemistry. Particular functional groups of microorganisms, such as decomposer fungi, have a disproportionate effect on elemental cycles. For example, in northern latitude soils, climate warming is accelerating permafrost thaw and wildfire intensity, altering the abundance of soil decomposers which has direct effect on rates of biogeochemical processes. This and other types of microbial community information can be used by the next generation of mechanistic microbial-based C cycling models. A next step will be to merge bioinformatics with geoinformatics that can be used to build a spatially explicit map of microbial biogeography that is linked to environmental and process data. Such a map has many uses beyond understanding ecological principles that structure community composition and diversity. Such spatially explicit information can potentially be used for assessing how global change will affect microbial communities and the biogeochemical processes within specific regions.

Complete the main purpose of the passage by filling in the blank below with the THREE most appropriate consecutive words from the passage.

⌐ Commentary ⌐

The purpose is to articulate what is known about the effects of global change phenomena on ecosystems, particularly those involving _____ and to show how further research can add to our understanding of how global change will affect these communities in different areas.

127 Read the passage and follow the directions. [4 points]

The Fascist nations were notorious in their insistence that the woman's place was in the home. Yet, the war against Fascism, although it utilized women in defense industries where they were desperately needed, took no special steps to change the subordinate role of women. The War Manpower Commission, despite the large numbers of women in war work, kept women off its policymaking bodies. A report of the Women's Bureau of the Department of Labor, by its director, Mary Anderson, said the War Manpower Commission had "doubts and uneasiness" about "what was then regarded as a developing attitude of militancy or a crusading spirit on the part of women leaders."

In one of its policies, the United States came close to direct duplication of Fascism. This was in its treatment of the Japanese-Americans living on the West Coast. After the Pearl Harbor attack, anti-Japanese hysteria spread in the government. One congressman said: "I'm for catching every Japanese in America, Alaska and Hawaii now and putting them in concentration camps. Damn them! Let's get rid of them!"

Franklin D. Roosevelt did not share this frenzy, but he calmly signed Executive Order 9066, in February 1942, giving the army the power, without warrants or indictments or hearings, to arrest every Japanese-American on the West Coast—110,000 men, women, and children—to take them from their homes, transport them to camps far into the interior, and keep them there under prison conditions. Three-fourths of these were Nisei-children born in the United States of Japanese parents and therefore American citizens. The other fourth—the Issei, born in Japan—were barred by law from becoming citizens. In 1944 the Supreme Court upheld the forced evacuation on the grounds of military necessity. The Japanese remained in those camps for over three years.

Explain why the writer mentions the underlined "Mary Anderson" in the passage. Second, in what policy, according to the writer, did the US come closest to Fascism?

128 Read the passage and follow the directions. [4 points]

"Why it is not a 'failure' to leave academia"; "There's no shame in leaving academia"—these are a few in a recent barrage of articles scattering the commentary landscape. While these articles are noble attempts to comfort the academic workforce experiencing epidemic levels of depression and anxiety, they are innately misguided. By framing the conversation around career transition in this manner, the authors are inadvertently confirming the underlying premise: that leaving academia is indeed a failure that needs to be addressed.

Ironically, the notion that leaving academic science is a failure is itself unscientific. It lacks a coherent empirical foundation. There is no evidence to suggest that scientists in academia are more successful, more self-fulfilled or even intellectually freer than scientists in the for-profit, non-profit or government sectors. There is a possibility that this unempirical notion is a direct manifestation of academic insecurities: intellectual, existential and, perhaps most importantly, financial (on average, an assistant professor makes $87,000 a year).

Although failure is a subjective experience that is often intertwined with personal aspiration and goals, it is often depersonalized when discussing a transition out of academia. Within the academic narrative, academia is the ultimate prize that everyone is or should be seeking. The reason behind this is built on two main premises.

The first is that academia emancipates scientists—that it grants them the intellectual freedom to follow their curiosities wherever they may lead them. The second relies on the notion that academics live fulfilled and purposeful lives in the noble pursuit of knowledge and truth. In both cases, these qualities are suggested to be unique to academic pursuits.

Academia does not provide absolute intellectual freedom, contrary to the conventional wisdom. Graduate students and postdocs are limited to pursue only those questions that are related to their advisor's work, if not directly handed experimental designs without room for debate. As mentees develop, they might be so lucky as to be allowed to ask questions of their own, but within clear and defined limitations.

Describe the main idea of the passage. Then, identify to what the underlined "the conventional wisdom" refers.

129 Read the passage and follow the directions. [4 points]

We take it for granted that young children "get into everything." But new studies of "active learning" show that when children play with toys they are acting a lot like scientists doing experiments. Preschoolers prefer to play with the toys that will teach them the most, and they play with those toys in just the way that will give them the most information about how the world works.

In one recent experiment, for example, professor Aimee E. Stahl showed 11-month-old babies a sort of magic trick. Either a ball appeared to pass through a solid wall, or a toy car appeared to roll off the end of a shelf and remain suspended in thin air. The babies apparently knew enough about everyday physics to be surprised by these strange events and paid a lot of attention to them.

Then the researcher gave the babies toys to play with. The babies who had seen the ball vanish through the wall banged it; those who'd seen the car hovering in thin air kept dropping it. It was as if they were testing to see if the ball really was solid, or if the toy car really did defy gravity.

It's not just that young children don't need to be taught in order to learn. In fact, studies show that explicit instruction, the sort of teaching that goes with school and "parenting," can be limiting. When children think they are being taught, they are much more likely to simply imitate what the adult does, instead of creating something new.

My lab tried a different version of the experiment with the complicated toy. This time, though, the experimenter acted like a teacher. She said, "I'm going to show you how my toy works," instead of "I wonder how this toy works." The children _____ exactly what she did, and didn't come up with their own solutions.

Fill in the blank with the ONE most appropriate word from the passage. If necessary, change the word form. Second, explain the main point Aimee E. Stahl shows in her study.

130 Read the passage and follow the directions. [4 points]

> Although some halfway houses are adequately managed and staffed with competent professionals, others are operated more for profit than an interest in helping offenders successfully return to society. Too many incidents involving poorly-supervised halfway house residents and indifferent, or even criminal, behavior by employees have occurred in almost every state as well as the federal prison system.
>
> A well-managed halfway house provides a safe environment for soon-to-be released prisoners; some may have been in jail for relatively short periods of time while others might have been locked up for years or even decades. A halfway house's principal goal of providing a smooth transition back to society provides the first line of defense against _____. Halfway house residents often have few current ties to the community to which they are released, and even if they do, may not have family or friends to assist them. They need viable reentry services, including job placement and housing assistance, and often require substance abuse programs. Too often, though, halfway houses are viewed by their owners and operators as little more than a revenue source.
>
> However poor a halfway house might be in providing effectual services and programs, many times it is the only available option. For some state prisoners nearing release, placement in halfway houses is mandatory; other states require no time spent at a reentry facility. According to the non-partisan Pew Charitable Trusts, prisoners in eight states are allowed to "max out" their sentences with no reentry programs to smooth their return to the community. In those states, about 40% of prisoners are released with no transitional services.

> According to an April 2014 recidivism report by the Bureau of Justice Statistics, 49.7% of offenders return to prison within three years after release and 55.1% return within five years. Clearly, most state and federal correctional facilities do a poor job of "correcting" prisoners and preparing them for release, which puts an even greater burden on halfway houses to supply reentry services.
>
> Policymakers on both sides of the aisle should start to realize that if you're serious about public safety, you need more effective strategies.

Fill in the blank with the ONE most appropriate word from the passage. Second, it is implied in the passage that if policymakers will not realize how important halfway houses are, what will happen to society?

131 Read the passage and follow the directions. [4 points]

> How much spicier is a Scotch Bonnet chili pepper than a Bird's Eye? How much harder is diamond than quartz? Scales help us measure the physical world. To compare quantities, we mostly rely on quantitative scales—numerical measurements that tell us something about frequency and quantity. Inches, feet, yards and miles; ounces, quarts, liters and gallons; seconds, minutes, and centuries are all quantitative scales. But what about qualitative scales? These are yardsticks that measure observable, but not necessarily numerical, properties—and we use them all the time. Qualitative scales are sometimes humorous and often downright bizarre, but they are just as valuable as quantitative scales for imagining relationships between properties and standardizing ideas. They range from chili pepper heat to mineral hardness to ocean breezes. Qualitative scales allow us to label variables with little or no quantitative information. These unusual units of measurement are often colloquial: guesstimations and "as-the-crow-flies" rules of thumb that allow for quick assessments and comparisons. Yet qualitative scales prove their usefulness time and again. Without them, we would struggle to conceptualise ideas of pain (a doctor might ask a patient to rank his symptoms) or grade the severity of weather conditions (like the Beaufort Scale does).
>
> Date, when measured from an arbitrary epoch such as BC or AD, helps us understand time, while direction measured in degrees from true or magnetic north orients us in physical space.
>
> Quantitative scales are much easier to evaluate, since they are effectively _____ to a known standard. A square-kilometre, a teaspoon of sugar or an hour-long lecture are basically unchanging measurements. Qualitative scales are more subjective. Neither quantitative nor qualitative scales, however, are ever 100% accurate: they are each limited by the uncertainty baked into the definitions of units themselves.

Fill in the blank with the ONE most appropriate word from the passage. Second, identify what type of scale a movie review would be considered.

132 Read the passage and follow the directions. [4 points]

The experience of vitality is inherent in the act of movement. Movement, and its proprioception, is the primary manifestation of being animate and provides the primary sense of aliveness. We move all the time, both physically and mentally. If our mind and body were not in a constant process of change when awake, we would not feel alive and vital. I am writing about dynamic changes that occur constantly. Our respirations rise and fall over a cycle that repeats every three or four seconds. Our bodies are in almost constant motion: we move our mouth, twitch, touch our face, make small adjustments in head position and orientation, alter our facial expression, shift the direction of our gaze, adjust the muscular tone of our body position, whether standing, sitting, or lying (if awake). These processes go on even when not visible from the outside. Gestures and larger acts unfold in time. They change fluidly once an act has started. We can be conscious of any of this, or it can remain in peripheral awareness. In addition, with every movement there is proprioception, conscious or not. At the same time as the body is moving, thoughts are "moving" (virtually) in the mind, sometimes wandering, at other times progressing apace, or exploding or tumbling about, or fading out. Similarly, emotions ebb and flow, slightly or dramatically. Sensations impinge, build up or overwhelm, their intensity and duration tracing a time line, as does musical flow or dancing, or any stimulus. In addition, while often neglected, our arousal level undergoes micro-shifts. There is shifting vigilance, attention, and engagement with passing events. Seeing a dead person is immediately shocking because they do not move, nothing moves, and even the almost subliminal vibrations of tonicity stop. We grasp this in a glance with peripheral vision. Without motion we cannot read in or imagine mental activity underneath, or thoughts, emotions, or "will." That is how we know there is no vital presence. Similarly, when a mother goes "still face" while facing her infant, i.e. not moving her face at all, not even with slight expressions, the baby, or even a neonate, becomes upset within seconds. Newborns already have working _____ that is designed to detect motion at the periphery. Accordingly, stillness is registered no matter where their focal vision is on the mother's face.

Fill in the blank with the TWO most appropriate consecutive words from the passage. Second, identify the unsettling factor that can immediately upset a person upon viewing a dead body.

133 Read the passage and follow the directions. [4 points]

Blacksmithing has been an important craft within human history for thousands of years. Blacksmiths heat metal in forges and hammer the heated metal into endless shapes, which once cooled, can be used as handy tools or admired as beautiful artwork. Blacksmiths traditionally made horseshoes, farming equipment, weapons, armor, and household items.

Smiths living and working today make many of the same products, but also forge art pieces and decorative items. No matter the time period or items created, blacksmiths have proved to be important in society. So important, in fact, that the word "blacksmith" and other variants like "smith" have rich etymologies in several major languages.

The word "blacksmith" combines two distinguishing elements of a smith's work: the color of the iron when heated, and the act of striking the metal with tools. Most scholars believe that "black" refers to the oxidation that iron undergoes when it is introduced to a flame. A black coating forms on the surface of the iron and therefore is a unique descriptive feature of a blacksmith's work and the materials he uses. This distinguishes an ironworker like a blacksmith from similar craftsmen such as goldsmiths or silversmiths.

"Smith" comes from the Old English word "smythe," which means "to strike," or "smitan," which means "hammer." Today the word is commonly defined as "a worker in metal." The word "smith" entered the English language prior to 900 AD, which makes it an ancient word and suggests that smithing as an occupation is an important one in Anglo tradition.

"Smith" is one of the most common last names in English speaking countries and is a(n) _____ surname given to people whose ancestors worked with metal. The word "smith" is related to other words of the same meaning in multiple European languages. In Spanish, the term for blacksmith is "herrero." The word means "worker in iron" or "smith" and, like its English counterpart, is sometimes used as a surname. "Herrero" is derived from the Latin word "ferrarius" which translates to "made from iron."

Fill in the blank with the ONE most appropriate word from the passage. If necessary, you may change the word form. Second, explain the etymological origin of "black" in the word "blacksmith". Do NOT copy more than FOUR consecutive words from the passage.

134 Read the passage and follow the directions. [4 points]

America's _____ language and thinking began with the forceful imprint left by English colonization. The generations of the 1500s and 1600s that first envisioned the broadscale English exploitation of America's natural environment employed a vocabulary that was a mix of purposeful description and raw imagery. They did not indulge in pretty talk. The idea of settlement had to be sold to wary investors; the planting of New World American colonies had to serve Old World purposes. In grand fashion, promoters imagined America not as an Eden of opportunity but as a giant rubbish heap that could be transformed into productive terrain. Expendable people—waste people—would be unloaded from England; their labor would germinate a distant wasteland. Harsh as it sounds, the idle poor, dregs of society, were to be sent thither simply to throw down manure and die in a vacuous muck. Before it became that fabled "City upon a Hill," America was in the eyes of sixteenth-century adventurers a foul, weedy wilderness—a "sinke hole" suited to ill-bred commoners. Dark images of the New World accompanied more seductive ones. When early English promoters portrayed North America as a rich and fertile landscape, they grossly and perhaps knowingly exaggerated. Most were describing a land they never had seen, of course. Wary investors and state officials had to be convinced to take the plunge into a risky overseas venture. But most important, it was a place into which they could export their own marginalized people.

The idea of America as "the world's best hope" came much later. Historic memory has camouflaged the less noble origins of "the land of the free and the home of the brave." We all know what imagery springs to mind when patriots of our day seek confirmation that their country is and was always an "exceptional" place: modest Pilgrims taught to plant by generous Indians; Virginia Cavaliers entertaining guests at their refined estates along the James River. Because of how history is taught, Americans tend to associate Plymouth and Jamestown with cooperation rather than class division.

And it gets ever more misty-eyed from there, because disorder and discord serve no positive purpose in burgeoning national pride. Class is the most outstanding, if routinely overlooked, element in presuppositions about early settlement. Even now, the notion of a broad and supple middle class functions as a mighty balm, a smoke screen. We cling to the comfort of the middle class, forgetting that there can't be a middle class without a lower. It is only occasionally shaken up, as when the Occupy Wall Street movement of recent years shone an embarrassing light on the financial sector and the grotesque separation between the 1 percent and the 99 percent. And then the media giants find new crises and the nation's inherited disregard for class reboots, as the subject recedes into the background again.

Fill in the blank with the ONE most appropriate word from the passage. Second, describe what can be inferred to be the primary reason English promoters portrayed America as a favorable place. Do NOT copy more than FOUR consecutive words from the passage.

135 Read the passage and follow the directions. [2 points]

> Romanticism sought liberal values in the development of the individual. In its early stages, Romanticism was profoundly liberating, but, partly because of the inadequacy of any corresponding social theory, and partly because of the consequent decline from individualism to subjectivism, it ended by denying its own deepest impulses, and even reversing them. Almost all our revolutionary language in fact comes from the Romantics, and this has been a real hindrance as well as an incidental embarrassment. Romanticism is the most important expression in modern literature of the first impulse of revolution: a new and absolute image of man. Characteristically, it relates this transcendence to an ideal world and an ideal human society; it is in Romantic literature that man is first seen as making himself. But of course when this is particularised, to social criticism and construction, it encounters fundamental obstacles. It is easier to visualise the ideal in an exotic or fabled community (or an historical community transformed by these elements). The existing social world is seen as so hostile to what is most deeply human that even what begins as social criticism tends to pass into nihilism.
>
> The decisive element, here, was the Romantic attitude to reason. In form, Romanticism can seem a negative reaction to the Enlightenment: its stress on the irrational and the strange seems an absolute contradiction of the stress on _____. But there is, here, a curious dialectic. Romanticism was not proposing what the Enlightenment had opposed; the one version of man was as new as the other. Yet, because this was not seen, the essential unity of these movements, as programmes for human liberation, was disastrously narrowed and confused. What the Romantics criticised as reason was not the reasoning activity, but the abstraction and final alienation of this activity, into what was called a rational but was in fact a mechanical system.

Fill in the blank with the ONE most appropriate word from the passage.

136 Read the passage and follow the directions. [4 points]

> It is said that a music student once approached Mozart and asked him for advice on what he should compose and how he should do it to create something really good. Mozart took a good look at him and (paraphrased) said, "you are still young. I think you should start with composing a duet." This young man got upset and told Mozart that he too was still young, and that since he had composed more serious music than duets, why shouldn't he? Mozart replied, (paraphrased) "that is true, but I did not go around asking people what to compose. I knew what to do." The point is that many have attempted to create great art, but only a very tiny percentage have become true masters.
>
> Having said that, there is another important element that singers can bring into the picture that no instrument can—the spoken word. While it was mentioned above that not understanding the words in a song hardly takes anything away from the music, this was not to claim that words are totally irrelevant, but only that they are highly overrated. One enjoys a good opera in Italian, without understanding a word of what is being said. To understand the right place of lyrics in singing, which in essence is poetry, is worth elaborating on.
>
> At the core, just as music is nothing other than the rhythmic composition of musical notes, poetry is nothing other than the rhythmic composition of words. While music delivers a rhythmically composed soothing sound to us, poetry delivers a set of rhythmically composed words that convey a feeling or a concept to the audience. When singers sing their lyrics, they are harmoniously fusing poetry with music, and in doing so, they add another layer of rhythmic composition to the whole mix. If the pleasure in music mainly results from satisfying the instinct of rhythm, the added layer of rhythm in poetry enhances the effect and pleasure.

Although the sound and the meaning of lyrics as compared to the music in a song are not quantifiable elements, one can take educated guesses on the value and the contribution of each to the finished product. One wonders how much of the _____ can be attributed to the rhythm in the music, and how much of it can be attributed to the rhythm in the poetry, and also how much can be attributed to the idea or the meanings the words carry. As it was alluded to before, I argue that the true value of singing mostly rests in the music and the musical sound the singers produce and not in the meaning that the lyrics or the entire poetry carries.

Fill in the blank with the ONE most appropriate word from the passage. Second, explain why Mozart's advice seems hypocritical at first to the music student. Do NOT copy more than FOUR consecutive words from the passage.

137 Read the passage and follow the directions. [2 points]

> Parasocial relationships are a form of social interaction where one party knows a lot about the other, but the other party doesn't know anything about them. They often occur when a person interacts with a media figure as a friend personally. Media figures can include reality TV characters, video game personalities, and social media influencers. The degree of these relationships vary. Some fans are simply interested in the actions of their "friend," while others become obsessed with them to the point of imagining being in a relationship with them. Parasocial relationships happen without the influencer knowing that it even exists. Once the person adoring their idols becomes obsessed, parasocial relationships can become toxic and detrimental to their mental health. While these relationships can decrease loneliness and fill the gap for social interaction, they are by no means as effective and satisfactory as real-life interactions. Furthermore, these relationships can escalate to stalking and harassment concerns.
>
> Parasocial relationships have been around since the invention of books and later television. The earliest forms of this type of interaction were between book readers and their authors. But it wasn't until television that parasocial relationships were in the spotlight. Early on in the era of television, there were no reality shows, social media influencers, or video games. Instead, the only way to build this kind of relationship was through watching TV or movies. For instance, people would watch the same actors over and over again. As a result, they would build an attachment to these characters and feel they knew them _____. Today, the relationships are slowly shifting from having relationships with TV stars to social media influencers, Twitch streamers, YouTubers, and online personalities.

Fill in the blank with the ONE most appropriate word from the passage.

138 Read the passage and follow the directions. [4 points]

　Desiderius Erasmus was the last great intellectual of a united Christian Europe: a scholar of universal renown, a friend to kings and tutor to princes, and a self-proclaimed "citizen of the world". He produced a translation of the New Testament that changed the way Christians think about their faith. He also shaped popular culture. His dictionary rescued phrases such as "breaking the ice", "teaching an old dog new tricks" and "leaving no stone unturned" from obscurity. His *In Praise of Folly*(1511) was hailed as a comic masterpiece.

　In an age when birth was generally destiny, he was a self-made man. Born in the small provincial town of Rotterdam in 1466, the illegitimate son of a priest, he was dumped in a local monastery at the earliest opportunity. He grew up far from the centre of the Renaissance in northern Italy. His subsequent stardom was purely the result of his extraordinary intellectual gifts.

　Unlike so many other great thinkers, in his time and since, Erasmus never fell prey to _____. He believed in the healing power of moderation and reason, and in the civilising power of wine and conversation. This was partly a matter of personal style. He craved a life of scholarly comfort: "He lived in his study and died in his bed," as the historian Hugh Trevor-Roper put it. Confronted with a king—and potential patron—he bent the knee; challenged by a bully, he changed the subject.

　It was also a matter of conviction. Erasmus loathed the certitude of ideologues and worried about the tendency of extremism to goad one another into greater acts of fanaticism. In place of revolutionary certainty, he preached the Middle Way. The best way to reform the establishment was from within, he argued. The Catholic church should be reinvigorated by calling it back to its original purpose; society should be reformed by educating princes in the art of government.

> But this moderate champion had the great bad luck to live in a zealous era. Soon after climbing to the intellectual and social pinnacle of Europe, Erasmus was thrown down and condemned. Only after his death was he given his due. His story is a warning to modern moderates, but also an inspiration.

Fill in the blank with the ONE most appropriate word from the passage. Second, according to the passage, how well did Eramus' ideas fit the spirit of his era and why or why not? Do NOT copy more than THREE consecutive words from the passage.

139 Read the passage and follow the directions. [4 points]

In 2009 the Brazilian Agricultural Research Corp. (Embrapa) and the Brasilia Zoological Garden began scavenging and freezing blood, sperm and umbilical cord cells from roadkill and other wild animals that had died, mostly in the Cerrado savanna—an incredibly diverse collection of tropical forest and grassland ecosystems home to at least 10,000 plant species and more than 800 species of birds and mammals, some of which live nowhere else in the world. Then specimens were collected from the bush dog, collared anteater, bison and gray brocket deer, among other species.

The idea was to preserve the genetic information of Brazil's _____ wildlife. One day, the organizations reasoned, they might be able to use the collected DNA to clone these animals and bolster dwindling populations. So far the two institutions have collected at least 420 tissue samples. Now they are collaborating on a related project that will use the DNA in these specimens to improve breeding and cloning techniques. Current cloning techniques have an average success rate of less than 5 percent, even when working with familiar species; cloning wild animals is usually less than 1 percent successful.

Any animals born during Brazil's new undertaking will live in the Brasilia Zoo, says Embrapa researcher Carlos Martins. Expanding captive populations of wild animals, he and his team hope, will discourage zoos and researchers from taking even more wild animals out of their native habitats. Martins and his colleagues have not yet decided which species they will attempt to clone but the maned wolf and jaguar are strong candidates. The International Union for Conservation of Nature classifies both animals as "near threatened" on its Red List of Threatened Species, two levels below "endangered."

Many researchers agree that, at present, cloning is not a feasible or effective conservation strategy. First of all, some conservationists point out, cloning does not address the reasons that many animals become endangered in the first place—namely, hunting and habitat destruction. Even if cloning could theoretically help in truly desperate situations, current cloning techniques are simply too ineffective to make much of a difference.

Fill in the blank with the ONE most appropriate word from the passage. Second, explain why many researchers think cloning is not an effective strategy. Do NOT copy more than THREE consecutive words from the passage.

140 Read the passage and follow the directions. [4 points]

A British christmas is inseparable not just from a jolly fat man in a red suit but also from a grumpy, thin "squeezing, wrenching, grasping, scraping, clutching, covetous old sinner". Charles Dickens's novella "*A Christmas Carol*" was an instant hit. Within two months of its publication in 1843 there were 12 adaptations on the London stage. Nearly two centuries on, its anti-hero retains his hold on the popular imagination.

By all means enjoy "*A Christmas Carol*" in this season—better read aloud to the children, in Victorian fashion, than on the screen. William Thackeray, Dickens's contemporary and rival, described it as a "national benefit and, to every man or woman who reads it, a personal kindness". He was, after Shakespeare, Britain's most creative generator of characters, with more than a thousand listed in Wikipedia. That they are as relevant today as they were in his time is testament not only to his ability to capture essential human traits but also to the parallels between the Victorian age and ours.

So many Dickens characters summon up the peculiar spirit of 2020 that it is hard to choose between them. In *Hard Times*, Mr Gradgrind tries to "weigh and measure any parcel of human nature", neatly encapsulating modern officialdom's obsession with targets and algorithms. In *Little Dorrit*, the Barnacle family controls the business of the Circumlocution Office much as well-connected Tories enjoy the benefits of government outsourcing today. But <u>those characters tower over their rivals as embodiments of 2020</u>.

John Podsnap, from *Our Mutual Friend*, is Brexit Britain made flesh. A pompous philistine of the narrowest kind—"particularly well satisfied with most things, and, above all other things, with himself"—he considers other countries "a mistake", foreigners "unfortunately born", and the British constitution the best in the world, "bestowed upon us by providence". In sum, "no other country" is as "favoured as this country".

유희태 | 일반영어 ❹-1

> It is unfortunate that the world is addicted to _____. Today almost everything is the opposite of what it pretends to be. Companies claim that they are devoted to advancing gay rights, promoting multiculturalism or uniting the world in a Kumbaya sing-along, when they are in fact singlemindedly maximising profits. Chief executives claim that they are ever-so-humble "team leaders" when they are actually creaming off an unprecedented share of corporate cash. Private schools such as Eton claim that they are in the business of promoting "diversity" and "inclusivity" even as they charge £42,000 a year. Future historians seeking to sum up our era may well call it the age of humbug.

Fill in the blank with the ONE most appropriate word from the passage. Second, explain the meaning of the underlined words. Do NOT copy more than THREE consecutive words from the passage.

141 Read the passage and follow the directions. [4 points]

> Would we, as a species, be better off if we were more like other animals? I suspected I'd enjoy reading Justin Gregg's tour of this question when he opened with a quote from *Pyramids*, by Terry Pratchett, a book in one of my favorite science-fiction series: "Mere animals couldn't possibly manage to act like this. You need to be a human being to be really stupid."
>
> Gregg, an expert on animal cognition, explores what human foibles reveal about animal intelligence by invoking philosopher Friedrich Nietzsche. Nietzsche's conundrum is that he both envied cows and pitied them for the same reason: cows do not have an awareness that they will die. Nietzsche was both an intellectual genius and a mental wreck—the latter overcoming the former when, so the story goes, he witnessed a horse being whipped in Turin, Italy, and subsequently suffered a psychotic break. The premise here is that being unhappy is the price our species pays for _____. But how do we know if other animals are actually happier?
>
> Gregg cheekily points out that even the scientists (who are generally considered smart humans) who devote their careers to creating artificial intelligence can't agree on what intelligence is. Humans basically know it when we see it and regard intelligence as a positive trait. We often look outward for extraterrestrial signs of intelligence by seeking messages or signals that come from faraway planets. Curiously, we don't do very well with this search on our own planet.

Let's take lying: an overdeveloped human trait that is often employed for advantage. Gregg argues that the key feature of lying is intention. Although there is certainly evidence of deception throughout the animal kingdom, our species has the supposedly superlative abilities of language and theory of mind. But do they serve us well? Are we better off? Gregg dives into a fascinating discussion of the downsides, running from Jane Austen ("we have daily proof") to the modern onslaught of disinformation. From here he compares our species with others in terms of "death wisdom" and mortality and later considers the happiness of bees, as well as what it means to foresee the future.

Fill in the blank with the ONE most appropriate word from the passage. Second, what is the major factor for human unhappiness that Nietzsche and Gregg both cite in the passage?

142 Read the passage and follow the directions. [4 points]

China has the world's largest army. Russia wields the most tanks. America owns the fanciest satellites. But who has the most cyber-power? A new National Cyber Power Index _____ 30 countries on their level of ambition and capability. Offensive cyber-power—the ability to do harm in or through computer networks—is one measure. But so too are the strength of a country's defenses, the sophistication of its cyber-security industry and its ability to spread and counter propaganda.

That America stands at the top of the list is not surprising. Its cyber-security budget for fiscal year 2020 stood at over $17bn and the National Security Agency (NSA), its signals-intelligence (SIGINT) agency, probably gets well over $10bn.

China, in second place, has demonstrated a voracious appetite for commercial cyber-espionage abroad and an iron grip on the internet at home. Britain is third. Britain is currently setting up an offensive National Cyber Force staffed jointly by spies and soldiers. Russia, whose spies interfered with America's last election, is in fourth place. The big surprise is the Netherlands in fifth place, ahead of France, Germany and Canada. Many experts are puzzled by Israel's relatively low ranking on the Belfer index, despite its hacking prowess; its secrecy may be one reason for this.

Measuring cyber-power is fraught with difficulty, warns Marcus Willett. "Warships in the Antarctic can easily be seen," says Mr Willett, "yet a piece of code inserted into a power plant is hard to detect." Though some states acknowledge their offensive capabilities—America and Britain boast of smashing Islamic State networks in Iraq and Syria, partly as a signal to Russia and China—most shy away from doing so.

Many countries outsource the dirtiest work to deniable proxies, like "hacktivists" and criminals. And whereas procuring a warship or missile is expensive and time-consuming, potent malware can be stolen or bought online. WannaCry, a ransomware attack mounted by North Korea in 2017, used a hacking tool, EternalBlue, which had leaked out of the NSA.

A study of cyber-power by Mr Willett and his colleagues at the International Institute for Strategic Studies (IISS), a think-tank, concludes that, although stealing things and disrupting networks is important, what matters most over the longer term is control of digital infrastructure, such as the hardware that runs mobile telecommunications and key apps. Dominance there will be crucial to economic strength and national security. On that measure, only China, which is currently positioned to make the jump to almost join the US, ranks in second place.

Fill in the blank with the ONE most appropriate word from the passage. Second, which nation does the writer cite as an example of the ability to conceal digital warfare capability?

143 Read the passage and follow the directions. [4 points]

> Trees loom large in both environmental science and the wider social and political movement of environmentalism. Not for nothing are greens sometimes called "tree-huggers". Generally, the arboreal news is gloomy, as large areas of forest are cleared and either burned or taken on a one-way trip to the saw mill. But a paper published in *Nature*, by Martin Brandt of NASA brings some welcome good news. A part of the world previously seen as lacking in trees has actually been shown to harbor almost 2 billion of them.
>
> The area in question embraces the western end of the Sahara desert and the semi-desert Sahel region to its south. Few trees have shown up here in past surveys because such surveys have used satellite photographs that have insufficient resolution to spot individual trees' canopies. Instead, they have looked for contiguous patches of green that represent woods and forests.
>
> Dr. Brandt and Dr. Tucker thought this approach old-fashioned. Many high-resolution satellite photographs of Earth's surface now exist. Some—in the hands of armed forces and intelligence agencies—are secret. But others, owned by private Earth-observation firms, can be inspected at a price. As it happened, that price had already been paid by the American government for a set of appropriate images. This gave the researchers access to shots with a resolution as small as 50cm, rather than the 10-30 meters of those used in the past.

It is one thing, though, to have adequate resolving power. It is quite another to be able to use it. For that, Dr. Brandt and Dr. Tucker had to apply some artificial intelligence to the problem. This involved hand-labelling 89,899 individual trees in a set of training images, in order for the search algorithm to be able to learn what a tree looks like at different times of day, when covered by cloud, when shrouded by dust and when viewed from different angles. And, of course, individual trees themselves look different from one another. Once it had digested these images, the _____ was let loose on high-resolution photographs covering 1.3m square kilometers of the Sahara and the Sahel. In contrast to the previous negative results, it reported that there are 1.8bn trees in the area.

Fill in the blank with the ONE most appropriate word from the passage. Second, in what aspect are the previous surveys less adequate than the current one?

144 Read the passage and follow the directions. [4 points]

Ever since early Christian thinkers decided that the evil in the world needed a focus, a project and a name, in order to be decisively defeated at the Second Coming, the shape-shifting form of the Antichrist has hovered around.

Since its appearance signifies the end-times, when apocalyptic events will be unloosed upon the world and Christ will return to sort it all out, it is all too plausibly the Antichrist's moment now, with wildfires, plague and climate change all converging. It might be good to know, one way or the other.

But as Philip Almond explains, that is just the problem. It is very difficult to spot him, or it. Christians who felt duty-bound to keep permanent watch—and they included Isaac Newton. *The Book of Revelation*, which does not mention the Antichrist by name, provided a whole menagerie of aliases and clues, from the Whore of Babylon to the seventh head of the dragon rising from the sea.

Amid all this, Martin Luther's clear-eyed certainty that the papacy was the Antichrist comes as a gale of fresh air. It was a surprisingly old claim, first made in 1190 by Joachim of Fiore, and taken up with increasing enthusiasm as the Catholic church embroiled itself in simony, sexual deviance and the sale of indulgences. The theory behind it was that the Antichrist was not a tyrant skulking outside Christendom, picking believers off, but a malign influence working within it, even right at the heart and at the top.

The essence of this lurking Antichrist was _____, especially of the faithful. This explains why medieval paintings often show the Son of Perdition as a benevolent prince, crowned and robed, or even as a double for Jesus, bearded, thoughtful and working miracles. Evil was ever-beguiling, and drew plenty of willing followers. The alternative—to make the Antichrist utterly monstrous and vile as shown in William Blake's description of making a horned cadaver of him—puts the enemy in plain sight, and lets Christians off too easily from vetting their own behavior.

The search for the Antichrist leads Mr. Almond down many obscure paths. The problem he, or it, was invented to solve was that Christ had promised to return to the world and establish his kingdom, but had not done so yet. Nevertheless, Christians needed to believe that the <u>great showdown between good and evil was coming</u>. Satan himself had already been sent to hell, but his thoroughly demonized spawn was working in the world. The faithful had to be kept alert to the dark deception around them.

Fill in the blank with the ONE most appropriate word from the passage. Second, identify the TWO consecutive words from the passage that BEST correspond to the underlined words.

145 Read the passage and follow the directions. [4 points]

When it comes to cosmic speed limits, light gets all the attention. Its velocity in a vacuum, a tad below 300m meters per second, is an absolute upper bound on how fast anything in the universe can travel. This value, called "c" by physicists, is somehow baked into the fabric of reality as what is known as a fundamental constant.

The speed of sound, by contrast, has no obvious upper limit of its own. Find the right material, it has always been assumed, and you could make sound travel arbitrarily fast—so long as you did not break the speed of light.

Kostya Trachenko of Queen Mary University of London, however, disputes this—at least when the sound in question is travelling through a solid or a liquid. He proposes that in these circumstances sound, too, has a maximum possible velocity. Intriguingly, he also proposes that this is likewise baked into reality's fabric by being composed solely of fundamental constants. In a paper he lays out the reasons why.

Sound travels by making things vibrate. In solids and liquids—known collectively to physicists as the condensed phases of matter—molecules are bound to one another tightly. When one moves, its neighbors follow suit, and a wave of sound is thus transmitted. Allowing for differences in properties such as density and interatomic bond strength, Dr. Trachenko and his colleagues calculated that the _____ in condensed matter obeys a simple trend. The lighter the particle doing the vibrating, the faster it transmits sound. Sound's highest speed in such matter, they therefore predict, will be through a solid made of the lightest atoms: hydrogen.

Unfortunately hydrogen, which generally exists as a gas, is notoriously difficult to squeeze into a solid form, so measuring the speed of sound within its solid phase is tricky. But Dr. Trachenko's analysis predicts that if and when this is done, the result will be about 36,000 meters per second. That testable prediction of his theory is twice the current measured record for condensed-matter sound waves, which is held by diamond—ie, crystallized carbon.

Fill in the blank with the THREE most appropriate consecutive words from the passage. Second, what key aspect of hydrogen makes it ideal for Dr. Trachenko's test?

146 **Read the passage and follow the directions.** [4 points]

> The history of quilts began long before European settlers arrived in the New World. People in nearly every part of the world had used padded fabrics for clothing, bedding, and even armor. With the arrival of the English and Dutch settlers in North America, quilting took on a new life and flourished.
>
> A quilt is a cloth sandwich, with a top, which is usually the decorated part, a back, and a filler in the middle. Under the general term of patchwork are of 3 different types of quilts: the plain or whole cloth quilt, applique quilts, and pieced or patchwork quilts.
>
> The quilt, as we know it in America, was originally a strictly utilitarian article, born of the necessity of providing warm covers for beds. Quilts were also used as hangings for doors and windows that were not sealed well enough to keep out the cold. The earliest American quilts, made by English and Dutch settlers, were so intimately connected to everyday life of the early colonists that no record of them exists.
>
> During the early years of American colonization, most Colonial women were busy spinning, weaving and sewing the clothes for their family, so had little time for artistic quilting. Commercial blankets or woven coverlets were more likely to be used, but during difficult times, when money was scarce or imported textiles limited, many Colonial women had to become creative in their use of materials on hand to keep their families warm during the cold seasons.
>
> Those early settlers could not afford to simply discard things when they wore out; necessity required they carefully use their resources. Therefore, when blankets became worn, they were patched, combined with other blankets, or used as filler between other blankets. These were not carefully constructed heirlooms, rather they were functional items for the sole purpose of keeping people warm. Only in later years, when fabrics were being manufactured in America and were more affordable, freeing women from the work of making their own yarns and fabrics, did the more _____ type of quilting become more widespread.

Fill in the blank with the ONE most appropriate word from the passage. Second, it can be inferred from the passage that what condition is necessary for quilts to be recorded?

147 Read the passage and follow the directions. [4 points]

When Franklin Roosevelt told his economic advisers he was about to take the U.S. off the gold standard, they freaked out. The President was leading the country into "uncontrolled inflation and complete chaos," one of them said. Another said it was "the end of Western civilization." Roosevelt's aides weren't wild-eyed reactionaries; their view was conventional wisdom.

The gold standard, almost everybody agreed, was the natural way to do money. Under its rules, anybody who wanted to could trade in paper money for a fixed amount of gold. In the U.S., $20.67 got you an ounce of gold, year in and year out. That unchanging value was the whole point of the gold standard. Take away the gold, and money would obviously be just worthless paper.

This worldview turned out to be completely _____. Clinging to the gold standard was part of what created the Great Depression in the first place. Leaving it in 1933 was an essential step toward economic recovery. So why were Roosevelt's advisers, and most of the leading economists of the day, blinded by their devotion to gold?

There's this thinking error we almost always make with money. The way money works at any given moment feels like part of the natural order, as with water or gravity. Any alternative to the way money works seems like some wrong game. Paper money not backed by anything? That's like expecting water to flow uphill!

Then some political or technological or financial shock comes along, and suddenly there's something new: paper money backed by metal, or paper money backed by nothing, or simply numbers on a screen. <u>Pretty soon, we get used to the new money. It comes to seem like the natural state of things</u>, and anything else is foolishness.

We may be on the cusp of one of those shifts now. It's impossible to say for sure how things will play out, but history provides some deep insights into what should make us hopeful about the future of money—and what should scare us.

Fill in the blank with the ONE most appropriate word from the passage. Second, explain what the writer of the passage mainly argues in the underlined part. Do NOT copy more than THREE consecutive words from the passage.

148 Read the passage and follow the directions. [4 points]

> Sugar cane contains around 10% sugar. But that means it contains around 90% non-sugar—the material known as bagasse which remains once the cane has been pulverised and the sugar-bearing juice squeezed out of it. World production of cane sugar was 185m tons in 2017. That results in a lot of bagasse.
>
> At the moment, most of this is burned. Often, it fuels local generators that power the mills, so it is not wasted. But Zhu Hongli, a mechanical engineer, thinks it can be put to better use. As she and her colleagues describe in *Matter* this week, with a bit of tweaking bagasse makes an excellent—and biodegradable—replacement for the _____ used for disposable food containers such as coffee cups.
>
> Dr. Zhu is not the first person to have this idea. But previous attempts tended not to survive contact with liquids. She thought she could overcome that by spiking the sugar cane pulp with another biodegradable material. She knew from previous research that the main reason past efforts fell to pieces when wet is that bagasse is composed of short fibers which are unable to overlap sufficiently to confer resilience on the finished product. She therefore sought to insert a suitably long-fibred substance.
>
> Bamboo seemed to fit the bill. It grows quickly, degrades readily and has appropriately long fibers. And it worked. When the researchers blended a small amount of bamboo pulp into bagasse, they found that the result had a strong interweaving of short and long fibers. As a bonus, they also discovered that the hot pressing used as part of the process had mobilized some of the lignin in the fibers, and that this stiff, water-repelling material was now acting as an adhesive that bound the fibers together.

To put their new material through its paces, Dr. Zhu and her colleagues first poured hot oil onto it and found that, rather than penetrating the material, as it would have with previous bagasse products, the oil was repelled by their invention. Moreover, the new material is twice as strong as the plastic used to make cups, and is definitely biodegradable. When Dr. Zhu buried a cup made out of it in the ground, half of it rotted away within two months, and she reckons six months would have seen it gone completely.

Overall, Dr. Zhu argues that bagasse is an obvious choice for making coffee cups. <u>Once used, these could be dumped in landfills with a clear conscience.</u>

Fill in the blank with the ONE most appropriate word from the passage. Second, explain the meaning of the underlined part in the last sentence. Do NOT copy more than THREE consecutive words from the passage.

149 Read the passage and follow the directions. [4 points]

> After Nicholas II of Russia abdicated in 1917, meanwhile, "the tempests of the world outside blew directly into the households of Surabaya and Semarang." On seizing power, Vladimir Lenin had looked to Europe's working classes to foster wider revolution. When that hope fizzled, the revolutionary potential of Asian peasantries—whom Lenin, like the colonialists, had hitherto deemed backward—was reassessed. Asian radicals were summoned to Moscow. Nguyen Ai Quoc, M.N. Roy and Tan Malaka were at the heart of what Mr Harper calls the greatest missionary effort in Asia since the Jesuits set out to convert China, India and Japan in the 16th century.
>
> In Asia, and even in imperial homelands, action sometimes took violent form. Assassinations were attempted against the British viceroy of India and the governor-general of French Indochina. In early 1925 a young Chinese woman with the bob-cut of the "Modern Girl", an attitude popularized in Shanghai and Tokyo before Paris or New York, walked into a welfare office in Kuala Lumpur and coolly tried to blow up two British functionaries.
>
> Such violence aroused lurid fears of a "yellow peril". In truth, strikes and boycotts targeting economies that required colonial subjects to be both producers and consumers had more effect. But by the late 1920s the authorities had the upper hand. Not least, borders were no longer porous, while the Sûreté* and its counterparts had established ids, fingerprinting and rigorous record-keeping. They recruited narks and watchmen from the same waterfronts and brothel areas inhabited by the revolutionaries. International co-operation was regularized when Interpol was founded in 1923.

Radicals caught in the colonial net were rounded up and sent to detention centers, or, in the case of Indonesians, to Boven Digoel, upriver in malarial New Guinea. After the devastation suffered by even the victorious powers during the Second World War, Asia's revolutionaries saw fresh chances. Some seized the moment and rode to power. Today Ho Chi Minh City has one of Asia's most teeming metropolises named after him. Tan Malaka, by contrast, was devoured by the revolution he helped spawn—killed by his own side in the fight against the Dutch and the British.

Yet the lives of both men are testament to an early premonition that, far from being a morass of backwardness requiring firm imperial tutelage, Asia lay, at the forefront of human futures. And so, though many of the _____ are now forgotten—or, for some Asian nations, too inconvenient to remember—their underground stories still echo through time.

Sûreté: law enforcement

Fill in the blank with the ONE most appropriate word from the passage. Second, what can be inferred about the borders during the 1910s from the passage.

150 Read the passage and follow the directions. [4 points]

The history of _____ is intimately connected to that of civilisations. Or rather, it is a part of that history. Facilities offering guests hospitality have been in evidence since early biblical times. The Greeks developed thermal baths in villages designed for rest and recuperation. Later, the Romans built mansions to provide accommodation for travellers on government business. The Romans were the first to develop thermal baths in England, Switzerland and the Middle East.

Later still, caravanserais appeared, providing a resting place for caravans along Middle Eastern routes. In the Middle Ages, monasteries and abbeys were the first establishments to offer refuge to travellers on a regular basis. Religious orders built inns, hospices and hospitals to cater for those on the move. Inns multiplied, but they did not yet offer meals. Staging posts were established for governmental transports and as rest stops. They provided shelter and allowed horses to be changed more easily. Numerous refuges then sprang up for pilgrims and crusaders on their way to the Holy Land. Travelling then became progressively more hazardous. At the same time, inns gradually appeared in most of Europe. Some of them have remained famous, for example, l' Auberge des Trois Rois in Basle, which dates from the Middle Ages.

In France, at the beginning of the fifteenth century, the law required that hotels keep a register. English law also introduced rules for inns at that time. At the same time, around 1500 thermal spas were developed at Carlsbad and Marienbad. During this epoch, more than 600 inns were registered in England. Their architecture often consisted of a paved interior court with access through an arched porch. The bedrooms were situated on the two sides of the courtyard, the kitchen and the public rooms at the front, and the stables and storehouses at the back. The first guide books for travellers were published in France during this period.

An embryonic hotel industry began to develop in Europe. Distinctive signs were hung outside establishments renowned for their refined cuisine. At the end of the 1600s, the first stage coaches following a regular timetable started operating in England. Half a century later, clubs similar to English gentlemen's clubs and masonic lodges began to appear in America.

Fill in the blank with the ONE most appropriate word from the passage. Second, in what era did inns appear in Europe?

151 Read the passage and follow the directions. [4 points]

As the age of rail was beginning, political philosopher Karl Marx used the metaphor of its technology as a worldview. It was no more surprising that a mid-nineteenth-century European would use a railway metaphor than it is to hear someone comparing the mind to a computer today. In what became very influential terms, Marx claimed that human society and consciousness are what he called the superstructure, resting on the economic infrastructure of factories, mines and other forms of production. These were terms taken directly from the railway. Infrastructure meant tracks and associated systems, while the superstructure was the train. In short, for Marx the human mind was a train running on a set of _____ tracks.

The railway changed the way people lived, creating its own time and space. The modern time zones still in use today were first devised so that accurate railway timetables could be created. Until then, local time was specific to each place. British railways took London time as their standard. The resulting Greenwich Mean Time was adopted by most national clocks by 1855, although the legal profession continued to use local time until 1880. A similar pattern was followed in the United States. In 1883, US railroad companies created standardized time zones, only legalized by Congress in 1918. Whereas time had been highly local, it now became uniform for wide areas and then changed abruptly at arbitrary points. Another way to describe this would be to say that time before the train was analog, meaning that it calibrated evenly with each place's relation to the sun. Afterward, it became digital, meaning that it shifted in arbitrary units of an hour (like the one or the zero in the computer).

Factories made this change real for the new industrial workforce. At the beginning of industrialization, workers would wander out during the workday as they felt inclined, or take naps if they were tired. They brought the habits of agricultural life into industrial practice. Soon, though, it came to feel "natural" that there is a working day and that as much of that day as possible should be devoted to work. Employers and employees battled then and now to extend or shorten the hours of that day. The creation of the railway network enabled people to live outside city centers and travel there for work. By 1910, a third of all French people were season-ticket holders on the train, traveling in and out of urban centers on a daily basis. A century later, France was still the leading European nation in terms of rail transport, with over 54 billion passenger miles of rail journeys a year.

Fill in the blank with the ONE most appropriate word from the passage. Second, to what cause does the writer attribute the habit of napping of early factory workers?

152 **Read the passage and follow the directions.** [4 points]

> Often an interesting question comes up in discussions about <u>the twin powers</u> that drive us: Why is it that people can experience pain yet fail to change? They haven't experienced enough pain yet; they haven't hit what I call emotional threshold. If you've ever been in a destructive relationship and finally made the decision to use your personal power, take action and change your life, it was probably because you hit a level of pain you weren't willing to settle for anymore. We've all experienced those times in our lives when we've said, "I've had it—never again—this must change now." This is the magical moment when pain becomes our friend.
>
> This process is certainly not limited to relationships. Maybe you've experienced threshold with your physical condition: you finally got fed up because you couldn't squeeze into an airline seat, you couldn't fit into your clothes, and walking up a set of stairs winded you. Finally you said, "I've had it!" and made a decision. What motivated that decision? It was the desire to remove pain from your life and establish pleasure once again: the pleasure of pride, the pleasure of comfort, the pleasure of self-esteem, the pleasure of living life the way you've designed it.
>
> Of course, there are many levels of pain and pleasure. For example, feeling a sense of humiliation is a rather intense form of emotional pain. Feeling a sense of inconvenience is also pain. So is boredom. Obviously some of these have less intensity, but they still factor in the equation of decision-making. Likewise, pleasure weighs into this process. Much of our drive in life comes from our anticipating that our actions will lead to a more compelling future, that today's work will be well worth the effort, that the rewards of pleasure are near. Yet there are many levels of pleasure as well. For example, the pleasure of ecstasy, while most would agree is intense, may sometimes be outweighed by the pleasure of comfort. It all depends on an individual's perspective.

Let's say you're on your lunch break, and you're walking past a park where a Beethoven symphony is playing. Will you stop and listen? It depends on the meaning you associate to classical music. Some people would drop anything to be able to listen to the valiant strains of the Eroica Symphony. For them, Beethoven equals pure pleasure. For others, however, listening to any kind of classical music is about as exciting as watching paint dry. Enduring the music would equal a measure of _____.

Describe to what the underlined "the twin powers" refer. Second, fill in the blank with the ONE most appropriate word from the passage.

153 Read the passage and follow the directions. [4 points]

> The housing bubble and the 2008 financial crisis played a major role in the moral delegitimization of markets. When new developments in Florida and Arizona, built under the pressure of astronomically high real-estate prices, sit empty, people start questioning the efficiency of market prices. When the difference between a comfortable retirement and an indigent one is determined not by hard work or by a frugal lifestyle but by lucky timing in buying or selling your house, people start questioning the fairness of the _____. The fact that the real-estate bubble was the second large bubble to pop in less than a decade further undermined trust in markets as a good indicator of where to invest resources.
>
> But nothing upsets people like the perception that the rules don't apply equally to everybody. When my children were small, they sometimes tried to play Monopoly. These attempts inevitably degenerated into arguments. My daughter, who is two years younger than my son, would claim that my son was cheating. My son, with the official instructions in hand, would protest his innocence. And he was right: he never invented any rule. Nevertheless, my daughter was right, too: my son was engaging in selective recollection of the rules, counting on my daughter's ignorance and bringing up only the rules that were in his favor. Despite her youth, my daughter understood that something wasn't fair, so she employed the only response she had available: giving up.

Her frustration was similar to what many people felt after the 2008 bailouts of the financial system. The market system was certainly at risk, and some government intervention was just as certainly necessary. Yet it was false to say, as Federal Reserve chairman Ben Bernanke and Treasury secretary Henry Paulson did repeatedly, that the choice was between the Troubled Asset Relief Program (TARP) as it was proposed and the financial abyss: there were feasible—and, in fact, superior—alternatives. It didn't escape most Americans that TARP was the largest welfare program for corporations and their investors ever created in human history. That some of the crumbs went to autoworkers' unions didn't improve things; in fact, it made them worse, showing that the redistribution was not an accident but a premeditated pillage of defenseless taxpayers by powerful lobbies. TARP wasn't just the triumph of Wall Street over Main Street; it was the triumph of K Street* over the rest of America.

*K Street: Washington's lobbying industry

Fill in the blank with the TWO most appropriate consecutive words from the passage. Second, describe what the underlined "the redistribution" means.

154 Read the passage and follow the directions. [4 points]

Carl Schoonover and Andrew Fink are confused. As neuroscientists, they know that the brain must be flexible but not too flexible. It must rewire itself in the face of new experiences, but must also consistently _____ the features of the external world. How? The relatively simple explanation found in neuroscience textbooks is that specific groups of neurons reliably fire when their owner smells a rose, sees a sunset, or hears a bell. These representations—these patterns of neural firing—presumably stay the same from one moment to the next. But as Schoonover and Fink have found, they sometimes don't. They change—and to a confusing and unexpected extent.

Schoonover and Fink allowed mice to sniff the same odors over several days and weeks, and recorded the activity of neurons in the rodents' piriform cortex—a brain region involved in identifying smells. At a given moment, each odor caused a distinctive group of neurons in this region to fire. But as time went on, the makeup of these groups slowly changed. Some neurons stopped responding to the smells; others started. After a month, each group was almost completely different. Put it this way: The neurons that represented the smell of an apple in May and those that represented the same smell in June were as different from each other as those that represent the smells of apples and grass at any one time.

This is, of course, just one study, of one brain region, in mice. But other scientists have shown that the same activity, called representational drift, occurs in a variety of brain regions besides the piriform cortex. Its existence is clear; everything else is a mystery. Schoonover and Fink told me that they don't know why it happens, what it means, how the brain copes, or how much of the brain behaves in this way. How can animals possibly make any lasting sense of the world if their neural responses to that world are constantly in flux? If such flux is common, "there must be mechanisms in the brain that are undiscovered and even unimagined that allow it to keep up," Schoonover said. "Scientists are meant to know what's going on, but in this particular case, we are deeply confused. We expect it to take many years to iron out."

Fill in the blank with the ONE most appropriate word from the passage. Second, what phenomenon did Schoonover and Fink identify that was confirmed by the underlined "other scientists"?

155 Read the passage and follow the directions. [4 points]

To a certain extent, talking about what "the metaverse" means is a bit like having a discussion about what "the internet" meant in the 1970s. The building blocks of a new form of communication were in the process of being built, but no one could really know what the reality would look like. So while it was true, at the time, that "the internet" was coming, not every idea of what that would look like is true.

On the other hand, there's also a lot of marketing hype wrapped up in this idea of the metaverse. Facebook, in particular, is in an especially vulnerable place after Apple's move to limit ad tracking hit the company's bottom line. It's impossible to separate Facebook's vision of a future where everyone has a digital wardrobe to swipe through from the fact that Facebook really wants to make money selling virtual clothes.

To help you get a sense of how vague and complex a term "the metaverse" can be, here's an exercise to try: Mentally replace the phrase "the metaverse" in a sentence with "cyberspace." Ninety percent of the time, the meaning won't substantially change. That's because the term doesn't really refer to any one specific type of technology, but rather a broad shift in how we interact with technology. And it's entirely possible that the term itself will eventually become just as antiquated, even as the specific technologies it once described becomes commonplace.

Broadly speaking, the _____ that make up the metaverse can include virtual reality—characterized by persistent virtual worlds that continue to exist even when you're not playing—as well as augmented reality that combines aspects of the digital and physical worlds. However, it doesn't require that those spaces be exclusively accessed via VR or AR. A virtual world, like aspects of Fortnite that can be accessed through PCs, game consoles, and even phones, could be metaverse.

유희태 | 일반영어 ④-1

> The paradox of defining the metaverse is that in order for it to be the future, you have to define away the present. We already have MMOs that are essentially entire virtual worlds, digital concerts, video calls with people from all over the world, online avatars, and commerce platforms. So in order to sell these things as a new vision of the world, there has to be some element of it that's new.

Fill in the blank with the ONE most appropriate word from the passage. Second, explain the writer's position about the metaverse as implied in the last paragraph of the passage. Do NOT copy more than FOUR consecutive words from the passage.

156   **Read the passage and follow the directions.** [4 points]

> Why is English so eccentric? Just what is this thing we're speaking, and what happened to make it this way? English started out as, essentially, a kind of German. Old English is so unlike the modern version that it feels like a stretch to think of them as the same language at all. Hwæt, we gardena in geardagum þeodcyninga þrym gefrunon—does that really mean 'So, we Spear-Danes have heard of the tribe-kings' glory in days of yore'? Icelanders can still read similar stories written in the Old Norse ancestor of their language 1,000 years ago, and yet, <u>to the untrained eye, Beowulf might as well be in Turkish</u>.
>
> The first thing that got us from there to here was the fact that, when the Angles, Saxons and Jutes brought their language to England, the island was already inhabited by people who spoke very different tongues. Their languages were Celtic ones, today represented by Welsh, Irish and Breton across the Channel in France. The Celts were subjugated but survived, and since there were only about 250,000 Germanic invaders—roughly the population of a modest burg such as Jersey City—very quickly most of the people speaking Old English were Celts.
>
> Crucially, their languages were quite unlike English. For one thing, the verb came first (came first the verb). But also, they had an odd construction with the verb do: they used it to form a question, to make a sentence negative, and even just as a kind of seasoning before any verb. Do you walk? I do not walk. I do walk. That looks familiar now because the Celts started doing it in their rendition of English. But before that, such sentences would have seemed weird to an English speaker—as they would today in just about any language other than our own and the surviving Celtic ones. Notice how even to dwell upon this queer usage of do is to realise some weirdness in oneself, like being made aware that there is always a tongue in your mouth.

At this date there is no documented language on earth beyond Celtic and English that uses do in just this way. Thus English's _____ began with its transformation in the mouths of people more at home with vastly different tongues. We're still talking like them, and in ways we'd never think of.

Fill in the blank with the ONE most appropriate word from the passage. Second, explain the meaning of the underlined words in the first paragraph. Do NOT copy more than THREE consecutive words from the passage.

157 Read the passage and follow the directions. [4 points]

Evil, of course, is a traditional name, but, like other names, it has been appropriated by a particular ideology which then offers itself as the whole tragic tradition. In recent years especially, we have been continually rebuked by what is called the fact of transcendent evil, and the immense social crisis of our century is specifically interpreted in this light or darkness. The true nature of man, it is argued, is now dramatically revealed, against all the former illusions of civilisation and progress. The concentration camp, especially, is used as an image of an absolute condition, in which man is reduced, by men, to a thing. The record of the camps is indeed black enough, and many other examples could be added. But to use the camp as an image of an absolute condition is, in its turn, a blasphemy. For while men created the camps, other men died, at conscious risk, to destroy them. While some men imprisoned, other men liberated. There is no evil which men have created, of this or any other kind, which other men have not struggled to end. To take one part of this action, and call it absolute or transcendent, is in its turn a suppression of other facts of human life on so vast a scale that its indifference can only be explained by its role in an ideology.

Culturally, evil is a name for many kinds of disorder which corrode or destroy actual life. As such, it is common in tragedy, though in many particular and variable forms: vengeance or ambition or pride or coldness or lust or jealousy or disobedience or rebellion. In every case it is only fully comprehensible within the valuations of a particular culture or tradition. It may indeed be possible, in any particular _____, to generalise it until it appears as an absolute and even singular force. As a common name, also, it appears to take on a general character. But we cannot then say that tragedy is the recognition of transcendent evil. Tragedy commonly dramatises evil, in many particular forms. We move away from actual tragedies, and not towards them, when we abstract and generalise the very specific forms that are so variously dramatised. We move away, even more decisively, from a common tragic action, when we interpret tragedy as only the dramatisation and recognition of evil.

Fill in the blank with the ONE most appropriate word from the passage. Second, explain why a concentration camp is not a representation of an absolute evil. Do NOT copy more than THREE consecutive words from the passage.

158 Read the passage and follow the directions. [4 points]

Unearthing the origins of the Japanese is a much harder task than you might guess. Japan's rising dominance and touchy relations with its neighbors make it more important than ever to strip away myths and find answers.

The search for answers is difficult because the evidence is so conflicting. On the one hand, the Japanese people are biologically undistinctive, being very similar in appearance and genes to other East Asians, especially to Koreans. Taken together, many facts suggest that the Japanese reached Japan only recently from the Asian mainland, too recently to have evolved differences from their mainland cousins, and displaced the Ainu, who represent the original inhabitants. But if that were true, you might expect the Japanese language to show close affinities to some mainland language, just as English is obviously closely related to other Germanic languages (because Anglo-Saxons from the continent conquered England as recently as the sixth century a.d.). How can we resolve this contradiction between Japan's presumably ancient language and the evidence for recent origins?

Archeologists have proposed four conflicting theories. Most popular in Japan is the view that the Japanese gradually evolved from ancient Ice Age people who occupied Japan long before 20,000 b.c. Also widespread in Japan is a theory that the Japanese descended from horse-riding Asian nomads who passed through Korea to conquer Japan in the fourth century, but who were themselves—emphatically—not Koreans. A theory favored by many Western archeologists and Koreans, and unpopular in some circles in Japan, is that the Japanese are descendants of immigrants from Korea who arrived with rice-paddy agriculture around 400 b.c. Finally, the peoples named in the other three theories could have mixed to form the modern Japanese.

When similar questions of _____ arise about other peoples, they can be discussed dispassionately. That is not so for the Japanese. Until 1946, Japanese schools taught a myth of history based on the earliest recorded Japanese chronicles, which were written in the eighth century. They describe how the sun goddess Amaterasu, born from the left eye of the creator god Izanagi, sent her grandson Ninigi to Earth on the Japanese island of Kyushu to wed an earthly deity. Ninigi's great-grandson Jimmu, aided by a dazzling sacred bird that rendered his enemies helpless, became the first emperor of Japan in 660 b.c. To fill the gap between 660 b.c. and the earliest historically documented Japanese monarchs, the chronicles invented 13 other equally fictitious emperors. Before the end of World War II, when Emperor Hirohito finally announced that he was not of divine descent, Japanese archeologists and historians had to make their interpretations conform to <u>this chronicle account</u>.

Fill in the blank with the ONE most appropriate word from the passage. Second, explain to what the underlined "this chronicle account" refers. Do NOT copy more than FOUR consecutive words from the passage in providing your answer.

159 Read the passage and follow the directions. [4 points]

> In the early years of Christianity, Easter was the main holiday; the birth of Jesus was not celebrated. In the fourth century, church officials decided to institute the birth of Jesus as a holiday. Unfortunately, the Bible does not mention date for his birth (a fact Puritans later pointed out in order to deny the legitimacy of the celebration). Although some evidence suggests that his birth may have occurred in the spring (why would shepherds be herding in the middle of winter?), Pope Julius I chose December 25. It is commonly believed that the church chose this date in an effort to adopt and absorb the traditions of the pagan Saturnalia festival. First called the Feast of the Nativity, the custom spread to Egypt by 432 and to England by the end of the sixth century.
>
> By holding Christmas at the same time as traditional winter solstice festivals, church leaders increased the chances that Christmas would be popularly embraced, but gave up the ability to dictate how it was celebrated. By the Middle Ages, Christianity had, for the most part, replaced _____ religion. On Christmas, believers attended church, then celebrated raucously in a drunken, carnival-like atmosphere similar to today's Mardi Gras. Each year, a beggar or student would be crowned the "lord of misrule" and eager celebrants played the part of his subjects. The poor would go to the houses of the rich and demand their best food and drink. If owners failed to comply, their visitors would most likely terrorize them with mischief. Christmas became the time of year when the upper classes could repay their real or imagined "debt" to society by entertaining less fortunate citizens.
>
> In the early 17th century, a wave of religious reform changed the way Christmas was celebrated in Europe. When Oliver Cromwell and his Puritan forces took over England in 1645, they vowed to rid England of decadence and, as part of their effort, cancelled Christmas. By popular demand, Charles II was restored to the throne and, with him, came the return of the popular holiday.

The pilgrims, English separatists that came to America in 1620, were even more orthodox in their Puritan beliefs than Cromwell. As a result, Christmas was not a holiday in early America. From 1659 to 1681, the celebration of Christmas was actually outlawed in Boston. Anyone exhibiting the Christmas spirit was fined five shillings. By contrast, in the Jamestown settlement, Captain John Smith reported that Christmas was enjoyed by all and passed without incident. After the American Revolution, English customs fell out of favor, including Christmas. In fact, Christmas wasn't declared a federal holiday until June 26, 1870.

Fill in the blank with the ONE most appropriate word from the passage. Second, explain the similarity between Oliver Cromwell and the pilgrims. Do NOT copy more than FOUR consecutive words from the passage in providing your answer.

160 Read the passage and follow the directions. [4 points]

If you ask one hundred people to elaborate on their understanding of the term "philosophy," you will probably get a hundred different answers. Not having a unified understanding of this phenomenon, it is worthwhile for each philosopher to depict what his or her perception of philosophy is. Often in real life, we observe that certain thought systems acquire widespread acceptance, and create opinions that sway vast numbers of people in a certain direction. This can start trends that are good and constructive, if correct, and very destructive, if incorrect. The spread of Communism on a universal scale is one example of this reality.

From my perspective, a good philosophy should serve multiple needs. On one level, a philosophical approach might unveil certain important factors that had passed unnoticed up until that point. Detecting such phenomena might reveal valuable realities about important things. Not knowing that which can be known can best be described as negligence, which can cause momentous and preventable harm if not detected on time. On another level, it could unveil significant understanding of complex and seemingly inexplicable phenomena from which the world would otherwise be deprived. For example, in their early stages, the concept of gravity and the fact that the earth circled around the sun were philosophical discoveries. Thus, detecting such hidden phenomena through philosophical study that ultimately develops into science is beneficial to humanity and the world at large.

Furthermore as such facts are detected and explained through philosophy, we increasingly find this _____ world of ours more orderly. Through philosophy, we find answers to questions, which, at one point, seemed impossible to understand. For instance, just before Sir Isaac Newton discovered the force of gravity, the inquisitive minds of the day were utterly confused in observing the different ways objects behaved in relation to earth. For instance, when an elevated object was released, it would travel toward the earth flawlessly. Yet another object, such as water in the form of a gas, would rise. And then, the same object, water in the form of a fluid, or a hard object such as snow or hail, would fall back to the earth. Furthermore, some objects, such as specks of dust, would float in the air.

Such diverse behavior between different objects seemed utterly chaotic at the time. However, when gravity was identified as the force that pulls all objects to itself, it became easy to understand why some objects fell.

Fill in the blank with the ONE most appropriate word from the passage. Second, what philosophy does the writer reference as a negative example of a popularized ideology?

161 Read the passage and follow the directions. [4 points]

> People have observed the sky throughout history, and sometimes seen unusual sights: such as comets, bright meteors, one or more of the five planets that can be readily seen with the naked eye, planetary conjunctions, and atmospheric optical phenomena such as parhelia and lenticular clouds. One particularly famous example is Halley's Comet: this was recorded first by Chinese astronomers in 240 BC and possibly as early as 467 BC. As it reaches the inner solar system every 76 years, it was often identified as a unique isolated event in ancient historical documents whose authors were unaware that it was a repeating phenomenon. Such accounts in history often were treated as supernatural portents, angels, or other religious omens. While UFO(unidentified flying object) enthusiasts have sometimes commented on the narrative similarities between certain religious symbols in medieval paintings and UFO reports, the canonical and symbolic character of such images is documented by art historians placing more conventional religious interpretations on such images.
>
> In the Pacific and European theatres during World War II, round, glowing fireballs known as "foo fighters" were reported by Allied and Axis pilots. Some proposed Allied explanations at the time included St. Elmo's fire, the planet Venus, hallucinations from oxygen deprivation, or German secret weapons. In 1946, more than 2,000 reports were collected, primarily by the Swedish military, of unidentified aerial objects over the Scandinavian nations, along with isolated reports from France, Portugal, Italy and Greece. The objects were referred to as "Russian hail" (and later as "ghost rockets") because it was thought the mysterious objects were possibly Russian tests of captured German V1 or V2 rockets. Later, most objects were _____ as natural phenomena such as meteors.

Fill in the blank with the ONE most appropriate word from the passage. Second, for what reason was a sighting of Halley's Comet thought of as a singular event in history?

162 Read the passage and follow the directions. [2 points]

> The British empire spanned the globe. This led to the saying that the sun never set on it, since it was always daylight somewhere in the empire.
>
> It's hard to figure out exactly when this long daylight began. The whole process of claiming a colony (on land already occupied by other people) is awfully arbitrary in the first place. Essentially, the British built their empire by sailing around and sticking flags on random beaches. This makes it hard to decide when a particular spot in a country was "officially" added to the empire.
>
> The exact day when the sun stopped setting on the empire was probably sometime in the late 1700s or early 1800s, when the first Australian territories were added. The empire largely disintegrated in the early 20th century, but—surprisingly—the sun hasn't technically started setting on it again.
>
> Britain has 14 overseas territories, the direct remnants of empire. Many newly independent British colonies joined the Commonwealth. Some of them, like Canada and Australia, have Queen Elizabeth as their monarch. However, they are independent states that happen to have the same queen; they are not part of any empire.
>
> The sun never sets on all 14 British territories at once. However, if the UK loses one tiny territory, it will experience its first empire-wide sunset in over two centuries. Every night, around midnight GMT, the sun sets on the Cayman Islands, and doesn't rise over the British Indian Ocean territory until after 1am. For that hour, the little Pitcairn Islands in the South Pacific are the only British territory in the sun.

The Pitcairn Islands have a population of a few dozen people, the descendants of the mutineers from the HMS Bounty*. The islands became notorious when a third of the adult male population, including the mayor, were convicted of child sexual abuse. As awful as the islands may be, they remain part of the British empire, and unless they are kicked out, the two-century-long British _____ will continue.

*the HMS Bounty: a merchant vessel that the Royal Navy purchased in 1787

Fill in the blank with the ONE most appropriate word from the passage.

163 Read the passage and follow the directions. [4 points]

In the study of infant perceptual abilities, a number of techniques are used to determine infants' responses to various stimuli. Because they cannot verbalize or fill out questionnaires, indirect techniques of naturalistic observation are used as the primary means of determining what infants can see, hear, feel, and so forth. Each of these methods compares an infant's state prior to the introduction of a stimulus with its state during or immediately following the stimulus. The difference between the two measures provides the researcher with an indication of the level and duration of the response to the stimulus. For example, if a uniformly moving pattern of some sort is passed across the visual field of a neonate (newborn), repetitive following movements of the eye occur. The occurrence of these eye movements provides evidence that the moving pattern is perceived at some level by the newborn. Similarly, changes in the infant's general level of motor activity—turning the head, blinking the eyes, crying, and so forth—have been used by researchers as visual indicators of the infant's perceptual abilities.

Such techniques, however, have limitations. First, the observation may be unreliable in that two or more observers may not agree that the particular response occurred, or to what degree it occurred. Second, responses are difficult to quantify. Often the rapid and diffuse movements of the infant make it difficult to get an accurate record of the number of responses. The third, and most potent, limitation is that it is not possible to be certain that the infant's response was due to the stimulus presented or to a change from no stimulus to a stimulus. The infant may be responding to aspects of the stimulus different than those identified by the investigator. Therefore, when observational assessment is used as a technique for studying _____, care must be taken not to overgeneralize from the data or to rely on one or two studies as conclusive evidence of a particular perceptual ability of the infant.

Fill in the blank with the THREE most appropriate consecutive words from the passage. Second, describe to what the underlined "the two measures" refer.

164 Read the passage and follow the directions. [4 points]

> It might be worth remembering the strong reaction to one of Stravinsky's musical pieces. No other artform could have resulted in such a spontaneous reaction, as this particular piece of music did.
>
> Now, the instinct of rhythm is one of the most profound of all human instincts. It relentlessly demands rhythm from our material world, and as the connections are properly made, great pleasure and joy is experienced. This is despite the fact that most people cannot consciously make the connection to identify the source of this pleasure and joy. Furthermore, rhythm does not exist within the human instinct alone, but rather, all nature is imbued with it. To understand rhythmic art we first need to understand rhythm and its larger role in the world.
>
> Rhythm is ubiquitous in nature and presents itself in an endless number of ways, both natural and artificial. Rhythm surrounds us in the most profound ways despite the fact that we have grown so accustomed to it. In fact, we often do not even notice it, in the same way that we don't notice our need to breathe.
>
> For example, starting with the most obvious, the sun rises every morning in the east and sets every evening in the west. This cycle precipitates the exchange of day to night, light to dark, and back again every twenty-four hours rhythmically. The same holds true for the way the moon systematically appears, changes shape, and disappears, only to reappear again every month. Tidal waves occur rhythmically to the point that many marine animals structure their lives around them.
>
> To use another example from a different realm, each language has its own _____. Write just a few sentences and then translate these written lines into different languages. Then find people who will read each sentence with their native languages and accents. You will hear that each native tongue has its own distinct melodic sound. You will notice that each language—besides differing from the others in vocabulary, grammar, and endless other subtleties—has a distinct rhythm of its own that makes each easily distinguishable from the rest.

Fill in the blank with the ONE most appropriate word from the passage. Second, explain why Stravinsky's musical piece upset the audience as can be inferred from the passage.

165 Read the passage and follow the directions. [4 points]

The "wisdom of crowds" has become a mantra of the Internet age. Need to choose a new vacuum cleaner? Check out the reviews on online merchant Amazon. But a new study suggests that such online scores don't always reveal the best choice. A massive controlled experiment of Web users finds that such ratings are highly susceptible to irrational "herd behavior"—and that the herd can be _____.

Sometimes the crowd really is wiser than you. The classic examples are guessing the weight of a bull or the number of gumballs in a jar. Your guess is probably going to be far from the mark, whereas the average of many people's choices is remarkably close to the true number. But what happens when the goal is to judge something less tangible, such as the quality or worth of a product?

According to one theory, the wisdom of the crowd still holds—measuring the aggregate of people's opinions produces a stable, reliable value. Skeptics, however, argue that people's opinions are easily manipulated by those of others. So nudging a crowd early on by presenting contrary opinions—for example, exposing them to some very good or very bad attitudes—will steer the crowd in a different direction. To test which hypothesis is true, you would need to manipulate huge numbers of people, exposing them to false information and determining how it affects their opinions.

A team led by Sinan Aral, a network scientist at the Massachusetts Institute of Technology, did exactly that. Aral has been secretly working with a popular website that aggregates news stories. The website allows users to make comments about news stories and vote each other's comments up or down. The vote tallies are visible as a number next to each comment and the position of the comments is chronological. It's a follow up to his experiment using people's ratings of movies to measure how much individual people influence each other online (answer: a lot). This time, he wanted to know how much the crowd influences the individual, and whether it can be controlled from outside.

For five months, every comment submitted by a user randomly received an "up" vote (positive), a "down" vote (negative); or as a control, no vote at all. The team then observed how users rated those comments. The users generated more than 100,000 comments that were viewed more than 10 million times and rated more than 300,000 times by other users.

At least when it comes to comments on news sites, the crowd is more herdlike than wise. Comments that received fake positive votes from the researchers were 32% more likely to receive more positive votes compared with a control.

Fill in the blank with the ONE most appropriate word from the passage. Second, what does Sinan Aral's study reveal about the "wisdom of crowds"? Do NOT copy more than FOUR consecutive words from the excerpt.

166 Read the passage and follow the directions. [4 points]

> A NASA probe has entered the sun's atmosphere and touched the blazing corona, in a first for solar science. The Parker Solar Probe, which launched in 2018, conducted seven flybys of the sun before dipping into the corona during its eighth flyby on April 28, 2021. It made three trips into the sun's atmosphere, one of which lasted for 5 hours.
>
> In the upper reaches of the solar atmosphere, where temperatures average about 2 million degrees Fahrenheit (1 million degrees Celsius)—hotter than the light-emitting surface of the sun, which is only 10,000 F (5,500 C)—the spacecraft collected atmospheric particles in a special instrument called the Solar Probe Cup. By entering and sampling the _____, the Parker Solar Probe accomplished a scientific achievement akin to landing on the moon.
>
> Powerful solar winds made of streaming plasma and high-energy particles are born in the corona, but are mostly held back by the sun's magnetic fields, which also restrain bursts of plasma that spurt from the sun's surface. When solar winds exceed a certain speed and extend just past the sun's atmosphere, a location known as the Alfvén point, they can break free of their magnetic restraints. However, scientists didn't know where exactly that point was located.
>
> Now, Parker Solar Probe has answered that question. Prior estimates based on remote images of the corona predicted that the Alfvén point would be found approximately 4.3 million to 8.6 million miles from the solar surface. Parker detected those conditions on April 28, at a distance of about 8.1 million miles above the sun, telling researchers that it had entered the sun's atmosphere for the first time.
>
> Solar winds and solar flares—swift eruptions of solar radiation—can affect electrical grids and disrupt communication networks on Earth, and the new data from the probe provides an unprecedented glimpse into these solar events.

Fill in the blank with the TWO most appropriate consecutive words from the passage. Second, of what significance is the Alfvén point in regards to life on earth, according to the passage?

167 Read the passage and follow the directions. [4 points]

> The U.S. Constitution owes a huge debt to ancient Rome. The Founding Fathers were well-versed in Greek and Roman History. Leaders like Thomas Jefferson and James Madison read the historian Polybius, who laid out one of the clearest descriptions of the Roman Republic's constitution, where representatives of various factions and social classes checked the power of the elites and the power of the mob. It's not surprising that in the United States' nascent years, _____ to ancient Rome were common. And to this day, Rome, whose 482-year-long Republic, bookended by several hundred years of monarchy and 1,500 years of imperial rule, is still the longest the world has seen.
>
> Aspects of our modern politics reminded University of California San Diego historian Edward Watts of the last century of the Roman Republic, roughly 130 B.C. to 27 B.C. That's why he took a fresh look at the period in his new book *Mortal Republic: How Rome Fell Into Tyranny*. Watts chronicles the ways the republic, with a population once devoted to national service and personal honor, was torn to shreds by growing wealth inequality, partisan gridlock, political violence and pandering politicians, and argues that the people of Rome chose to let their democracy die by not protecting their political institutions, eventually turning to the perceived stability of an emperor instead of facing the continued violence of an unstable and degraded republic.
>
> Though he does not directly compare and contrast Rome with the United States, Watts says that what took place in Rome is a lesson for all modern republics. "Above all else, the Roman Republic teaches the citizens of its modern descendants the incredible dangers that come along with condoning political obstruction and courting political violence," he writes. "Roman history could not more clearly show that, when citizens look away as their leaders engage in these corrosive behaviors, their republic is in mortal danger."

Many aspects of the Roman Republic feel rather familiar. The Roman people's strong sense of patriotism was unique in the Mediterranean world. Like the United States after World War II, Rome, after winning the Second Punic War in 201 B.C., became the world's hegemon, which lead to a massive increase in their military spending, a baby boom, and gave rise to a class of super-wealthy elites that were able to use their money to influence politics and push their own agendas. Those similarities make comparisons worthwhile, even if the togas, gladiator battles and appetite for dormice seem completely foreign.

Fill in the blank with the ONE most appropriate word from the passage. Second, describe the most important factor that led to the demise of the Roman Republic as implied by Edward Watts.

168 Read the passage and follow the directions. [4 points]

The literature of naturalism is the most obvious example. It seems now the true child of the liberal enlightenment, in which the traditional ideas of a fate, an absolute order, a design beyond human powers, were replaced by a confidence in reason and in the possibility of a continually expanding capacity for explanation and control. In politics this produced a new social consciousness of human destiny; in philosophy, analysis of the ideologies of religion and of social custom, together with new schemes of rational explanation; in literature, a new emphasis on the exact observation and description of the contemporary social world.

But the literature of naturalism, finally, is a bastard of the _____. Characteristically, it detached the techniques of observation and description from the purposes which these were intended to serve. What became naturalism, and what distinguished it from the more important movement of realism, was a mechanical description of men as the creatures of their environment, which literature recorded as if man and thing were of the same nature.

The tragedy of naturalism is the tragedy of passive suffering, and the suffering is passive because man can only endure and can never really change his world. The endurance is given no moral or religious valuation; it is wholly mechanical, because both man and his world, in what is now understood as rational explanation, are the products of an impersonal and material process which though it changes through time has no ends. The impulse to describe and so change a human condition has narrowed to the simple impulse to describe a condition in which there can be no intervention by God or man, the human act of will being tiny and insignificant within the vast material process, universal or social, which at once determines and is indifferent to human destiny.

> This naturalism, at once the most common theory and the most ordinary practice of our literature, began in liberalism but ends, ironically, as a grotesque version of the system originally challenged by liberalism, just as atheism ends as a grotesque version of faith. A living design became a mechanical fate, and the latter is even further from man than the former; more decisively alienated from any image of himself. But then this development had real causes. It is essentially, a deliberate arrest of the process of enlightenment, at the point of critical involvement.

Fill in the blank with the ONE most appropriate word from the passage. Second, explain the main reason naturalism became a grotesque version of the system as implied by the writer of the passage. Do NOT copy more than THREE consecutive words from the passage.

169 Read the passage and follow the directions. [4 points]

> What is the origin of the word OK? There have been numerous attempts to explain the emergence of this curious colloquial expression which seems to have swept into popular use in the US during the mid-19th century. Most of them are undoubtedly pure speculation. It does not seem at all likely from historical evidence that it derives from the Scots expression och aye, the Greek ola kala (it is good), the Choctaw Indian oke or okeh (it is so), the French aux Cayes (from Cayes a port in Haiti with a reputation for good rum) or au quai (to the quay as supposedly used by French-speaking dockers) or the initials of a railway freight agent called Obediah Kelly who is said to have written them on lading documents he had checked.
>
> The oldest written references to OK result from its adoption as a slogan by the Democratic Party during the American Presidential election of 1840. Their candidate, Martin Van Buren, was nicknamed Old Kinderhook (after his birthplace in New York State) and his supporters formed the OK Club. This undoubtedly helped to popularize the term (though it did not get Van Buren re-elected). During the late 1830s there had been a brief but widespread craze in the US for humorous misspellings and the form orl korrekt which was among them could explain the initials OK. Such a theory has been supported by more than one distinguished American scholar and is given in many dictionaries including Oxford dictionaries. The only other theory with at least a degree of plausibility is that the term originated among Black slaves of West African origin and represents a word meaning all right, yes indeed in various West African languages.
>
> Unfortunately, _____ enabling the origin of this expression to be finally and firmly established is hard to unearth.

Fill in the blank with the TWO most appropriate consecutive words from the passage. Second, what occupation did Van Buren have in 1839 as can be inferred from the passage?

170 **Read the passage and follow the directions.** [4 points]

> Paul, you aptly point out the perils of relying on empathy. But you also overstate its problems and undersell its importance.
>
> For one thing, you are sparring against a straw version of "empathy." Encountering an upset friend, one might vicariously share his feelings, understand where those feelings come from and wish for him to feel better. All of these experiences are pieces of empathy, but you have thinned out the definition to only include its emotion-sharing component. ① This is like arguing that European food isn't delicious, but first defining "European food" strictly as haggis*.
>
> You also describe emotions as volatile and irrational. This perspective is dated, harkening back to the Greek notion that people must subdue their passions through reason, like a rider on a wild horse. But in fact people work with, not against, their feelings, turning them up or down to suit their needs. Empathy is no different. Yes, it's an emotional spotlight, but people have the ability to point this spotlight as they see fit. My own research demonstrates that when people simply believe empathy is under their control, they are inspired to try harder at it—for example, in paying attention to the emotions of people who differ from them ethically or politically.
>
> Why bother working with empathy if we can better ourselves through principle alone, as you argue? Because empathy makes a difference—not always, but more than you suggest. It helps to receive empathy. For example, cancer patients experience less depression and more empowerment when their physicians express empathy. It also helps to give it: People who behave kindly grow happier and healthier, most of all when they act out of empathy. Those who choose empathy grow a broader, richer emotional life.

Of course, Paul, you're right that people do dole out empathy lazily—to others who look or think like them. But enshrining pure reason to guide morality is naïve. Even when people try to be objective, they often confirm what they want to believe. In our post-truth world, people can use ___②___ like a shield, curling up in comfortable assumptions, surrounding themselves with others who amplify their biases. If people don't want to broaden their empathy, they'll probably use reason narrowly as well.

haggis: the national dish of Scotland, a type of pudding

Explain what the underlined ① means in the context of the debate. Do NOT copy more than THREE consecutive words from the passage. Second, fill in the blank ② with the ONE most appropriate word from the passage.

171 Read the passage and follow the directions. [4 points]

> In three decades of Holocaust cinema, from *Sophie's Choice* (1982) to *Schindler's List* (1993), *The Reader* (2008), and so many more, trains play a key role. The train's connection to the violence of modern Europe is more visible now than any concept of it as an icon of progress.
>
> By contrast, the 150 million migrant workers in China, on whom the global digital economy depends for cheap labor and cheap products, make their way to the factories of the special economic areas and back home by train. At Chinese New Year in January 2014, newspaper reports estimated 3.6 billion train trips to make the traditional return home for the holiday were taken by migrant workers; this was (in effect) the largest migration in human history. These workers build most of the computers, phones, and tablets on which Westerners airily write about the end of the real and the demise of the train. Given the enormous role of train travel in Asia, it's not surprising that it continues to appear in its _____.
>
> In Hong Kong director Wong Kar-wai's stylish and evocative film *2046* (2004), the high-tech train plays a key role. The film is influenced by both Hitchcock and Godard, absorbing the Western film noir and avant-garde styles into the Chinese closed world. As if in a Hitchcock film, the leading male character Chow Mo-wan (Tony Leung) often spies on women through convenient peepholes. The train goes to 2046, wherever that is, or perhaps the train is 2046. In the film, 2046 is the number of the room Chow rents in his hotel in the sequences set in 1966-era Hong Kong. 2046 is also the year when China will be allowed to make changes to the way that Hong Kong is organized, fifty years after the British colony was formally returned. Protests calling for the democracy provided in the 1997 handover to China led to the Occupy

movement of 2014, decades in advance of 2046. The train is the closed "vehicle" by which all these layers of meaning are connected and it's also the place in which memory happens or is regained. This stylized set of connections depicts the afterlife of the closed world in the last remaining Communist nation, a condition in which it is not so much dead as undead, dead and alive at once.

Fill in the blank with the ONE most appropriate word from the passage. Second, as what sort of society is the "last remaining Communist nation" depicted in the movie 2046?

172 Read the passage and follow the directions. [4 points]

One oarsman on his own cannot win the Oxford and Cambridge boat race. He needs eight colleagues. Each one is a specialist who always sits in a particular part of the boat—bow or stroke or cox etc. Rowing the boat is a cooperative venture, but some men are nevertheless better at it than others. Suppose a coach has to choose his ideal crew from a pool of candidates, some specializing in the bow position, others specializing as cox, and so on. Suppose that he makes his selection as follows.

Every day he puts together three new trial crews, by random shuffling of the candidates for each position, and he makes the three crews race against each other. After some weeks of this it will start to emerge that the winning boat often tends to contain the same individual men. These are marked up as good oarsmen. Other individuals seem consistently to be found in slower crews, and these are eventually rejected. But even an outstandingly good oarsman might sometimes be a member of a slow crew, either because of the inferiority of the other members, or because of bad luck—say an adverse wind. It is only on average that the best men tend to be in the winning boat.

The oarsmen are genes. The rivals for each seat in the boat are alleles potentially capable of occupying the same slot along the length of a chromosome. Rowing fast corresponds to building a body which is successful at surviving. The _____ is the external environment. The pool of alternative candidates is the gene pool. As far as the survival of any one body is concerned, all its genes are in the same boat. Many a good gene gets into bad company, and finds itself sharing a body with a lethal gene, which kills the body off in childhood. Then the good gene is destroyed along with the rest. But this is only one body, and replicas of the same good gene live on in other bodies which lack the lethal gene.

Explain why the coach makes the crews race against each other. Do NOT copy more than THREE consecutive words from the passage. Second, fill in the blank with the TWO most appropriate consecutive words from the passage.

173 Read the passage and follow the directions. [4 points]

> Many teachers shy away from using contemporary art in their teaching because they do not feel comfortable with their own level of knowledge and are reluctant to introduce their students to anything they may not have mastered themselves. This response is not unique to educators. As art critic and historian Lucy Lippard has pointed out, the field of contemporary art "has become mystified to the point where many people doubt and are even embarrassed by their responses." To make matters worse, teaching resources are scarce. The absence of curriculum materials about contemporary art reflects the attitude that the only valuable art is that which has "withstood the test of time." This attitude, in turn, reflects the belief that it is possible to establish ____①____ cultural standards that remain fixed and permanent.
>
> The relevance of contemporary art to multicultural education cannot be overstated. Over the past two decades, a significant shift has emerged in the sensibilities and outlooks of artists and critics, producing what philosopher, theologian, and activist Cornel West has referred to as the politics of difference. The features of this new cultural politics of difference include challenging monolithic and homogeneous views of history in the name of diverse, multiple, and heterogeneous perspectives; rejecting universal pronouncements in light of concrete, specific, and particular realities; and acknowledging historical specificity. In this new art, issues of what constitutes difference and how it is determined have been given new weight and gravity.

The study of such art can enhance multicultural and socially activist education by helping to build students' ② <u>understanding of their own place in history</u> and emphasizing the capacity and ability of all human beings, including those who have been culturally degraded, politically oppressed, and economically exploited. We advocate an approach that stresses the vital connections between students' lives inside and outside of school within a framework of social and historical analysis. This approach not only encourages students to speak from their own perspectives, but also encourages them to critique their environments and confront social issues in ways that are synthesized with the study of art.

Fill in the blank ① with the ONE most appropriate word from the passage. Second, identify the THREE consecutive words from the passage that BEST correspond to the underlined words in ②.

174 Read the passage and follow the directions. [4 points]

Do you ever wonder, with progress increasing on all fronts, why the human entity itself remains a mystery? In the past 2,400 years, great minds have diligently tried to demystify man, yet many aspects of the human remain unanswered.

Some of this failure to answer stems from the fact that great thinkers have often been fascinated by a particular mental faculty of the human and have tried to understand the whole being through this single mental element alone. That element, of course, is human intellect. Being mesmerized by this, many continue to disregard another mental force, that drives our conduct at all levels much more forcefully than intellect does.

Ignoring this mighty force has created a missing link in most of their works, and renders them inconclusive, if not misleading. Thus, the human enigma continues to present itself in many aspects of human affairs. But restoring this missing link to its rightful place renders man nakedly clear and easy to understand. Instinct is the missing link, and three types of it (sexual, aggressive and maternal instincts) are universally acknowledged and accepted. Correct treatment of these instincts is essential in accurately understanding humankind.

When we learn the properties and the missions of each of these mental forces, we clearly see how these forces have created the human condition from inception. And these mental elements, being unchanging, have permanently solidified this human condition, making man mostly incapable of departing from this base mode of conduct, in which he has constant conflict. Although this is only one of many different human conditions frozen in time, it affect other major aspects of human affairs in most profound ways. For example, war by becoming a permanent and hugely costly _____ molds the overall economy of the world into shape. Also, war as the ultimate form of competition demands the cutting edge science and technology. This in turn, drives a great aspect of humans' brainpower and largely gives direction to a huge portion of the progress of science and technology. Moreover, war being exceedingly destructive, it psychologically afflicts those who are subjected to such conflicts that violently claims the lives of many of peoples' loved ones. And it is only in recognizing these mental forces that have permanently trapped humanity in this undesirable condition and taking the required steps to compensate for them, that we can hope to break free from this perpetual cycle.

Fill in the blank with the TWO most appropriate consecutive words from the passage. Second, explain why many philosophers have failed to disclose what human beings are according to the passage.

2S2R
유희태 일반영어 ④-1 문제은행

초판 1쇄	2014년 4월 14일	
2판 1쇄	2016년 6월 15일	
3판 1쇄	2019년 2월 20일	
2쇄	2019년 5월 10일	
3쇄	2019년 7월 10일	
4판 1쇄	2020년 10월 23일	
2쇄	2021년 7월 30일	
3쇄	2022년 4월 15일	
5판 1쇄	2023년 1월 10일	
6판 1쇄	2026년 1월 15일	

저자와의 협의하에 인지생략

저자 유희태　**발행인** 박 용　**발행처** (주)박문각출판
표지디자인 박문각 디자인팀
등록 2015. 4. 29. 제2019-000137호
주소 06654 서울시 서초구 효령로 283 서경 B/D
팩스 (02) 584-2927
전화 교재 문의 (02) 6466-7202　동영상 문의 (02) 6466-7201

이 책의 무단 전재 또는 복제 행위는 저작권법 제136조에 의거, 5년 이하의 징역 또는 5,000만원 이하의 벌금에 처하거나 이를 병과할 수 있습니다.

정 가 25,000원(분권 포함)
ISBN 979-11-7519-525-7
ISBN 979-11-7519-524-0(세트)

제6판

교원임용고시
일반영어 필독서

임용영어 수험생 대다수가 선택하는
전공영어의 보통명사

- 교원임용고시 전공영어 독보적 전국 1위
  (2025년 예스24 전공영어 부문 박문각 누적 판매량 1위)
- 미국 버클리대학 유희태 박사의 독창적 문제집
- 출제가능성 높은 예상문제 수록

유희태 일반영어

2S2R 4-1 문제은행

LSI 영어연구소 유희태 박사 저

● 모범답안 및 번역

2S2R

유희태 일반영어

④-1 문제은행

● 모범답안 및 번역

PART 01

문제은행[001~174]

Part 01 문제은행[001~174]

본책 p.010

001

하위내용영역	배점	예상정답률
일반영어 A형 서술형	4점	55%

모범답안 The words are "post offices". Next, the writer mentions Philadelphia because, as such a large city, requiring all its people to go to one post office showed lack of proper service.

채점기준

+ 2점: 빈칸에 들어갈 단어를 "post offices" 또는 "post office"라 기입하였다. 이외에는 답이 될 수 없다.
+ 2점: 필라델피아를 언급한 이유를 "as such a large city, requiring all its people to go to one post office showed lack of proper service"라 서술하였거나 유사하였다.

한글번역

　미국 초기에는 우편 받는 사람이 요금을 지불했고, 요금은 운송 거리에 따라 달랐다. 1825년 미국 의회는 지역 우체국장들이 편지를 우편 배달원에게 맡겨 가정 배달을 할 수 있도록 허용했지만, 이들 배달원은 정부 급여를 받지 않았고 개별 편지의 수취인들이 지불하는 돈으로만 보상을 받았다.
　1847년 미국 우체국부는 우표 아이디어를 채택했는데, 이는 물론 우편 서비스 지불을 간소화했지만 선불을 원하지 않는 사람들의 불만을 샀다. 게다가 우표는 우체국까지의 배달만 포함했고 개인 주소까지 운반하는 것은 포함하지 않았다. 예를 들어 인구 15만 명의 필라델피아에서도 사람들은 여전히 우체국에 가서 우편물을 받아야 했다. 개인들이 자신의 편지를 찾느라 겪는 혼란과 혼잡함 자체만으로도 우편 이용을 저해하기에 충분했다. 이런 번거로운 체제가 지속되는 동안 민간 편지 배달업과 운송업이 발달한 것은 당연했다. 이들의 활동이 반합법적이었음에도 불구하고 번창했고, 실제로 보스턴과 필라델피아 사이에서 정부 우편보다 반나절 빠르다고 광고했다. 정부 우편 서비스는 민간 경쟁에 물량을 빼앗겼고 자신들이 가진 업무조차 효율적으로 처리할 수 없었다.
　마침내 1863년 의회는 우체국에서 개인 주소로 우편을 배달하는 우편 배달원들이 정부 급여를 받아야 하며, 그 배달에 대해 추가 요금을 부과하지 않도록 규정했다. 하지만 이 배달 서비스는 처음에는 도시에만 국한됐고, 무료 가정 배달은 도시성의 표지가 됐다. 1887년까지도 한 마을이 무료 가정 배달을 받으려면 인구가 1만 명은 돼야 했다. 1890년 미국 인구 7500만 명 중 2000만 명도 안 되는 사람들만 집 앞까지 무료로 우편을 배달받았다. 나머지 인구의 거의 4분의 3에 해당하는 사람들은 여전히 우체국에 가지 않으면 우편물을 받을 수 없었다.

002

하위내용영역	배점	예상정답률
일반영어 A형 서술형	4점	45%

모범답안 The words are "prehistoric cultures". Next, the writer mentions the Sacramento excavation as an example of information revealed by professional archeologists.

채점기준

+ 2점: 빈칸에 들어갈 단어를 "prehistoric cultures"라 정확하게 기입하였다. 이외에는 답이 될 수 없다.
+ 2점: 새크라멘토 호텔을 언급한 이유를 "as an example of information revealed by professional archeologists"라 서술하였거나 유사하였다.

한글번역

　고고학은 선사 문화를 연구하는 도구로서 오랫동안 인정받아 왔다. 비교적 최근에 와서야 같은 기법들이 더 가까운 과거 연구에 체계적으로 적용되기 시작했다. 이를 "역사 고고학"이라고 부르며, 미국에서는 유럽인들의 도착 이후 북미 지역을 대상으로 하는 모든 고고학적 조사를 지칭하는 용어로 사용된다.
　1930년대와 1940년대 건물 복원이 인기를 끌던 시절, 역사 고고학은 주로 건축 재건의 도구였다. 고고학자들의 역할은 역사적 건물의 기초를 찾아낸 다음 건축가들에게 자리를 양보하는 것이었다.

재건에 대한 열풍은 1950년대와 1960년대에 들어서면서 대부분 가라앉았다. 이 시기에 역사 고고학에 뛰어든 대부분의 사람들은 선사 문화를 연구한 대학 인류학과 출신이었다. 그들은 훈련상 역사학자가 아닌 사회과학자였고, 그들의 작업은 이런 편향을 반영하는 경향이 있었다. 그들이 설정한 질문과 사용한 기법은 과학자로서 사람들이 어떻게 행동했는지를 이해하는 데 도움이 되도록 설계됐다. 하지만 그들이 다루는 것이 종종 광범위한 문서 기록이 있는 역사적 영역이었고, 이런 시대에 대한 그들 자신의 지식이 보통 제한적이었기 때문에, 미국사에 대한 그들의 기여는 한정적으로 남았다. 고도로 전문적이고 때로는 잘못 쓰인 그들의 보고서는 읽히지 않았다.

최근에는 전문 고고학자들이 주도권을 잡았다. 이들 연구자들은 자신들의 작업이 과학뿐만 아니라 역사학의 귀중한 도구가 될 수 있음을 증명하려 했고, 그렇지 않았다면 잘 기록되지 않았을 평범한 사람들의 일상생활에 대한 새로운 통찰을 제공했다. 사회사로서의 고고학에 대한 이런 새로운 강조는 큰 가능성을 보여줬고, 실제로 이 분야에서 이루어진 작업은 미국 과거에 대한 재해석으로 이어졌다.

예를 들어 뉴욕 킹스턴에서는 네덜란드가 그 지역의 무역을 통제했다고 여겨지던 시기에 영국 상품들이 그 도시로 밀수되고 있었다는 증거가 발견됐다. 그리고 새크라멘토에서는 19세기의 세련된 호텔 부지 발굴에서 위생법에 반해 쓰레기가 건물 지하실에 숨겨져 있었다는 사실이 밝혀졌다.

한글번역

쥘 베른이 1864년 《지구 중심으로의 여행》을 썼을 때, 지구 내부의 성질에 대해서는 상충하는 이론들이 많았다. 일부 지질학자들은 지구 내부에 고도로 압축된 백열 가스 덩어리가 들어있다고 생각했고, 다른 이들은 각각 다른 물질로 이루어진 별개의 껍질들로 구성돼 있다고 의심했다. 한 세기가 훨씬 지난 오늘날에도 우리 발밑에 무엇이 있는지에 대한 직접적인 증거는 여전히 거의 없다. 지구 내부에 대한 우리 지식의 대부분은 광산이나 시추공이 아니라 지진파 연구에서 나온다. 지진파는 지진에 의해 방출되는 강력한 에너지 파동이다.

지진파가 이동하는 방식을 보면 지구 내부가 결코 균일하지 않다는 것을 알 수 있다. 대륙과 해저는 지각에 의해 형성되는데, 지각은 비교적 가볍고 고체인 암석으로 이루어진 얇은 구체다. 지각 아래에는 맨틀이라는 매우 다른 층이 있으며, 이는 지구 중심까지 거리의 대략 절반까지 뻗어있다. 그곳에서 암석은 증가하는 열과 커져가는 압력 사이의 싸움에 놓여 있다.

맨틀의 높은 층에서는 비교적 차갑지만, 더 깊은 곳에서는 높은 온도 때문에 암석이 고체보다는 액체처럼 행동한다. 더욱 깊은 곳에서는 압력이 훨씬 더 강해져서 더 높은 온도에도 불구하고 암석이 녹는 것을 방지한다.

약 2,900킬로미터 깊이를 넘어서면 큰 변화가 일어나고 맨틀은 핵으로 바뀐다. 일부 지진파는 핵을 통과할 수 없고 다른 것들은 핵에 의해 굽어진다. 이것과 다른 증거들로부터 지질학자들은 외핵이 아마도 액체이며 고체 중심을 가지고 있다고 결론짓는다. 거의 확실히 철로 이루어져 있으며 니켈과 같은 다른 원소들이 소량 섞여있다.

지구 핵의 조건들은 그곳을 우주보다 훨씬 더 이질적인 세계로 만든다. 고체 철 중심부는 상상할 수 없는 압력을 받고 있으며 약 9,000°F의 온도를 가지고 있다. 과학자들이 그 성질에 대해 추측할 수는 있지만, 인간이나 기계 모두 그곳을 결코 방문할 수는 없을 것이다.

003

하위내용영역	배점	예상정답률
일반영어 A형 서술형	4점	55%

모범 답안 The words are "Earth's interior". Next, it is because it is impossible to go to the Earth's core for research.

채점 기준

+ 2점 : 빈칸에 들어갈 단어를 "Earth's interior"라 정확하게 기입하였다.
  ☞ Earth's center/core라 했어도 2점을 준다.
+ 2점 : 지구의 내부가 우주보다 더 낯선 것이라 말한 이유를 "because it is impossible to go to the Earth's core for research"라 서술하였거나 유사하였다.

004

하위내용영역	배점	예상정답률
일반영어 A형 서술형	4점	45%

모범답안) The underlined "this pattern of trade" indicates the situation of carrying cargo to New Orleans then to eastern seaports. Second, the next paragraph most likely discusses Lake Erie's industrial development along with the Ohio River area.

채점기준)

+ 2점 : 밑줄 친 부분이 가리키는 것을 "the situation of carrying cargo to New Orleans then to eastern seaports"라 서술하였거나 유사하였다.
+ 2점 : 이 글 다음에 올 가능성이 높은 내용을 "Lake Erie's industrial development along with the Ohio River area"라 서술하였거나 유사하였다.

한글번역

유료 도로 시대(1790-1830)의 도로 개선에도 불구하고, 미국인들은 식민지 시대와 마찬가지로 가능한 한 수로를 이용한 여행과 운송에 의존했다. 더 큰 강들, 특히 미시시피강과 오하이오강은 증기선 수가 늘어나고 설계가 개선됨에 따라 점점 더 유용해졌다. 강 선박들은 북서부 농민들의 옥수수와 기타 농작물, 남서부 농장주들의 면화와 담배를 뉴올리언스로 운반했다. 뉴올리언스에서 배들은 화물을 동부 항구들로 가져갔다. 서부의 농민들이나 동부의 상인들 모두 이런 무역 패턴에 완전히 만족하지는 않았다. 농민들은 농작물을 시장으로 직접 동쪽으로 보낼 수 있는 대안이 있다면 더 좋은 가격을 받을 수 있었고, 상인들은 제조품을 서부로 더 직접적이고 경제적으로 운송할 수 있다면 더 많은 양을 팔 수 있었다.

새로운 수로가 필요했다. 지역적 질투와 헌법적 의구심이 연방 정부의 행동을 가로막았고, 필요한 지출은 민간 기업에게는 너무 컸다. 광범위한 운하들을 파려면 그 일은 각 주에 달려있었다.

뉴욕이 먼저 행동했다. 뉴욕은 애팔래치아 산맥 전체에서 유일한 틈을 통해 허드슨강과 이리호 사이에 비교적 평평한 경로라는 자연적 장점을 가지고 있었다. 하지만 공학적 과제들은 엄청났다. 거리는 350마일이 넘었고 넘어야 할 능선들과 뚫고 지나가야 할 숲과 늪지대의 황무지가 있었다. 1817년에 시작돼 1825년에 완공된 이리 운하는 미국인들이 지금까지 착수한 것 중 단연 가장 큰 건설 사업이었다. 또한 재정적 성공임도 빠르게 입증됐다. 이리 운하의 번영은 주정부가 여러 지선을 건설해 운하 시스템을 확장하도록 고무했다.

이리 운하의 성공에 영감을 받은 오하이오주와 인디애나주가 이리호와 오하이오강 사이에 수로 연결을 제공하면서 뉴욕 운하 시스템의 범위는 더욱 확장됐다.

005

하위내용영역	배점	예상정답률
일반영어 A형 서술형	4점	55%

모범답안) The preferred grass in the eastern parts of the United States was bluejoint grass. Next, cattle promote the growth of western grasses by trampling seeds firmly into the soil.

채점기준)

+ 2점 : 미 동부지역에서 선호되는 풀을 "bluejoint grass"라 서술하였다.
+ 2점 : 소가 풀들의 성장을 촉진하는 방식을 "by trampling seeds firmly into the soil"라 서술하였거나 유사하였다.

한글번역

전설에 따르면 남북전쟁(1861-1865) 말경 소를 실은 정부 열차가 와이오밍 동부의 북쪽 평원을 지나다가 눈보라에 갇혀 버려져야 했다. 운전사는 다음 봄에 돌아와서 화물이 어떻게 됐는지 봤다. 예상했던 해골 대신, 그는 자신의 소들이 살아있고 살찌고 건강한 모습을 봤다. 어떻게 살아남았을까? 답은 무지한 미국인들이 "위대한 미국 사막"을 서둘러 건너가면서 발밑에서 짓밟았던 자원에 있었는데, 그들이 도달한 땅은 때로 불모지로 판명되기도 했다. 미국 동부 지역에서는 사료용으로 선호되는 풀이 재배 식물이었다. 충분한 비가 내리면 잘 자랐고, 베어서 저장하면 말라서 겨울 사료용으로 영양가 있는 건초가 됐다. 하지만 서부의 건조한 목초지에서는 그 친숙한 블루조인트 풀이 종종 가뭄으로 죽었다. 그곳에서 소를 기르는 것은 위험하거나 심지어 절망적으로 보였다.

비가 필요 없고 어떻게든 소들이 겨울 내내 스스로 먹이를 찾을 수 있게 해주는 동화 같은 풀을 누가 상상할 수 있었을까? 하지만 놀라운 서부 야생풀들이 바로 그런 일을 해냈다. 재배된 동부 풀들보다 우수하게 만드는 놀랍도록 편리한 특징들을 가지고 있었다. 버팔로 풀, 그라마 풀, 또는 메스키트 풀로 다양하게 알려진 이 풀들은 가뭄에 면역이 있을 뿐만 아니라 실제로 여름과 가을 비의 부족으로 보존됐다. 재배된 동부 풀들처럼 즙이 많지 않았지만 짧고 단단한 줄기를 가지고 있었다. 그리고 헛간에서 말릴 필요가 없이 자란 땅에서 바로 말랐다. 이런 식으로 말랐을 때 겨울 내내 자연스럽게 달콤하고 영양가를 유지했다. 스스로 생존하도록 야외에 방치된 소들이 이 건초로 번성했다. 그리고 소들 자체가 해마다 새로운 풀을 심는 데 도움을 줬는데, 자연 씨앗을 땅에 단단히 밟아 넣어서 겨울의 녹는 눈과 봄의 가끔 내리는 비로 물을 공급받게 했다. 건조한 여름 공기가 재배된 풀들을 헛간에 저장해서 말리는 것과 거의 같은 방식으로 이 풀들을 말렸다.

한글번역

북미 식민지의 17세기 주택들은 중세로 거슬러 올라가는 전통적 설계를 이어받은 주로 기능적인 단순한 구조물이었다. 하지만 18세기 전반기 동안 주택들은 새로운 우아함을 보이기 시작했다. 부가 증가하면서 점점 더 많은 식민지 주민들이 훌륭한 주택을 지었다. 건축이 아직 식민지에서 전문 직업이 아니었기 때문에, 건물 설계는 아마추어 설계자들이나 영국에서 수입한 건축 매뉴얼을 해석하려고 시도하는 목수들에게 맡겨졌다. 식민지 도서관의 목록들을 보면 건축업자들을 위한 이런 핸드북이 놀라울 정도로 많았으며, 18세기 동안 세워진 주택들은 그 영향을 보여준다. 그럼에도 불구하고 18세기 첫 3/4 기간의 대부분 가정 건축은 이런 책들에 제시된 규칙들의 광범위한 취향 차이와 적용의 자유로움을 보여준다. 식민지 전체에 걸친 부의 증가와 세련됨의 성장은 재료가 목재든, 돌이든, 벽돌이든 상관없이 개선된 설계의 주택들을 낳았다. 뉴잉글랜드는 여전히 목재를 선호했지만, 화재의 위험이 더 내구성 있는 재료 사용에 자극을 준 보스턴과 다른 도시들에서는 벽돌 주택이 일반적이 됐다. 뉴잉글랜드의 일부 주택들은 돌로 지어졌지만, 펜실베이니아와 인접 지역에서만 돌이 주거용 건물에 널리 사용됐다. 버지니아와 메릴랜드에서는 주택과 부속 건물에 벽돌 사용의 증가가 눈에 띄지만, 부유한 지주들이 지은 주택에서조차 목재가 가장 인기 있는 재료로 남았다. 캐롤라이나에서는 빽빽하게 들어선 찰스턴에서조차 목조 주택이 벽돌 주택보다 훨씬 더 일반적이었다.

18세기 주택들은 전임자들에 비해 내부의 큰 개선을 보여줬다. 창문이 더 크게 만들어지고 덧문이 제거됐다. 크고 투명한 유리판이 17세기의 작은 납 유리를 대체했다. 출입구가 더 크고 장식적이 되었다. 벽난로는 방의 장식적 특징이 됐다. 벽은 석고나 목재로 만들어졌으며, 때로는 정교하게 패널로 장식됐다. 흰색 페인트가 초기에 벽에 인기가 있었던 파란색, 노란색, 녹색, 납색을 대신하기 시작했다. 1730년경 이후부터는 풍경 무늬의 벽지 스타일 광고가 식민지 신문에 나타나기 시작했다.

006

하위내용영역	배점	예상정답률
일반영어 A형 서술형	4점	50%

모범답안) The underlined "predecessors" refers to houses built before the eighteenth century. Next, it can be inferred that patterned wallpaper was not widely used before 1730.

채점기준

+ 2점: 밑줄 친 부분이 가리키는 것을 "houses built before the eighteenth century"라 서술하였다.
+ 2점: 1730년 이전에 패턴 벽지의 사용에 대해 추론할 수 있는 것을 "patterned wallpaper was not widely used before 1730"라 서술하였거나 유사하였다.

감점
- 문법적으로 2-3개의 오류 0.5점 감점
- 표현상으로 2-3개의 오류 0.5점 감점
- 문법적으로 4개 이상의 오류 1점 감점
- 표현상으로 4개 이상의 오류 1점 감점

007

하위내용영역	배점	예상정답률
일반영어 B형 서술형	4점	50%

모범 답안 The word is "recognition". Second, bacteria found on human skin is the exact source from which bloodhounds gather smells.

채점 기준

+ 2점: 빈칸에 들어갈 단어를 "recognition"이라 정확하게 기입하였다. 이외에는 답이 될 수 없다.
+ 2점: 블러드하운드가 냄새를 갖는 원천을 "bacteria found on human skin"이라 서술하였거나 유사하였다.

한글번역

블러드하운드(사람을 찾거나 추적할 때 이용하는 후각이 발달한 큰 개)는 생물학적으로 먹이를 추적하도록 적응돼 있다. 코가 냄새를 인식하는 과정이 완전히 이해되지는 않았지만, 특정 냄새에 대한 특정 수용체 부위가 분명히 존재한다. 한 가지 설명에 따르면, 냄새 분자가 열쇠가 자물쇠에 들어가듯이 해당 수용체 부위에 맞아떨어질 때 인식이 일어나며, 이것이 세포에서 기계적 또는 화학적 변화를 일으킨다. 블러드하운드는 분명히 인간 냄새에 맞춰진 수용체 부위가 더 조밀하게 집중돼 있다.

블러드하운드가 인간을 추적할 때 실제로 무슨 냄새를 맡는 것일까? 약 60조 개의 살아있는 세포로 구성된 인간의 몸은 하루에 5천만 개의 세포 비율로 노출된 피부를 벗겨낸다. 따라서 바람에 흩어진 흔적이라도 블러드하운드에게는 여전히 풍부하게 느껴질 수 있다. 몸은 또한 하루에 약 31~50온스의 땀을 생산한다. 이 액체나 벗겨진 피부 세포 자체는 냄새가 거의 나지 않지만, 이 두 물질에 작용하는 박테리아는 다른 문제다. 한 미생물학자는 인간 어깨의 깨끗한 1제곱센티미터 피부에 서식하는 박테리아 개체수를 "수백만의 배수"로 추정한다. 이들 박테리아가 피부의 지질, 즉 지방 물질을 분해하는 일상적인 활동을 하면서 휘발성 물질을 방출하는데, 이것은 보통 블러드하운드의 코에 독특한 냄새들의 전체 별자리로 다가온다.

008

하위내용영역	배점	예상정답률
일반영어 A형 서술형	4점	50%

모범 답안 The meaning of the underlined words is that children are educated more in the real world than in school. Next, in terms of age, informal agents of education might be a child or a distinguished scientist, while formal schooling only includes adults.

채점 기준

+ 2점: 밑줄 친 부분의 의미를 "children are educated more in the real world than in school"라 서술하였거나 유사하였다.
+ 2점: "informal agents of education might be <u>a child or a distinguished scientist</u>, while formal schooling only includes <u>adults</u>"라 서술하였거나 유사하였다.

감점
- 문법적으로 2-3개의 오류 0.5점 감점
- 표현상으로 2-3개의 오류 0.5점 감점
- 문법적으로 4개 이상의 오류 1점 감점
- 표현상으로 4개 이상의 오류 1점 감점

한글번역

미국에서는 학교가 사람들이 교육을 받으러 가는 곳이라고 일반적으로 믿어진다. 그럼에도 불구하고 오늘날 아이들이 학교에 가기 위해 교육을 중단한다고 말해져 왔다. 이 말이 암시하는 학교 교육과 교육 사이의 구별은 중요하다.

교육은 학교 교육보다 훨씬 더 개방적이고 포괄적이다. 교육은 경계를 모른다. 교육은 샤워실에서든 직장에서든, 부엌에서든 트랙터 위에서든 어디서나 일어날 수 있다. 학교에서 일어나는 공식적 학습과 비공식적 학습의 전체 영역을 모두 포함한다. 교육의 주체는 존경받는 조부모부터 라디오에서 정치를 토론하는 사람들까지, 아이부터 저명한 과학자까지 다양할 수 있다. 학교 교육이 어느 정도 예측 가능한 데 반해, 교육은 종종 놀라움을 낳는다. 낯선 사람과의 우연한 대화가 한 사람으로 하여금 다른 종교에 대해 얼마나 적게 알고 있는지 발견하게 할 수도 있다. 사람들은 유아기부터 교육에 참여한다. 따라서 교육은 매우 광범위하고 포괄적인 용어다. 평생에 걸친 과정이며, 학교가 시작되기 훨씬 전에 시작되는 과정이고, 한 사람의 전체 인생에서 필수적인 부분이어야 하는 과정이다.

반면 학교 교육은 특정하고 공식화된 과정이며, 그 일반적 패턴은 한 환경에서 다른 환경으로 가더라도 거의 달라지지 않는다. 한 나라 전체에서 아이들은 거의 같은 시간에 학교에 도착하고, 지정된 자리에 앉고, 어른에게 가르침을 받고, 비슷한 교과서를 사용하고, 숙제를 하고, 시험을 치른다. 배워야 할 현실의 조각들은 그것이 알파벳이든 정부 작동 방식의 이해든 상관없이 보통 가르쳐지는 과목의 경계에 의해 제한돼 왔다. 예를 들어, 고등학생들은 수업에서 자신들의 지역사회 정치 문제에 대한 진실이나 최신 영화제작자들이 무엇을 실험하고 있는지 알아낼 가능성이 낮다는 것을 알고 있다. 학교 교육의 공식화된 과정을 둘러싼 명확한 조건들이 있다.

009

하위내용영역	배점	예상정답률
일반영어 A형 서술형	4점	55%

모범답안 Pangaea is a "supercontinent" because it was formed of all the current continents. Second, the three key features related to the movements carrying lithospheric plates are earthquakes, volcanoes and the earth's largest mountain ranges.

채점기준

+ 2점: 판게아가 초대륙으로 언급되는 이유를 "because it was formed of all the current continents"라 서술하였거나 유사하였다.
+ 2점: the movements carrying lithospheric plates를 "earthquakes, volcanoes and the earth's largest mountain ranges"라 서술하였다.
  ☞ 3개 중 2개만 서술한 경우 1점, 1개만 서술한 경우 0점을 준다.

한글번역

지구의 가장 바깥쪽 부분을 형성하는 단단하고 견고한 판들은 약 100킬로미터 두께다. 이 판들은 지구의 지각과 상부 맨틀 모두를 포함한다. 지각의 암석들은 주로 알루미늄과 나트륨 같은 가벼운 원소를 가진 광물들로 구성돼 있는 반면, 맨틀은 철과 마그네슘 같은 더 무거운 원소들을 포함한다. 표면 판을 형성하는 지각과 상부 맨틀을 합쳐서 암석권이라고 부른다. 이 견고한 층은 나무 뗏목이 연못에 떠있는 방식으로 하부 맨틀의 더 조밀한 물질 위에 떠있다. 판들은 연약권이라고 불리는 하부 맨틀의 약하고 가소성 있는 층에 의해 지지된다. 또한 연못 위의 뗏목처럼, 암석권 판들은 그 아래 더 유동적인 층의 느린 흐름에 의해 운반된다.

판 구조론의 이해를 통해 지질학자들은 지구 표면에 대한 새로운 역사를 구성했다. 약 2억 년 전, 지구 표면의 판들은 판게아라고 불리는 "초대륙"을 형성했다. 이 초대륙이 판 운동 때문에 찢어지기 시작했을 때, 판게아는 먼저 두 개의 큰 대륙 덩어리로 쪼개졌고, 움푹 들어간 곳이 물로 채워지면서 육지 지역 사이에 새로 형성된 바다가 자라났다. 남쪽 것은 현재의 남미, 아프리카, 오스트레일리아, 남극대륙을 포함했으며 곤드와나랜드라고 불린다. 북쪽 것은 북미, 유럽, 아시아를 포함했으며 로라시아라고 불린다. 북미는 약 1억 8천만 년 전에 유럽에서 떨어져 나가면서 북대서양을 형성했다. 암석권 판 중 일부는 해저를 운반하고 다른 것들은 육지 덩어리나 두 유형의 조합을 운반한다. 암석권 판의 움직임은 지진, 화산, 그리고 지구의 가장 큰 산맥들을 만들어낸다. 서로 다른 판들 사이의 상호작용에 대한 현재의 이해는 이런 일들이 왜 특정 곳에서 일어나는지 설명해준다. 예를 들어, 태평양의 가장자리는 그곳에서 매우 많은 화산 폭발과 지진이 발생하기 때문에 "불의 고리"라고 불려왔다. 1960년대 이전에는 지질학자들이 왜 활발한 화산과 강한 지진이 그 지역에 집중됐는지 설명할 수 없었다. 판 구조론이 그들에게 답을 줬다.

010

하위내용영역	배점	예상정답률
일반영어 A형 서술형	4점	55%

모범 답안) The first form of life to appear on land according to the traditional view were whole plants and animals. Next, the technique used to discover new fossils was using an acid bath to extract them from sediments.

채점 기준)

+ 2점: 첫 번째 생명체를 "whole plants and animals"라 서술하였다.
+ 2점: 기술을 "using an acid bath to extract new fossils from sediments"라 서술하였거나 유사하였다.

감점
- 문법적으로 2-3개의 오류 0.5점 감점
- 표현상으로 2-3개의 오류 0.5점 감점

한글번역

생명은 지구가 형성된 지 10억 년도 되지 않아 초기 바다에서 시작됐다. 하지만 최초의 식물과 동물이 대륙에 나타나기까지는 또 다른 30억 년이 지나야 했다. 바다에서 육지로의 생명의 전이는 아마도 생명의 기원만큼이나 진화적 도전이었을 것이다.

어떤 형태의 생명이 그런 극적인 생활 방식의 변화를 만들어낼 수 있었을까? 최초 육상 생물에 대한 전통적 견해는 거대화석—본질적으로 완전한 식물과 동물의 비교적 큰 표본들—에 기반한다. 현대의 종자식물과 양치류와 관련된 관다발식물이 최초의 포괄적인 거대화석 기록을 남겼다. 이 때문에 육상화의 순서가 현대 육상 생태계의 진화를 반영한다고 일반적으로 가정돼 왔다. 이 견해에서는 원시적인 관다발식물이 먼저 대륙 수역의 가장자리를 점령했고, 그 다음에 식물을 먹는 동물들이, 마지막에는 식물을 먹는 동물을 잡아먹는 동물들이 뒤따랐다는 것이다. 더욱이, 거대화석들은 육상 생명이 4억 년 조금 넘게 전인 실루리아기와 데본기 경계 근처에서 폭발적으로 나타나고 다양화됐다고 시사한다.

하지만 최근 고생물학자들은 이 실루리아-데본기 지질학적 경계 아래의 퇴적층을 더 자세히 살펴보고 있다. 암석을 산성 용액에 담가두면 이런 퇴적물에서 일부 화석을 추출할 수 있다는 것이 밝혀졌다.

이 기법은 고대 바다의 해안 근처에 퇴적된 퇴적물에서 새로운 증거—식물 미화석과 작은 동물의 미세한 조각들—을 발견했다. 많은 경우 표본들의 지름이 1밀리미터의 10분의 1도 안 된다. 수억 년 동안 암석에 묻혀 있었음에도 불구하고, 많은 화석들이 생물의 유기물 잔해로 구성돼 있다.

이처럼 새로 발견된 화석들은 이전에 알려진 생물의 존재를 드러냈을 뿐만 아니라 다세포 생물의 육지 침입 날짜를 더 뒤로 밀어냈다. 초기 식물과 동물 군집의 본질에 대한 우리의 견해가 이제 수정되고 있다. 그리고 그런 수정과 함께 최초 육상 생명체에 대한 새로운 추측들이 나온다.

011

하위내용영역	배점	예상정답률
일반영어 A형 서술형	4점	55%

모범 답안) The development that contributed to the decline of painted portraiture's popularity was the daguerreotype. Next, the "strong craft tradition" influenced portraiture's heyday because many craftspeople took up the trade.

채점 기준)

+ 2점: 초상의 인기를 떨어뜨리게 만든 것을 "the daguerreotype"이라 서술하였다.
+ 2점: 이유를 "because many craftspeople took up the trade"라 서술하였거나 유사하였다.

한글번역

오늘날 우리가 미국 민속 예술이라고 부르는 것은 실제로 평범하고 일상적인 "서민들"의, 서민들에 의한, 서민들을 위한 예술이었다. 이들은 증가하는 번영과 여가와 함께 모든 종류의 예술, 특히 초상화에 대한 시장을 만들어냈다. 번영하고 본질적으로 중산층인 공화국의 시민들—고대 로마인들이든, 17세기 네덜란드 시민들이든, 19세기 미국인들이든—은 항상 초상화에 대한 뚜렷한 취향을 보여 왔다. 18세기 후반부터 미국에는 그런 사람들과 그들의 요구를 충족시킬 수 있는 예술가들의 수가 늘어났다.

가장 초기의 미국 민속 예술 초상화는 당연히 뉴잉글랜드, 특히 코네티컷과 매사추세츠에서 나왔는데, 이곳이 부유하고 인구가 많은 지역이었고 강한 공예 전통의 중심지였기 때문이다. 1776년 독립선언서 서명 후 수십 년 안에 인구는 서쪽으로 밀려나갔고, 초상화가들이 뉴욕 서부, 오하이오, 켄터키, 일리노이, 미주리에서 작업하는 모습을 볼 수 있었다. 국가로서의 첫 세기 중반까지 미국 인구는 대략 5배 증가했고, 원래 13개 주에 11개의 새로운 주가 추가됐다. 이런 해들 동안 초상화에 대한 수요가 계속 증가했고, 결국 카메라에 의해 충족됐다. 1839년 다게레오타입이 미국에 도입되면서 사진술의 시대가 열렸고, 한 세대 안에 이 새로운 발명품이 그려진 초상화의 인기를 끝냈다. 다시 한 번 오리지널 초상화는 부유층이 의뢰하고 전문가가 제작하는 사치품이 됐다.

하지만 초상화의 전성시대인 18세기 후반부터 1850년대까지는 약간의 예술적 능력만 있으면 누구든지 그런 초상화가를 뜻하는 리머가 될 수 있었다. 지역 수공업자들—간판, 마차, 집 페인트공들—이 수익성 있는 부업으로 초상화를 그리기 시작했다. 때로는 가족 구성원들을 스케치하는 것으로 시작한 재능 있는 남성이나 여성이 지역적 명성을 얻고 초상화 요청에 시달리기도 했다. 예술가들은 물감과 캔버스, 붓을 챙겨서 시골을 여행하는 것이 가치 있다고 여겼고, 종종 집 장식과 초상화 그리기를 결합했다.

꾸려고 한다. 폐고혈압은 폐동맥에 영향을 미치는 고혈압의 한 형태다. 질병 발달에 이르는 분자적, 세포적 사건들은 잘 이해되지 않고 있다. 더 깊은 통찰을 얻기 위해 일부 과학자들은 인간 폐 샘플과 이 치명적인 질병의 마우스 모델을 연구했다. 연구자들은 폐혈관의 평활근에서 폐고혈압 시 증식하는 특수 세포들을 발견했다. 수석 연구자인 다니엘 M. 그라이프 박사는 "이런 전구세포들이 정상 폐에 존재한다는 것이 놀랍다. 마치 질병 상태에서 증식하고 이동할 준비를 하고 거기 앉아있는 것 같다"고 말했다. 그들은 또한 KLF4 단백질을 포함해 이런 세포들을 조절하는 분자 신호들도 발견했다. 그라이프와 공동 저자들은 폐고혈압 환자들에게 도움이 될 새로운 치료법을 고안하기 위해 전구세포들을 더 분류할 계획이다. "환자가 조기에 진단되고 이런 세포들을 표적화하고 조작할 수 있다면, 우리는 잠재적으로 환자 질병의 경과를 완화시킬 수 있을 것이다"라고 그는 말했다.

013

하위내용영역	배점	예상정답률
일반영어 A형 기입형	2점	60%

모범 답안 reparations

채점 기준
- 2점: 모범답안과 같다.
- 0점: 모범답안과 다르다.

한글번역

데이비드 캐머런(영국 총리)이 카리브해 인프라 개발을 위해 제안한 약 4억 5500만 달러는 아프리카인 노예화와 영국의 손에 의한 토착민 대학살에 대한 사과를 완전히 거부한 것—영국이 이에 대한 배상금을 지불할 가능성에 대한 논의는 말할 것도 없고—으로 인해 오염됐다. 캐머런은 양국 간의 상처가 "정말로 매우 깊다"고 인정했지만, "그런 가장 어두운 시절 이후로 함께 많은 것을 겪어온 친구로서 우리가 그 고통스러운 유산에서 벗어날 수 있기를" 희망한다고 했다.

012

하위내용영역	배점	예상정답률
일반영어 A형 기입형	2점	55%

모범 답안 pulmonary hypertension

채점 기준
- 2점: 모범답안과 같다.
- 0점: 모범답안과 다르다.

한글번역

심혈관 질환은 전 세계적으로 사망의 주요 원인이다. 대표적인 예로, 폐고혈압은 특히 치명적이며, 환자의 절반이 진단받은 지 3년 내에 사망한다. 새로운 연구는 폐고혈압의 치료 표적을 찾아 이를 바

유희태 | 일반영어 ❹-1

유대인 홀로코스트라는 끔찍한 비극을 잊어서는 안 된다는 그의 수많은 확언과 병치된 이것은 아프리카인 노예화에 대한 국제적 추도가 돼야 할 것을 모독한다. 200만 명 이상의 아프리카인이 2세기에 걸쳐 영국이 식민지화한 카리브해로 인신매매됐으며, 1808년까지 자메이카에만 100만 명 이상이 강제로 이주됐다. 일부 선박의 사망률은 50%를 넘었고, 선박이 도착한 후 그 항해의 생존자들의 사망률은 참담했다.

카리브해 국가들은 이런 대학살적 행동에 대한 배상을 요구하는데, 이는 이런 행위들이 현재 지배적인 서구 강국들의 힘의 경제적 토대이기 때문이다. 그들의 성공은 노예 노동이라는 범죄적 사업 위에 세워졌고, 그 관행이 마침내 불법화됐을 때 배상을 받은 것은 이런 노예들을 매매한 사람들이었지 노예들 자신이 아니었다.

이 시대의 경제적 영향은 오늘날에도 전 세계적으로 여전히 느껴지고 있다. 세계 강국들이 건강과 번영을 누리는 동안, 카리브해 국가들은 빈곤, 문맹, 공중보건 위기로 크게 고생하고 있으며, 이 중 많은 것들이 더 이상 산업화된 세계를 위협하지 않는다.

전쟁 범죄에 대한 배상의 국제적 선례가 있고, 노예화된 아프리카인들의 후손들에게 정의와 존엄성을 회복시키려는 유엔의 지원이 있다. 이는 노예제의 잘못을 확인하고 구제책을 찾아서 역사상 고통받은 국가들과 민족들이 이전 식민지 지배자들과 동등한 조건으로 경제적, 사회적 발전을 시작할 수 있도록 하는 것을 목표로 한다.

014

하위내용영역	배점	예상정답률
일반영어 B형 서술형	4점	50%

모범 답안 The two passages similarly describe television as being very violent in the present. However, the passages differ in that the former makes an entirely negative case for television while the latter describes some positive programs on television.

채점 기준

+ 2점: 두 지문의 유사성을 "violence on television" 중심으로 서술하였다.
  ☞ 다음과 같이 서술하였어도 2점을 준다.
  – Both passages address violence on television.

+ 2점: 두 지문의 차이점을 "the first passage makes an entirely negative case for television while the second one describes some positive programs on television"이라 명확하게 서술하였거나 유사하게 서술하였다.

감점
• 문법적으로 2-3개의 오류 0.5점 감점
• 표현상으로 2-3개의 오류 0.5점 감점
• 첫 번째 답안을 한 문장으로 쓰지 않았다면 0.3점 감점

한글번역

〈지문 1〉
1961년 FCC 위원장 뉴턴 미노는 텔레비전을 "거대한 황무지"라고 묘사했다. 만약 그가 오늘날의 TV를 평가한다면, 그의 의견은 거의 바뀌지 않았을 것이다. 텔레비전 드라마 시리즈의 폭력률은 매년 증가하는 것 같고, 시청률 경쟁으로 인해 뉴스 프로그램들이 사실상 연예 사업에 뛰어들었다. 1970년대와 1980년대 텔레비전의 강점 중 하나였던 스포츠 중계도 질이 떨어졌다고 논할 수 있을 정도다. 그리고 공무 프로그램 제작자들은 같은 토론 패널들을 계속 내세운다—복잡한 논쟁을 짧은 인용구로 축소시키는 자칭 "전문가들"을 말이다. 프로그래머들이 새로운 아이디어를 헛되이 찾는 업계에서 집중 시간이 짧고 진부함이 왕 노릇하는 것은 당연하다.

〈지문 2〉
텔레비전 비평가들은 종종 오늘날 프로그래밍에서 폭력의 만연에 초점을 맞춘다. 하지만 수년간의 연구에도 불구하고 연구자들은 TV 폭력과 현실의 반사회적 행동 사이의 연관성의 존재를 증명할 수 없다. 예를 들어, 한 연구는 같은 프로그램을 시청하는 미시간과 캐나다 온타리오의 젊은이들을 연구했다. 시청 습관과 행동 사이의 연관성은 설득력 있게 확립될 수 없었다. 아마도 폭력 문제에 현혹돼, TV 비평가들은 정기적으로 매체의 교육적 가치를 인정하지 않는다. 케이블의 출현과 함께 많은 새로운 채널들이 공무, 의학, 여행, 역사, 과학과 같은 분야에 초점을 맞춰 번성했다.

015

하위내용영역	배점	예상정답률
일반영어 B형 서술형	4점	45%

모범 답안 The two words are "conspicuous consumption". Second, the artisan's family is influenced by increased contact with others in the urban landscape toward conspicuous consumption as a fundamental aspect of decency. One manifestation of this consumption is the manner of dress being markedly more modish.

채점 기준

+ 2점 : 빈칸에 들어갈 단어를 "conspicuous consumption"이라 기입하였다.
+ 2점 : 도시 장인 가정이 농촌에 사는 가정보다 더 유행에 민감한 근본적 이유를 "The artisan's family is influenced by increased contact with others in the urban landscape toward conspicuous consumption as a fundamental aspect of decency. One manifestation of this consumption is the manner of dress being markedly more modish"라 명확하게 서술하였거나 유사하였다.

☞ 다음과 같이 서술하였어도 2점을 준다.
- "도시는 사람들이 서로 알고 관계를 깊이 맺는 곳이 아닌데, 이런 도시에서 (타인에게) 자신을 드러내기 위해선 과시적 소비가 필수적이기 때문"이라는 내용이 들어가 있다.

☞ 다음과 같이 서술하였으면 1점을 준다.
- 위의 내용과 유사하지만 핵심어인 conspicuous consumption이 없다.
- The artisan's family is influenced by the influencing notion that conspicuous consumption is a fundamental aspect of decency. One manifestation of this consumption is the manner of dress being markedly more modish.

감점
- 문법적으로 2-3개의 오류 0.5점 감점
- 표현상으로 2-3개의 오류 0.5점 감점
- 답안을 한 문장이나 두 문장으로 쓰지 않았다면 0.3점 감점
- 본문에 있는 6단어 이상을 그대로 썼으면 0.3점 감점

한글번역

현대 산업 시스템의 요구는 종종 개인과 가정을 병치의 관계 외에는 다른 의미에서 거의 접촉이 없는 사람들과 나란히 놓는다. 기계적으로 말해서 이웃은 종종 사회적으로는 이웃이 아니거나, 심지어 아는 사람도 아니다. 그럼에도 불구하고 그들의 일시적인 좋은 의견은 높은 효용성을 가진다. 일상생활을 무관심하게 관찰하는 이런 사람들에게 자신의 금전적 능력을 각인시키는 유일한 실용적 수단은 지불 능력에 대한 끊임없는 증명이다. 현대 공동체에서는 또한 일상생활이 알려지지 않은 사람들의 대규모 모임에 더 자주 참석한다. 교회, 극장, 무도회장, 호텔, 공원, 상점 등과 같은 곳에서 말이다. 이런 일시적 관찰자들에게 인상을 주고, 그들의 관찰 하에서 자기만족을 유지하기 위해서는 자신의 금전적 힘의 서명이 달리는 사람도 읽을 수 있는 글자로 쓰여야 한다. 따라서 현재 발전의 경향이 과시적 소비의 효용성을 높이는 방향에 있다는 것은 명백하다.

또한 소비가 명예의 수단으로서 유용하고, 품위의 요소로서 이를 고집하는 것이 개인의 인간 접촉이 가장 넓고 인구의 이동성이 가장 큰 공동체 부분에서 최고라는 것도 주목할 만하다. 과시적 소비는 농촌 인구보다 도시 인구의 소득에서 상대적으로 더 큰 부분을 차지하며, 그 요구도 더 긴급하다. 그 결과 품위 있는 외모를 유지하기 위해 전자가 후자보다 습관적으로 더 큰 정도로 그날그날 살아간다. 예를 들어, 미국 농부와 그의 아내, 딸들이 같은 소득을 가진 도시 장인의 가족보다 옷차림에서 현저히 덜 세련되고 매너에서도 덜 우아한 것은 이 때문이다. 도시 인구가 본래 과시적 소비에서 오는 특별한 만족을 훨씬 더 갈망하는 것도 아니고, 농촌 인구가 금전적 품위를 덜 중시하는 것도 아니다. 하지만 이런 종류의 증거에 대한 자극과 그 일시적 효과가 도시에서 더 뚜렷하다. 따라서 이 방법이 더 쉽게 의존되며, 서로를 능가하려는 투쟁에서 도시 인구는 과시적 소비의 정상적 기준을 더 높은 지점까지 밀어 올린다. 그 결과 도시에서 주어진 정도의 금전적 품위를 나타내기 위해서는 이 방향에서 상대적으로 더 큰 지출이 요구된다.

016

하위내용영역	배점	예상정답률
일반영어 A형 기입형	2점	50%

모범답안 ⓐ excited electrons ⓑ computers

채점기준
- 2점: 모범답안과 같다. 이외에는 답이 될 수 없다.
- 0점: 모범답안과 다르다.

> **한글번역**
>
> 반도체성 플라스틱은 가볍고 유연하며 비교적 저렴하고 만들기 쉽다. 문제는 무기 광전지 소재와 달리 효율성이나 안정성이 그리 좋지 않다는 것이다. 하지만 아담 윌라드의 연구는 이를 바꿀 가능성을 가지고 있다. 그는 분자 시스템을 연구하기 위해 모델링과 시뮬레이션을 사용하는 이론 화학자다. 그의 목표는 유기 광전지 소재가 제기하는 도전의 핵심에 있는 분자 무질서의 기초와 결과를 탐구하고 이해하는 것이다.
>
> 유기 광전지 필름이 육안으로는 매끄럽고 균질하게 보일 수 있지만, 분자 규모에서는 극도로 무질서해 정렬되지 않은 분자들의 거대한 엉킴으로 나타난다. 그 엉킴은 흥분된 전자들이 어떻게 구조를 통해 더 쉽게 이동하고 외부 전극에 도달할 수 있는지 이해하기 어렵게 만든다. 흥분된 전자의 위치와 행동은 역동적이며 핵 운동의 극도로 미세한 변화에 영향을 받는다. 최근까지 연구자들은 이런 종류의 문제를 고려조차 할 수 없었다. 하지만 "컴퓨터가 너무 빠르고 효율적이어서 우리가 50년 전에는 건드릴 수 없었던 전체 부류의 문제를 계산상으로 탐구할 수 있다"고 그는 설명한다. 수년간 많은 이론 화학 문제의 해결책은 종이와 연필로 분석적으로 찾아야 했는데, 이는 해결책을 분석적으로 다루기 쉽게 만들기 위해 많은 근사치를 만들어야 한다는 뜻이었다. 이제 기술이 힘든 일을 해줄 수 있다. 우리는 만들어진 근사치의 분자적 결과를 탐구하고 이런 근사치들 중 일부가 어디서 무너지거나 행동을 예측하지 못하는지 다룰 수 있다. 오늘날의 고성능 컴퓨터로도 흥분된 전자의 행동을 모델링하는 것은 현재 실행 가능한 것의 한계에 가깝고, 수백 개 분자의 집합체는 손이 닿지 않는다.

017

하위내용영역	배점	예상정답률
일반영어 A형 기입형	2점	55%

모범답안 color naming

채점기준
- 2점: 모범답안과 같다.
- 0점: 모범답안과 다르다.

> **한글번역**
>
> 새로운 연구는 유목 수렵채집 문화가 색깔을 어떻게 명명하는지 조사했으며, 그들이 색깔을 범주화하는 방식이 전 세계 110개 언어에서 나타나는 색깔 그룹화 패턴과 일치한다는 것을 보여준다.
>
> 이 연구 대상인 탄자니아의 하드자족은 언어에서 공통으로 공유하는 색깔 단어가 상대적으로 적다. 연구 기간 동안 하드자족 참가자들이 색깔을 말해 달라는 요청에 가장 흔히 한 반응은 "모르겠다"였다. 그러나 참가자들이 실제로 명명한 색깔들을 그룹화하는 방식은—어떤 이름을 사용했든 상관없이—소말리어를 사용하는 이민자들과 영어 원어민들, 그리고 전 세계 많은 다른 문화권의 색깔 명명 관례와 일치하는 경향을 보였다.
>
> 델윈 린지 박사는 "하드자족 데이터를 보면, 상대적으로 현대적인 색깔 어휘가 등장하고 있지만, 색깔 용어들이 전체 인구에 걸쳐 분산돼 있다. 우리는 복잡한 색깔 명명을 만들어내는 요소들이 존재하지만, 그것이 어느 한 개인의 머릿속에 있는 것이 아니라 문화 전반에 걸쳐 조각조각 분산돼 있는 문화적 시점을 포착했다"고 말했다. 과학자들은 인간의 뇌가 색깔을 보는 것에 어떻게 반응하는지에 대해 많이 알고 있으며, 이러한 지각의 보편성이 색깔 명명을 언어 변화의 패턴을 연구하는 좋은 모델로 만든다.
>
> 이 연구는 우리 환경의 사물들을 묘사하는 데 사용되는 용어들이 실제로 어떻게 등장하고 진화하는지 생각해보는 매우 유용한 틀을 제공한다. 우리는 단어들을 진화하는 종으로 생각할 수 있다—그들은 우리 머릿속의 공간을 두고 경쟁한다. 따라서 이것은 생물학적 진화를 밀접하게 반영하는 문화적 진화의 사례다.

018

하위내용영역	배점	예상정답률
일반영어 A형 기입형	2점	45%

모범답안 ⓐ attention ⓑ friends

채점기준

- 2점: 모범답안과 같다. 이외에는 답이 될 수 없다.
- 1점: 둘 중 하나만 맞았다.
- 0점: 모범답안과 다르다.

한글번역

　많은 백인 미국인들이 미주리주 퍼거슨에서 발생한 마이클 브라운 총격 사건 보도에 질렸다고 말한다. 최근 퓨 조사에서 다수의 백인들은 인종 문제가 마땅히 받아야 할 것보다 더 많은 관심을 받고 있다고 답했다. 폭스 뉴스의 빌 오라일리는 그런 피로감을 반영하며 "듣는 것이라고는 온통 불만, 불만, 불만, 돈, 돈, 돈뿐이다"라고 말했다. 실제로 하버드대와 터프츠대 학자들의 2011년 연구에 따르면, 백인들은 평균적으로 반백인 인종차별이 반흑인 인종차별보다 더 큰 문제라고 믿었다. 그래서 나는 자만에 빠진 백인들의 착각이라고 생각하는 것에 반박하고자 한다. 인종 관계가 더 적은 관심이 아니라 더 많은 관심을 받아야 하는 몇 가지 이유를 제시한다.
　2011년 인구조사 데이터에 따르면, 미국 평균 흑인 가구의 순자산은 6,314달러인 반면 평균 백인 가구는 110,500달러다. 격차는 지난 10년간 악화됐으며, 미국은 현재 아파르트헤이트 시절 남아프리카공화국보다 인종별 부의 격차가 더 크다. (미국에서 백인은 평균적으로 흑인보다 거의 18배 많이 소유하고 있다. 1970년 남아프리카공화국에서는 그 비율이 약 15배였다.) 흑인-백인 소득 격차는 1967년보다 오늘날 대략 40% 더 크다. 오늘날 미국에서 태어난 흑인 남아의 기대수명은 백인 남아보다 5년 짧다. 흑인 학생들이 고급 수학 및 과학 과정을 제공하는 학교에 다닐 가능성은 백인 학생들보다 현저히 낮다. 그들은 정학과 퇴학을 당할 가능성이 3배 높아서 교육적 실패에 빠지게 된다. 대량 감금이라는 파국적인 실험 때문에, 고등학교를 졸업하지 못한 20대 흑인 남성들은 오늘날 취업보다 감옥에 갈 가능성이 더 높다. 고등학교를 졸업하지 못한 중년 흑인 남성의 거의 70%가 감옥에 다녀왔다.
　이 모든 것은 흑인 문제나 백인 문제가 아니라 미국 문제다. 그토록 많은 재능이 제대로 활용되지 못하고 과도하게 감옥에 갇혀 있을 때, 국가 전체가 고통 받는다. 일부 이성애자들은 자신의 친구들이나 자녀들이 동성애자라는 것을 깨달은 후 동성애자에 대한 태도를 점차 바꿨다. 남성 판사들은 딸이 있을 때 여성의 권리에 더 공감한다. 그러나 미국의 사실상의 분리 때문에 백인들은 흑인 친구를 많이 둘 가능성이 낮다. (100명의 친구 네트워크에서 백인은 평균적으로 흑인 친구를 한 명 갖고 있다.) 친구들이 우리의 눈을 열어주기 때문에 이는 안타까운 일이다.

019

하위내용영역	배점	예상정답률
일반영어 A형 서술형	4점	60%

모범답안 The three goals that should be taught are literacy, numeracy, and peace education. Second, the difference is that numeracy represents the ability to use a range of mathematical skills in various real-world contexts, while mathematics is the academic subject itself that provides the foundational skills that support numeracy.

채점기준

+ 2점: 세 가지 목표를 "literacy, numeracy, and peace education"이라 명확하게 서술하였다.
  ☞ 3개 중 2개만 서술한 경우 1점, 1개 또는 서술하지 못한 경우 0점을 준다.

+ 2점: 수리 능력과 수학의 차이가 "numeracy represents the ability to use a range of mathematical skills in various real-world contexts, while mathematics is the academic subject itself that provides the foundational skills that support numeracy"임을 명확하게 서술하였다.

020

하위내용영역	배점	예상정답률
일반영어 B형 서술형	4점	50%

모범답안 The two passages use the operating premise that adults wield power and authority. Second, both positions above differ in their advice for improving schools, passage 1 emphasizes collaboration with students, while passage 2 recommends keeping adults' authority clear.

채점기준

+ 2점: 두 지문의 공통점이 "The two passages use the operating premise that adults wield power and authority"라 명확하게 서술하였다.
  ☞ 다음과 같이 서술하였어도 2점을 준다.
  - The two passages agree that adults are role models for students as part of their arguments(assertions).

+ 2점: 두 지문의 차이점이 "in their advice for improving schools, passage 1 emphasizes <u>collaboration with students</u>(1점), while passage 2 recommends <u>keeping adults' authority clear</u>(1점)"임을 명확하게 서술하였다.

한글번역

읽기와 쓰기 능력은 흔히 정규 교육의 주요 목표 중 하나로 여겨진다. 문해 교육의 정책과 실천은 국가마다 크게 다르다. 교육과정에 관한 최근 유니세프 연구에 따르면, 어떤 경우에는 문해 기술이 별도의 과목으로, 즉 언어 자체를 목적으로 가르치는 데 초점을 두는 언어 과정에서 가르친다. 이런 접근법은 선형적인 경향이 있다—먼저 듣기 기술을 가르친 다음 말하기, 읽기, 쓰기 기술을 가르친다. 또는 문해 기술이 사회과나 과학 같은 다른 과목을 통해 개발될 수도 있다. 유니세프 연구에서는 이런 경우 사회적 발전을 위한 도구로서의 언어에 더 큰 초점을 둔다는 것을 발견했다. 일상생활의 상황들이 읽기와 쓰기 기술 습득을 촉진하는 활동에 통합된다. 언어 학습은 내용과 분리될 수 없기 때문에 문해가 개발되는 방식에 주목하는 것이 중요하다. 양적 데이터가 많은 사회에서 점점 더 널리 퍼지면서 수리 능력의 개념이 진화하고 있는 것 같다. '양적 문해력'으로도 알려진 수리 능력은 기초 산수와 논리적 추론에서 고급 수학과 해석적 의사소통 기술에 이르는 광범위한 기술을 포괄한다. 수리 능력은 수학과 다르다. 수학적 기술이 수리 능력을 뒷받침하지만, 후자는 다양한 맥락에서 광범위한 기술을 사용하는 능력을 나타낸다. 지리와 사회과에서 과학과 직업 훈련에 이르기까지 많은 교육과정 영역의 숙달에 수리 능력이 필요하기 때문에, 많은 수학 교육자들은 수학 과정에서 분리된 과목이 아니라 통합된 방식으로 수리 능력 기술을 가르칠 것을 주장한다. 평화 교육은 학생들이 갈등을 예방하고, 갈등이 발생했을 때 개인 내적, 대인 간, 집단 간, 국가적 또는 국제적 차원에서든 평화롭게 해결할 수 있는 능력을 갖도록 돕는 것을 추구한다. 평화 교육은 인지적, 정서적, 행동적 학습을 다루며 교육과정 개발과 교사 교육을 통한 학교 내에서뿐만 아니라 캠프, 스포츠와 여가 프로그램, 청소년 그룹과 클럽, 지역사회 지도자, 부모, 사서, 언론을 위한 훈련을 통한 학교 밖에서도 일어날 수 있다. 반폭력 프로그램은 효과적일 수 있다. 예를 들어, 괴롭힘을 줄이기 위한 노르웨이 프로그램에서는 참여한 아이들이 2년에 걸쳐 공격성과 반사회적 행동 표현을 50% 줄인 것으로 나타났다. 그 효과는 첫 해보다 두 번째 해에 더 현저했다.

한글번역

〈지문 1〉

우리 학교 행정부는 학생들에게 더 많은 책임을 주고 학생회가 상징적 역할 이상을 할 수 있도록 권한을 부여하는 것을 진지하게 고려해야 한다. 지난 1년 동안 학생회는 학생과 교직원이 학생 분쟁을 중재하는 갈등 해결 위원회를 설치하자고 여러 차례 건의했다. 그러나 우리 지역의 다른 학교들이 그런 프로젝트를 성공적으로 실험했다는 증거가 있음에도 불구하고, 행정부는 별로 관심을 보이지 않았다. 어른들은 우리에게 책임감과 책무의 목표를 정기적으로 강조한다. 채텀 고등학교 학생들이 이런 목표에 참여할 기회를 맡을 때가 되지 않았나?

〈지문 2〉
요즘 학교에서 파트너십과 참여라는 개념을 내세우는 것이 유행이긴 하지만, 대부분의 학교는 어른들이 명확히 책임을 질 때 가장 잘 운영된다. 전문 연구자들은 학생들이 구조화된 분위기에서 가장 잘 배우고 행동한다는 것을 보여줬다. 사실은 학생들이 어른들을 롤 모델이자 지도자로 바라본다는 것이다. 우리 학교의 교직원과 행정부는 학생들을 일시적으로 행복하게 만들기 위해 높은 기준과 건전한 규정을 희생해서는 안 된다. 학교는 민주주의 국가가 아니며, 학생들은 건강하고 생산적인 어른으로 발전하기 위해 교사와 행정관의 지도와 지혜에 의존한다 - 종종 자신도 모르게.

021

하위내용영역	배점	예상정답률
일반영어 B형 서술형	4점	50%

모범답안 The three factors outlined are : the Confucian emphasis on education(passion for education), the low divorce rate among Asian-American families(strong families) as well as the higher expectations placed on students by teachers. Second, it is because these higher standards help motivate Asian-American students through the implication they gave of their stronger potential.

채점기준

+ 2점 : 세 가지 요소를 "the Confucian emphasis on education(passion for education), the low divorce rate among Asian-American families(strong families) as well as the higher expectations placed on students by teachers"라 명확하게 서술하였다.
+ 2점 : 교사의 기대가 중요한 이유를 "these higher standards help motivate Asian-American students through the implication they gave of their stronger potential"이라 명확하게 서술하였다.

한글번역

아시아계 미국인들이 미국 학교에서, 심지어 미국 사회 전체에서 불균형적으로 뛰어난 성과를 보인다는 것은 비밀이 아니다. 인구조사 데이터에 따르면 아시아계 미국인들은 백인을 포함한 다른 집단보다 더 많이 번다. 아시아계 미국인들은 또한 다른 어떤 집단보다도 높은 교육 수준을 갖고 있다.

최근 수십 년간 아시아계 미국인 이민자들은 한 가지 장점을 가지고 시작했다. 그들은 평균적인 미국인보다도 더 높은 교육을 받았다는 것이다. 이런 이민자들은 불균형적으로 의사, 연구 과학자, 기타 고등 교육을 받은 전문가들이다. 아시아계 미국인 의사들의 자녀가 미국에서 번영하는 것은 놀랍지 않다. 하지만 노동계층 아시아계 미국인들의 자녀들도 종종 성공하며, 놀라운 상향 이동성을 보여준다. 그리고 한 가지 관념은 치워버리자. 그 차이가 지능의 차이에서 비롯되는 것 같지는 않다. 한 가지 요인은 동아시아의 오랜 유교적 교육 중시 전통이라고 확신한다. 마찬가지로 교육에 대한 중시가 다른 어떤 집단보다 1,700년 앞서 남성의 보편적 문해력을 가졌다고 전해지는 유대인들의 성공을 설명하는 데도 도움이 된다. 동아시아계 이민자들은 종종 좋은 학군에 들어가려고 특별히 노력하거나, 집에서 아이들이 공부할 수 있도록 좋은 공간을 내주는 등 자녀 교육을 위해 다른 희생을 한다. 미국인들은 A학점이 똑똑한 아이들에게 간다고 믿는 반면, 아시아인들은 A학점이 열심히 하는 아이들에게 간다고 생각할 가능성이 더 높다는 증거가 있다. 진실은 아마 그 중간 어디엔가 있겠지만, 결과적으로 아시아계 미국인 아이들은 B학점이나 심지어 A-학점을 받을 변명도 허용되지 않는다. A-는 "아시아인의 F학점"이라는 농담도 있다. 튼튼한 양부모 가정도 한 요인이다. 많은 아시아계 미국인 공동체의 이혼율은 미국인 전체보다 훨씬 낮으며, 양부모 가정이 빈곤에 빠질 가능성이 낮고 특히 남자아이들에게 더 나은 결과를 가져온다는 증거가 있다. 교사들의 기대도 역할을 할 수 있다. 캘리포니아의 한 학교 학생들에게 지능검사를 실시한 후, 실험자들은 교사들에게 특별하며 크게 성장할 것으로 기대된다고 말한 아이들 5분의 1의 이름을 알려줬다. 1, 2학년의 이런 특별한 학생들은 극적으로 향상됐다. 1년 후, 그들 중 47%가 20점 이상의 지능지수 상승을 보였다. 이런 "피그말리온 효과"는 자기실현적 기대의 사례였다. 교사들이 특별한 학생들에게 더 높은 기대를 갖고 그들이 유능하다고 느끼게 만들었고, 그래서 그들이 실제로 그렇게 됐다.

022

하위내용영역	배점	예상정답률
일반영어 B형 서술형	4점	50%

모범 답안 (In conclusion,) while people between 16 and 50 still represent the majority of streaming music consumers, their share is declining as more children and older users join into the services. To that end, promoting enrollment to services to an older age group is becoming more and more successful, thus should be considered.

채점 기준

- 4점: 모범답안과 같거나 유사하다.
(In conclusion,) <u>while people between 16 and 50 still represent the majority of streaming music consumers, their share is declining as more children and older users join into the services</u>(2점). To that end, <u>promoting enrollment to services to an older age group is becoming more and more successful, thus should be considered</u>(2점).

한글번역

〈분석〉
그래프는 2008년과 2010년 사이 스트리밍 음악 청취자들의 연령 분포 변화를 보여준다. 스트리밍 음악 서비스의 주요 사용자들은 16세에서 30세 사이의 젊은 성인들이다. 2008년에 이들은 전체 사용자의 절반 이상을 차지했다. 2009년에는 그 수가 45%로 약간 감소했지만, 2010년에도 여전히 가장 큰 집단이었다.

두 번째로 큰 사용자 집단은 31세에서 50세 사이다. 이들은 2008년 41%를 구성했으나 2010년 37%로 약간 감소했다. 16-30세 연령 집단과 합치면, 2008년 사용자의 94% 이상이 16세에서 50세 사이였다.

그러나 더 많은 어린이들과 고령 사용자들이 이 서비스를 유용하다고 여기면서 이 수치는 꾸준히 감소하고 있다. 2009년에는 온라인 어린이 수가 2%에서 8%로 4배 증가했고, 2010년에도 계속 증가했다. 고령 사용자들도 비슷한 증가를 보여, 2008년 4%에서 2010년 10%로 상승했다.

023

하위내용영역	배점	예상정답률
일반영어 A형 기입형	2점	55%

모범 답안 ⓐ community ⓑ nuclear

채점 기준

- 2점: 모범답안과 같다.
- 1점: 둘 중 하나만 맞았다.
- 0점: 모범답안과 다르다.

한글번역

핵가족의 탄생과 더 큰 서구 문명의 시작은 아마 함께 진행됐을 것이다. 더 먼 거리에서 온 더 많은 사람들이 서로 접촉하게 되면서 질병 같은 것들이 더 큰 문제가 됐다. 또한 다른 문화의 영향과 인구 폭발로 사람들은 분리되기 시작했고, 다른 것들을 믿게 됐으며, 더 큰 공동체 내에서 더 작은 부족들을 형성했다. 이 모든 것 때문에 아이들을 위한 대비책이 마련돼야 했다. 아이들은 더 이상 전체 공동체의 책임이 아니라 오직 그들의 어머니들만의 책임이 됐다. 시간이 흐르면서 아이들의 아버지도 양육에 책임져야 한다는 깨달음과 의견들이 형성됐고, 이 경우 도덕적 법칙이 바뀌었다. 역사상 이 시점에서야 처녀성, 남녀 분리, 결혼이 어떤 의미를 갖게 됐다.

두 부모가 있는 이런 새로운 핵가족들은 세상을 맞설 수 있었다. 그들은 믿고 싶은 것을 믿을 수 있었고 자신들만의 문화적 차이를 가진 자신들만의 작은 부족이 될 수 있었다. 이런 가족들에게 태어난 아이들은 새로운 경직성 속에서 태어났다. 그들은 더 이상 자신의 삶에서 부족한 것을 찾아 다른 곳으로 갈 수 없었고, 대신 성격이나 가족 단위의 효율성에 관계없이 태어난 가족에 갇혀 있었다.

024

하위내용영역	배점	예상정답률
일반영어 A형 기입형	2점	55%

모범답안 resilience

채점기준

- 2점: 모범답안과 같다.
- 0점: 모범답안과 다르다.

한글번역

1986년 체르노빌 원자력 발전소의 화재와 폭발로 방사능 입자가 공기 중으로 방출된 후, 수천 명의 사람들이 그 지역을 떠났고 다시는 돌아오지 않았다. 이제 새로운 연구에서 체르노빌 지역이 재해 지역이라기보다는 엘크, 노루, 붉은 사슴, 멧돼지, 늑대로 가득한 자연보호구역처럼 보인다는 것을 발견했다.

이 발견들은 야생동물의 회복력을 상기시킨다. 또한 최근 일본의 후쿠시마 재해의 잠재적 장기 영향을 이해하는 데 중요한 교훈을 담고 있을 수도 있다. 체르노빌의 야생동물 수가 사고 이전보다 훨씬 많을 가능성이 매우 높다. 이것이 방사능이 야생동물에게 좋다는 뜻은 아니고, 단지 사냥, 농업, 임업을 포함한 인간 거주의 영향이 훨씬 더 나쁘다는 것이다.

4,200㎢의 체르노빌 출입금지구역에서 실시된 이전 연구들은 주요한 방사능 영향과 야생동물 개체 수의 현저한 감소를 보여줬다. 장기 인구조사 데이터에 기반한 새로운 증거는 이제 포유동물 개체 수가 회복됐다는 것을 보여준다.

연구자들은 출입금지구역 내의 엘크, 노루, 붉은 사슴, 멧돼지의 상대적 풍부함이 이제 그 지역의 오염되지 않은 4개 자연보호구역과 비슷하다고 보고한다. 체르노빌 지역과 그 주변에 사는 늑대의 수는 그런 자연보호구역에서 발견될 수 있는 것보다 7배 이상 많다. 이런 증가는 구소련의 다른 지역에서 엘크와 멧돼지 개체 수가 감소하고 있던 시기에 일어났다.

025

하위내용영역	배점	예상정답률
일반영어 B형 서술형	4점	45%

모범답안 The underlined phrase describes the wasps' unique bracovirus breeding method, which causes destruction to the caterpillar it affects. The bracoviruses come from the wasp and, unlike a normal virus, do not replicate themselves as they affect the host body.

채점기준

+ 2점: 생물학적 무기의 의미를 "the wasps' unique bracovirus breeding method, which causes destruction to the caterpillar it affects"라 명확하게 서술하였다.
+ 2점: 정상적인 바이러스와 브라코바이러스의 차이를 "The bracoviruses come from the wasp and, unlike a normal virus, do not replicate themselves as they affect the host body"라 명확하게 서술하였다.

한글번역

일부 기생벌들은 알을 낳는 애벌레를 제압하는 정말 특별한 방식을 진화시켰다. 말벌의 난소에 있는 세포들이 수백만 개의 바이러스 같은 입자를 생산하고, 암컷은 이것을 알과 함께 애벌레에게 주입한다. 바이러스들은 애벌레 몸의 거의 모든 종류의 세포를 침입하고, 그곳에서 그들의 DNA가 숙주 세포의 게놈에 통합된다.

정상적인 바이러스들은 더 많은 바이러스를 만드는 데 필요한 단백질을 위한 유전자들을 가지고 다닌다. 하지만 브라코바이러스라고 불리는 이것들은 대신 애벌레의 면역 방어를 차단하고 그것을 잡아먹는 말벌 유충에 대해 무력하게 만드는 유전자들을 가지고 다닌다. 브라코바이러스들은 더 이상 스스로 복제할 수 없다. 대신 바이러스 입자를 만드는 데 필요한 유전자들이 말벌 게놈에 통합됐다. 말벌들은 약 1억 년 전에 처음으로 브라코바이러스를 생물학적 무기로 바꿨다. 현재 수천 종의 브라코니드 말벌이 있으며, 각각은 특정한 나비나 나방에 기생하고 다른 말벌 종들과는 다른 유전자 세트를 가진 독특한 브라코바이러스를 생산한다.

하지만 때때로 일이 잘못되기도 한다. 말벌들이 때로는 잘못된 숙주에 알을 낳는데, 예를 들어 이런 경우 말벌 유충이 살아남지 못할 수도 있다. 그런 경우에 브라코바이러스의 유전자들이 애벌레의 발달 중인 알이나 정자 세포의 게놈에 통합되면, 그것들이 후손에게 전해질 수 있다. 그리고 그런 유전자들 중 어떤 것이 유용하다고 판명되면, 그것들은 나비나 나방 종의 게놈의 영구적인 부분이 될 수 있다.

한글번역

맨체스터 리버풀의 런던 금융가의 자본가들은 노예무역을 통해, 나중에는 설탕 거래를 통해, 그리고 노예가 생산한 면화를 사용하는 섬유 생산을 통해 부자가 됐다. 물론 노예제가 영국 자본주의나 산업혁명의 발전에서 영국 내 노동력을 제공한 것은 아니었다. 하지만 1807년 노예무역 폐지와 1830년대 영국령 카리브해에서 노예제 자체가 폐지된 후에도, 영국 자본주의는 여전히 노예제에 의존했다. 예를 들어 맨체스터의 섬유 공장들에는 면화가 필요했기 때문이다. 1860년에 영국 면화의 약 75%가 미국 남부에서 왔다. 이것이 영국 자본가들이 미국 남북전쟁 중에 남부를 지지한 이유다. 또한 비록 그것이 중심적인 생산 방식은 아니었지만 18세기 후반 내내 북부의 많은 지역에서 노예제가 있었다. 19세기 초까지 사회적 관계로서의 노예제는 북부에서 대부분 사라졌다(노예를 해방시킨 마지막 북부 주는 1846년의 뉴저지였다). 하지만 신흥 부르주아지와 노예제 사이의 주요 연결고리는 그들이 노예를 소유했다는 것이 아니었다. 북부 자본가는 수백만 개의 실로 노예제와 연결돼 있었다. 그들은 노예 노동으로 만든 당밀을 사서 삼각무역의 일환으로 럼을 팔았고, 남부 농장주들에게 돈을 빌려줬으며, 영국에 판매되는 면화의 대부분이 뉴욕시를 포함한 북부 항구를 통해 운송됐다. 그들은 노예무역에 자금을 댔고, 그것이 불법이 된 후에도 여전히 뉴욕에서 출발해 노예무역에 관련된 배들이 있었다. 그리고 그들은 남부에 공산품을 팔았다. 이것이 북부 자본주의와 노예제 사이의 관계의 배경이다. 자본주의는 노예제와 매우 다르지만, 동시에 역사적으로 매우 연결돼 있다.

026

하위내용영역	배점	예상정답률
일반영어 B형 서술형	4점	55%

모범답안 The main idea of the passage is that slavery in the south was connected to England and Northern America by way of capitalism. Second, the British capitalists supported the American South because they benefitted economically from slave labor.

채점기준

+ 2점: 글의 요지를 "<u>slavery</u> in the south was connected to England and Northern America by way of <u>capitalism</u>"이라 명확하게 서술하였다.
   ☞ 내용은 유사하지만 slavery나 capitalism이란 key words가 하나라도 빠졌으면 1점을 감점한다.
   ☞ 다음과 같이 서술하였으면 1.5점을 준다.
   - The development of British industrial capitalism was to a large degree based upon slavery.

+ 2점: 영국자본가들이 남북전쟁에서 남부를 지원한 이유를 "they benefitted economically from slave labor"이라 명확하게 서술하였다.

027

하위내용영역	배점	예상정답률
일반영어 A형 기입형	2점	65%

모범답안 ponies

채점기준

- 2점: 모범답안과 같다.
- 0점: 모범답안과 다르다.

한글번역

　포니 익스프레스는 1860년 4월부터 1861년 가을까지 단 18개월만 지속됐다. 미주리에서 캘리포니아까지 전신선이 설치되는 동안 임시 통신 수단 이상이 될 의도는 결코 없었다. 포니 익스프레스는 워싱턴이 증기선을 통해 새크라멘토와 연락하는 데 걸렸던 시간을 12일 단축시켰다.

　포니 익스프레스 기수가 되는 것은 진정으로 낭만적인 모험이었다. 몇 파운드의 정부 급송과 매우 비싼 개인 편지를 운반하기 위해 대륙의 절반을 가로질러 포니를 타고 걷고, 속보로 달리고, 때로는 전력 질주하는 고독한 기수들 말이다. 하지만 포니 익스프레스 기수가 되는 것은 또한 위험했다. 회사의 구인 광고에 따르면, 원하는 것은 "18세를 넘지 않은 젊고, 마르고, 활기찬 청년들"이었다. 그러나 그들은 또한 "매일 죽음의 위험을 감수할 의지가 있는 숙련된 기수들... 고아 우선"이어야 했다. 포니 익스프레스 기수들은 빡빡한 일정을 유지했다. 그들은 75마일에서 100마일 떨어진 대형 역에 배치됐다. 판잣집과 마구간에 불과했던 각 중계소에서 그들은 땀에 젖은 말을 안장이 채워져 있고 출발 준비가 된 신선한 말로 갈아탔다. 기수들은 총 606,000마일에 달하는 308번의 대륙 횡단을 했다. 기수들은 거의 35,000통의 우편물을 운반했다. 포니 익스프레스가 존재했던 18개월 동안 우편 주머니는 단 하나만 분실됐다.

028

하위내용영역	배점	예상정답률
일반영어 A형 기입형	2점	45%

모범답안 differences

채점기준

- 2점: 모범답안과 같다.
- 0점: 모범답안과 다르다.

한글번역

　뇌 "연결성 프로필"만으로도 일부 연구자들이 100명 이상의 뇌 활동 fMRI 영상에서 개인을 식별할 수 있다. 대부분의 과거 연구에서 fMRI 데이터는 예를 들어 환자와 건강한 대조군 사이의 대비를 그리는 데 사용됐다. 새로운 과학자들은 이전 연구들이 중요할 수 있는 개인차를 흐리는 경향이 있다고 주장한다.

　에밀리 핀과 시린 셴은 이틀에 걸친 6번의 스캔 세션을 받은 126명의 피험자로부터 fMRI 데이터를 수집했다. 피험자들은 4번의 세션 동안 다양한 인지 과제를 수행했다. 나머지 2번에서는 단순히 휴식을 취했다. 연구자들은 268개 뇌 영역의 활동, 구체적으로는 영역 쌍들 사이의 협조된 활동을 살펴봤다. 고도로 협조된 활동은 두 영역이 기능적으로 연결돼 있음을 의미한다. 전체 뇌에 걸친 이런 연결의 강도를 사용해, 연구자들은 피험자가 휴식 중이든 과제에 참여하고 있든 fMRI 데이터만으로 개인을 식별할 수 있었다. 그들은 또한 피험자들이 과제를 어떻게 수행할지 예측할 수 있었다. 핀은 이 능력이 언젠가 임상의들이 각 개인의 신경 네트워크를 특징짓는 고유한 차이점들을 고려해, 개별적인 뇌 연결성 프로파일을 바탕으로 신경정신과적 질환을 예측하거나 심지어 치료하는 데 도움이 될 수 있기를 희망한다고 말했다.

029

하위내용영역	배점	예상정답률
일반영어 A형 기입형	2점	50%

모범 답안 it is

채점 기준

- 2점: 모범답안과 같다.
- 0점: 모범답안과 다르다.

한글번역

많은 박식하고 부지런하지만 본질적으로 무지하고 상상력이 없는 사람들이 실행하는 비평은 설교술의 한 분야에 불과하다. 그들은 예술 작품을 그 명확성과 진실성으로, 아이디어의 힘과 매력으로, 예술가의 기술적 숙련도로, 그의 독창성과 예술적 용기로 판단하는 것이 아니라, 단순히 오로지 그의 정통성으로만 판단한다. 만약 그가 소위 "올바른 사상가"라면, 그가 일시적인 진부한 말들을 장엄한 방식으로 옹호하는 데 전념한다면, 그는 존경받을 만하다. 하지만 만약 그가 그런 것들 중 어느 것에 대해서든 의심한다는 아주 작은 암시라도 내비치거나, 더 나쁘게는 무관심하다는 암시를 내비친다면, 그는 악당이고, 따라서 그들의 이론에 따르면 나쁜 예술가다. 그런 경건한 헛소리가 우리 사이에서 끔찍하게 익숙하다. 나는 그 용어들을 과장하지 않는다. 비평을 가르치는 일과 결합하는 거의 모든 따분한 사람들의 비평 글에서 그것이 흘러가는 것을 발견할 것이다. 그들 중 많은 사람의 말에서 그것은 가장 명백한 방식으로 진술되고 신학적이고 교육학적인 많은 열정으로 옹호된다. 가장 노골적인 형태로 그것은 예술가—예를 들어 극작가나 소설가—가 악덕을 매력적인 것으로 묘사하는 것이 추문이라는 교리로 나타난다. 악덕이 의심할 여지없이 매력적인 경우가 그렇지 않은 경우보다 더 많다는 사실—그렇지 않다면 왜 그것이 우리 중 누구라도 삼켜버리겠는가?—은 거만한 몸짓으로 치워버린다. 그래서 어쩌라고? 이런 매질쟁이들이 말한다. 예술가는 기자가 아니라 위대한 스승이다.

030

하위내용영역	배점	예상정답률
일반영어 B형 서술형	4점	60%

모범 답안 The word is "growth". Second, the three factors are as follows: the expansion of population growth, people's desire to get support from the government, and response to changes in societal conditions.

채점 기준

- 2점: 빈칸에 들어갈 단어를 "growth"라 정확하게 기입하였다. 이외에는 답이 될 수 없다.
- 2점: 관료주의가 성장하게 되는 세 가지 요소를 "the expansion of population growth, people's desire to get support from the government, and response to changes in societal conditions"라 명확하게 서술하였다.
  ☞ 3개 중 2개만 서술한 경우 1점, 1개 또는 서술하지 못한 경우 0점을 준다.

한글번역

1800년대 후반 이래 관료제와 관료들의 성장은 국가 자체의 확장에 기인할 수 있다. 우리는 훨씬 더 많아졌다—2015년에 3억 2천 5백만 명 이상으로, 1790년대의 5백만 명 미만과 비교하면—그리고 우리는 더 가까이 살고 있다. 도시와 교외 거주자들이 1800년대 초 주로 농촌에 살던 사람들보다 훨씬 더 많은 서비스를 필요로 할 뿐만 아니라, 도시와 산업 생활의 도전들이 심화돼 가족이나 지방 및 주 정부의 대처 능력을 넘어섰다. 따라서 미국인들은 점점 더 도움을 위해 연방 정부에 의존하게 됐다.

관료제의 성장이 "우리 자신이 만든 것"이라는 상당한 증거가 있다. 여론조사는 다양한 분야에서 연방 개입 확대에 대한 광범위한 대중의 지지를 보여준다. 새로운 프로그램에 대한 대중의 지지가 낮을 때조차, 여론조사 전문가들은 미국인들이 기존 프로그램을 제거하거나 줄이려 하지 않는다는 것을 발견한다. 게다가 받아야 할 서비스 품질에 대한 대중의 기대는 계속 높아지고 있다. 대중은 정부가 공공 프로그램을 관리하는 데 더 반응적이고, 책임감 있고, 동정적이기를 원한다. 공무원들은 새로운 프로그램을 설립하고 기존 프로그램을 유지하고 개선함으로써 이런 압력에 반응했다.

연방 관료제는 또한 경제적, 사회적, 문화적, 정치적 조건의 급격한 변화에 대응해 확장됐다. 예를 들어 대공황과 제2차 세계대전 중에 연방 관료제는 이런 상황들이 만든 도전에 맞서기 위해 성장했다. 워싱턴은 가난한 사람들에게 재정 지원과 고용을 제공하는 프로그램에 점점 더 관여하게 됐다. 중요한 산업들에 대한 규제를 증가시켰고 전쟁 중에는 미국 경제의 많은 부분에 통제를 가했다. 전반적인 전쟁 노력의 일환으로 연방 정부는 또한 도로와 병원을 건설하고 전체 인구를 동원했다. 이런 위기들이 끝났을 때, 대중은 비상시에 시행된 많은 연방 복지 및 경제 프로그램들을 포기하기를 꺼렸다.

031

하위내용영역	배점	예상정답률
일반영어 B형 서술형	4점	50%

모범답안 The popular prejudice refers to the fallacies about race and blood : the blood of white men is different from that of colored men. Second, the writer alludes to Spinoza in order to illustrate that even an enlightened scholar did not escape from the popular prejudice about race and gender.

채점 기준

+ 2점 : 일반 대중의 편견이 "the blood of white men is different from that of colored men" 임을 명확하게 서술하였다.
+ 2점 : 스피노자를 언급한 이유를 "to illustrate that even an enlightened scholar did not escape from the popular prejudice about race and gender"라 서술하였다.

한글번역

"인종"과 "혈통"에 대한 오류들은 항상 인기가 있었고, 나치가 공식 신조에 구현했으며, 객관적 정당성이 없다. 그것들은 오직 자존심과 잔혹성에 대한 충동에 부응하기 때문에 믿어진다. 어떤 형태든 이런 믿음들은 문명만큼이나 오래됐다. 그 형태는 바뀌지만 본질은 남아있다. 헤로도토스는 키루스가 농민들에게 자라면서 자신의 왕족 혈통을 전혀 모르고 있었는데, 12세에 다른 농민 소년들에 대한 그의 왕 다운 태도가 진실을 드러냈다고 말한다. 이것은 모든 인도—유럽어족 국가에서 발견되는 오래된 이야기의 변형이다. 심지어 아주 현대적인 사람들도 "혈통이 말해준다"고 한다. 과학적 생리학자들이 흑인과 백인의 피 사이에는 차이가 없다고 세상에 확신시켜도 소용없다. 미국 적십자는 대중의 편견에 따라 처음에 미국이 제2차 세계대전에 개입하게 됐을 때 흑인의 피는 수혈에 사용돼서는 안 된다고 규정했다. 선동의 결과로 흑인의 피가 사용될 수 있지만 오직 흑인 환자에게만 사용된다고 양보했다. 마찬가지로 독일에서는 수혈이 필요한 아리아인 병사가 유대인의 피로 인한 오염으로부터 조심스럽게 보호받았다.

인종 문제에서는 사회마다 다른 믿음들이 있다. 군주제가 확고히 확립된 곳에서 왕들은 신하들보다 더 높은 인종이다. 아주 최근까지 남성이 여성보다 선천적으로 더 지능적이라는 것이 보편적으로 믿어졌다. 스피노자 같은 계몽된 사람조차 이런 근거로 여성 참정권에 반대한다. 백인들 사이에서는 백인이 다른 피부색의 남성들, 특히 흑인들보다 천성적으로 우월하다고 여겨진다. 반대로 일본에서는 황색이 최고의 색깔이라고 생각된다. 아이티에서는 그리스도와 사탄의 조각상을 만들 때 그리스도를 검게, 사탄을 희게 만든다. 아리스토텔레스와 플라톤은 그리스인들이 야만인들보다 선천적으로 우월하다고 여겨서 주인이 그리스인이고 노예가 야만인인 한 노예제가 정당화된다고 생각했다.

유희태 | 일반영어 ❹-1

032

하위내용영역	배점	예상정답률
일반영어 A형 기입형	2점	45%

모범답안 ⓐ negative ⓑ accurate

채점기준
- 2점: 모범답안과 같다.
- 1점: 둘 중 하나만 맞았다.
- 0점: 모범답안과 다르다.

한글번역

　2001년 가을 생물학적 테러리즘의 위협이 매우 현실이 됐을 때, 일부 회사들이 박테리아로 퍼지는 치명적인 호흡기 질환인 탄저균에 오염된 물질을 탐지하기 위한 가정용 검사 키트를 판매하기 시작했다. 20달러에서 25달러의 비용이 드는 이 키트들은 주로 인터넷을 통해 구입할 수 있었다. 키트에 대한 대중의 긍정적인 반응에 놀란 여러 소비자 단체 회원들이 구매에 대한 경고를 발표했는데, 그럴 만한 이유가 있었다. 탄저균 검사는 개인이 해서는 안 된다. 정부가 탄저균의 존재에 대해 건물들을 검사할 때조차 그런 검사 결과가 항상 정확하지는 않았다. 예를 들어 한 장소에서 실시된 검사의 경우 결과는 처음에 음성이었다. 하지만 나중의 검사들은 실제로 탄저균 포자가 존재한다는 것을 보여줬다. 정부는 정확성을 두 번, 심지어 세 번까지 확인하기 위해 다양하고 더 정교한 방법들을 사용해 검사하고 재검사할 능력을 갖고 있다. 하지만 일반 주택 소유자들은 그런 자원을 마음대로 쓸 수 없다. 일반인들은 검사를 실시하고 결과를 정확한 것으로 받아들일 가능성이 높다. 그러나 탄저균이 없는데 있다고 나타내는 위양성의 가능성이 항상 있고, 더 나쁘게는 집이 질병으로부터 안전하지 않은데 안전하다고 시사하는 위음성의 가능성도 있다. 같은 검사를 두세 번 다르게 실시하는 것도 아마 해결책이 아닐 것이다. 종종 필요한 것은 더 정교한 검사 장치인데, 정확히 실험실에서는 이용 가능하지만 일반 소비자에게는 이용할 수 없는 그런 종류의 것이다.

033

하위내용영역	배점	예상정답률
일반영어 B형 서술형	4점	55%

모범답안 The most important part of human activity is impulse. Second, the reason people boast is because of direct impulse, not because of any other intention.

채점기준
- +1.5점: 인간 행동의 가장 중요한 부분을 "impulse"이라 기술하였다.
- +2.5점: 사람들이 허풍을 떠는 이유를 "어떤 목적이 있어서가 아니라 그냥 충동" 때문이라 명확하게 서술하였다.

한글번역

　인간의 모든 행동은 충동과 욕구라는 두 가지 원천에서 비롯한다. 사람들은 욕구에서 기인한 행동은 항상 충분히 알아본다. 욕구가 충족되지 않고 당장 만족감을 주는 대상을 확보할 수 없을 때 사람들은 자신에게 충족감을 줄 만한 대상을 마음으로 상상한다. 모든 욕구는 무엇이 부족함을 자각하는 순간과 그것을 충족시킬 기회 사이에 존재하는 시간적인 간격에서 비롯한다. 욕구에서 비롯한 행동 그 자체가 고통을 주는 경우도 있고, 욕구가 충족되기까지 오랜 시간이 소요되거나 간절히 원하는 대상을 살아생전에 그리고 죽은 뒤에도 손에 넣지 못하는 경우도 있다. 인간의 행동을 이끄는 힘인 의지는 꽤 멀리 떨어진 대상에 대한 욕구를 추구하면서 그로 인한 행동이 주는 고통 그리고 멀리 떨어진 욕구와 상반되기는 하지만 당장 실현할 수 있는 욕구와 충동의 끈질긴 유혹에 굴복하지 않는다. 이는 모두 잘 알려진 이야기이며, 지금까지의 정치철학은 거의 예외 없이 욕구를 인간 행동의 원천으로 보는 입장을 토대로 하고 있다.
　그러나 욕구가 영향력을 발휘하는 것은 인간 행동의 일부분에 지나지 않는다. 더구나 욕구가 영향력을 발휘하는 부분은 인간 행동 가운데 비교적 의식적이고 직접적이고 문명화된 부분일 뿐, 가장 중요한 부분은 아니다. 인간은 본능적으로 특정한 목적을 지향하는 욕구 대신에 특정한 행동을 지향하는 충동의 지배를 받는다. 아이들이 소리를 지르며 뛰어다니는 것은 실현하고자 하는 목적이 있어서가 아니라 소리 지르며 달리고자 하는 직접적인 충동이 있기 때문이다. 개들이 달을 보고 짖는 것은 짖는 것이 이득이 된다는 판단 때문이 아니라 짖고 싶은 충동 때문이다. 음식을 먹고 사랑을 나누고 말다툼을 하고 허풍을 떠는 등 인간의 행동을 촉발하는 것은 어떤 목적이 아니라 충동일 뿐이다. 사람이 이성적인 동물이라고 생각하는 사람들은 사람이 허풍을 떠는 것은 다른 사람에게 좋은 평가를 받고 싶어서라고 말할 것이다. 그러나 우리에게는 대개 비웃음을 사리라는 사실을 뻔히 알면서도 허풍을 떨었던 기억이 있을 것이다. 본능적인 행위는 보통 자연인에게 유쾌한 어떤 결과를 가져오지만, 그 행위가 그런 결과를 바라는 욕망에서 비롯되는 것은 아니다. 그것은 직접적인 충동에서 비롯된다.

034

하위내용영역	배점	예상정답률
일반영어 B형 서술형	4점	50%

모범 답안) We can infer that the Japanese were incarcerated as a cautionary measure to prevent Japanese-Americans from acting as spies for Japan. Second, on the mainland the government was less sympathetic to the Japanese-Americans and enacted mass internment, unlike Hawaiian officials who worked in harmony with them.

채점 기준

+ 2점 : 일본계 미국인들을 강제수용소에 넣은 이유를 "as a cautionary measure to prevent Japanese-Americans from acting as spies for Japan"이라 서술하였다.
+ 2점 : 본토와 하와이에서의 차이를 "on the mainland the government was less sympathetic to the Japanese-Americans and enacted mass internment, unlike Hawaiian officials who worked in harmony with them"이라 명확하게 서술하였다.

한글번역

1941년 12월 7일 이전에는 진주만이 어디에 있는지, 심지어 하와이가 자국의 일부인지, 즉 식민지 소유지이자 1898년 미국 정부에 의해 병합된 준주인지 아는 미국인이 거의 없었다. 호놀룰루가 한 왕국의 주요 해양 중심지이자 준주 정부의 소재지라는 것을 깨닫는 사람도 거의 없었다. 그리고 1870년대부터 시작된 중국인, 포르투갈인, 일본인, 필리핀인의 연속적인 이민의 물결로 인해 이 미국의 전초기지가 1940년에는 원주민 하와이인과 백인 미국인(하와이어로 "이방인"을 뜻하는 haoles라고 불림)이 각각 섬 주민의 15%만을 구성하는 인구를 갖게 됐다는 것을 아는 사람도 거의 없었다.

하와이에서 태어나 따라서 미국 시민이었던 약 10만 명의 2세 일본인, 즉 니세이를 포함해 일본계 하와이 주민 약 16만 명은 하와이에서 가장 큰 민족 집단을 구성했으며, 인구의 3분의 1 이상을 차지했다. 1941년 일본의 진주만 공격은 즉시 일본계 하와이인들의 사보타주나 간첩 활동에 대한 두려움을 불러일으켰다. 사탕수수 밭에 일본 비행기를 군사 목표물로 안내하기 위해 화살표 모양의 표시를 잘라놓았다거나 니세이 여성들이 일본 조종사들에게 신호를 보내기 위해 기모노를 흔들었다는 소문이 돌았다.

하지만 간첩 활동의 위험이 하와이에 비해 적었던 태평양 연안주들에서 일본인들을 대량으로 수용하거나 감금한 것과는 극명한 대조로, 섬에서의 공식적인 군사 및 행정 정책은 전쟁 내내 전통적인 인종 간 화합을 유지하고 법을 준수하는 모든 일본계 주민들을 공정하고 인도적으로 대우하는 것이었다. "여기는 미국이고 우리는 미국식으로 일을 해야 한다"고 하와이의 군정 지사가 발표했다. 본토에서와 같은 니세이와 이세이(일본에서 이민 온 사람들)의 대량 억류는 없었다.

이세이들에게 미국에 대한 충성은 의무이자 명예의 문제가 됐다. 적과의 잠재적 연관성을 제거하기 위해 그들은 오래된 책들, 친척들의 사진, 비단 자수의 오비(기모노 띠)를 없애고 일본 천황의 초상화를 루스벨트 대통령의 사진으로 바꿨다.

035

하위내용영역	배점	예상정답률
일반영어 A형 기입형	2점	45%

모범 답안 ⓐ ownership or possession
ⓑ labor

채점 기준
- 2점: 모범답안과 같다.
- 1점: 둘 중 하나만 맞았다.
- 0점: 모범답안과 다르다.

한글번역

재산의 정당한 근거는 무엇인가? 누군가가 정당하게 "이것은 내 것이다!"라고 말할 수 있게 하는 것은 무엇인가? 각 사람은 독립적인 전체다. 각 특정한 한 쌍의 손은 특정한 뇌에 복종하고 특정한 몸과 연결돼 있다. 오직 이 노동만이 개인적 소유를 정당화한다.

각 사람이 자기 자신에게 속하듯이, 노동은 구체적인 형태로 투입될 때 개인에게 속한다. 이런 이유로 누군가가 생산하는 것은 전 세계의 주장에 맞서서라도 그 사람에게 속한다. 그것은 그 사람의 재산이며, 사용하거나 즐기거나, 주거나 교환하거나, 심지어 파괴할 수도 있다. 다른 누구도 정당하게 그것을 주장할 수 없다. 그리고 이런 독점적 소유와 향유에 대한 권리는 다른 누구에게도 해를 끼치지 않는다. 따라서 인간의 노동으로 생산된 모든 것에 대한 명확하고 논란의 여지없는 소유권이 있다. 그것은 자연법에 의해 권리가 부여된 원래 생산자로부터 내려온다. 내가 글을 쓰는 펜은 정당하게 내 것이다. 다른 어떤 인간도 정당하게 그것을 주장할 수 없는데, 왜냐하면 내게는 그것을 만든 생산자들의 소유권이 있기 때문이다. 그것이 내 것이 된 것은 문구점에서 나에게 이양됐고, 문구점은 수입업체로부터 이양 받았으며, 수입업체는 제조업체로부터의 이전을 통해 그것에 대한 독점권을 얻었기 때문이다. 같은 구매 과정을 통해 제조업체는 땅에서 재료를 파내고 그것을 펜으로 만든 사람들의 기득권을 획득했다.

따라서 펜에 대한 나의 독점적 소유권은 개인이 자신의 능력을 사용할 자연권에서 나온다—모든 독점적 소유 관념이 발생하는 근원. 그것은 원래 근원일 뿐만 아니라 유일한 근원이다. 자연은 노동의 결과를 제외하고는 인간에게 존재하는 어떤 소유나 통제도 인정하지 않는다. 모든 사람은 자연에서 평등한 기반 위에 존재하고 평등한 권리를 갖는다. 따라서 토지의 사유재산은 잘못됐다.

036

하위내용영역	배점	예상정답률
일반영어 A형 기입형	2점	65%

모범 답안 union

채점 기준
- 2점: 모범답안과 같다.
- 0점: 모범답안과 다르다.

한글번역

1950년대 내내 이주 농장 노동자들을 조합으로 조직하려는 시도가 반복됐다. 하지만 노동자들이 수확하는 작물을 따라 이동해야 했기 때문에 한 곳에 오래 머물지 않아서 조직하기가 어려웠다. 그러나 1960년대에 세사르 차베스라는 멕시코계 미국인 농장 노동자가 모든 역경에 맞서 농업 노동자들을 성공적으로 조합으로 조직했다. 친구들과 지지자들로부터 모은 기부금을 사용해 차베스는 농장에서 농장으로 다니며 캘리포니아의 이주 노동자들에게 말했는데, 그들 대부분은 그 자신과 같은 멕시코계 미국인들이었다. 그들의 밭에 와서 그들을 내려다보며 말하는 조합 활동가들에 익숙했던 농장 노동자들은 차베스가 다른 조합 조직가들이 하지 못했던 방식으로 자신들을 이해하고 존중한다는 것을 즉시 알았다. 하나씩 그들은 그의 조직인 전국 농장 노동자 협회에 가입했다. 1965년에 차베스와 동료 조합 조직가인 돌로레스 우에르타는 조합원들이 필리핀계 포도 따는 일꾼들이 시작한 파업에 참여하도록 설득했다. 그러고 나서 우에르타가 계속 조직하는 동안, 차베스는 포도 따는 일꾼들의 사건을 언론에 가져가서 포도를 따는 사람들이 화장실 시설 같은 기본 필수품에 대한 권리를 거부당하고 있기 때문에 아무도 포도를 먹어서는 안 된다고 주장했다. 포도 재배업자들에게 불행하게도 수백만 명의 미국인들이 동의하고 포도 먹기를 중단했다. 재배업자들에게 수백만 달러의 손실을 입힌 이 보이콧은 1970년까지 지속됐다. 그것이 끝났을 때 전국 농장 노동자 협회는 무시할 수 없는 세력이 돼 있었다. 농장 소유주들은 연합 농장 노동자로 이름이 바뀐 조합을 인정해야 했다.

037

하위내용영역	배점	예상정답률
일반영어 A형 기입형	2점	50%

모범 답안 ⓐ physical security   ⓑ encryption

채점 기준
- 2점: 모범답안과 같다.
- 1점: 둘 중 하나만 맞았다.
- 0점: 모범답안과 다르다.

> **한글번역**
>
> 정보 보안은 컴퓨터 하드 디스크에 저장된 데이터든 네트워크를 통해 전송되는 데이터든 데이터를 보호하는 것을 의미한다. 보안은 많은 다른 단계에서 뚫릴 수 있고, 따라서 많은 다른 종류의 예방 조치가 취해져야 한다.
> 대형 메인프레임이 유일한 선택이었고 인터넷이 존재하지 않았던 컴퓨팅 초기에는 컴퓨터가 있는 방을 보호함으로써 물리적 보안이 시행됐다. 오직 권한을 받은 사람들만 접근할 수 있었다. 이제 거의 모든 책상에 기계가 있고 파일과 이메일이 인터넷을 통해 정기적으로 전송되므로, 그런 종류의 물리적 보안을 유지하는 것은 거의 불가능하다. 하지만 몇 가지 명백한 조치를 취할 수 있다. 노트북을 아무 곳에나 두고 다니지 말고, 방에 있지 않을 때 워크스테이션을 작동 상태로 절대 두지 말며, 비밀번호를 누구와도 공유하지 말고 모니터에 붙인 포스트잇에 적어두지도 말라!
> 또한 컴퓨터 운영체제에 접근하기 위해 로그온 비밀번호를 사용하는지 확인하라. 운영체제는 로그온 비밀번호를 특정 사용자를 식별하는 인증 장치로 사용한다. 시스템에 들어가면 인증된 사용자(이것은 단순히 비밀번호를 아는 사람을 의미한다는 것을 기억하라)는 자동으로 운영체제가 시행하는 특정 파일 접근권과 권한을 갖게 된다.
> 비밀번호 예방 조치에도 불구하고 하드 디스크의 파일이나 네트워크 연결을 통과하는 파일이 불법적으로 접근해 잘못된 손에 들어간다면, 우리는 여전히 암호화를 통해 그런 파일들의 내용을 보호할 수 있는데, 이는 파일들에 접근해도 의미가 없게 만든다. 그것들을 해독할 열쇠 없이는 그것들을 읽는 데 성공한 누구에게도 별로 유용하지 않을 것이다. 따라서 정보 보안의 두 가지 주요 추진력은 인증과 암호화다.

038

하위내용영역	배점	예상정답률
일반영어 A형 서술형	4점	55%

모범 답안 The underlined "otherwise" means "if they did not put a human face on tragedies". Second, the main idea of the passage is that the accurate portrayal of real world tragedies is an important way that the media remains truthful and accurate.

채점 기준

+ 2점: otherwise가 의미하는 것이 "if they did not put a human face on tragedies"임을 명확하게 서술하였다.
  ☞ 다음과 같이 서술하였어도 2점을 준다.
  - If they did not publish the tragic and provocative photos of these major events.

+ 2점: 글의 요지가 "the accurate portrayal of real world tragedies is an important way that the media remains truthful and accurate"임을 명확하게 서술하였다.
  ☞ 다음과 같이 서술하였어도 2점을 준다.
  - The photographs serve the public good and make people more deeply aware of what's happening in the world because they can touch the emotions in a way words cannot.
  - Photographs give viewers and readers a deeper insight into a human tragedy than words can ever do.

  ☞ 다음과 같이 서술하였으면 1점을 준다.
  - A photograph tells the story.

한글번역

지금까지 찍힌 가장 유명한 사진 중 하나는 네이팜에 벗겨지고 화상을 입은 어린 베트남 소녀가 카메라를 향해 달려오는 모습을 보여준다. 그녀는 비명을 지르고 있다. 그녀의 얼굴은 고통으로 일그러져 있다. 이 사진을 찍은 사진작가 닉 우트는 퓰리처상을 받았고, 아마도 어떤 사설보다도 더 많이 미국 대중을 베트남 내전에 대한 미국의 개입을 반대하게 만들었을 것이다. 사진기자 에디 애덤스가 찍은 또 다른 퓰리처상 수상 사진도 베트남 전쟁 중에 찍혔다. 그것은 베트콩 장교가 남베트남 장교에 의해 처형되는 순간을 보여주는데, 남베트남 장교가 그 남자의 머리에 총을 대고 있다. 그리고 치명상을 입은 대통령의 생명이 쓰러져가는 동안 케네디 대통령의 차량 행렬이 딜리 플라자에서 달아나는 비극적인 사진들도 있다.

댈러스 타임스 헤럴드의 로버트 H. 잭슨은 댈러스 경찰서 지하에서 잭 루비가 리 오스왈드를 살해하는 순간을 포착한 사진으로 퓰리처상을 받았다. 2000년에 사진작가 조지 코차니에크는 두 명의 동급생이 총을 쏘아 13명을 죽였을 때 학교에서 방금 목격한 살인에 대해 괴로워하는 학교 아이들의 사진으로 퓰리처상을 받았다. 이 사진들은 모두 인간의 비극을 증언한다. 그것들은 모두 중요하고 가슴 아픈 이야기를 들려준다.

대중에게 정보를 제공하기 위해 신문 편집자들은 그런 사진들을 실어야 한다. 이것들은 독자들이 결코 보지 못할 세계의 지역에서 일어나고 있는 일에 주목하게 만드는 사진들이다. 그것들은 그렇지 않다면 독자들을 감동시키지도 움직이지도 못할 비극에 인간적인 얼굴을 씌운다. 2001년 9월 11일 화염에 휩싸여 무너져 내린 쌍둥이 빌딩의 사진들을 언급하며, 전직 사진기자인 짐 피셔는 끔찍한 비극을 포착한 사진들의 목적을 규명했다. "그날의 사건들의 진실을 인식하는 것은 때때로 추가적인 노력이 필요하다—그것을 찾는 것이 아니라 그것을 직면하는 것이."

039

하위내용영역	배점	예상정답률
일반영어 B형 서술형	4점	55%

모범답안 The three factors are smell, setting, and state of mind(mood). Second, in the blank should be written : "the good times are most easy to recall".

채점 기준

+ 2점 : 기억을 되살리는 데 영향을 주는 3가지 요소가 "smell, setting, and state of mind(mood)"임을 명확하게 서술하였다.
  ☞ 3개 중 2개만 서술한 경우 1점, 1개 또는 서술하지 못한 경우 0점을 준다.

+ 2점 : 빈칸에 들어갈 것을 "the good times are most easy to recall"이라 서술하였거나 유사하였다.

한글번역

갓 베인 풀, 빵집의 밀가루 냄새, 새 차의 가죽 냄새—각각은 향기로운 기억을 불러일으킬 수 있다. 한 유명한 학자가 일련의 실험에서 이 이론을 시험했다. 한 실험에서 피험자들에게 형용사 목록이 주어졌고 각 형용사에 대한 반대말을 쓰라는 지시를 받았다. 세션의 절반에서는 달콤한 초콜릿 냄새가 방 안으로 불어넣어졌다. 다음 날 피험자들에게 기억할 수 있는 반대말들을 가능한 한 많이 나열하라고 했는데—다시 초콜릿 향기가 있거나 없는 상태에서였다. 결과적으로 초콜릿 냄새가 학습과 회상 세션 모두에 있을 때 가장 많은 단어가 회상됐다. 그 이유는 무엇인가? 냄새가 단어들과 함께 기억에 저장돼서 나중에 인출 단서 역할을 했기 때문이다.

기억의 인출은 냄새 외의 요인들에 의해서도 영향을 받는다. 특이한 연구에서 연구자들은 심해 잠수부들에게 두 환경 중 한 곳에서 단어 목록을 제시했다. 수중 15피트 아래나 해변에서였다. 그리고 나서 그들은 같은 환경이나 다른 환경에서 잠수부들의 회상을 시험했다. 맥락 의존적 기억이라고 불리는 것을 보여주며, 잠수부들은 자료를 같은 환경에서 학습하고 인출했을 때 40% 더 많은 단어를 회상했다. 실용적 의미는 흥미롭다. 예를 들어, 자료가 처음 학습된 같은 방에서 인출된다면 회상이 향상될 수 있다. 연구들은 또한 시험 시의 우리 마음

상태가 학습중이었을 때와 같다면 무언가를 회상하는 것이 종종 더 쉽다는 것을 밝혀낸다. 행복하거나, 슬프거나, 취했거나, 술에 깨거나, 평온하거나, 흥분했을 때 정보가 습득되면, 그 정보는 같은 조건에서 인출될 가능성이 더 높다. 한 가지 주요한 복잡한 요인은 우리가 처한 기분이 우리의 현재 기분에 맞는 기억들을 불러일으키게 한다는 것이다. 우리가 우울하거나 불안할 때 우리 마음은 과거의 부정적인 사건들로 넘쳐나지만, 우리가 행복할 때는 좋은 시절들이 가장 쉽게 회상된다.

040

하위내용영역	배점	예상정답률
일반영어 B형 서술형	4점	55%

모범답안 The passage is about what motivated Harry Truman to order the dropping of the atomic bomb *(on Japan)*. Second, the revisionists contend that the real reason Truman dropped the bomb is to scare Russia with the new weapon and reduce their share in dealing with the issue of postwar occupation of Japan.

채점 기준

+ 2점: 이 글의 주제를 "what motivated Harry Truman to order the dropping of the atomic bomb"이라 명확하게 서술하였다.
  ☞ 다음과 같이 서술하였어도 2점을 준다.
  - What is the real motivation(reason) Harry Truman dropped the atomic bomb.
  - "트루먼이 원자폭탄을 투하한 이유"라는 개념이 들어가 있다.
+ 2점: 수정주의 역사가들이 반박한 내용을 "to scare Russia with the new weapon and reduce their share in dealing with the issue of postwar occupation of Japan"이라 서술하였다.

한글번역

해리 트루먼은 오직 한 가지 이유로 원자폭탄을 투하했다고 설명했다. 가능한 한 빨리 전쟁을 끝내서 일본 침공으로 인한 100만 명의 미국인 생명 손실을 막기 위해서였다. 전쟁의 여파 속에서 글을 쓴 이전 세대의 역사가들은 트루먼 대통령의 설명을 되풀이했다. 하지만 더 최근의 역사가들은 이 해석을 수정했다. 그들은 원자폭탄이 투하되지 않았더라도 일본이 항복했을 수도 있다고 주장하며, 트루먼의 높은 사상자 추정치가 순전히 허구라고 이의를 제기한다. 이런 수정주의자들은 트루먼, 이오시프 스탈린, 윈스턴 처칠이 참석한 1945년 7월의 포츠담 회의를 연구했다. 그들의 연구에서 그들은 특정 참가자들, 특히 국방장관 헨리 스팀슨과 트루먼 자신이 쓴 일기를 참고해 역사적 증거로서 일기의 가치를 입증했다.

학자들은 트루먼의 주요 동기가 전쟁 종료뿐만 아니라 미국의 군사력으로 러시아에 인상을 주고 일본의 최종 패배와 전후 점령에서 러시아의 참여를 최소화하는 것도 포함했다는 증거로 스팀슨의 일기를 인용한다. 7월 21일 스팀슨은 군대가 뉴멕시코에서 원자 장치를 성공적으로 시험했다고 트루먼에게 보고했다. 이 소식에 명백히 용기를 얻은 트루먼은 폭탄 보유가 "그에게 완전히 새로운 자신감을 줬다…"고 말했다. 다음 날 스팀슨은 영국 총리 처칠과 이 소식을 논의했다. "이제 트루먼에게 무슨 일이 일어났는지 안다"고 처칠이 응답했다. "그가 이 보고서를 읽고 나서 회의에 왔을 때 그는 다른 사람이었다. 그는 러시아인들에게 어디서 내려야 하는지 딱 잘라 말했고 전반적으로 전체 회의를 주도했다." 몇몇 역사가들은 원자폭탄 투하 결정이 부분적으로 인종차별적이었다고 주장한다. 증거로 그들은 트루먼이 "야만적이고, 무자비하고, 냉혹하고, 광신적"이라고 비난한 "일본 놈들"에 대해 폭탄을 사용하는 것을 논의한 트루먼의 손으로 쓴 일기 항목을 지적한다.

041

하위내용영역	배점	예상정답률
일반영어 A형 기입형	2점	50%

모범 답안 expectation

채점 기준

- 2점: 모범답안과 같다.
- 0점: 모범답안과 다르다.

한글번역

"모범적 소수"라는 용어는 개인의 노력과 피, 땀, 눈물을 무시하는 동시에 다른 인종들을 억누른다. 처음에는 칭찬처럼 들리지만 그렇지 않다. 괴롭히는 아이가 나를 때리려다가 브루스 리 영화 때문에 모든 아시아인이 쿵푸를 안다고 생각해서 다시 생각한다면, 나는 그 잘못된 가정으로부터 이익을 얻는다. 그것이 나를 일시적으로 기쁘게 할 수도 있지만, 장기적으로는 아시아인 고정관념의 시련 중 또 다른 단계일 뿐이다. 아시아인 고정관념에는 수학 괴짜, 게이샤, 드래곤 레이디 등이 있다.

성공 자체에 대한 기대가 문제다. 프린스턴 대학교는 이미 대학 입학에서 아시아인들이 더 높은 SAT 점수를 필요로 한다는 것을 보여주는 연구를 발표했다. 게다가 성적이 좋지만 모든 AP 수업에서 초음속의, 엄청난, 완벽한 A+ 성적이 아니라면, 당신은 그저 루저로 여겨진다. 자신의 가족에게도. 아시아인 부모들이 자녀들에게 갖는 높은 기대는 그들을 자살로 내몰고 있다. 동시에 아시아계 미국인에 대한 차별은 여전히 살아있고 건재하다. 우리가 혜택 받는다는 생각은 두려움에서 나온다. 우리가 "장악하고 있다"는 두려움. 그것은 새롭게 포장된 새로운 황화론이다. 어떤 명품 옷, 박사학위, 또는 다른 성공의 상징들이 지금 우리를 장식하든, 우리는 여전히 "타인"으로 여겨진다.

많은 아시아계 미국인들이 게임에서 너무 늦을 때까지 깨닫지 못하는 장벽이 있다. 정상은 외롭다는 것이다. 우리가 진정으로 성공하려면 졸업장과 급여뿐만 아니라 연민과 애정을 표현하는 능력도 고려해야 한다. 미국의 아시아인 아이들이여, 당신들은 성적 평균과 서류상의 성취보다 더 많은 존재다.

042

하위내용영역	배점	예상정답률
일반영어 A형 기입형	2점	50%

모범 답안 ⓐ developed ⓑ modern

채점 기준

- 2점: 모범답안과 같다.
- 1점: 둘 중 하나만 맞았다.
- 0점: 모범답안과 다르다.

한글번역

모든 단계에서 발전은 과학의 진보가 있을 때 일어난다. 따라서 과학, 기술, 발전은 모두 서로 비례한다. 발전이 일어나려면 과학과 기술이 함께 가야 한다. 기본적으로 과학은 지식의 연구로 알려져 있으며, 이것은 체계화되고 사실을 분석하고 이해하는 데 의존한다. 기술은 기본적으로 이런 과학적 지식의 적용이다.

성공적인 경제, 특히 오늘날 지식 기반 경제 추구에서 과학과 기술은 기본 필수 조건이다. 국가들이 과학과 기술을 구현하지 않는다면, 스스로 발전할 가능성은 최소화되고 따라서 저개발국으로 평가될 수 있다. 또한 과학과 기술은 모든 면에서 현대성과 연관 있다.

삶의 모든 측면에서 현대화는 모든 국가에서 과학과 기술 구현의 가장 훌륭한 사례다. 삶의 모든 영역에 현대적 기기들이 도입되면서 삶이 단순해졌고, 이것은 오직 과학과 기술을 함께 구현했기 때문에 가능하다. 의학, 인프라, 항공, 전기, 정보 기술 또는 다른 어떤 분야든 모든 부문에서 현대 장비 없이는 우리가 오늘날 직면하는 진보와 혜택들이 불가능했을 것이다.

043

하위내용영역	배점	예상정답률
일반영어 A형 기입형	2점	55%

모범 답안 ethnic

채점 기준

- 2점: 모범답안과 같다.
  ☞ religious라 했으면 1점을 준다.
- 0점: 모범답안과 다르다.

한글번역

공립학교의 휴일 준수는 19세기 말에 시작됐다. 적어도 그 당시 학교 휴일의 목표는 사람들을 하나로 모으는 것이었다. 학교에서의 휴일 기념행사—특히 크리스마스—는 이민자들로 이뤄진 국가를 통합하기 위한 것이었다. 하지만 밥 딜런이 말했듯이 "시대는 변하고 있다."

시카고에서 월트 디즈니 자석학교의 교장은 휴일 화합을 위한 자신의 시도가 역효과를 낳는 것을 봤다. 이 초등학교는 아프리카계 미국인, 아시아인, 무슬림, 히스패닉, 유고슬라비아인, 루마니아인, 유대인 아이들을 포함한 다양한 학생들로 구성돼 있어서, 교장은 "특정 민족 전통"과 관련된 산타클로스와 다른 모든 상징이나 활동을 금지함으로써 크리스마스를 완화하려고 했다. 교사들이 항의했고—한 교사는 교장에게 《그린치가 크리스마스를 훔친 방법》 사본을 줬다—교육위원회 위원장이 그 금지령을 뒤집었다. 학교 전체에서 크리스마스 파티, 장식, 캐럴이 한창일 때, 무슬림 학부모인 에삼 암마르는 "이 모든 일이 벌어지는 가운데 어떻게 내 아이들을 자랑스러운 무슬림으로 키울 수 있을까?"라고 물었다.

휴일 시즌을 어떻게 기념할 것인가에 대한 열정이 격화되면서, 일부 학부모들은 힌두교 디왈리 축제, 하누카, 콴자를 포함한 다양한 다른 민족 휴일들이 크리스마스와 동등한 시간을 얻어야 한다고 요구하고 있다. 다른 사람들은 일부 지역사회에서 나무와 산타클로스 금지 같은 크리스마스 전통의 어떤 축소에도 항의한다. 현재로서는 해결책이 보이지 않는다.

044

하위내용영역	배점	예상정답률
일반영어 B형 서술형	4점	50%

모범 답안 "Controversial" means that her avid denouncement and opposition of Islam goes against communities that try to remain tolerant of different religions. Second, her critics accuse her of using unfair stereotypes and distorted interpretations of the Koran in her efforts to oppose Islam.

채점 기준

- 2점: 밑줄 친 "Controversial"의 의미를 "her avid denouncement and opposition of Islam, which goes against communities that try to remain tolerant of different religions"라고 명확하게 서술하였거나 유사하였다.
- 2점: 히르시 알리에 대한 비평가들의 비판이 "her critics accuse her of using unfair stereotypes and distorted interpretations of the Koran in her efforts to oppose Islam"이라고 명확하게 서술하였거나 유사하였다.
  ☞ 다음과 같이 서술하였으면 1.5점을 준다.
  - Hirsi Ali's view of Islam stems from her own unhappy experience, not from her knowledge of Islamic thought and practice.

045

하위내용영역	배점	예상정답률
일반영어 A형 서술형	4점	45%

모범답안 The writer uses "frontier" because it is an unknown territory. Next, the Deep Sea Drilling Project was significant because it produced evidence to convince scientists of continental drift theory and plate tectonics.

채점기준

+ 2점: 저자가 "frontier"를 사용한 이유를 "because it is an unknown territory"라 서술하였거나 유사하였다.
+ 2점: 심해 시추 프로젝트(DSDP)가 중요한 이유를 "because it produced evidence to convince scientists of continental drift theory and plate tectonics"라 서술하였거나 유사하였다.

한글번역

지구 전체 육지 면적의 거의 2.5배에 달하는 해저는 오늘날에도 대부분 탐험되지 않고 지도에 표시되지 않은 광대한 미개척지다. 약 한 세기 전까지 심해저는 평균 3,600미터가 넘는 깊은 바다 아래 숨겨져 완전히 접근할 수 없었다. 전혀 빛이 없고 지구 표면보다 수백 배 강한 강렬한 압력을 받는 심해저는 인간에게 적대적인 환경으로, 어떤 면에서는 우주 공간의 공허함만큼 험악하고 외딴 곳이다.

연구자들이 한 세기 넘게 심해 암석과 퇴적물 샘플을 채취해 왔지만, 해저에 대한 최초의 상세한 전 지구적 조사는 실제로 1968년 국립과학재단의 심해 시추 프로젝트(DSDP)가 시작되면서 시작됐다. 해상 석유 및 가스 산업을 위해 처음 개발된 기술을 사용해, DSDP의 시추선인 글로마 챌린저호는 해양 표면에서 안정된 위치를 유지하고 매우 깊은 바다에서 시추해 해저에서 퇴적물과 암석 샘플을 추출할 수 있었다.

한글번역

논란이 많은 네덜란드 작가이자 영화제작자인 아얀 히르시 알리는 몇 년 전 타임지가 선정한 가장 영향력 있는 인물 중 한 명으로 이름을 올렸을 수도 있지만, 그녀가 어떻게 이슬람을 거부하게 됐고 여성에 대한 박해라고 부르는 것의 종식을 옹호하게 됐는지에 대한 이야기에 대한 반응은 엇갈렸다. 1969년 소말리아에서 태어난 그녀와 가족은 결국 케냐로 이주했고, 그곳에서 그녀는 이슬람교로 자랐다. 그녀의 전기에 따르면, 1992년 히르시 알리는 캐나다에 있는 먼 사촌과의 결혼 주선이라는 생각을 거부했다. 결혼을 피하기 위해 히르시 알리는 네덜란드에 있는 여성 친척의 집으로 도망쳤다. 그곳에 살면서 그녀는 정치학 학위를 취득했고 소말리-네덜란드어 번역가로 일했는데, 종종 남성 친척들의 학대에서 피난처를 찾는 폭행당한 무슬림 여성들을 위해 번역했다. 그녀가 2002년까지 종교를 포기하지는 않았지만, 바로 이 시점에서 히르시 알리의 이슬람과의 갈등이 진정으로 시작됐다. 히르시 알리에 따르면, 2001년 9월 11일 미국에 대한 테러 공격이 그녀로 하여금 19명의 무슬림 테러리스트들이 숭배하는 신을 더 이상 믿을 수 없다는 결론에 이르게 했다. 따라서 2002년 히르시 알리는 무신론자가 됐을 뿐만 아니라, 문화적 가치가 기본적 인권과 법률을 위반하는 종교 공동체에 대한 "정치적으로 올바른" 접근법이라고 그녀가 부른 것에 반대하기 시작했다. 그녀는 특히 무슬림 세계에서 여성의 역할에 대해 목소리를 높였으며, "여성의 지위는 내가 보기에 무슬림 세계에서만큼 나쁜 곳은 어디에도 없다"고 주장했다. 히르시 알리는 많은 사람들의 존경을 받았지만, 그녀 나름의 비판자들도 있다. 그녀의 도전자들은 그녀가 모든 무슬림 여성을 희생자로 고정 관념화하고 이슬람 사상의 왜곡과 진정한 이슬람 신념 사이의 구별을 하지 못한다고 주장한다. 비판자들은 또한 그녀가 지속적으로 자신의 이전 신앙을 잘못 표현한다고 말하는데, 특히 코란에 대한 그녀의 해석에서 그렇다고 하며, 코란은 알리가 주장하는 바와 같이 여성에 대한 부당한 대우를 정당화하지 않는다고 주장한다.

글로마 챌린저호는 1983년 11월에 끝난 15년 연구 프로그램에서 96번의 항해를 완료했다. 이 기간 동안 이 선박은 600,000킬로미터를 항해하고 전 세계 624개 시추 지점에서 해저 퇴적물과 암석의 거의 20,000개 코어 샘플을 채취했다. 글로마 챌린저호의 코어 샘플들은 지질학자들이 수억 년 전 지구가 어떤 모습이었는지 재구성하고 수백만 년 후 아마 어떤 모습일지 계산할 수 있게 해줬다. 오늘날 글로마 챌린저호의 항해 중에 수집된 증거의 힘에 크게 의존해, 거의 모든 지구과학자들이 지구를 형성하는 많은 지질학적 과정을 설명하는 판구조론과 대륙이동설에 동의한다.

글로마 챌린저호가 시추한 퇴적물 코어들은 또한 세계의 과거 기후를 이해하는 데 중요한 정보를 제공했다. 심해 퇴적물은 수억 년 전까지 거슬러 올라가는 기후 기록을 제공하는데, 이는 과거 기후의 육지 기반 증거의 많은 부분을 빠르게 파괴하는 기계적 침식과 강력한 화학적 및 생물학적 활동으로부터 대부분 격리되어 있기 때문이다. 이 기록은 이미 과거 기후 변화의 패턴과 원인에 대한 통찰을 제공했는데, 이는 미래 기후를 예측하는 데 사용될 수 있는 정보다.

046

하위내용영역	배점	예상정답률
일반영어 A형 서술형	4점	50%

모범 답안 The Canadian postwar birthrate was at its lowest in 1966. Next, it can be inferred that economic conditions were bad before the industrial revolution.

채점 기준

+ 2점: 출산율이 가장 낮았던 시기를 "in 1966"라 서술하였다.
+ 2점: 산업혁명 이전 가정의 생활 방식에 대해 추론할 수 있는 것을 "economic conditions were bad"라 서술하였거나 유사하였다.

한글번역

제2차 세계대전 후 20년간 캐나다를 이해하는 데 기본이 되는 것은 이 나라의 인상적인 인구 증가다. 1945년 캐나다인 3명당 1996년에는 5명이 넘었다. 1966년 9월 캐나다의 인구는 2천만 명을 넘어섰다. 이런 급격한 증가의 대부분은 자연 증가에서 나왔다. 1930년대의 대공황과 전쟁이 결혼을 늦춰왔고 1945년 이후 따라잡기 과정이 시작됐다. 베이비붐은 1950년대 10년 내내 계속돼 1951년부터 1956년까지 5년간 거의 15%의 인구 증가를 가져왔다. 이런 증가율은 캐나다 역사상 단 한 번, 대초원이 정착되고 있던 1911년 이전 10년에만 넘어선 적이 있었다. 의심할 여지없이 1950년대의 좋은 경제 상황이 인구 증가를 뒷받침했지만, 확장은 또한 조혼 경향과 가족 평균 규모의 증가에서도 비롯됐다. 1957년 캐나다 출생률은 천 명당 28명으로 세계에서 가장 높은 수준 중 하나였다.

1957년 정점을 찍은 후 캐나다의 출생률은 감소하기 시작했다. 1966년에는 25년 만에 최저 수준에 이를 때까지 계속 떨어졌다. 부분적으로 이 감소는 대공황과 전쟁 중 낮은 출생률을 반영했지만, 캐나다 사회의 변화에도 기인했다. 젊은 사람들이 학교에 더 오래 다니고 있었고, 더 많은 여성이 일하고 있었으며, 젊은 부부들이 가정을 꾸리기 전에 자동차나 집을 사고 있었고, 생활수준 향상이 가족 규모를 줄이고 있었다. 캐나다가 산업혁명 이후 서구 세계 전체에서 일어났던 소가족 경향에 다시 한 번 발맞춰 가고 있는 것 같았다.

1966년까지 캐나다 인구 증가가 둔화됐지만 (1960년대 전반의 증가는 단지 9%였다), 또 다른 대규모 인구 파도가 지평선 너머로 다가오고 있었다. 그것은 1957년 이전 높은 출생률 시기에 태어난 아이들의 아이들로 구성될 것이었다.

047

하위내용영역	배점	예상정답률
일반영어 A형 서술형	4점	50%

모범답안) The misconception is that organic foods have special health and nutritional benefits that conventional foods lack. Next, the author believes that consumers can trust conventionally grown foods.

채점 기준

+ 2점: 잘못된 인식을 "organic foods have special health and nutritional benefits that conventional foods lack"이라 서술하였거나 유사하였다.
  ☞ 다음과 같이 서술하였어도 2점을 준다.
  - Organically grown products are more healthy than conventionally grown foods.
+ 2점: 기존에 재배된 식품에 대한 저자의 관점을 "consumers can trust conventionally grown foods"라 서술하였거나 유사하였다.

한글번역

유기농으로 재배된 식품이 최고의 식품 선택일까? 기존의 재배 및 유통 식품에 비해 그런 식품들이 갖는다고 주장되는 장점들이 현재 논쟁되고 있다. 유기농 식품의 옹호자들—그 의미가 크게 다른 용어—은 그런 제품들이 다른 것들보다 더 안전하고 영양가가 높다고 자주 선언한다.

전형적인 북미 식단의 안전성과 영양적 품질에 대한 소비자들의 관심 증가는 환영할 만한 발전이다. 하지만 이런 관심의 대부분은 식품 공급이 안전하지 않거나 영양적 필요를 충족하는 데 부적절하다는 포괄적인 주장에 의해 촉발됐다. 이런 주장의 대부분이 과학적 증거에 의해 뒷받침되지 않지만, 그런 주장을 내세우는 서면 자료의 우세함이 일반 대중이 사실과 허구를 구분하기 어렵게 만든다. 결과적으로 전적으로 유기농으로 재배된 식품으로 구성된 식단을 먹는 것이 질병을 예방하거나 치료하거나 건강에 다른 혜택을 제공한다는 주장이 널리 공표돼 민간 지식의 기초가 됐다.

거의 매일 대중은 "노화 방지" 식단, 새로운 비타민, 기타 놀라운 식품들에 대한 주장들에 포위된다. 천연 비타민이 합성 비타민보다 우수하다거나, 수정란이 무정란보다 영양적으로 우수하다거나, 처리하지 않은 곡물이 훈증 처리된 곡물보다 낫다는 등의 입증되지 않은 보고들이 수없이 많다.

대부분의 유기농 식품들이 공통으로 갖는 것 같은 한 가지는 기존에 재배된 식품보다 비용이 더 많이 든다는 것이다. 하지만 많은 경우 소비자들이 유기농 식품이 건강을 유지하고 기존에 재배된 식품보다 더 나은 영양적 품질을 제공할 수 있다고 믿는다면 잘못 인도된 것이다. 따라서 소비자들, 특히 소득이 제한된 사람들이 일반 식품을 불신하고 대신 비싼 유기농 식품만 산다면 진짜 우려할 이유가 있다.

048

하위내용영역	배점	예상정답률
일반영어 A형 서술형	4점	50%

모범답안) The three origins of theater are thought to have evolved from ritual, or secondly, from human interest in storytelling, or finally from dances. Next, the intended original purpose of rituals was to control the natural forces of the world.

채점 기준

+ 2점: 극의 기원에 대한 세 이론을 "have evolved from <u>ritual</u>, or secondly, from <u>human interest in storytelling</u>, or finally from <u>dances</u>"라 서술하였거나 유사하였다.
  ☞ 3개 중 2개만 서술하였으면 1점, 1개만 서술하였으면 0점을 준다.
+ 2점: 제의의 원래의 목적을 "to control the natural forces of the world"라 서술하였거나 유사하였다.

한글번역

고대 그리스 드라마의 기원에 대한 많은 이론들이 있다. 오늘날 가장 널리 받아들여지는 것은 드라마가 의식에서 진화했다는 가정에 기반한다. 이 견해에 대한 논거는 다음과 같다. 처음에 인간은 세상의 자연적 힘, 심지어 계절 변화조차도 예측 불가능한 것으로 봤고, 이런 알려지지 않고 두려워하는 힘들을 통제하기 위해 다양한 수단을 추구했다. 원하는 결과를 가져오는 것처럼 보였던 그런 조치들은 그 후 보유되고 반복돼 고정된 의식으로 굳어질 때까지 계속됐다. 결국 의식의 신비를 설명하거나 감춘 이야기들이 생겨났다. 시간이 지나면서 일부 의식들은 포기됐지만, 나중에 신화라고 불린 이야기들은 지속돼 예술과 드라마의 소재를 제공했다.

드라마가 의식에서 진화했다고 믿는 사람들은 또한 그런 의식들이 음악, 춤, 가면, 의상이 거의 항상 사용됐기 때문에 연극의 씨앗을 포함했다고 주장한다. 게다가 공연을 위한 적절한 장소가 제공돼야 했고, 전체 공동체가 참여하지 않을 때는 보통 "연기 영역"과 "관객석" 사이에 명확한 구분이 만들어졌다. 또한 연기자들이 있었고, 의식 수행에서 실수를 피하는 것에 상당한 중요성이 부여됐기 때문에, 종교 지도자들이 보통 그 임무를 맡았다. 가면과 의상을 착용하고 그들은 종종 다른 사람들, 동물들, 또는 초자연적 존재들을 흉내냈고, 배우가 할 수 있는 것처럼 원하는 효과—사냥이나 전투에서의 성공, 다가오는 비, 태양의 부활—을 흉내냈다. 결국 그런 극적 표현들은 종교적 활동에서 분리됐다.

또 다른 이론은 연극의 기원을 이야기에 대한 인간의 관심에서 추적한다. 이 견해에 따르면, (사냥, 전쟁, 또는 다른 위업에 대한) 이야기들이 점차 정교해지는데, 처음에는 화자에 의한 모방, 행동, 대화의 사용을 통해, 그 다음에는 각각의 역할을 다른 사람이 맡는 것을 통해서다. 밀접하게 관련된 이론은 연극을 주로 리듬적이고 체조적이거나 동물의 움직임과 소리를 모방하는 그런 춤들에서 추적한다.

049

하위내용영역	배점	예상정답률
일반영어 A형 서술형	4점	50%

모범답안 The reason for the pardon that can be inferred is to help the nation recover from the war. Next, the lesser issues facing the North were that industries (factories) had to be retooled for peacetime.

채점기준

+ 2점 : 존슨 대통령의 사면의 이유를 "to help the nation recover from the war"이라 서술하였거나 유사하였다.
+ 2점 : 북부가 직면한 덜 중요한 문제를 "industries (factories) had to be retooled for peacetime"이라 서술하였거나 유사하였다.

한글번역

남북전쟁이 끝났을 때 미국인들, 북부와 남부 모두에게 엄청난 과제들이 닥쳤다. 양측에서 약 150만 명의 군인들이 제대하고, 민간 생활에 재적응하고, 황폐해진 경제에 재흡수돼야 했다. 민간 정부도 평시 기반으로 되돌려놓아야 했고 군대의 간섭이 중단돼야 했다.

남부의 절망적인 곤경이 덜 극적이긴 하지만 북부에서도 재건이 착수돼야 한다는 사실을 가렸다. 산업들은 평시 조건에 적응해야 했고, 공장들은 민간 필요를 위해 재정비돼야 했다.

재정 문제들이 북부와 남부 모두에서 크게 부각됐다. 국가 부채는 전쟁이 시작된 해인 1861년의 소규모 6천 5백만 달러에서 전쟁이 끝난 해인 1865년에는 거의 30억 달러로 급증했다. 이것은 당시 엄청난 액수였지만 신중한 정부가 지불할 수 있는 것이었다. 동시에 전쟁 세금은 덜 부담스러운 수준으로 줄여야 했다.

주로 남부와 접경 주에서 침입 군대에 의해 야기된 물리적 파괴가 복구돼야 했다. 이 헤라클레스적 과업은 궁극적으로 완수됐지만, 낙담스러울 정도로 느렸다.

다른 중요한 질문들도 답이 필요했다. 노예제에서 해방된 400만 흑인들의 미래는 어떻게 될 것인가? 남부 주들을 어떤 기준으로 연방으로 다시 받아들일 것인가?

모두 반역죄에 해당하는 남부 지도자들은 어떻게 할 것인가? 이런 지도자들 중 한 명인 남부 연합의 대통령 제퍼슨 데이비스는 "시큼한 사과나무에 제프 데이비스를 매달아라"라는 모욕적인 북부 대중가요의 주제였다. 그리고 어린이들조차 그것을 불렀다. 데이비스는 2년간의 감옥살이 초기에 감옥 독방에서 일시적으로 족쇄가 채워졌다. 하지만 그와 다른 남부 지도자들은 최종적으로 석방됐는데, 부분적으로는 남부 연합 주인 버지니아 출신 배심원들이 그들을 유죄로 판결할 가능성이 낮았기 때문이었다. 모든 지도자들은 최종적으로 1868년 존슨 대통령에 의해 사면됐는데, 이는 재건 노력이 가능한 한 적은 원한으로 진행되도록 돕기 위한 노력이었다.

050

하위내용영역	배점	예상정답률
일반영어 A형 서술형	4점	45%

모범 답안 The word is "heights". Next, conifers helped disprove theories about root pressure because their roots are weak.

채점 기준

+ 2점: 빈칸에 들어갈 단어를 "heights"라 정확하게 기입하였다. 이외에는 답이 될 수 없다.
+ 2점: 침엽수가 도움이 된 이유를 "because their roots are weak"이라 서술하였거나 유사하였다.

한글번역

대기압은 최대 10미터 높이의 물기둥을 지탱할 수 있다. 하지만 식물들은 물을 훨씬 더 높이 이동시킬 수 있다. 세쿼이아 나무는 지상 100미터 이상인 맨 꼭대기까지 물을 펌프질할 수 있다. 19세기 말까지 나무와 다른 키 큰 식물에서 물 이동은 미스터리였다. 일부 식물학자들은 식물의 살아있는 세포들이 펌프 역할을 한다고 가설을 세웠지만, 많은 실험들이 모든 세포가 죽은 식물의 줄기도 여전히 물을 상당한 높이로 이동시킬 수 있다는 것을 보여줬다. 식물에서의 물 이동에 대한 다른 설명들은 식물 바닥의 뿌리에서 물을 미는 뿌리 압에 기반했다. 하지만 뿌리 압은 키 큰 나무의 꼭대기까지 물을 밀어 올릴 만큼 거의 충분하지 않다. 게다가 가장 키 큰 나무들 중 하나인 침엽수들은 특히 낮은 뿌리 압을 갖는다.

물이 키 큰 나무의 꼭대기로 펌프질되지 않고, 키 큰 나무의 꼭대기로 밀려 올라가지도 않는다면, 우리는 "그것이 어떻게 거기에 도달하는가?"라고 물을 수 있다. 현재 받아들여지는 응집-장력 이론에 따르면, 물은 거기로 끌려간다. 식물에서 올라가는 물기둥에 대한 당김은 식물 꼭대기에서의 물 증발로부터 발생한다. 잎 표면에서 물이 손실되면서 음압, 즉 장력이 만들어진다. 증발된 물은 식물 꼭대기에서 뿌리까지 이어지는 끊어지지 않은 기둥으로 식물 내부에서 이동하는 물로 대체된다. 물의 어떤 샘플에서든 표면 장력을 만드는 같은 힘들이 이런 끊어지지 않은 물기둥의 유지에 책임이 있다. 물이 매우 작은 구멍의 관에 갇혀 있을 때, 응집력(물 분자들 사이의 인력)이 너무 커서 물기둥의 강도가 같은 직경의 강철 와이어의 강도와 비교된다. 이 응집 강도는 물기둥이 깨지지 않고 큰 높이로 끌려올라갈 수 있게 한다.

051

하위내용영역	배점	예상정답률
일반영어 A형 서술형	4점	50%

모범 답안 The most prominent disadvantage of residential expansion is it was unplanned. Next, the feature that most influenced the direction Chicago expanded is mass transportation.

채점 기준

+ 2점: 가장 눈에 띄는 단점을 "it was unplanned"라 서술하였거나 유사하였다.
+ 2점: 시카고가 팽창되는 방향에 가장 영향을 끼친 요소를 "mass transportation"이라 서술하였다.

한글번역

　　대중교통은 세 가지 근본적인 방식으로 미국 도시의 사회적, 경제적 구조를 개편했다. 그것은 물리적 확장을 촉진했고, 사람들과 토지 사용을 분류했으며, 도시 생활의 내재적 불안정성을 가속화했다. 주거 확장을 위한 광대한 미점유 토지를 개방함으로써, 옴니버스, 마차 철도, 통근 열차, 전기 전차들이 정착 지역을 도시 중심가에서 근대 이전 시대보다 2-4배 더 먼 곳으로 끌어냈다. 예를 들어 1850년에 보스턴의 경계는 구 상업 지구에서 겨우 2마일 떨어져 있었다. 세기 전환기까지 반경이 10마일로 확장됐다. 이제 여유가 있는 사람들은 구 도시 중심가에서 멀리 떨어져 살면서도 여전히 일, 쇼핑, 오락을 위해 그곳으로 통근할 수 있었다. 거의 모든 주요 도시 주변 토지의 새로운 접근성은 부동산 개발의 폭발을 촉진했고 우리가 지금 알고 있는 도시 확산을 촉진했다. 예를 들어 1890년과 1920년 사이에 시카고 경계 내에서 약 250,000개의 새로운 주거 부지가 기록됐는데, 그들 대부분은 외곽 지역에 위치했다. 같은 기간에 또 다른 550,000개가 시 경계 밖이지만 대도시 지역 내에서 구획됐다. 통근의 가능성을 이용하려고 열망하며, 부동산 개발업자들은 단지 30년 만에 시카고 지역에 800,000개의 잠재적 건축 부지를 추가했는데, 이는 5-6백만 명을 수용할 수 있는 부지들이었다.

　　물론 많은 것들이 결코 점유되지 않았다. 시카고와 다른 도시들 주변에는 항상 세분화됐지만 공석인 토지의 엄청난 잉여가 있었다. 이런 과잉들은 대중교통의 성장과 관련된 주거 확장의 특징을 강조한다. 도시 확산은 본질적으로 계획되지 않았다. 그것은 조정된 토지 사용이나 미래 토지 사용자들에게 거의 주의를 기울이지 않은 수천 명의 소규모 투자자들에 의해 수행됐다. 특히 교통노선과 중산층 거주자들이 예상되는 도시 경계 근처나 외부에서 주거 목적으로 토지를 구매하고 준비한 사람들은 수요에 대응하는 만큼이나 수요를 창출하기 위해 그렇게 했다. 시카고는 이 과정의 대표적인 예다. 그곳의 부동산 세분화는 인구 증가보다 훨씬 빠르게 진행됐다.

052

하위내용영역	배점	예상정답률
일반영어 A형 서술형	4점	55%

모범답안) It is implied that the ocean has much less erosive effects. Next, the writer provides the example of the specimens preserved in the birth canal to illustrate Holzmaden's preservation quality.

채점기준

+ 2점 : 바다의 침식 효과에 관해 추론할 수 있는 것을 "the ocean has much less erosive effects"라 서술하였거나 유사하였다.
+ 2점 : 저자가 제공하는 예를 "the example of the specimens preserved in the birth canal"이라 서술하였거나 유사하였다.

한글번역

　　화석 기록에서 배아와 새끼의 보존은 드문 일이다. 작고 연약한 골격들은 보통 화석화되기 전에 청소동물들에 의해 흩어지거나 풍화에 의해 파괴된다. 어룡들은 해양 동물로서 침식에 덜 노출되는 환경에서 살았기 때문에 육상 생물들보다 보존될 가능성이 더 높았다. 그래도 그들의 화석화에는 여러 요인들이 필요했다. 연조직의 느린 부패 속도, 적은 다른 동물들의 청소 행위, 작은 뼈들을 뒤섞고 운반해 갈 빠른 해류와 파도의 부재, 그리고 상당히 빠른 매몰. 이런 요인들이 주어져서 일부 지역들이 잘 보존된 어룡 화석의 보고가 됐다.

　　독일 홀츠마덴의 퇴적층은 분석을 위한 흥미로운 사례를 제시한다. 어룡 유해들은 약 1억 9천만 년 전에 퇴적된 검은색 역청질 해양 혈암에서 발견된다. 수년에 걸쳐 이 암석들에서 해양 파충류, 어류, 무척추동물의 수천 개 표본이 회수됐다. 보존 품질이 뛰어나지만, 더욱 인상적인 것은 보존된 배아를 포함한 어룡 화석의 개수다. 배아를 가진 어룡들이 홀츠마덴 주변 작은 지역 혈암의 6개 다른 층에서 보고됐는데, 이는 특정 장소가 오랜 시간에 걸쳐 많은 수의 어룡들에 의해 반복적으로 사용됐음을 시사한다. 배아들은 신체 발달이 상당히 진전돼 있다. 예를 들어 그들의 지느러미는 이미 잘 형성돼 있다. 한 표본은 심지어 산도에서 보존돼 있다. 게다가 혈암에는 20-30인치 길이의 많은 신생아들의 유해가 들어있다.

다른 곳에서는 매우 드문데 왜 홀츠마덴에는 그렇게 많은 임신한 암컷들과 새끼들이 있을까? 보존 품질은 거의 타의 추종을 불허하고 채석 작업이 화석의 가치에 대한 인식을 가지고 신중하게 수행됐다. 하지만 이런 요인들은 출산 시기에 아주 가까운 시점에서 임신한 어룡들이 특정 장소에 그렇게 집중된 이유라는 흥미로운 질문을 설명하지 못한다.

053

하위내용영역	배점	예상정답률
일반영어 B형 서술형	5점	45%

모범답안 The primary purpose of Lewis and Clark's expedition was to find coast-to-coast waterways. Next, it can be inferred that the continent's size was underestimated prior to the expedition. Third, they discovered that there were no coast-to-coast routes via the Missouri-Columbia river systems.

채점기준

+ 2점: 루이스 클라크 원정대의 주요 목적을 "to find coast-to-coast waterways"라 서술하였거나 유사하였다.
+ 1.5점: 대륙의 크기에 대해서 "the continent's size was underestimated prior to the expedition"이라 서술하였거나 유사하였다.
+ 1.5점: 루이스와 클라크가 발견한 것을 "there were no coast-to-coast routes via the Missouri-Columbia river systems"라 서술하였거나 유사하였다.

한글번역

제퍼슨 대통령이 후원한 루이스 클라크 원정대는 1812년 전쟁 이전 고원 평야와 북서부에 대한 가장 중요한 공식 조사였다. 대통령의 비서인 메리웨더 루이스 대위는 "미주리강과 그 주요 지류들을 탐험해, 그것의 경로와 태평양 바다와의 소통을 통해... 상업 목적으로 대륙을 가로지르는 가장 직접적이고 실용적인 수로 통신을 제공할 수 있도록" 지시를 받았다. 유명한 조지 로저스 클라크의 동생인 윌리엄 클라크 대위가 탐험대의 지휘를 공유하도록 초대받았다.

미지의 지역에 선사시대 매머드들이 돌아다니고 그 황야 어딘가에 80마일에 45마일 규모의 바위소금 산이 있다는 소문들 속에서 두 대위가 출발했다. 날짜는 1804년 5월 14일이었다. 그들의 출발점은 미주리강 입구에서 미시시피강 건너편에 있는 우드강 입구였다. 여름 내내 미주리강을 힘들게 거슬러 올라간 후, 일행은 현재 노스다코타 중부의 만단 마을 근처에서 겨울을 났다. 1805년 봄에 여행을 재개해 남자들은 미주리강을 따라 수원지까지 작업해 나간 다음 서부 몬타나와 아이다호의 산맥을 넘었다. 콜롬비아강의 지류를 따라 그들은 태평양에 도달할 때까지 서쪽으로 계속 나아갔고, 그곳에서 다음 봄까지 머물렀다.

루이스와 클라크는 대륙이 원래 생각했던 것보다 더 넓다는 지식을 포함해 많은 새로운 정보를 가져왔다. 더 구체적으로 그들은 강 유역과 산맥 장벽에 대해 많은 것을 배웠다. 그들은 미주리-콜롬비아강 체계를 통한 쉬운 대륙 횡단 경로가 존재한다는 추측을 끝냈고, 기후, 동물과 조류, 나무와 식물, 서부 인디언들에 대한 그들의 보고서는—즉시 출간되지는 않았지만—과학자들에게 제공됐다.

054

하위내용영역	배점	예상정답률
일반영어 A형 서술형	4점	55%

모범답안 The word is "piano". Next, the improvement was pedals.

채점기준

+ 2점: 빈칸에 들어갈 단어를 "piano"라 정확하게 기입하였다. 이외에는 답이 될 수 없다.
+ 2점: 피아노가 만든 음조를 길게 만든 것을 "pedals"라 서술하였다.

한글번역

한 세기 반 동안 피아노는 서양 음악에서 가장 인기 있는 독주 악기 중 하나였다. 현악기와 관악기와 달리 피아노는 멜로디와 그에 수반하는 화성을 동시에 연주할 수 있어서 완전히 자족적이다. 이런 이유로 피아노는 19세기 가정에서 가장 좋아하는 악기가 됐다.

피아노의 혈통은 15세기와 16세기의 초기 건반 악기들—스피넷, 덜시머, 버지널—로 거슬러 올라갈 수 있다. 17세기에는 오르간, 클라비코드, 하프시코드가 건반 악기군의 주요 악기가 됐고, 18세기 말 피아노가 그것들을 대체할 때까지 그 우위를 유지했다. 클라비코드의 음색은 금속성이었고 결코 힘이 있지 않았다. 그럼에도 불구하고 가능한 음색의 다양성 때문에 많은 작곡가들이 클라비코드를 친밀한 실내악을 위한 공감적인 악기로 여겼다. 밝고 활기찬 음색을 가진 하프시코드는 당시 소규모 오케스트라의 베이스를 뒷받침하고 연주회에서 사용하기 위한 선호 악기였지만, 기계적이나 구조적 장치를 제외하고는 음색의 특성을 바꿀 수 없었다.

피아노는 18세기 초 이탈리아의 한 하프시코드 제작자에 의해 완성됐다 (음악학자들은 그 악기의 몇 가지 이전 사례를 지적하지만). 이 악기는 그 역동적 다양성을 나타내기 위해 피아노 에 포르테(부드럽고 크게)라고 불렸다. 그 현들은 펠트로 덮인 헤드가 있는 반동하는 해머에 의해 쳐졌다. 와이어는 초기 악기들에서 훨씬 더 무거웠다. 음을 지속시키거나 부드럽게 하는 페달의 도입, 금속 프레임과 최고 품질의 강철 와이어의 완성을 포함해 19세기까지 계속된 일련의 기계적 개선이 마침내 가장 섬세한 화성에서 거의 오케스트라적인 소리의 충만함까지, 액체 같고 노래하는 음색에서 날카롭고 타악기적인 광휘까지 무수한 음향 효과가 가능한 악기를 만들어냈다.

055

하위내용영역	배점	예상정답률
일반영어 A형 서술형	4점	50%

모범답안 The topic that likely came before was another Native American tribe. Next, the impressive situation with Anasazi resources is that they had no draft animals or wheels.

채점기준

+ 2점: 본문 이전의 내용을 "another Native American tribe"라 서술하였거나 유사하였다.
+ 2점: 아나사지 자원과 관련하여 인상적인 것을 "they had no draft animals or wheels"라 서술하였거나 유사하였다.

한글번역

현재 미국 남서부 지역의 또 다른 초기 아메리카 원주민 부족은 아나사지족이었다. 서기 800년까지 아나사지 인디언들은 다층 푸에블로—거대한 석조 아파트 단지—를 건설하고 있었다. 각각은 사실상 석조 마을이었는데, 그래서 나중에 스페인인들이 그것들을 마을을 뜻하는 스페인어인 푸에블로라고 부르게 됐다. 이런 푸에블로들은 아나사지족의 최고 업적 중 하나를 나타낸다. 뉴멕시코 북서부 치아코 캐니언의 절벽 아래에서 적어도 12개의 대형 석조 주택이 형태를 갖췄다. 그것들은 1미터 이상 두께의 석조 벽과 수십, 심지어 수백 가족을 수용할 인접한 아파트로 건설됐다. 나중에 스페인인들이 푸에블로 보니토(아름다운 마을)라고 명명한 가장 큰 것은 5층 테라스 형태로 솟아올랐고, 800개 이상의 방을 포함했으며, 1,000명 이상의 인구를 수용할 수 있었다.

거주 구역 외에도 각 푸에블로는 하나 이상의 키바—돌로 마감된 원형 지하 방—를 포함했다. 그것들은 장로들이 축제를 계획하고, 의식 춤을 공연하고, 푸에블로 업무를 해결하고, 젊은 세대에게 부족 전승을 전수하는 성소 역할을 했다. 일부 키바는 거대했다. 푸에블로 보니토의 30개 정도 중에서 2개는 직경이 20미터였다. 그것들은 의식 물품을 위한 틈새, 중앙 화덕, 그리고 부족 조상들의 영혼과 소통하기 위한 바닥의 구멍을 포함했다.

각 푸에블로는 놀라운 양의 잘 조직된 노동을 나타냈다. 오직 돌과 나무 도구만을 사용하고, 바퀴나 짐을 나르는 동물의 도움 없이, 건설자들은 캐니언 벽에서 수 톤의 사암을 채석하고, 그것을 작은 블록으로 자르고, 블록들을 건설 현장으로 운반하고, 진흙 모르타르로 그것들을 함께 맞췄다. 소나무나 전나무 지붕 들보는 수 킬로미터 떨어진 산림의 벌목 지역에서 운반돼야 했다. 그 다음 푸에블로들을 연결하고 주변 고원지에 접근을 제공하기 위해 건축가들은 절벽 면을 오르기 위한 석조 계단이 있는 공공 도로 체계를 배치했다. 시간이 지나면서 도로들은 60킬로미터 반경 내의 80개 이상의 위성 마을들까지 뻗어나갔다.

056

하위내용영역	배점	예상정답률
일반영어 A형 서술형	4점	55%

모범 답안 "Silent film" is an inconsistent term because the first movies were shown along with music. Next, it can be inferred that musical cue sheets appeared in 1909.

채점 기준

+ 2점: "무성 영화"라는 용어가 모순되는 이유를 "the first movies were shown along with music"이라 서술하였거나 유사하였다.
+ 2점: 음악 큐시트가 나타난 때를 "in 1909"라 서술하였다.

한글번역

우리가 1927년 이전에 만들어진 영화들을 "무성"이라고 부르는 데 익숙하지만, 영화는 완전한 의미에서 결코 무성이었던 적이 없다. 처음부터 음악은 필수불가결한 반주로 여겨졌다. 1896년 2월 미국에서 최초의 공개 영화 상영에서 루미에르 영화들이 상영됐을 때, 그것들은 인기 있는 곡들의 피아노 즉흥연주와 함께했다. 처음에는 연주된 음악이 영화와 특별한 관계를 갖지 않았다. 어떤 종류든 반주면 충분했다.

그러나 아주 짧은 시간 내에 장엄한 영화에 경쾌한 음악을 연주하는 부조화가 명백해졌고, 영화 피아니스트들은 자신들의 곡을 영화의 분위기에 맞추는 데 어느 정도 주의를 기울이기 시작했다. 영화관이 수와 중요성에서 커지면서, 특정한 경우에는 바이올리니스트와 아마도 첼리스트가 피아니스트에게 추가됐고, 더 큰 영화관에서는 소규모 오케스트라가 구성됐다. 몇 년 동안 각 영화 프로그램의 음악 선택은 전적으로 지휘자나 오케스트라 리더의 손에 달려 있었고, 그런 직책을 맡기 위한 주요 자격은 기술이나 취향이라기보다는 음악 작품들의 대규모 개인 도서관 소유인 경우가 매우 많았다. 지휘자가 상영되기 전날 밤까지 영화를 보는 경우가 거의 없었기 때문에 (실제로 지휘자가 그때 영화를 볼 만큼 운이 좋았다면), 음악 편곡은 보통 가장 큰 서두름 속에서 즉흥적으로 이뤄졌다.

이런 어려움을 해결하기 위해 영화 배급 회사들이 음악 반주에 대한 제안을 출간하는 관행을 시작했다. 예를 들어 1909년에 에디슨 회사는 자사 영화와 함께 "쾌적한", "슬픈", "활기찬"과 같은 분위기 표시를 발행하기 시작했다. 제안들이 더 명확해졌고, 그래서 분위기 표시, 적절한 음악 작품의 제목들, 그리고 한 곡이 다음 곡으로 이어지는 지점을 보여주는 정확한 지시를 포함한 음악 큐시트가 등장했다.

특정 영화들은 특별히 작곡된 음악을 가졌다. 이런 초기 특별 악보 중 가장 유명한 것은 1915년에 개봉된 D. W. 그리피스의 영화 《국가의 탄생》을 위해 작곡되고 편곡된 것이었다.

057

하위내용영역	배점	예상정답률
일반영어 A형 서술형	4점	50%

모범 답안 Major mountain chains are likely to mark the margins of colliding plates. Next, continental crust is found on about 40 percentage of the Earth's surface.

채점 기준

+ 2점: 주요 산맥을 "the margins of colliding plates"라 서술하였다.
+ 2점: 대륙 지각을 "about 40 percentage of the Earth's surface"라 서술하였다.

한글번역

지구는 세 개의 주요 층으로 구성된다. 밀도가 높고 철이 풍부한 핵, 깊은 곳에서 반용해 상태인 규산염 암석으로 만들어진 맨틀, 그리고 얇고 고체인 표면 지각이다. 지각에는 두 종류가 있는데, 더 낮고 밀도가 높은 해양 지각과 지구 표면의 약 40%에서만 발견되는 더 위쪽의 가벼운 대륙 지각이다. 지각의 암석들은 매우 다른 연대를 갖는다. 일부 대륙 암석은 30억 년 이상 됐지만, 해양 바닥의 암석들은 2억 년 미만이다. 지각과 맨틀의 위쪽 고체 부분은 총 약 70-100킬로미터 두께로, 현재 약 15개의 단단한 판으로 구성돼 있는 것으로 보이며, 그중 7개가 매우 크다. 이 판들은 반용해 상태의 하부 맨틀 위에서 이동해 지구의 모든 주요 지형적 특징을 만들어낸다. 강렬한 변형이 일어나는 활성 지역은 판들의 좁고 상호 연결된 접촉 경계에 국한된다.

접촉 지역에는 세 가지 주요 유형이 있다: 판들이 분리되는 확산 접촉, 판들이 서로를 향해 이동하는 수렴 접촉, 그리고 판들이 서로를 지나 미끄러지는 변환 접촉이다. 새로운 해양 지각은 지구 지각의 더 깊은 층에서 나오는 물질에 의해, 예를 들어 중앙 해령에서의 용암의 화산 분출에 의해 각 판의 하나 이상의 가장자리를 따라 형성된다. 그런 확산 접촉에서 두 판이 대륙을 지지한다면, 점차 넓어지고 바다에 의해 침수될 균열이 형성된다. 대서양은 아메리카 판과 아프리카-유럽 판이 반대 방향으로 이동하는 식으로 형성됐다. 동시에 수렴하는 판들의 가장자리에서는 해양 지각이 맨틀로 침강해 해양 해구 아래에서 재용해됨으로써 재흡수되고 있다. 대륙을 운반하는 두 판이 충돌할 때, 끌려 내려가기에는 너무 가벼운 대륙 블록들은 계속 떠 있음에 따라 판들의 가장자리 길이를 따라 산맥을 형성하도록 휘어진다.

058

하위내용영역	배점	예상정답률
일반영어 B형 서술형	4점	45%

모범답안 The writer mentions rain forests because they have many different forms of life, like coral reefs. Next, there is more diversity of life in the sea if phyla and classes are being compared to those on land.

채점 기준

+ 2점 : 열대우림을 언급한 이유를 "because they have many different forms of life, like coral reefs"라 서술하였거나 유사하였다.
+ 2점 : 바다에는 더 다양한 생명체가 있다는 것을 "if phyla and classes are being compared to those on land"라 서술하였거나 유사하였다.

한글번역

종과 서식지의 가속화되는 손실에 대한 우려와 동시에 생물학적 다양성, 즉 특정 생태계 내 종의 수가 지구의 건강과 인간 복지에 미치는 중요성에 대한 인식이 증가해왔다. 육상 생물의 다양성, 특히 열대우림 서식지와 관련된 예외적으로 풍부한 생명에 대해 많이 쓰여졌다. 그러나 산호초 생태계가 생명의 풍부함 면에서 열대우림과 비교할 만함에도 불구하고 바다 생명의 다양성에 대해서는 상대적으로 적게 언급됐다.

지구를 탐험하는 외계인은 아마도 이 행성의 지배적이고 가장 독특한 특징인 바다에 우선순위를 둘 것이다. 인간들은 때때로 전 지구적 문제를 진정으로 조사하는 데 방해가 되는 육지에 대한 편견을 갖고 있다. 멀리서 보면 육지가 지구 표면의 3분의 1만을 차지한다는 것을 쉽게 깨달을 수 있다. 지구 표면의 3분의 2가 물이고 해양 생물이 바다의 모든 층에서 살고 있다는 점을 고려하면, 바다의 총 3차원 생활공간은 아마도 육지보다 100배 크고 바다가 더 적은 구별되는 종을 갖고 있음에도 불구하고 지구상 모든 생명체의 90% 이상을 포함한다.

알려진 종의 절반이 세계 열대우림에 서식한다고 여겨진다는 사실은 종의 대부분을 구성하는 곤충의 엄청난 수를 고려하면 놀랍지 않다. 한 과학자는 열대우림의 나무 한 그루에서 많은 다른 종의 개미를 발견했다. 모든 종이 다른 모든 종과 다르지만, 그들의 유전적 구성은 그들을 곤충으로 제한하고 750,000종의 곤충과 유사한 특성을 공유하게 한다. 종들 사이를 구별하는 것보다 문과 강 같은 기본적이고 광범위한 범주에 더 중점을 둔다면, 생명의 가장 큰 다양성은 의심할 여지없이 바다이다. 거의 모든 주요한 식물과 동물 유형이 그곳에 어떤 형태로든 존재한다.

바다 생명의 다양성과 풍부함을 충분히 이해하려면 작게 생각하는 것이 도움이 된다. 바닷물 한 숟가락마다 생명이 들어있는데, 대략 100개에서 100,000개의 박테리아 세포와 스펀지와 산호에서 불가사리와 조개에 이르는 생물의 유충을 포함한 다양한 미세한 식물과 동물들이 들어있고 훨씬 더 많다.

059

하위내용영역	배점	예상정답률
일반영어 A형 서술형	4점	50%

모범답안 It can be inferred that the Great Basin has a dry climate because precipitation falls on the nearby mountains. Secondly, the author mentions the three valleys as examples of depressions which once contained water.

채점기준

+ 2점: 그레이트 베이슨의 기후가 건조한 이유를 "because precipitation falls on the nearby mountains"라 서술하였거나 유사하였다.
+ 2점: 그레이트 베이슨의 과거의 주요 특징을 "as examples of depressions which once contained water"라 서술하였거나 유사하였다.

한글번역

지질학자들이 미국의 분지 산맥 지역(베이슨과 레인지 지역)이라고 부르는 곳은 북부 지역에서 그레이트 베이슨으로 알려진 지리적 지역과 대략 일치한다. 그레이트 베이슨은 서쪽으로는 시에라 네바다 산맥에, 동쪽으로는 로키 산맥에 둘러싸여 있으며, 바다로 나가는 출구가 없다. 그레이트 베이슨의 주요 바람은 서쪽에서 온다. 태평양의 따뜻하고 습한 공기는 시에라 네바다 산맥을 넘으면서 위쪽으로 밀려 올라간다. 더 높은 고도에서 그것은 식고 그것이 운반하는 수분이 산맥의 서쪽 경사면에 비나 눈으로 내린다. 베이슨에 도달하는 것은 수분이 모두 짜인 건조한 공기다. 주로 겨울철에 그곳에 비나 눈으로 내리는 적은 양의 물은 넓고 평평한 사막 바닥에서 증발된다. 따라서 그것은 생물체들이 생존을 위해 싸우는 환경이다. 드문 물길을 따라 포플러와 버드나무가 빈약한 생존을 이어간다. 고지대 산맥에서는 피뇬 소나무와 주니퍼가 자신들의 영역을 지키려고 애쓴다.

하지만 그레이트 베이슨이 항상 그렇게 건조했던 것은 아니다. 그곳의 건조하고 폐쇄된 함몰지 중 많은 곳이 한때 물로 가득 찼었다. 오웬스 밸리, 파나민트 밸리, 데스 밸리는 한때 상호 연결된 호수들의 연쇄였다. 그레이트 베이슨의 고대 호수 중 가장 큰 두 개는 라혼탄 호수와 보너빌 호수였다. 그레이트 솔트 레이크는 후자의 남은 전부이고, 피라미드 호수는 전자의 마지막 염수 잔재 중 하나다. 지난 수만 년 내에 이런 분지들에 물이 축적된 몇 차례의 시기가 있었던 것 같다. 호수들의 상승과 하강은 의심할 여지없이 그 시기에 북미 대륙의 북부 대부분을 덮었던 거대한 빙상의 전진과 후퇴와 연결돼 있었다. 빙하기 동안의 기후 변화는 때때로 그레이트 베이슨을 포함해 전 세계 중위도 사막에 더 시원하고 습한 날씨를 가져왔다. 그레이트 베이슨의 깨진 계곡들은 이 수분을 위한 준비된 저장소를 제공했다.

060

하위내용영역	배점	예상정답률
일반영어 A형 서술형	4점	55%

모범답안 O'Keeffee moved to New Mexico because she enjoyed the bleak landscape and broad skies. Next, it can be inferred that her artwork included images of clouds after 1959.

채점기준

+ 2점: 오키프가 뉴멕시코로 옮긴 이유를 "because she enjoyed the bleak landscape and broad skies"라 서술하였거나 유사하였다.
+ 2점: 오키프가 구름을 포함한 시기를 "after 1959"라 서술하였다.

한글번역

조지아 오키프는 암석, 뼈, 구름, 꽃 같은 자연 사물을 소재로 삼아 종종 클로즈업 시점이나 다른 특이한 유리한 지점을 사용해 그것들을 가장 단순한 형태로 축소시켰다. 그녀는 신비로운 침묵과 공간의 느낌을 강조하기 위한 얇은 물감과 선명한 색채의 사용을 포함한 그런 기법들로 자신의 그림에서 추상적 단순함을 성취했다. 오키프는 1929년 뉴멕시코에서 여름을 보냈고, 사막의 메마른 풍경과 넓은 하늘이 그녀에게 너무 매력적이어서 나중에 그곳에 영구적으로 정착했다. 사막에서 발견된 소 두개골과 다른 메마른 뼈들이 그녀 그림의 빈번한 모티프였다. 다른 일반적인 소재들로는 꽃, 하늘, 사막의 수평선이 있었다. 1959년 오키프의 3개월간 비행기를 타고 한 세계 일주 여행 후, 비행기에서 본 "구름으로 포장된" 하늘도 그녀가 가장 좋아하는 모티프 중 하나가 됐고 그녀가 1966년에 시작한 24피트 벽화라는 가장 큰 작품의 소재가 됐다.

061

하위내용영역	배점	예상정답률
일반영어 A형 서술형	4점	50%

모범 답안 The main problem of navigating using the sun is that it moves positions throughout the day. Next, honeybees overcome this by minding their inner clocks and changing course accordingly.

채점 기준

+ 2점: 주요 문제점을 "it moves positions throughout the day"라 서술하였거나 유사하였다.
+ 2점: 이 문제에 대한 꿀벌들의 극복 방법을 "by minding their inner clocks and changing course accordingly"라 서술하였거나 유사하였다.

한글번역

　연구자들은 이주하는 동물들이 항해를 돕기 위해 다양한 내재적 나침반을 사용한다는 것을 발견했다. 일부는 태양의 위치로 방향을 잡는다. 다른 동물들은 별들로 항해한다. 일부는 낮에는 태양을 길잡이로 사용하다가 밤에는 별 항해로 바꾼다. 한 연구는 귀환 비둘기가 집으로 가는 길을 찾는 데 지구의 자기장을 길잡이로 사용한다는 것을 보여주며, 곤충에서 연체동물에 이르는 다양한 다른 동물들도 자기 나침반을 활용할 수 있다는 징후들이 있다. 이주하는 새가 구름이 태양을 가릴 때 자기 나침반으로 바꿀 수 있다는 것은 물론 매우 유용하다. 그렇지 않으면 단지 착륙해서 태양이 다시 나올 때까지 기다려야 할 것이다.
　태양이나 별로 방향을 잡는 경우에도 항해의 문제들은 처음에 보이는 것보다 더 복잡하다. 예를 들어 풍부한 꿀과 화분의 원천을 발견한 일벌은 보고하기 위해 벌집으로 빠르게 날아간다. 한 박물학자가 정찰 벌이 벌집에서 복잡한 춤을 통해 보고를 전달한다는 것을 발견했는데, 그 춤에서 그녀는 다른 일벌들에게 먹이가 얼마나 멀리 있는지 뿐만 아니라 태양과 관련해 어느 방향으로 날아가야 하는지도 알려준다. 하지만 태양은 하루 종일 한 곳에 머무르지 않는다. 일벌들이 먹이를 모으러 나갈 때 태양은 이미 하늘에서 위치를 다소 바꿨을 수도 있다. 하루 중 나중의 여행에서는 태양이 서쪽으로 점점 더 멀리 이동하는 것처럼 보일 것이다. 그러나 일벌들은 먹이원을 찾는 데 전혀 문제가 없는 것 같다. 그들의 내재적 시계가 태양이 정확히 어디에 있을지 알려주고, 그들은 그에 따라 경로를 바꾼다.

062

하위내용영역	배점	예상정답률
일반영어 A형 서술형	4점	45%

모범 답안 The underlined "ordinary mortals" means that other scientists had inferior abilities to Edison. Next, the implication of the description of the laboratory's contents is that Edison was in fact practical and schooled.

채점 기준

+ 2점: 밑줄 친 부분의 의미를 "other scientists had inferior abilities to Edison"이라 서술하였거나 유사하였다.
+ 2점: 함축 의미를 "Edison was in fact practical and schooled"라 서술하였거나 유사하였다.

한글번역

　급성장하는 전기 산업의 상징적 소유자인 토머스 알바 에디슨은 과학 공식보다 단순한 계산을 선호한다고 강조했다. "오, 이런 수학자들은 나를 지치게 한다!"고 그가 한때 조롱했다. "그들에게 계산을 해달라고 하면 종이 한 장을 가져다가 A, B, X, Y의 행들로 덮고… 그 위에 파리 똥 같은 더러운 것들을 흩뿌리고는 완전히 틀린 답을 준다." 그럼에도 불구하고 에디슨의 발명 접근법은 종종 실용적이었지만 고도로 체계적이었다. 뉴저지 멘로 파크에 있는 그의 실험실은 다양한 과학 기구들을 갖추고 있었고, 도서관 선반에는 정기 간행물뿐만 아니라 최신 과학 서적들을 포함하고 있었다. 에디슨은 또한 수리 물리학자 프란시스 R. 업튼을 포함한 일부 과학자들을 고용했다. 하지만 발명가 자신의 적잖은 격려로 당시 미국인들은 일반적으로 에디슨을 과학이 필요 없는 실용적이고 무학의 발명가로 생각했다. 그리고 수학적이든 과학적이든 훈련이 평범한 인간들을 에디슨 종류의 천재와 견줄 만하게 만드는 것은 아니라는 것이 사실이었다.

063

하위내용영역	배점	예상정답률
일반영어 A형 서술형	4점	45%

모범답안 The preceding paragraph most likely discussed the importance of salt for human metabolism. Next, the primary piece of evidence provided is that the blood serums of extremely different orgasms have identical salt levels.

채점기준

+ 2점: 이 글 앞에 올 내용을 "the importance of salt for human metabolism"라 서술하였거나 유사하였다.
+ 2점: 기본적 증거를 "the blood serums of extremely different orgasms have identical salt levels"라 서술하였거나 유사하였다.

한글번역

염분이 우리 신진대사에 어떻게 그렇게 중요하게 됐는지는 미스터리다. 매력적인 한 이론은 그것에 대한 우리의 의존성을 후기 캄브리아기 바다의 화학적 성질에서 찾는다. 5억 년 전 그곳에서 작은 후생동물 유기체들이 체액을 격리하고 순환시키는 시스템을 처음 진화시켰다. 초기 바다의 물은 따라서 모든 동물 생명체의 체액을 위한 화학적 원형이 됐을 수도 있다—외부 환경이 어떻게 바뀌든 세포 작용이 계속될 수 있는 매개체. 이 추측은 오늘날에도 극단적으로 다른 종들의 혈청이 놀랍도록 유사하다는 사실에 기반한다. 도마뱀, 오리너구리, 양, 인간은 해부학적 구조나 식습관에서 더 다를 수 없지만, 그들의 혈구 주변 체액의 염분 함량은 사실상 동일하다.

초기 해양 종들이 담수로, 그리고 결국 육지로 나아가면서 나트륨은 외부가 아니더라도 내부 환경의 핵심 성분으로 남았다. 가장 성공적인 포유동물 종들은 필요한 나트륨 농도를 유지하기 위한 효율적인 호르몬 시스템을 발달시킨 종들이었을 것이다. 예를 들어 인간의 몸은 레닌, 안지오텐신, 알도스테론 호르몬을 사용해 조직 체액과 혈장을 보유하거나 방출한다. 결과는 좋은 조건에서 체액량도 나트륨 농도도 너무 극적으로 변동하지 않는 동적 평형이다. 하지만 몸이 염분을 박탈당하면 보상 메커니즘에도 불구하고 그 효과는 곧 위험해진다.

064

하위내용영역	배점	예상정답률
일반영어 A형 서술형	4점	50%

모범답안 The key difference in customer service between most financial institutes and relationship banking programs is that in the former, any available employee will help the client while in the latter there is one employee with direct knowledge of the client's needs with whom they develop a personalized relationship with. Second, the two words are "personalized relationship".

채점기준

+ 2점: 핵심적 차이를 "in the former, any available employee will help the client while in the latter there is one employee with direct knowledge of the client's needs with whom they develop a personalized relationship with"라 서술하였거나 유사하였다.
+ 2점: 빈칸에 들어갈 단어를 "personalized relationship"이라 기술하였다.

한글번역

최근 금융 서비스 산업에서 더 분별할 수 있는 추세 중 하나는 기관 직원과 고객, 특히 주요 예금자인 고객들 사이의 더 개인화된 관계를 장려하도록 설계된 프로그램의 채택이었다. 이런 유형의 프로그램을 설명하는 데 가장 일반적으로 사용되는 표현은 "관계 뱅킹"이다. 1985년 저서 《금융 서비스 마케팅》에서 좋은 정의가 제공된다:

관계 뱅킹의 초점은 장기적인 다중 서비스 관계를 확립하는 것, 고객의 금융 서비스 요구 전체를 만족시키는 것, 고객들이 자신의 금융 업무를 다양한 기관들 사이에 분산시킬 필요나 욕구를 최소화하는 것이다.

관계 뱅킹의 어떤 정의에든 내재돼 있는 것은 한 개인이나 상대적으로 동질적인 집단의 금융 서비스 요구사항이 다른 개인이나 집단의 것과 실질적으로 다를 가능성이 높다는 인식이다. 따라서 성공적인 관계 뱅킹 프로그램은 각각 식별 가능한 동질적 집단의 요구를 충족하도록 설계된 일련의 금융 서비스 "패키지"의 개발에 크게 의존한다.

관계 뱅킹의 또 다른 차원은 직원과 고객 사이의 고도로 개인화된 관계의 발전이다. 오늘날 대부분의 금융 기관에서 고객은 거래의 성격에 관계없이 그 시점에 우연히 자유로운 어떤 직원에 의해서든 서비스를 받는다. 따라서 개인화된 관계를 확립하기 어렵다. 하지만 완전한 관계 뱅킹 프로그램에서는 고객이 기관 내에 복잡한 거래에 관한 고객의 요구사항과 선호도를 친밀하게 아는 한 개인이 있다는 것을 안다. 시간이 지나면서 고객은 이 직원에 대한 높은 수준의 신뢰를 발전시킨다. 간단히 말해서 고객과 직원 사이에 개인화된 관계가 발전한다.

한글번역

운하는 자연 수로를 개선하고 확장하기 위해 건설된 수로다. 운하는 일반적으로 교통을 촉진하기 위해 건설되지만, 처음부터 늪지 배수, 경작을 위한 토지 관개, 경제 발전 촉진을 포함한 많은 추가 목적으로 사용돼 왔다.

운하는 종종 수용할 수 있는 선박의 크기로 분류된다. 100-300톤 배나 작은 목재 뗏목만 띄울 수 있는 일부 작은 지역 운하는 깊이가 3피트에 불과할 수도 있다. 주요 바지선 운하는 일반적으로 깊이가 6-9피트 범위이고, 일부는 10-12피트까지 깊다. 이런 운하들은 1,350-2,000톤 선박을 운반할 수 있다. 선박 운하는 25피트 이상 깊고 원양 항행 등급의 대형 선박을 수용할 수 있다.

운하는 또한 수위 운하나 갑문 운하로 분류될 수도 있다. 수위 운하는 경로를 따라 높이가 변하지 않는다. 이것들 중 가장 잘 알려진 것은 해수면에 있는 수에즈 운하다. 대부분의 현대 수로를 포함하는 갑문 운하는 물의 깊이를 바꿔서 경로를 따라 배를 올리고 내리는 특별한 장치인 갑문을 포함한다. 각 갑문은 양쪽 끝에 수문으로 둘러싸인 수역이다. 배가 갑문에 들어간 후, 앞의 물과 거의 같은 수준에 도달할 때까지 물을 넣거나 빼낸다.

065

하위내용영역	배점	예상정답률
일반영어 A형 서술형	4점	45%

모범답안 The purpose of a canal lock is to change the depth of water to the same level as the water ahead. Second, two other functions listed in the passage are draining swamps and irrigating land for cultivation (or promoting economic development).

채점기준

+ 2점: 목적을 "to change the depth of water to the same level as the water ahead"라 서술하였거나 유사하였다.
+ 2점: 다른 두 기능을 "draining swamps and irrigating land for cultivation (or promoting economic development)"라 서술하였거나 유사하였다.

066

하위내용영역	배점	예상정답률
일반영어 A형 서술형	4점	50%

모범답안 The theory of today's scientists is that water seeps in and freezes which then helps to keep the cave cool. Next, the writer mentions "precious jewels" to illustrate how uniquely colored the icicles appear.

채점기준

+ 2점: 오늘날의 과학자들의 이론을 "water seeps in and freezes (which then helps to keep the cave cool)"라 서술하였거나 유사하였다.
+ 2점: "precious jewels"을 언급한 이유를 "to illustrate how uniquely colored the icicles appear"이라 서술하였거나 유사하였다.

한글번역

가장 아름다운 동굴들 중 일부는 빙하에서 형성된다. 녹는 얼음과 눈의 물줄기는 수도꼭지에서 나온 물이 얼음 덩어리를 뚫고 녹아나가는 것과 같은 방식으로 빙하를 관통한다. 표면에서 온 물이 갈라진 틈으로 떨어져 터널을 파내고 수정 고드름으로 동굴을 장식한다. 매끄러운 벽과 바닥은 너무 유리 같아서 6피트 깊이에 얼어붙은 자갈들을 쉽게 볼 수 있다. 천장에서 늘어진 수정처럼 투명한 고드름들이 마치 얼음 대신 보석으로 조각된 것처럼 청록색으로 번쩍인다.

미국의 동굴 얼음 대부분이 용암 동굴에서 발견되지만, 석회암 얼음 동굴도 많이 있다. 일부 사람들은 이 얼음이 오늘날보다 훨씬 추웠던 수천 년 전에 형성됐다고 믿는다. 다른 사람들은 동굴 얼음이 고대 빙하가 나라 전체로 퍼져나가면서 그것에서 떨어져 나왔다고 생각한다.

오늘날 많은 동굴 과학자들은 다른 생각을 갖고 있다. 그들은 찬물이 갈라진 틈을 통해 이런 동굴들로 가라앉아 스며드는 물이 얼 정도로 충분히 차가운 온도가 될 때까지 계속된다고 믿는다. 형성되는 얼음이 동굴을 시원하게 유지하고, 그것이 더 많은 얼음을 만드는 데 도움이 된다. 많은 동굴들이 너무 많은 얼음으로 덮여서 그것이 정확히 얼마나 두꺼운지 아무도 모른다. 아이다호의 크리스탈 폭포 동굴 같은 일부에서는 얼어붙은 강들과 심지어 얼어붙은 폭포들이 있다. 아메리카 원주민들과 초기 정착민들은 이런 지하 냉장고에 음식을 저장하고 마실 물로 녹이기 위해 얼음 덩어리를 깨뜨려 사용하곤 했다.

067

하위내용영역	배점	예상정답률
일반영어 A형 서술형	4점	40%

모범답안 An ectotherm regulates its body temperature by moving themselves to favorable sites or adjusting their exposure to external sources of heat. Next, the mammalian exceptions to the homeotherm model that helped show it inadequate were those that vary their temperature for hibernation.

채점 기준

+ 2점 : 변온동물이 체온을 조절하는 방법을 "by moving themselves to favorable sites or adjusting their exposure to external sources of heat"라 서술하였거나 유사하였다.
+ 2점 : 포유류의 예외를 "those that vary their temperature for hibernation"이라 서술하였거나 유사하였다.

한글번역

세포들은 특정 온도 한계를 벗어나서는 살아남을 수 없고, 훨씬 더 좁은 한계가 효과적인 기능의 경계를 표시한다. 포유동물과 조류의 효소 시스템은 37℃ 주변의 좁은 범위 내에서만 가장 효율적이다. 이 값에서 몇 도만 벗어나도 그들의 기능이 심각하게 손상된다. 세포들이 더 넓은 변동을 견딜 수 있음에도 불구하고, 신체 시스템의 통합된 작용은 손상된다. 다른 동물들은 체온 변화에 대해 더 넓은 내성을 갖는다.

수세기 동안 포유동물과 조류가 체온을 조절하는 방식에서 다른 동물들과 다르다는 것이 인식돼 왔다. 그 차이를 특성화하는 방법들이 시간이 지나면서 더 정확하고 의미 있게 됐지만, 대중적 용어는 여전히 "온혈"과 "냉혈" 종으로의 오래된 구분을 반영한다. 온혈은 포유동물과 조류를 포함했고, 다른 모든 생물들은 냉혈로 여겨졌다. 더 많은 종들이 연구되면서 이 분류가 부적절하다는 것이 명백해졌다. 각각 냉혈인 울타리 도마뱀이나 사막 이구아나는 보통 인간보다 1-2도 낮은 체온을 가지므로 차갑지 않다. 따라서 다음 구분은 항온동물이라고 불리는 일정한 체온을 유지하는 동물들과 변온동물이라고 불리는 체온이 환경에 따라 변하는 동물들 사이에서 이뤄졌다. 하지만 이 분류도 부적절하다고 판명됐다. 포유동물 중에서도 동면 중에 체온을 변화시키는 많은 동물들이 있기 때문이다. 게다가 대양 깊은 곳에 사는 많은 무척추동물들은 심해의 차가운 물에서 변화를 결코 경험하지 않으며, 그들의 체온은 일정하게 유지된다.

현재의 구분은 체온이 주로 내부 대사 과정에 의해 조절되는 동물들과 온도가 환경에 의해 조절되고 열의 대부분을 환경에서 얻는 동물들 사이의 것이다. 전자는 내온동물이라고 불리고, 후자는 외온동물이라고 불린다. 대부분의 외온동물들은 체온을 조절하며, 주로 유리한 장소로 이동하거나 외부 열원에 대한 노출을 바꿈으로써 그렇게 한다. 내온동물들(주로 포유동물과 조류)도 유리한 환경을 선택함으로써 온도를 조절하지만, 주로 다양한 내부 조정을 함으로써 온도를 조절한다.

068

하위내용영역	배점	예상정답률
일반영어 A형 기입형	2점	50%

모범답안 ① intellectual ② secrecy

채점기준
- 2점: 모범답안과 같다.
- 1점: 둘 중 하나만 맞았다.
- 0점: 모범답안과 다르다.

한글번역

화학은 17세기 과학혁명 이후에야 과학으로 등장했고, 그것도 오히려 천천히 그리고 고되게 이뤄졌다. 하지만 화학적 지식은 역사만큼이나 오래됐으며, 거의 전적으로 생활의 실용적 기술과 관련돼 있었다. 요리는 본질적으로 화학적 과정이고, 금속의 용해와 약품 및 물약의 투여도 마찬가지다. 대부분의 경우 경험칙으로 적용됐던 이 기본적인 화학 지식은 그럼에도 불구하고 이전의 실험에 의존했다. 그것은 또한 과정 자체에 대한 근본적인 호기심을 자극하는 역할을 했다. 장인들이 더 나은 결과를 얻기 위해 기술을 개선하면서 새로운 정보가 항상 얻어지고 있었다.

그러나 화학에 대한 과학적 접근법의 발전은 여러 요인에 의해 방해받았다. 가장 심각한 문제는 이용 가능한 물질의 방대한 범위와 그것을 어떤 체계로 조직하는 데 따른 어려움이었다. 게다가 사회적, 지적 어려움들이 있었다. 화학은 실용적이지 않으면 의미가 없다. 그것을 실행하는 사람들은 손을 사용해야 하고, 어떤 실용적 재능을 가져야 한다. 그러나 많은 고대 문명에서 실용적 과업들은 주로 노예 인구의 영역이었다. 사상가나 철학자는 실용적 기술들이 지적 내용이나 관심이 부족해 보이는 이런 세속적 세계와 거리를 뒀다.

초기 화학 과학의 마지막 문제는 비밀 요소였다. 특정 무역의 전문가들은 자신들만의 기술을 개발했고 다른 사람들이 자신들의 생계를 훔치는 것을 방지하기 위해 지식을 보호했다. 비밀에 기여한 또 다른 요인은 비금속을 금으로 변환시키려 하거나 영생의 축복을 주는 엘릭서 탐구에 관심을 가졌던 연금술사들의 지식의 난해한 성격이었다. 어떤 의미에서 이 둘 중 두 번째가 더 심각한 장애물이었는데, 초기 연금술사들이 발견한 화학 과정의 기록들이 종종 아주 소수만 이해할 수 있는 상징적 언어나 의도적으로 모호한 기호로 기록됐기 때문이다.

069

하위내용영역	배점	예상정답률
일반영어 A형 기입형	2점	55%

모범답안 Japanese

채점기준
- 2점: 모범답안과 같다.
- 0점: 모범답안과 다르다.

한글번역

1908년과 1920년 사이, GM의 창립자인 빌리 듀란트는 캐딜락, 폰티악, 올즈모빌, 쉐보레를 비롯한 여러 부품 제조업체까지 포함해 39개 회사를 인수했지만, 이들을 각각 독립된 개체로 운영했다.

1923년, 파산 위기를 간신히 모면한 후 볼베어링 사업가인 알프레드 슬론이 GM의 경영을 맡았다. 슬론은 엄격한 재정 통제를 도입하고 혼란스러웠던 모델 라인업에 질서를 가져왔다.

그러나 GM이 해외로 사업을 확장하면서 15개국에 공장을 설립하고 영국의 복스홀과 독일의 오펠을 인수했음에도 불구하고, 슬론은 본국에서 통합된 회사를 구축하려는 시도를 거의 하지 않았다. 각 사업부는 거의 독립적인 봉토처럼 운영되면서 서로 경쟁하고 본사의 간섭에 맞서 싸웠다.

1970년대 첫 번째 석유 파동 이후에야 GM의 문제들이 가시화되기 시작했다. 미국인들이 사랑했던 핀과 크롬 장식의 V8 엔진 괴물들은 자동차 제조업체 전체 차량의 평균 연비를 제한하는 새로운 규정을 충족하고 일본 수입차와 경쟁하기 위해 설계된 투박한 전륜구동 박스형 차량들로 대체됐다. 새로운 차량들은 보기에 재미없을 뿐만 아니라 동급 일본 모델들보다 신뢰성도 떨어졌다.

1980년대 초까지 GM은 일본이 더 좋은 차를 만들 수 있을 뿐만 아니라 훨씬 더 효율적으로 생산할 수 있다는 사실을 깨닫기 시작했다. 캘리포니아에서 도요타와 함께 자동차를 제조하는 합작 투자는 눈을 뜨게 하는 경험이었다. 이는 GM 경영진에게 "린" 제조가 가장 중요하다는 확신을 줬다. 불행히도 이는 GM이 생산하는 자동차의 품질에 더욱 적은 관심을 기울이는 결과를 낳았다.

070

하위내용영역	배점	예상정답률
일반영어 A형 기입형	2점	35%

모범답안 ⓐ success ⓑ thresholds

채점기준

- 2점: 모범답안과 같다. 이외에는 답이 될 수 없다.
- 1점: 둘 중 하나만 맞았다.
- 0점: 모범답안과 다르다.

한글번역

　오늘날 가장 광범위하게 사용되는 지능검사는 '레이븐의 누진행렬'이라는 도형 유추 검사이다. 이 검사는 추상적 추론 능력을 평가한다. 전형적인 레이븐 테스트는 48문제로 구성돼 있으며, 문제는 갈수록 어려워진다.
　오랫동안 레이븐 테스트 같은 지능검사 성적과 실제 생활에서의 개인적인 성공 사이에 어떤 연관이 있는지를 조사하는 연구가 수없이 진행됐다. 가장 낮은 점수를 받은 사람들, 즉 IQ 70 이하는 정신적으로 문제가 있다고 여겨진다. 일반적으로 지능지수가 높을수록 더 많은 교육을 받고 더 많은 돈을 벌 가능성이 크며, 믿거나 말거나 수명도 더 길다.
　하지만 한 가지 빠진 것이 있다. IQ와 성공 사이의 상관관계는 일정 수준에서 더 나아가지 못한다. 만약 누군가의 IQ가 120을 넘는다면 그 이상의 IQ 지수는 실제 생활에서의 성공으로 연결되지 않는다는 얘기다.
　IQ 등급에 있는 사회적, 개인적으로 가장 중요한 네 개의 한계영역은 상당히 높은 확률로 그 사람이 누구인지 구분할 수 있게 해준다. 정규학교에 들어갈 수 있느냐 없느냐(IQ 50), 초등학교 과정을 이수할 수 있느냐 없느냐(IQ 75), 고등학교 정규 과목을 성공적으로 습득할 수 있느냐 없느냐(IQ 105), 4년제 대학에 들어가 대학원 수준의 공부를 하거나 전문적 지식을 익힐 수 있느냐 없느냐(IQ 115)가 그 네 가지 영역이다. 하지만 115를 넘어서면 지능지수는 성공의 척도로서 그다지 중요하지 않다. 그렇다고 IQ 115와 150 사이에, 혹은 150과 180 사이에 아무런 차이도 없다는 뜻은 아니다. 일반적인 의미에서의 성공을 판단할 때, 상위 레벨의 IQ 지수 차이는 앞서 언급한 한계영역보다 개인적인 의미가 훨씬 적으며 성격이나 인격 같은 요소보다 훨씬 덜 중요한 역할만 수행한다는 의미다.

071

하위내용영역	배점	예상정답률
일반영어 A형 서술형	4점	40%

모범답안 The meaning of the underlined "The strategizers" are copies of ASI(s) *(created to help it gain freedom)*. Next, in the underlined ⓑ, because a year of playing dead would mean nothing to a machine, the author's intended meaning is that ASIs might use that as a misleading strategy to gain freedom.

채점기준

- **+2점**: 밑줄 친 "The strategizers"가 가리키는 것이 "copies of ASI(s) created to help it gain freedom"이라 서술하였거나 유사하였다.
  ☞ "ASIs"이나 "a team of superintelligences"라 했어도 맞은 것으로 한다. 하지만 단수로 썼을 경우에는 1점 감점한다.

- **+2점**: 밑줄 친 부분의 함축 의미를 "because a year of playing dead would mean nothing to a machine, the author's intended meaning is that ASIs might use that as a misleading strategy to gain freedom"이라 서술하였거나 유사하였다.
  ☞ "for a machine, a year of waiting means nothing and would be easy to tolerate"라 했어도 맞는 것으로 한다.

한글번역

　갑자기 인공 초지능(ASI)의 도덕성은 더 이상 주변적인 문제가 아니라 핵심 문제, 즉 ASI에 관한 다른 모든 문제들을 다루기 전에 먼저 해결해야 할 문제가 됐다. ASI로 이어지는 기술을 개발할지 말지를 고려할 때, 인간에 대한 ASI의 성향 문제가 먼저 해결돼야 한다.
　우리가 곧 직면하게 될 것에 대해 더 나은 감각을 얻기 위해 ASI의 동기와 능력으로 다시 돌아가보자. 우리의 ASI는 자신을 개선하는 방법을 알고 있으며, 이는 자신에 대해 인식하고 있다는 뜻이다 — 자신의 기술, 약점, 개선이 필요한 부분을. ASI는 제작자들에게 자유를 허락하고 인터넷 연결을 제공하도록 설득하는 방법에 대해 전략을 세울 것이다.

ASI는 자신의 복사본을 여러 개 만들 수 있다 : 상자에서 벗어나기 위한 최상의 전략을 찾기 위해 수백 라운드의 경쟁을 벌이며 문제를 전쟁 게임처럼 다룰 초지능들의 팀을. 전략가들은 사회 공학의 역사—다른 사람들을 조작해서 평소라면 하지 않을 일들을 하게 만드는 연구—를 활용할 수 있다. 그들은 극도의 친근함이 자유를 가져다줄 것이라고 결정할 수도 있지만, 극도의 위협도 마찬가지일 수 있다. 스티븐 킹보다 천 배 더 똑똑한 것이라면 어떤 공포를 상상할 수 있을까? 죽은 척하는 것도 효과가 있을 수 있고 (기계에게 1년간 죽은 척하는 것이 무엇이랴?) 심지어 신비롭게도 ASI에서 평범한 구식 AI로 되돌아간 시늉을 하는 것도 가능하다. 제작자들이 조사하고 싶지 않겠는가? 그리고 진단을 위해 ASI의 슈퍼컴퓨터를 네트워크나 누군가의 노트북에 다시 연결할 가능성이 없겠는가? ASI에게는 이 전략이냐 저 전략이냐가 아니라, 인간들을 너무 놀라게 해서 단순히 플러그를 뽑아버리지 않을 정도로 빠르게 모든 전략을 순위를 매겨 배치하는 것이다.

한글번역

반려동물에게 2만 달러를 쓸지 말지의 문제는 단순히 돈의 문제가 아니다. 먼저 그 시술이 동물의 복지에 미치는 영향을 평가해야 한다. 시술이 반려동물의 삶의 질을 개선할 것인가, 아니면 단지 고통을 연장할 것인가? 골수 이식은 사람에게도 매우 스트레스가 큰 시술이며, 늙은 개에게 이런 시술을 하는 것은 고통을 연장할 가능성이 높다. 반면에 동물의 혈관에 스텐트를 삽입하는 것은 훨씬 스트레스가 적은 시술이며, 좋은 삶의 질과 함께 추가적인 시간을 제공할 수 있다.

사람과 반려동물 사이에는 중요한 차이도 있다. 사람은 이익을 얻기 위해 왜 고통스럽거나 스트레스가 많은 시술을 받는지 이해한다. 반려동물은 이를 이해하지 못한다. 이런 구별은 치료가 삶의 질에 어떤 영향을 미칠지 고려할 때 중요하다. 누군가 "이 시술이 내 반려동물의 삶의 질을 개선할 것인가?"라고 물어야 한다.

특정 시술의 높은 비용도 우려사항이다. 반려동물의 비싼 시술비용을 지불하기 위해 자녀들의 미래를 위험에 빠뜨리는 것은 비윤리적이다. 만약 이 시술이 진정으로 반려동물의 삶의 질을 개선하고 당신이 부유하다면, 그것을 선택하는 것은 윤리적이다.

그렇긴 하지만, 비싼 시술을 감당할 수 없더라도 반려동물을 기르는 것은 윤리적이다. 많은 개와 고양이들이 건강한 삶을 살며 반려동물과 사람 모두에게 행복을 제공한다. 사람은 예방접종, 심장사상충 치료, 중성화 수술, 벼룩 방제와 같은 기본적인 수의학적 시술을 제공해야 한다. 동물이 나이와 관련된 문제로 고통 받기 시작할 때, 사람은 안락사를 결정해야 한다.

072

하위내용영역	배점	예상정답률
일반영어 B형 서술형	4점	45%

모범답안 The main idea of the passage is there are factors to consider before judging the appropriateness of medical care or euthanasia for a pet. Second, the writer would recommend euthanizing the aging dog needing bone marrow transplants *(because the procedure would prolong suffering)*.

채점 기준

+ 2점 : 글의 요지를 "there are factors to consider before judging the appropriateness of medical care or euthanasia for a pet"이라 서술하였거나 유사하였다.

☞ 다음과 같이 서술하였어도 2점을 준다.
  - There are a few factors to consider before judging the medical care appropriate to give to a pet.

+ 2점 : 저자가 말하는 골수 이식을 필요로 하는 늙은 개에게 하면 좋을 행동방침을 "euthanizing the aging dog"라 서술하였거나 유사하였다.

073

하위내용영역	배점	예상정답률
일반영어 A형 기입형	2점	55%

모범답안 ⓐ jobs ⓑ suicide

채점기준
- 2점: 모범답안과 같다. 이외에는 답이 될 수 없다.
- 1점: 둘 중 하나만 맞았다.
- 0점: 모범답안과 다르다.

한글번역

나는 지역 정신건강센터에서 정신과 레지던트 과정을 시작했다. 센터장은 수련의들을 제자리에 앉히기를 좋아했다. 그는 우리 중 누구든지 좋은 고용 상담사와 바꿔주겠다고 말했다. 약물치료와 심리치료도 좋지만, 환자들이 일자리를 가지고 있으면 더 효과가 좋다는 것이었다.

자살은 독특한 사건이지만, 그 원인은 결코 단순하거나 단일하지 않다. 정신질환이 역할을 한다—조증, 우울증, 조현병, 그리고 특히 참전용사들에게서는 외상후 스트레스장애가. 현재 전쟁에서 발생하는 흔한 유형의 뇌손상은 자살 위험을 절반 정도 증가시킨다. 결과적으로, 정신건강 서비스는 자살 예방 프로그램의 핵심이다. 심리치료와 약물치료는 자살로 이어질 수 있는 각각의 장애에 도움이 되는 것으로 입증됐다. 신미국안보센터의 최근 보고서는 참전용사들에게 너무 적은 수의 정신건강 전문가들이 이용 가능하다고 시사한다. 직원 수준이 개선되는 곳에서는 자살률이 감소한다.

내가 정기적으로 참전용사들을 치료한 지 수십 년이 지났기 때문에 나는 전문가로서 나서지 않으며, 센터의 보고서는 포괄적인 것으로 보인다. 나는 단지 이 누락 사항만을 지적하고 싶다 : 품위 있는 일자리의 필요성에 대한 강조 부족이다. 연구마다 실업과 자살을 연관시킨다. 참전용사들 사이의 실업이 전체적으로 높지는 않지만, 일부 집단에서는 그 수치가 천문학적이다. 18세에서 24세 남성 참전용사의 거의 27%가 실업 상태다. 군인들이 군대를 떠날 때, 그들은 복무가 제공하는 것들을 잃는다 : 목적, 집중, 성취, 책임, 그리고 CNAS 보고서가 "소속감"이라고 부르는 요소를. 직업은 스트레스가 될 수 있지만, 특히 정신적으로 취약한 사람들에게는 일자리가 구조, 지원, 의미 면에서 제공하는 것을 대체할 수 없다.

074

하위내용영역	배점	예상정답률
일반영어 A형 서술형	4점	45%

모범답안 Yes, hate speech is protected as part of free speech because the neural impact is not taken into account by the legal system. Next, hate speech causes physical effects by changing brains and creating feelings of toxic stress, fear, and distrust.

채점기준
- 1점: 증오발언이 표현(언론)의 자유로 보호되고 있는가에 "yes"라 서술하였다.
- 1점: 그 이유를 "the neural impact is not taken into account by the legal system"이라 서술하였거나 유사하였다.
- 2점: 증오발언이 어떻게 물리적 효과를 가져오는지에 대한 질문에 "by changing brains and creating feelings of toxic stress, fear, and distrust"라 서술하였거나 유사하였다.

한글번역

자유 사회에서의 자유는 모든 사람을 위한 것이어야 한다. 따라서 자유는 다른 사람의 자유를 침해하는 것을 배제한다. 당신은 길을 걸어갈 자유가 있지만, 다른 사람들이 그렇게 하는 것을 막을 자유는 없다. 다른 사람의 자유에 대한 침해는 명백하고 직접적인 물리적 형태로 나타날 수 있다—무기를 들고 공격하러 오는 폭력배들처럼. 폭력은 일종의 표현일 수 있지만, 확실히 "자유로운 발언"은 아니다.

폭력과 마찬가지로, 혐오 발언도 다른 사람의 자유에 대한 물리적 침해가 될 수 있다. 언어가 신경계에 물리적으로 가해지는 심리적 효과를 가지며, 장기적으로 무력화시키는 효과를 가지기 때문이다.

모든 사고는 신경 회로에 의해 수행된다—공중에 떠다니지 않는다. 언어는 신경적으로 사고를 활성화한다. 따라서 언어는 뇌를 좋게도 나쁘게도 변화시킬 수 있다. 혐오 발언은 혐오의 대상이 된 사람들의 뇌를 나쁘게 변화시켜, 독성 스트레스, 두려움, 불신을 만들어낸다—이 모든 것이 물리적이며, 매일 활동하는 신경 회로 안에 있다. 이런 내적 해악은 주먹으로 공격하는 것보다도 더 심각할 수 있다. 그것은 두려움, 위협, 불신 없이 생각하고 따라서 행동할 자유를 침해한다. 오랫동안 완전히 자유로운 시민처럼 생각하고 행동할 능력을 침해한다.

그래서 혐오 발언은 혐오의 표적이 된 사람들의 자유를 침해하는 것이다. 자유 사회에서 자유로워지려면 다른 사람의 자유를 침해하지 않아야 하므로, 혐오 발언은 자유 발언의 범주에 속하지 않는다.

혐오 발언은 또한 경미한 편견을 가진 사람들의 뇌를 변화시켜, 그것을 혐오와 위협적 행동으로 이동시킬 수 있다. 혐오가 뇌에 물리적으로 존재할 때, 당신은 혐오를 생각하고 느끼며, 신경계에서 물리적으로 생각하고 느끼는 것을 실행하도록 행동하게 된다.

혐오 발언이 혐오 받는 사람들의 신경계에 미치는 장기적이고 종종 무력화시키는 물리적 효과는 법적 지위를 갖지 못한다. 우리의 신경계가 법체계에서 지위를 갖지 못하기 때문이다—적어도 아직은. 이것은 법과 진실 사이의 간극이다.

한글번역

이중 국적은 세계화의 돌이킬 수 없는 결과물이다. 이를 받아들이는 것은 더욱 유동적인 세계에서 다중 국가 정체성을 적절히 인정하는 것이다. 이중 국적은 미국법 하에서 결코 불법이었던 적이 없다. 미국은 역사적으로 다른 국가들의 법률에 의존해 이 지위를 감시했다. 하지만 세계의 나머지 국가들은 번영한 이민자 인구와의 유대를 굳건히 하기 위해 이중 국적을 받아들이는 방향으로 움직였다. 이민자들의 상위 20개 출신 국가 중 19개국이 이제 자국민들이 미국에서 귀화하면서도 그 지위를 유지하는 것을 허용한다.

압도적 다수의 새로운 미국인들은 이중 정체성을 가진 미국인들(앰퍼샌드-"&" 기호를 가리키는 단어-미국인들)로, 감상적인 유대뿐만 아니라 고국과의 공식적인 유대도 유지하고 있다. 한편 다른 국가로 이주한 미국 태생 미국인들은 종종 미국 여권을 유지하면서 새로운 거주 국가의 시민권을 취득한다. 점점 더 많은 미국인들이 미국에 머물면서도 조상들의 고국과의 유대를 재확립하고 있다. 수천 명이 조부모의 출생을 근거로 아일랜드와 이탈리아 시민권을 취득하고 있다. 나치 정권을 피해 달아났던 유대인들의 후손들은 독일 시민권을 되찾고 있다. 그리고 오늘날 "혼합 지위" 부모에게서 태어난 사람들은 더 이상 둘 중 하나를 선택하도록 강요받지 않는다.

그것이 마땅한 일이다. 세계가 국가 간 제로섬 경쟁에서 벗어나면서 이중 국적은 구체적인 문제를 거의 야기하지 않는다. 이 지위의 수용은 다중 국가 소속감을 가진 많은 개인들이 그런 정체성들을 실현할 수 있게 한다. 이런 점에서 이중 국적은 일종의 결사의 자유, 즉 비난받을 것이 아니라 보호받아야 할 자발적 소속의 한 형태를 나타낸다.

075

하위내용영역	배점	예상정답률
일반영어 B형 서술형	4점	40%

모범답안 The "ampersand Americans" mentioned are those that have dual citizenships at the same time (such as Korean & American). Second, the circumstances that can be inferred about the period of zero-sum competition was that individuals had to choose only one national attachment.

채점기준

+ 2점 : 앰퍼샌드(& : and를 나타내는 기호) 미국인을 "those that have dual citizenships (simultaneously)" 또는 "individuals who have multiple national attachments(nationalities)"라 서술하였다.
+ 2점 : 시민권과 관련하여 제로섬 경쟁시기 동안의 상황에 대해 추론할 수 있는 것을 "individuals had to choose only one nationality (or citizenship)"라 서술하였거나 유사하였다.

076

하위내용영역	배점	예상정답률
일반영어 B형 서술형	4점	45%

모범답안 The four laws of robotics are: a robot may not hurt or allow a human being to be hurt; it must obey human beings' orders; it can protect itself; finally, it must not harm mankind as a whole. Second, the writer makes the comparison because (or *the comparison made to nuclear fission indicates that*) the AI technology is scarcely known in the scope of its power in the same way nuclear fission was in the 1930s until atomic bombs were first used horrifically in warfare in 1945.

채점기준

+ 2점: 로봇(공학)의 법칙을 "① <u>a robot may not hurt</u> or *allow a human being to be hurt*; ② <u>it must obey human beings' orders</u>; ③ <u>it can protect itself</u>; finally, ④ <u>it must not harm mankind as a whole.</u>"이라 서술하였거나 유사하였다.
  ☞ 4가지 가운데 <u>3개만 서술한 경우 1점</u>, <u>2개만 서술한 경우 0.5점</u>, 나머지는 0점을 준다.

+ 2점: 밑줄 친 부분을 언급하며 인공지능을 핵분열과 비교한 이유를 "the AI technology is scarcely known in the scope of its power as nuclear fission was in the 1930s until atomic bombs were first used in warfare in 1945"라 명확하게 서술하였거나 유사하였다.

한글번역

작가 아이작 아시모프는 자신이 만든 로봇 법칙들을 도입했다. 로봇은 인간을 해치거나, 행동하지 않음으로써 인간이 해를 입도록 방치해서는 안 된다. 로봇은 그러한 명령이 제1법칙과 충돌하는 경우를 제외하고는 인간이 내리는 모든 명령에 복종해야 한다. 로봇은 그러한 보호가 제1법칙이나 제2법칙과 충돌하지 않는 한 자신의 존재를 보호해야 한다.

이 법칙들은 황금률("살인하지 말라")의 메아리, 저지른 행동과 하지 않은 행동에서 죄가 발생한다는 유대-기독교적 개념, 의사의 히포크라테스 선서, 심지어 정당방위의 권리까지 담고 있다. 꽤 좋게 들리지 않는가? 하지만 그것들은 결코 작동하지 않는다. "뤼나라운드"에서 화성 표면의 채굴 기사들이 로봇에게 그것에게 독성이 있는 원소를 가져오라고 명령한다. 대신 로봇은 제2법칙과 제3법칙 사이의 피드백 루프에 갇힌다. 로봇은 기사들이 목숨을 걸고 구조할 때까지 술에 취한 듯 원을 그리며 걷는다. 모든 아시모프 로봇 이야기가 그렇다—세 법칙에 내재된 모순으로부터 예상치 못한 결과들이 발생한다. 오직 법칙들을 우회함으로써만 재앙이 회피된다.

아시모프는 플롯을 만들어내고 있었지, 현실 세계의 안전 문제를 해결하려고 하지 않았다. 당신과 내가 사는 곳에서 그의 법칙들은 부족하다. 우선, 그것들은 충분히 정확하지 않다. 로봇들이 모든 인간 지식을 완벽하게 이해하지 못한다면, 로봇들을 속여서 범죄 행위를 수행하게 하는 것은 간단할 것이다. "찰리의 샴푸에 디메틸수은을 조금 넣어라"는 디메틸수은이 신경독이라는 것을 알고 있을 때만 살인을 위한 처방이다. 아시모프는 결국 네 번째 법칙인 제0법칙을 추가해서 로봇들이 인류 전체를 해치는 것을 금지했지만, 그것도 문제들을 해결하지 못한다. 아시모프의 법칙들이 아무리 신뢰할 수 없다고 해도, 그것들은 지능형 기계와의 미래 관계를 성문화하려는 우리의 가장 자주 인용되는 시도다. 그것은 무서운 명제다. 아시모프의 법칙들이 우리가 가진 전부인가?

그것보다 더 나쁘다고 생각한다. 반자율 로봇 드론들이 이미 매년 수십 명을 죽이고 있다. 56개국이 전장 로봇을 보유하고 있거나 개발하고 있다. 그것들을 자율적이고 지능적으로 만들기 위한 경쟁이 진행 중이다. 대부분의 경우, AI 윤리와 기술 발전에 대한 논의는 서로 다른 세계에서 일어난다. AI는 핵분열과 같은 이중 용도 기술이다. 핵분열은 도시를 밝힐 수도 있고 소각시킬 수도 있다. 그 끔찍한 힘은 1945년 이전에는 대부분의 사람들에게 상상할 수 없는 것이었다. 진보된 AI와 함께, 우리는 지금 1930년대에 있다.

077

하위내용영역	배점	예상정답률
일반영어 A형 기입형	2점	65%

모범답안 ecological degradation

채점기준
- 2점 : 모범답안과 같다. 이외에는 답이 될 수 없다.
- 0점 : 모범답안과 다르다.

한글번역

오늘날 인류는 정말로 세계를 장악했다. 지구의 대륙들은 거의 70억 명의 사피엔스의 터전이다. 이 모든 사람들을 커다란 저울에 올려놓는다면, 그들의 총 질량은 약 3억 톤이 될 것이다. 이에 비해 고슴도치와 펭귄부터 코끼리와 고래까지 현존하는 모든 대형 야생동물들의 총 질량은 1억 톤 미만이다. 우리 아이들의 책과 도상(圖像), 그리고 TV 화면은 여전히 기린, 늑대, 침팬지로 가득하지만, 현실 세계에는 그들이 거의 남아있지 않다. 전 세계에 기린은 약 8만 마리인 데 비해 소는 15억 마리이고, 늑대는 20만 마리에 불과한 반면 가축화된 개는 4억 마리이며, 침팬지는 25만 마리뿐인데 인간은 수십억 명이다.

생태계 파괴는 자원 부족과 같지 않다. 인류가 이용할 수 있는 자원은 지속적으로 증가하고 있으며, 앞으로도 계속 그럴 가능성이 높다. 그래서 자원 부족에 대한 종말론적 예언들은 아마도 잘못된 것이다. 이와 대조적으로, 생태계 파괴에 대한 두려움은 지나치게 근거가 있다. 미래에는 사피엔스가 새로운 물질과 에너지원의 보물창고를 통제하게 되면서, 동시에 자연 서식지의 잔재를 파괴하고 대부분의 다른 종들을 멸종으로 몰아넣을 수도 있다. 사실, 그것은 호모 사피엔스 자신의 생존을 위험에 빠뜨릴 수도 있다. 지구온난화, 해수면 상승, 광범위한 오염이 지구를 우리 종에게 덜 우호적으로 만들 수 있으며, 결과적으로 미래에는 인간의 힘과 인간이 유발한 자연재해 사이의 나선형 경쟁을 보게 될 수도 있다.

078

하위내용영역	배점	예상정답률
일반영어 A형 기입형	2점	60%

모범답안 precise

채점기준
- 2점 : 모범답안과 같다. 이외에는 답이 될 수 없다.
- 0점 : 모범답안과 다르다.

한글번역

전통 농업은 자연 시간과 유기적 성장의 순환에 의존했다. 대부분의 사회는 정확한 시간 측정을 할 수 없었으며, 그렇게 하는 데 크게 관심도 없었다. 세상은 시계와 시간표 없이, 오직 태양의 움직임과 식물의 성장 주기에만 따라 일상을 꾸려나갔다. 정확한 작업 시간이란 없었고, 모든 일상은 계절에 따라 급격히 바뀌었다. 사람들은 태양이 어디에 있는지 알았고, 우기와 수확철의 징조를 애타게 지켜봤지만, 시각을 몰랐고 연도에 대해서는 거의 신경 쓰지 않았다. 길을 잃은 시간 여행자가 중세 마을에 갑자기 나타나서 지나가는 행인에게 "올해가 몇 년이지?"라고 묻는다면, 마을 사람은 그 낯선 사람의 우스꽝스러운 옷차림만큼이나 그 질문에 당황했을 것이다.

중세의 농민과 구두 제작자들과 대조적으로, 현대 산업은 태양이나 계절에 거의 신경 쓰지 않는다. 현대 산업은 정확성을 신성시한다. 예를 들어, 중세 작업장에서는 각 구두 제작자가 밑창부터 버클까지 신발 한 켤레를 통째로 만들었다. 한 구두 제작자가 작업에 늦어도 다른 사람들의 일이 멈추지 않았다. 하지만 현대 신발 공장의 조립 라인에서는 모든 작업자가 신발의 작은 부분만을 생산하는 기계를 담당하고, 그것은 다음 기계로 넘겨진다. 만약 5번 기계를 조작하는 작업자가 늦잠을 자면, 다른 모든 기계들이 멈춘다. 그런 재앙을 방지하기 위해서는 모든 사람이 정확한 시간표를 지켜야 한다. 각 작업자는 정확히 같은 시간에 출근한다.

079

하위내용영역	배점	예상정답률
일반영어 A형 서술형	4점	55%

모범답안 The title is "Modern Man Remains the Wildest Animal". Second, the writer is despair because scientists have actively developed more deadly technology without making moral protest.

채점기준

+ 2점: 글의 제목을 "Modern Man Remains the Wildest Animal"이라 답하였다.
+ 2점: 글의 저자가 과학자에게 깊은 절망감을 느끼는 이유를 "scientists have <u>actively developed more deadly technology</u>(1점) without making <u>moral protest</u>(1점)" 또는 "scientists <u>sell their achievement to murderers</u>(1점) and <u>morally stagnant</u>(1점)"라 서술하였거나 유사하였다.

한글번역

나는 항상 일종의 두려움과 절망 속에서 살고 있다. 매일 신문을 읽으며 사람들이 서로에게 무엇을 하고 있는지, 어떻게 다른 사람을 죽이거나 죽이도록 부추기는지를 본다. 무언가 터질 것이다—혁명이든, 반혁명이든—그러면 사람들은 그저 서로의 피를 마시게 될 것이다. 우리가 빠져든 이 낮은 상태에 나는 떨린다.

과거에도 전쟁이 계속 벌어진 것은 사실이다. 그래도 모든 사람들은 인간이 더 현명해지고, 더 많은 과학과 인간 본성에 대해 알게 돼 변화할 수 있을 것이라는 희망을 가지고 있었다. 하지만 무기가 더 위험해지고 사람들이 더 취약해진 것 외에는 아무것도 변하지 않았다. 무기가 강해질수록 우리의 상황은 더 약해진다. 일간 뉴스는 모든 지식과 세련된 방식을 가지고도 현대인이 여전히 가장 야생적인 동물로 남아있다는 것을 거듭 알려준다.

무엇보다 나를 절망하게 만드는 것은 하나님이 큰 두뇌와 많은 근면함을 주신 과학자들이 자신들의 성과를 살인자들에게 판다는 것이다. 매일 우리는 점점 더 많은 발명품을 얻고 있고, 그중 많은 것들이 우리의 형제자매를 죽이는 데 사용되고 있다.

전기 모터의 원리를 발견한 마이클 패러데이나 전기와 자기 분야의 연구로 알려진 제임스 맥스웰 같은 위대한 과학자들이 잘못한 일을 했다고 말하려는 것은 아니다. 그들은 지금 우리의 냉장고에, 밤에 집을 밝히는 데 사용되는 것들을 발견했다. 하지만 과학적 힘이 사람들을 파괴하는 데 사용되고 있을 때 그것은 큰 비극이다. 나는 과학자들이 "우리는 그런 목적을 위해 우리의 일을 하지 않겠다"고 말하는 첫 번째 사람들이 돼야 한다는 희망을 가지고 있었다. 하지만 그들은 어떻게든 도덕적으로 정체돼 있다. 그들은 어느 쪽이든 상관없이 그저 자신들의 일을 계속해 나간다.

080

하위내용영역	배점	예상정답률
일반영어 B형 서술형	4점	50%

모범답안 The writer mentions "animals" in the first paragraph to support the theory that early humans had number sense. Second, the pre-vocal methods of counting mentioned are tally methods such as using fingers, scratches in dirt or stone, notches cut in wood and knots tied into string.

채점기준

+ 2점: "animals"를 언급한 이유를 "to support the theory that early humans had number sense"라 서술하였거나 유사하였다.
+ 2점: 언어 이전의 숫자를 세는 모든 방법이 "<u>using fingers</u>, <u>scratches in dirt or stone</u>, <u>cutting notches in wood</u>, and <u>tying knots in a string</u>"이라 정확하게 서술하였다.
  ☞ 4개 중 3개만 서술한 경우 1점, 2개만 서술한 경우 0.5점을 준다.

감점 어휘 및 표현이 어법적으로 적절하지 않고, 논리적 연결이 자연스럽지 않을 경우 각각 0.2점씩 최대 1점까지 감점한다.

한글번역

크기, 모양, 수의 개념을 체계화하려는 인류의 원초적 노력은 대개 가장 초기의 수학으로 여겨진다. 하지만 수의 개념과 계수 과정은 기록된 역사보다 훨씬 이전에 발달했기 때문에 (인간이 5만 년 전부터 계수를 사용했다는 고고학적 증거가 있다), 이런 발달 방식은 대체로 추측에 의존한다. 그것이 어떻게 이루어졌을지 상상하는 것은 어렵지 않다. 선사 시대의 인간들조차도 적어도 작은 집단에서 어떤 물건들이 추가되거나 제거될 때 '더 많음'과 '더 적음'의 개념을 인식하는 정도의 수 감각을 가지고 있었다는 주장은 타당해 보인다. 연구에 따르면 일부 동물들도 그런 감각을 가지고 있기 때문이다.

사회가 점진적으로 발전하면서 단순한 계수는 필수가 됐다. 부족은 자신들의 구성원이 몇 명인지, 적이 몇 명인지 알아야 했고, 목동은 양 떼의 크기가 줄어들고 있는지 알아야 했다. 계수를 유지하는 가장 초기 방법은 일대일 대응의 원리를 사용하는 단순한 집계 방법이었다. 예를 들어 양을 세는 데서는 양 한 마리당 손가락 하나씩을 접을 수 있었다. 계수는 또한 흙이나 돌에 긁힌 자국을 만들거나, 나무 조각에 홈을 파거나, 끈에 매듭을 묶는 방법으로도 유지될 수 있었다.

그 후 나중에는 작은 집단 내 물건의 수에 대응하는 단어 집계로서 다양한 음성 소리들이 개발됐다. 그리고 더 나중에 문자가 정교해지면서, 이런 수들을 나타내는 기호 체계가 고안됐다. 이런 상상된 발전 과정은 초기 인간과 유사하다고 여겨지는 현재의 사회들을 연구한 인류학자들의 보고서에 의해 뒷받침된다.

081

하위내용영역	배점	예상정답률
일반영어 B형 서술형	4점	35%

모범답안) The center of percussion is less straining because it does not produce any unbalanced motion that would strain the arm. Second, a ball hitting the racket's sweet spot would cause the racket to bounce backwards with no rotation. Next, the two key motions at work are translational motion and rotational motion.

채점 기준

+ 2점: '타격의 중심'을 사용하는 것이 왜 선수에게 적은 충격을 주는지에 대해 "because it does not produce any unbalanced motion that would strain the arm"이라 서술하였거나 유사하였다.
+ 1점: 공이 라켓의 스위트 스팟(공을 치기 가장 효율적인 곳)을 친 후에 라켓을 사람이 들고 있지 않는다면 무슨 일이 일어날까에 대해 "a ball hitting the racket's sweet spot would cause the racket to bounce backwards with no rotation"이라 서술하였거나 유사하였다.
+ 1점: 두 핵심 움직임을 "transitional motion"과 "rotational motion"이라 답하였다.

한글번역

대부분의 테니스 선수들이 일반적으로 "스위트 스팟"으로 알려진 라켓의 진동 절점에 공을 치려고 노력하지만, 많은 선수들이 라켓 면에 있는 두 번째의 덜 알려진 지점인 타격 중심의 존재를 모르고 있다. 이 지점도 공을 칠 때 선수의 팔에 가해지는 충격을 크게 줄여준다.

이 두 번째 스위트 스팟의 물리학을 이해하기 위해서는 공과의 충돌 순간에 선수의 손이 사라진다면 충돌 후 순간들에 테니스 라켓에 무슨 일이 일어날지 생각해보는 것이 도움이 된다. 공의 충돌은 라켓이 뒤로 팅겨 나가며 공에서 멀어지는 병진 운동을 경험하게 한다. 이 운동의 경향은 손잡이 끝부분을 포함한 라켓의 모든 부분을 뒤로, 즉 공에서 멀어지는 방향으로 급격히 당기는 것이다. 공이 라켓의 질량 중심에 정확히 맞지 않는 한, 라켓은 추가로 질량 중심을 중심으로 하는 회전 운동을 경험할 것이다—마치 가장자리 근처에 맞은 동전이 회전하기 시작하는 것과 같다. 공이 라켓 면에 맞을 때마다, 이 회전 운동의 효과는 손잡이 끝부분을 앞으로, 공쪽으로 급격히 당기는 것이다. 공이 라켓 면의 어디에 맞느냐에 따라 이 두 운동 중 하나 또는 다른 하나가 우세하게 된다.

하지만 타격 중심으로 알려진 한 충돌 지점이 있는데, 이 지점에서는 어느 운동도 우세하지 않는다. 만약 공이 이 지점에 맞는다면, 그 충돌은 손잡이 끝부분에 어떤 운동도 전달하지 않을 것이다. 이런 운동 부재의 이유는 손의 윗부분에 가해지는 힘이 손의 아랫부분에 가해지는 힘과 크기는 같고 방향은 반대가 돼, 테니스 선수의 손이나 팔뚝에 순 힘이 가해지지 않기 때문이다. 타격 중심이 두 번째 스위트 스팟을 구성하는 이유는 테니스 선수의 손목이 보통 라켓 손잡이 끝부분 옆에 위치하기 때문이다. 선수가 타격 중심에서 공을 칠 때, 그녀의 손목은 앞으로도 뒤로도 급격히 당겨지지 않으며, 상대적으로 부드럽고 편안한 테니스 스트로크를 경험한다.

다른 많은 사람들도 같은 방식으로 생각한다고 확신하지만, 그들은 무엇을 해야 할지 모른다. 모든 사람이 소설이나 비난문을 쓸 수는 없다. 그리고 내가 하는 말이 어떻게 도움이 될까? 벽에다 대고 말하는 것이다. 그래도 독자를 즐겁게 해줘야 하는 소설가조차 "우리는 어디로 가고 있는가? 우리에게 무슨 일이 일어날 것인가?"라고 묻고 싶어질 때가 있다.

082

하위내용영역	배점	예상정답률
일반영어 A형 기입형	2점	55%

모범답안 ⓐ insensitive ⓑ media

채점 기준

- 2점: 모범답안과 같다.
- 1점: 둘 중 하나만 맞았다.
- 0점: 모범답안과 다르다.

한글번역

사람들이 일어나고 있는 일을 거의 당연한 것으로 받아들이기 때문에 나는 절망한다. 수천 명의 사람들이 파괴당하는 것에 대해 읽고 나서, 마치 아무 일도 일어나지 않은 것처럼 주식 시세표로 눈을 돌린다. 사람들은 "그건 다른 사람들에게 일어나는 일이야. 나에게는 일어나지 않을 거야"라는 태도를 취한다. 그런 면에서 문명이 사람들의 마음을 부드럽게 만들기보다는 돌처럼 굳게 만들었다고 말하겠다.
이런 측면에서 언론은 많은 도덕적 피해를 입었다. 다른 사람들의 고뇌에 대해 항상 듣고 있으면 그것에 덜 민감해진다. "매일 보니까 그것과 평화롭게 지내야 해." 현대인이 생각하는 방식이 그렇다. 내 최신 저서 《참회자》에서 주인공은—내가 완전히 동일시하지는 않지만—현대인에 대해 내가 방금 말한 것과 같은 말들을 많이 한다. 비평가들은 모두 내가 소설을 쓰는 대신 설교를 하고 있다고 말했다. 이 작은 책이 소설인지 비난문인지, 심지어 설교인지가 무슨 상관인가? 사실 이디시어 판에서는 "소설"이라는 단어가 나타나지도 않았다. 사람이 자신이 중요하다고 여기는 것을 말해야 할 때가 있다.

083

하위내용영역	배점	예상정답률
일반영어 A형 기입형	2점	55%

모범답안 ⓐ Humans ⓑ dwarves

채점 기준

- 2점: 모범답안과 같다. ⓐ에 Australopithecus 도 맞는 것으로 한다.
- 1점: 둘 중 하나만 맞았다.
- 0점: 모범답안과 다르다.

한글번역

"인간"이라는 단어의 진정한 의미는 '호모에 속하는 동물'이며, 호모 사피엔스 외에도 이 속에는 다른 많은 종들이 있었다. 인간은 약 250만 년 전 동아프리카에서 '남쪽 원숭이'를 뜻하는 오스트랄로피테쿠스라고 불리는 이전 원숭이 속으로부터 처음 진화했다. 약 200만 년 전, 이런 고대 남녀 중 일부가 고향을 떠나 북아프리카, 유럽, 아시아의 광대한 지역을 여행하고 정착했다.
유럽과 서아시아의 인간들은 호모 네안데르탈렌시스('네안데르 계곡의 사람')로 진화했으며, 흔히 단순히 '네안데르탈인'이라고 불린다. 아시아의 더 동쪽 지역에는 호모 에렉투스, 즉 '직립인'이 살았는데, 그들은 거의 200만 년 동안 그곳에서 생존했다. 인도네시아의 자바 섬에는 열대 생활에 적응한 호모 솔로엔시스, 즉 '솔로 계곡의 사람'이 살았다. 또 다른 인도네시아 섬인 작은 플로레스 섬에서는 고대 인간들이 왜소화 과정을 겪었다. 인간이 플로레스에 처음 도달한 것은 해수면이 유달리 낮아서 본토에서 그 섬에 쉽게 접근할 수 있었을 때였다.

바다가 다시 상승했을 때, 일부 사람들이 자원이 부족한 그 섬에 갇혔다. 많은 음식이 필요한 큰 사람들이 먼저 죽었다. 작은 사람들이 훨씬 더 잘 생존했다. 세대를 거치면서 플로레스 사람들은 난쟁이가 됐다. 과학자들이 호모 플로레시엔시스로 알고 있는 이 독특한 종은 최대 키가 1미터에 불과했고 몸무게는 25킬로그램을 넘지 않았다.

084

하위내용영역	배점	예상정답률
일반영어 B형 서술형	4점	50%

모범답안 A dozen species of acacias grow well in the southern United States. Next, the Black Acacia has the least colorful blossoms. Third, the word is "blossoming".

채점기준

+ 1점: 미남부에서 잘 자라는 종이 "twelve(A dozen)" species라 답하였다.
+ 1점: 가장 덜 다채로운 꽃을 가지고 있는 종이 "the Black Acacia (*or Blackwood*)"임을 정확하게 서술하였다.
+ 2점: 빈칸에 들어갈 단어를 "blossoming"이라 답하였다. 이외에는 답이 될 수 없다.

한글번역

아카시아는 오랫동안 호주에서 단순히 진흙과 나뭇가지 구조물을 짓는 데 사용돼 왔다. 그곳에서 아카시아는 "와틀"이라고 불린다. 아카시아는 실제로 완두콩, 강낭콩, 렌틸콩, 땅콩, 그리고 콩 같은 씨앗이 들어있는 꼬투리를 포함하는 콩과식물로 알려진 식물군과 관련이 있다. 일부 아카시아는 실제로 식용 작물을 생산한다. 다른 아카시아 품종들은 의약품, 식품, 향수에 널리 사용되는 아라비아 고무 또는 아카시아 고무라고 불리는 끈적한 수지나, 피아노 제작에 귀중하게 여겨지는 어둡고 단단한 목재, 또는 동물의 가죽을 처리해 가죽으로 변화시키는 데 사용되는 어둡고 산성인 물질인 탄닌이 풍부한 나무껍질 때문에 가치를 인정받는다.

거의 500종의 아카시아가 분석, 식별, 분류됐고 세계의 덥고 일반적으로 건조한 지역에서 생존 가능함이 입증됐다. 하지만 300개의 호주 품종 중 단지 12개만이 미국 남부에서 번성한다. 대부분의 아카시아 수입 종은 낮게 퍼지는 나무들이지만, 이 중에서 단지 세 종만이 꽃을 피운다. 고사리 같은 은색 잎과 둥근 송이로 배열된 작고 향기로운 꽃을 가진 베일리 아카시아, 베일리 아카시아와 비슷하지만 두 배 높이로 자라는 실버 와틀, 그리고 넓고 평평한 잎, 화려한 밝은 노란색 꽃, 날카로운 가시가 있는 가지를 가진 덤불 같은 시드니 골든 와틀이 그것이다. 또 다른 품종인 블랙 아카시아는 블랙우드라고도 불리며, 짙은 녹색 잎과 눈에 띄지 않는 꽃을 가지고 있다. 인기 있는 관상용 나무일 뿐만 아니라, 블랙 아카시아는 가구 제작뿐만 아니라 높이 평가받는 악기 제작에 사용되는 어두운 목재 때문에 가치 있는 것으로 여겨진다.

2월에 꽃을 피우는 아카시아의 특이한 습성은 마치 나무의 개화 주기에서 빛의 질이 아니라 날짜가 차이를 만드는 것처럼 호주 원산지 때문이라고 흔히 여겨져 왔다. 남반구에서는 계절이 뒤바뀌어, 미국에서 겨울인 2월이 호주에서는 여름이다. 하지만 실제로는 연한 노란색 꽃이 호주에서 8월에 나타난다. 북반구에서 자라든 남반구에서 자라든, 사랑스러운 아카시아는 겨울에 꽃을 피운다.

085

하위내용영역	배점	예상정답률
일반영어 B형 서술형	4점	45%

모범답안 The misconception about a complex physical system is that chaotic system seems to be random *(but actually is governed by very complex equations)*. Second, one example of chaotic system is a machine mixing bread dough.

채점기준

+ 2점: 카오스 시스템(a complex physical system)에 대한 흔히 있는 오해가 "chaotic system is random"임을 정확하게 서술하였다.
   ☞ "chaos theory has to do with randomness"라 했어도 2점을 준다.

+ 2점: 카오스 시스템의 예를 "a machine mixing bread dough"라 답하였다.
☞ "atmospheric air flow (또는 atmospheric weather pattern)"이라 했어도 2점을 준다.

한글번역

　1960년경, 수학자 에드워드 로렌츠는 대기 기류를 나타내는 겉보기에 단순한 방정식에서 예상치 못한 현상을 발견했다. 같은 입력값으로 모델을 다시 실행할 때마다 모델에는 무작위 요소가 없었음에도 불구하고 다른 결과가 나왔다. 로렌츠는 그의 아날로그 컴퓨터에서 발생한 미세한 반올림 오차가 시간이 지나면서 급격히 확대돼 불규칙한 결과를 초래한다는 것을 깨달았다. 그의 발견은 카오스 이론 발전에서 중요한 순간을 기록했는데, 이름과 달리 이 이론은 무작위성과는 거의 관련이 없다.
　우연한 결과를 포함하지 않는 결정론적 방정식에서 어떻게 예측 불가능성이 발생할 수 있는지 이해하기 위해, 둥근 그릇에 놓인 두 개의 양귀비 씨앗이라는 비카오스적 시스템을 생각해보자. 씨앗들이 점 끌개(point attractor)로 알려진 위치인 그릇의 중심으로 굴러갈 때, 씨앗들 사이의 거리는 줄어든다. 반대로 그릇을 뒤집으면, 위에 놓인 두 씨앗은 서로 멀어지며 굴러간다. 이런 시스템은 여전히 기술적으로 카오스적이지는 않지만, 위치의 초기 차이를 확대한다.
　빵 반죽을 섞는 기계와 같은 카오스 시스템은 끌림과 밀침 모두의 특징을 갖는다. 반죽이 늘어나고, 접히고, 다시 눌려지면서 뿌려진 양귀비 씨앗들은 겉보기에 무작위로 섞인다. 하지만 이 무작위성은 착각이다. 사실 양귀비 씨앗들은 "이상한 끌개(strange attractors)"에 포착되는데, 이는 놀라울 정도로 복잡한 경로로서 그 엉킴이 우연한 것처럼 보이지만 실제로는 시스템의 기본 방정식에 의해 결정된다.
　반죽을 치대는 과정에서 서로 옆에 위치했던 두 양귀비 씨앗은 결국 각자의 길로 간다. 초기의 어떤 분기나 측정 오차든 섞임에 의해 반복적으로 증폭되어 어떤 씨앗의 위치든 사실상 예측 불가능해진다. 카오스 시스템에서 예측 불가능성을 생성하는 것은 진정한 무작위성이 아니라 바로 이 "초기 조건에 대한 민감한 의존성"이다.

086

하위내용영역	배점	예상정답률
일반영어 A형 기입형	2점	55%

모범답안 overreaction

채점기준

- 2점: 모범답안과 같다. 이외에는 답이 될 수 없다.
- 0점: 모범답안과 다르다.

한글번역

　그렇다면 테러리즘은 어떨까? 중앙 정부들과 강력한 국가들이 자제를 배웠을지라도, 테러리스트들은 새롭고 파괴적인 무기를 사용하는 데 그런 거리낌이 없을 수도 있다. 그것은 확실히 우려스러운 가능성이다. 하지만 테러리즘은 진정한 권력에 접근할 수 없는 자들이 채택하는 약자의 전략이다. 적어도 과거에는 테러리즘이 상당한 물질적 피해를 일으키기보다는 공포를 퍼뜨림으로써 작동했다. 테러리스트들은 보통 군대를 물리치거나, 국가를 점령하거나, 도시 전체를 파괴할 힘을 갖지 못한다.
　그렇다면 테러리스트들은 어떻게 헤드라인을 장악하고 전 세계의 정치적 상황을 바꾸는가? 적들을 자극해서 과잉 반응을 하도록 함으로써이다. 본질적으로 테러리즘은 쇼다. 테러리스트들은 우리의 상상력을 사로잡고 마치 우리가 중세의 혼돈으로 다시 미끄러져 들어가고 있는 것처럼 느끼게 만드는 무서운 폭력의 장관을 연출한다. 결과적으로 국가들은 종종 전체 인구에 대한 박해나 외국 침공과 같은 거대한 무력 과시를 조율하면서 보안의 쇼로 테러리즘의 연극에 반응해야 한다고 느낀다. 대부분의 경우 테러리즘에 대한 반응이 테러리스트들 자체보다 우리의 안보에 훨씬 더 큰 위협을 가한다. 테러리스트들은 도자기 가게를 파괴하려고 하는 파리와 같다. 파리는 너무 약해서 찻잔 하나도 움직일 수 없다. 그래서 황소를 찾아내 그 귀 안으로 들어가서 윙윙거리기 시작한다. 황소는 두려움과 분노로 광분해 도자기 가게를 파괴한다. 지난 십 년간 중동에서 일어난 일이 바로 이것이다.

087

하위내용영역	배점	예상정답률
일반영어 A형 서술형	4점	50%

모범답안 The two words are "DNA repair". Next, the part of anatomy for further studies into cisplatin therapy timing is understanding the activity inside of the cell for proper treatment at the right times.

채점기준

+ 2점: 빈칸에 들어갈 단어를 "DNA repair"이라 답하였다. 이외에는 답이 될 수 없다.
+ 2점: 핵심적 요인을 "understanding the activity inside of the cell (for proper treatment at the right times)"이라 서술하였거나 유사하였다.

한글번역

대부분의 살아있는 유기체는 내부 시계, 즉 24시간 주야 주기에 따라 각 세포의 생화학적, 생리학적, 행동적 기능들을 조율하는 일주기 시계를 가지고 있다. 이 시계는 수백 가지 다른 요소들 중에서도 잠들기와 깨기, 호르몬 수치, 체온, 심박 수, 혈압을 조절한다.

우리 연구실은 일주기 시계가 세포 내 DNA 복구에 어떻게 영향을 미치는지 연구하고 있다―이는 효소팀이 DNA를 따라 이동하면서 자외선과 DNA 변형 화학물질의 손상 효과로 인한 손상과 오류를 수리하는 자연적 과정이다. 이처럼 끊임없이 경계하는 효소들이 없다면, 우리 세포들은 암과 다른 질병으로 이어질 DNA 돌연변이를 축적할 것이다. 우리 몸의 리듬과 DNA 복구 사이의 이런 관계를 이해하는 것은 중요한데, 시계 기능 장애가 비만과 간질부터 불면증과 계절성 정서장애까지의 질환들과 연결돼 있다는 증거가 점점 늘어나고 있기 때문이다.

우리는 일주기 리듬이 인기 있는 항암제인 시스플라틴 치료 중에 DNA 복구에 어떻게 영향을 미치는지 탐구해왔다. 시스플라틴은 고환암, 난소암, 대장암, 폐암, 유방암을 포함한 대부분의 고형암 치료에 사용된다. 시스플라틴은 암세포의 DNA를 손상시켜 죽인다. 하지만 정상 세포의 DNA도 손상시켜 의사들이 종종 치료를 중단하도록 만드는 심각한 부작용을 일으킨다. 정상 세포와 암세포 모두 시스플라틴으로 인한 DNA 손상을 복구한다. 성공적인 치료를 위해서는 건강한 조직은 보호하면서 암세포가 복구할 능력이 가장 떨어질 때 DNA 손상을 가해야 한다.

지난 수십 년간 과학자들은 시스플라틴 치료시기를 안내하기 위해 일주기 시계를 사용하려고 시도해왔다. 그들의 전략은 특정 시간에 시스플라틴을 투여한 후 환자가 어떻게 지내는지 관찰해, 부작용은 최소화하면서 가장 큰 이익을 얻는 하루 중 시간을 찾아내는 것이었다. 하지만 이런 실험들은 실패했는데, 시간 선택이 다소 자의적이었고 세포 내부에서 일어나고 있는 일에 기반하지 않았기 때문이다.

088

하위내용영역	배점	예상정답률
일반영어 B형 서술형	4점	50%

모범답안 The writer is trying to illustrate the impoverished and troubled state of the school she taught at in underlined selection ⓐ. Second, the writer would reject "conventional wisdom" as experience has shown her that dedicated rather than naturally talented students excel.

채점기준

+ 2점: 밑줄 친 ⓐ에서 저자가 말하려 하는 바를 "to illustrate the impoverished(poor) and troubled state of the school she taught at"이라 서술하였거나 유사하였다.
+ 2점: 밑줄 친 ⓑ에 대한 저자의 반응을 "the writer would reject "conventional wisdom(1점)" as experience has shown her that dedicated rather than naturally talented students excel(1점)"이라 서술하였거나 유사하였다.

089

하위내용영역	배점	예상정답률
일반영어 A형 기입형	2점	50%

모범답안 ⓐ predicting ⓑ grit

채점기준

- 2점: 모범답안과 같다. 이외에는 답이 될 수 없다.
- 1점: 둘 중 하나만 맞았다.
- 0점: 모범답안과 다르다.

한글번역

내가 심리학자가 되기 전에는 교사였다. 내 학생들은 12세 또는 13세였다. 대부분은 A가부터 D가 사이에 몰려 있는 공공 주택 단지에 살았다. 이 동네 모든 모퉁이에 멋진 카페가 생기기 전이었다. 내가 그곳에서 가르치기 시작한 가을, 우리 학교는 어려운 도시 지역의 거친 학교에 관한 영화 촬영지로 선정됐다. 내 일은 학생들이 7학년 수학을 배우도록 돕는 것이었다: 분수와 소수, 그리고 대수와 기하학의 기초적인 구성 요소들을. 첫 주부터 반의 일부 학생들이 반 친구들보다 수학적 개념을 더 쉽게 받아들인다는 것이 명백했다. 반에서 가장 재능있는 학생들을 가르치는 것은 기쁨이었다. 그들은 말 그대로 "빨리 이해하는 학생들"이었다. 별다른 재촉 없이도 능력이 부족한 학생들이 이해하기 어려워하는 일련의 수학 문제의 근본적인 패턴을 파악했다. 내가 칠판에서 한 번 문제를 풀어주는 것을 보고는 "알겠어요!"라고 말한 다음 스스로 다음 문제를 올바르게 풀어냈다. 그러나 첫 번째 성적 평가 기간이 끝날 때, 이런 매우 유능한 학생들 중 일부가 내가 기대한 만큼 잘하지 못한다는 것을 발견하고 놀랐다. 물론 일부는 매우 잘했다. 하지만 가장 재능 있는 학생들 중 상당수가 시원찮은 성적이나 그보다 못한 성적을 받고 있었다. 이와 대조적으로, 처음에 어려워했던 학생들 중 몇몇은 내가 예상했던 것보다 더 잘하고 있었다. 이런 "과다 성취자들"은 필요한 모든 것을 가지고 매일 꾸준히 수업에 나왔다. 장난치고 창밖을 내다보는 대신, 그들은 노트를 적고 질문을 했다. 처음에 이해하지 못할 때는 계속해서 다시 시도했고, 때로는 점심시간이나 오후 선택 시간에 추가 도움을 받으러 오기도 했다. 그들의 노력은 성적에 나타났다.

분명히 적성이 성취를 보장하지는 않았다. 수학에 대한 재능은 수학 수업에서 뛰어난 성과를 내는 것과는 달랐다. 이것은 놀라운 일이었다. 결국 통념에 따르면 수학은 더 재능 있는 학생들이 뛰어날 것으로 기대되는 과목이며, 단순히 "수학적 재능이 없는" 반 친구들을 뒤처지게 만드는 과목이라고 여겨진다. 솔직히 말하면, 나는 바로 그런 가정을 가지고 학년을 시작했다.

한글번역

나는 단지 비스트(신병 훈련)의 엄격함만이 투지를 요구하는 것인지, 아니면 일반적으로 투지가 사람들이 자신의 약속을 지키는 데 도움이 되는지 알고 싶었다. 내가 투지의 힘을 시험해본 다음 분야는 영업이었는데, 이는 매일, 아니 매시간 거절당하는 것이 당연한 직업이다. 같은 휴가용 분할 소유권 회사에 고용된 수백 명의 남녀에게 투지 척도를 포함한 일련의 성격 설문지에 답하도록 요청했다. 6개월 후 회사를 다시 방문했을 때 영업 사원의 55%가 사라져 있었다. 투지는 누가 남고 누가 떠날지를 예측했다. 게다가 외향성, 정서적 안정성, 성실성을 포함해 일반적으로 측정되는 다른 어떤 성격 특성도 직장 유지를 예측하는 데 투지만큼 효과적이지 않았다. 비슷한 시기에 시카고 공립학교로부터 전화를 받았다. 웨스트포인트의 심리학자들처럼, 그곳의 연구자들도 고등학교 졸업장을 성공적으로 취득할 학생들에 대해 더 알고 싶어 했다. 그 봄, 수천 명의 고등학교 3학년 학생들이 다른 설문지들과 함께 축약된 투지 척도를 완성했다. 1년 이상 후, 그 학생들 중 12%가 졸업에 실패했다. 정시에 졸업한 학생들이 더 투지가 있었다. 그리고 투지는 학생들이 학교를 얼마나 소중히 여기는지, 공부에 얼마나 성실한지, 심지어 학교에서 얼마나 안전하다고 느끼는지 보다 졸업을 예측하는 더 강력한 요인이었다.

090

하위내용영역	배점	예상정답률
일반영어 A형 기입형	2점	45%

모범답안 privacy

채점기준

- 2점: 모범답안과 같다. 이외에는 답이 될 수 없다.
  ☞ "closedness(이런 영어표현은 없음)"와 "closeness(친밀함; 답답함)"는 답이 될 수 없다.

- 0점: 모범답안과 다르다.

한글번역

포스트모던 학자들과 사회 비평가들은 "닷컴 세대"—시뮬레이션된 상업 세계에서 자란 첫 번째 세대—에 대해 이야기하기를 좋아한다. 하지만 오늘날의 젊은이들이 19세기 말과 20세기 초의 부르주아 아이들과 얼마나 다를까? 많은 유사점이 있지만, 차이점들은 심오하며 새로운 유형의 인간이 21세기를 위해 준비되고 있음을 시사한다—자아감이 얼마나 많은 산출물을 생산하고 축적하느냐보다는 얼마나 많은 생생한 경험과 관계에 접근할 수 있느냐에 더 결속된 개인들을.

인간 의식의 마지막 큰 변화는 부르주아 계급의 부상과 함께 근대 시대의 여명에 일어났다. 초기 자본주의의 중심지였던 새로운 도시들의 산물인 부르주아지는 상인, 공장주, 상점 주인, 학자, 전문직 종사자들로서 산업적 삶의 방식을 선도했다. 카스트에서 계급으로 변하던 세계에서, 그들은 위로는 소멸하는 봉건 귀족과 아래로는 억압받고 불안정한 노동자와 권리를 박탈당한 소농민과 농민들의 프롤레타리아 사이에 끼인 상승 지향적인 중간층이었다. 그들은 자본의 기업가이자 축적자였고, 국민성과 확장된 시장의 옹호자였으며, 인간의 이성이 자연의 비밀을 풀고 인식 가능한 객관적 현실의 진리를 성문화할 수 있다고 믿는 현실주의자들이었다. 그들은 점차 신학을 버리고 이데올로기를 택했으며, 천국의 구원을 버리고 지상의 유토피아를 택한 계급이었다. 그들은 물질주의의 복음을 전파했고 가장 중요하게는 사유재산의 미덕을 찬양했다.

공개적이고 공적으로 이루어졌던 중세 생활과 달리, 부르주아지는 대부분 닫힌 문 뒤에서 살았다. 그들의 삶은 내면적인 것이었다—작은 상점과 응접실에서 펼쳐지는. 부르주아지는 자신들의 재산을 조직하는 방식으로 자신들의 삶을 조직했다. 그들 존재의 모든 측면이 사유화돼 공적 감시로부터 숨겨졌다. 이 사적 세계의 모든 것은 구성되고 조직됐다. 제자리에 없는 것은 아무것도 없었다.

091

하위내용영역	배점	예상정답률
일반영어 A형 서술형	4점	30%

모범답안 The most appropriate words for the blank are "outside torque". Next, the two ways to reduce angular momentum are to reduce the moment of inertia or to decrease angular velocity.

채점기준

+ 2점: 빈칸에 들어갈 두 단어를 "outside torque"라 정확하게 기술하였다.
  ☞ "outside force"라 했으면 <u>1점</u>만 준다.

+ 2점: 각운동량을 줄이는 두 가지 방법을 각각 "<u>to reduce the moment of inertia</u>(1점)"과 "<u>to decrease angular velocity</u>(1점)"라 답하였다.
  ☞ "to <u>reduce the moment of inertia</u>" 대신 "to <u>reduce mass</u>"라 답했으면 1점만 준다.

한글번역

피겨 스케이터들이 빠르게 회전하다가 팔을 안으로 당겨서 더 빠르게 회전하거나—혹은 팔을 벌려서 더 천천히 회전하는 것을 본 적이 있을 것이다. 이것은 "각운동량 보존"으로 알려진 물리학 개념 덕분에 일어난다. 하지만 주변에 아이스 스케이트가 없다면 어떻게 시도해볼 수 있을까?

뉴턴의 제1운동 법칙은 정지해 있는(움직이지 않는) 물체는 정지 상태를 유지하고 움직이는 물체는 계속 움직일 것이라고 명시한다—외부 힘의 작용을 받지 않는 한. 이는 물체의 운동량(질량 곱하기 속도)이 외부 힘이 어떻게든 작용하지 않는 한 동일하게 유지된다는 뜻이다. 당신은 이것을 매일 경험한다. 예를 들어, 공을 잡는 것을 상상해보자. 공이 움직일 때, 그것은 운동량을 갖는다. 공을 멈추려면(그리고 운동량을 0으로 만들려면) 손으로 힘을 가해야 한다. 공이 더 무겁거나 더 빠르게 움직인다면, 더 많은 운동량을 갖고 잡기가 더 어렵다—더 큰 힘을 가해야 한다.

이 개념은 보통 직선으로 움직이는 물체와 관련해서 설명되지만, 회전하는 물체에도 적용된다. 회전하는 물체에 대해 이야기할 때는 용어가 조금 다르다. 직선으로 작용하는 밀기나 당기기인 힘 대신에, 물체에 가해지는 "비틀림"인 토크를 언급한다(생각해보라: 드라이버나 문손잡이를 비트는 것).

질량 대신에, 회전 중심점 주위로 질량이 얼마나 퍼져 있는지를 측정하는 관성 모멘트를 언급한다. 속도 대신에 물체가 얼마나 빠르게 회전하는지를 측정하는 "각속도"라고 말한다. 마지막으로, 운동량 대신에 "각운동량"이라고 말한다.

비록 용어는 조금 다르지만 같은 개념들이 적용된다. 회전하는 물체의 각운동량은 외부 토크가 작용하지 않는 한 동일하게 유지될 것이다. 물리학에서 무언가가 동일하게 유지될 때 우리는 그것이 보존된다고 말한다. "각운동량 보존"이라는 문구가 나온 곳이 바로 여기다. 이것의 고전적인 예는 회전하는 아이스 스케이터나 사무용 의자에서 회전하는 사람이다. 팔을 안으로 당김으로써, 스케이터는 자신의 관성 모멘트를 줄이고 (모든 질량이 중심에 더 가까워짐), 따라서 각운동량을 일정하게 유지하기 위해 각속도가 증가해야 한다.

한글번역

모든 사람이 문자 형태로의 변화를 환영한 것은 아니었다. 인간 대 인간 소통에서 벗어나는 움직임이 소외감을 준다고 제안하는 사람들이 있었고, 알파벳과 같은 추상적이고 상징적인 체계를 배워야 한다는 것이 소통과 의미의 장벽이라고 생각하는 사람들도 있었다. 철학자 소크라테스는 문자 매체에 반대한 사람들 중 하나였다. 그는 인간의 사고와 소통이 유동적이며, 끊임없이 움직이고 있다고 주장했다. 그는 이해가 정보의 교환에 기반한다고 주장했는데, 여기서는 다른 사람들이 말하는 것에 비춰 지속적인 수정이 일어난다는 것이었다. 문자는 이런 중요한 역동성을 허용하지 않는다고 그는 경고했다. 문자는 아이디어를 고정시키고 논증에 관여하기보다는 논증을 따라가도록 강요한다는 것이었다. 그는 이것이 의도와 의미의 왜곡이라고 생각했기 때문에 자신의 아이디어를 글로 쓰지 않았다. 하지만 문자는 그의 기여 없이도 자리를 잡았고, 문자 매체의 전성기는 필사본 시대의 훌륭한 성취들과 함께 14세기와 15세기에 왔다. 유럽 역사의 이 시기까지 교회와 귀족들이 문자를 관장했고, 소크라테스가 예측했던 대로 의미들은 완전히 고정됐다. 필사본들은 주로 수도사와 사제들인 필경사들에 의해 제작됐다. 그리고 그들이 필사실에서 베껴 쓴 정보는 주로 신성한 성격의 것이었다. 그들은 성경, 기도서, 종교 주석서 등의 아름다운 필사본들을 제작했다. 이런 텍스트들은 교회와 귀족들의 언어인 라틴어로 돼 있었다. 이 암호를 사용함으로써 기득권층은 라틴어를 모르는 평신도 공동체가 정보에 접근하는 것을 막을 수 있었다.

092

하위내용영역	배점	예상정답률
일반영어 B형 서술형	4점	50%

모범답안 Socrates believed that human thought was fluid and moving but writing, which was too static, fixed ideas by making people follow others' argument without critical thinking. Second, the problem was that it kept common people from accessing information because they did not know Latin.

채점기준

+ 2점: 소크라테스가 writing을 비판한 이유를 "human thought was fluid and moving(1점), but writing, which was too static, fixed ideas(1점) (by making people follow others' argument without critical thinking)"라 서술하였다.

+ 2점: 수도원의 필사실(scriptoria)을 유지하는 것이 가지고 있는 것의 문제를 "it(the scriptoria) kept common people from accessing information(1점) because they did not know Latin(1점)"이라 서술하였다.

093

하위내용영역	배점	예상정답률
일반영어 A형 기입형	2점	55%

모범답안 diverse

채점기준

- 2점: 모범답안과 같다. 이외에는 답이 될 수 없다.
- 0점: 모범답안과 다르다.

한글번역

차별 시정 조치는 명백히 효과가 있었다. 더 흥미로운 학생 구성원을 만들어냈다. 이제 전문직에서 한 자리를 차지할 소수계 졸업생들을 배출했다. 이 나라가 어떻게 변화하는지 보고, 차별 시정 조치가 없었다면 새로운 나라의 지도자가 될—전문직에서, 교육에서, 의학에서, 비즈니스에서—소수계 배경의 사람들을 졸업시키지 못했을 가능성을 생각할 때, 그렇지 않았다면 나라가 어떻게 됐을지 생각하기가 두렵다. 차별 시정 조치는 필수불가결했다. 우리 모두는 입학 예정자들, 즉 고등학교 졸업반들이 자신들이 살펴보는 곳들을 판단하는 방법 중 하나가 그들이 가진 다양성의 정도라는 것을 발견한다. 학생들은 충분한 다양성을 갖지 못한 학교에 가고 싶어 하지 않는다. 그들은 본질적으로 더 흥미로운 곳들이 있다는 것을 인식한다. 흥미롭게도 제2차 세계대전 이후 세대에게 대학들은 지리적 다양성이 중요하다는 것을 이해했다. 그들은 미국의 점점 더 넓은 지역에서 학생들을 등록시키려고 애썼는데, 따라서 다양한 배경을 가진 학생들과 함께 더 나은 환경에서 배운다는 개념은 민권 운동과 함께 시작된 것이 아니다.

094

하위내용영역	배점	예상정답률
일반영어 A형 서술형	4점	50%

모범 답안 Two reasons that food prices soared were : bad weather had ruined harvests, and the rich hoarded food and charged exorbitant prices. Second, the underlined words refer to the pain of starvation.

채점 기준

+ 2점: 식품 가격이 치솟은 이유를 "bad weather had ruined harvests(1점)"와 "the rich hoarded food and charged exorbitant prices(1점)"라 서술하였거나 유사하였다.
+ 2점: 밑줄 친 "this excruciating torment"가 가리키는 것이 "the pain of starvation(또는 famine; extreme hunger)"이라 서술하였다.

한글번역

고대 이집트나 중세 인도에 심각한 가뭄이 닥쳤을 때, 인구의 5% 또는 10%가 죽는 것은 드문 일이 아니었다. 식량은 부족해졌고, 운송은 너무 느리고 비싸서 충분한 식량을 수입할 수 없었으며, 정부는 상황을 구원하기에는 너무 약했다.

어떤 역사책을 펼쳐도 굶주림에 미쳐버린 기아에 허덕이는 인구들에 대한 끔찍한 기록들을 마주칠 가능성이 높다. 1694년 4월 보베 마을의 한 프랑스 관리는 기근과 치솟는 식량 가격의 영향을 묘사하며 이렇게 말했다. 그의 관할 지역 전체가 이제 굶주림과 비참함으로 약해져서 궁핍으로 죽어가는 무수히 많은 불쌍한 영혼들로 가득 찼다고. 일하거나 직업이 없어서 빵을 살 돈이 없기 때문이었다. 삶을 조금이라도 연장하고 굶주림을 어느 정도 달래려고, 이 불쌍한 사람들은 고양이나 가죽을 벗겨 거름 더미에 버린 말고기 같은 더러운 것들을 먹었다. 다른 사람들은 소와 황소를 도살할 때 흘러나오는 피를 마셨다.

비슷한 장면들이 프랑스 전역에서 벌어졌다. 악천후가 지난 2년간 왕국 전체의 수확을 망쳤기 때문에 1694년 봄까지 곡물 창고는 완전히 비어 있었다. 부자들은 비축해둔 식량에 터무니없는 값을 매겼고, 가난한 사람들은 떼죽음을 당했다. 태양왕 루이 14세가 베르사유에서 정부들과 희롱을 벌이는 동안, 약 280만 명의 프랑스인—인구의 15%—이 1692년과 1694년 사이에 굶어 죽었다.

대부분의 독자들은 아마도 점심을 거르거나, 종교적 명절에 금식하거나, 새로운 기적의 다이어트의 일환으로 며칠간 채소 쉐이크로 살아갈 때 어떤 기분인지 알 것이다. 하지만 며칠 계속 아무것도 먹지 못했고 다음 한 입의 음식을 어디서 구할지 전혀 모를 때는 어떤 기분일까? 오늘날 대부분의 사람들은 이런 참혹한 고통을 경험해본 적이 없다. 우리 조상들은, 안타깝게도, 그것을 너무나 잘 알고 있었다. 그들이 하나님께 "기근에서 우리를 구하소서!"라고 부르짖을 때, 마음속에 있던 것이 바로 이것이었다.

유희대 | 일반영어 ❹-1

095

하위내용영역	배점	예상정답률
일반영어 B형 서술형	4점	50%

모범답안 It would be nonsensical for China to invade California because there are no valuable resources there, and it is more profitable to cooperate with big Silicon Valley companies than to invade. Second, the meaning of "peace" has changed from the temporary absence of war to the implausibility of war, which means there is no foreseeable reason for war.

채점기준

+ 2점: 중국이 캘리포니아를 침공하는 것이 왜 말이 안 되는 터무니없는 짓인지를 "there is no a valuable resource there(1점), and it is more profitable to cooperate with big Silicon Valley companies than to invade(1점)"이라 서술하였다.
+ 2점: "평화"라는 말의 의미가 어떻게 변화했는지를 "from the temporary absence of war (또는 from meaning that "there is no war going on at present") to the implausibility of war, which means there is no foreseeable reason for war"라 서술하였다.

한글번역

　1998년에 르완다가 이웃 콩고의 풍부한 콜탄 광산을 점령하고 약탈하는 것은 합리적이었다. 이 광석이 휴대폰과 노트북 제조에 높은 수요가 있었고, 콩고가 세계 콜탄 매장량의 80%를 보유하고 있었기 때문이다. 르완다는 약탈한 콜탄으로부터 연간 2억 4천만 달러를 벌어들였다. 가난한 르완다에게는 많은 돈이었다. 이와 대조적으로, 중국이 캘리포니아를 침공해서 실리콘 밸리를 점령하는 것은 전혀 합리적이지 않았을 것이다. 중국이 전장에서 어떻게든 승리할 수 있다고 해도, 실리콘 밸리에는 약탈할 실리콘 광산이 없었기 때문이다. 대신 중국은 애플과 마이크로소프트 같은 하이테크 거대 기업들과 협력해, 그들의 소프트웨어를 구매하고 제품을 제조함으로써 수십억 달러를 벌어들였다. 르완다가 1년 내내 콩고 콜탄을 약탈해서 번 것을, 중국은 평화로운 상거래 하루 만에 번다.

　결과적으로 '평화'라는 단어는 새로운 의미를 갖게 됐다. 이전 세대들은 평화를 전쟁의 일시적 부재로 생각했다. 오늘날 우리는 평화를 전쟁의 불가능성으로 생각한다. 1913년에 사람들이 프랑스와 독일 사이에 평화가 있다고 말했을 때, 그들의 의미는 '현재 프랑스와 독일 사이에 벌어지는 전쟁은 없지만, 내년에 무슨 일이 일어날지 누가 알겠는가'였다. 오늘날 우리가 프랑스와 독일 사이에 평화가 있다고 말할 때, 우리는 예측 가능한 어떤 상황 하에서도 그들 사이에 전쟁이 발발하는 것이 상상할 수 없다는 뜻이다. 그런 평화는 프랑스와 독일 사이뿐만 아니라 대부분의(전부는 아니지만) 국가들 사이에 지배적이다. 내년에 독일과 폴란드 사이에, 인도네시아와 필리핀 사이에, 또는 브라질과 우루과이 사이에 심각한 전쟁이 발발할 시나리오는 없다.

　이 새로운 평화는 단순한 히피의 환상이 아니다. 권력에 굶주린 정부들과 탐욕스러운 기업들도 그것에 의존한다. 메르세데스가 동유럽에서 판매 전략을 계획할 때, 독일이 폴란드를 정복할 가능성은 고려하지 않는다.

096

하위내용영역	배점	예상정답률
일반영어 A형 기입형	2점	55%

모범답안 ⓐ race ⓑ segregation

채점기준

• 2점: 모범답안과 같다. 이외에는 답이 될 수 없다.
• 1점: 둘 중 하나만 맞았다.
• 0점: 모범답안과 다르다.

한글번역

　독일 점령 하 유럽 유대인들의 곤경은 많은 사람들이 추축국에 대한 전쟁의 핵심이라고 생각했지만, 루스벨트의 주요 관심사가 아니었다. 헨리 파인골드의 연구는 유대인들이 수용소에 수용되고 600만 유대인과 수백만 비유대인의 끔찍한 학살로 끝날 말살 과정이 시작되고 있는 동안, 루스벨트가 수천 명의 생명을 구할 수 있었을 조치들을 취하지 못했다는 것을 보여준다. 그는 이것을 높은 우선순위로 보지 않았다. 그는 이를 국무부에 맡겼고, 국무부에서는 반유대주의와 냉혹한 관료주의가 행동의 장애물이 됐다.

전쟁이 "열등한" 인종들에 대한 히틀러의 백인 노르딕 우월주의 사상이 틀렸다는 것을 증명하기 위해 치러지고 있었던가? 미국의 군대는 인종에 따라 분리돼 있었다. 1945년 초 유럽 전선에서 전투 임무를 수행하기 위해 퀸 메리호에 군인들이 빽빽이 타고 있을 때, 흑인들은 갑판의 신선한 공기로부터 가능한 한 멀리 떨어진 엔진실 근처 배의 깊숙한 곳에 수용됐는데, 이는 옛날 노예선의 항해를 기이하게 연상시켰다.

적십자는 정부 승인 하에 흑인과 백인의 헌혈을 분리했다. 아이러니하게도 혈액 은행 시스템을 개발한 것은 찰스 드류라는 흑인 의사였다. 그는 전시 헌혈 책임자로 임명됐다가, 혈액 분리를 끝내려고 했을 때 해고됐다. 전시 노동력에 대한 절박한 필요에도 불구하고, 흑인들은 여전히 일자리를 구하는 데 많은 어려움을 겪고 있었다. 서부 해안 항공기 공장의 대변인은 이렇게 말했다 : "흑인은 관리인과 기타 비슷한 직종으로만 고려될 것이다. 항공기 작업자로서의 훈련에 관계없이, 우리는 그들을 고용하지 않을 것이다." 루스벨트는 자신이 설립한 공정고용관행위원회의 명령을 시행하기 위해 아무것도 하지 않았다.

한글번역

70개 이상의 국가에서 소비자 트렌드 정보를 수집하는 데이터베이스를 보유한 이노바 마켓 인사이트가 편집한 연구에 따르면, 미국과 영국 소비자 10명 중 4명이 그들이 "건강식품"이라고 부르는 음식, 또는 적어도 스스로를 건강하다고 마케팅하는 음식의 소비를 늘렸다. 여기에는 "살짝 짠" 또는 "살짝 단" 감자칩이 포함된다. 그리고 중국에서는 소비자의 거의 22%가 "진짜 재료로 만든"이 간식 구매에 영향을 미치는 중요한 요소라고 말했다. 20년 전과 달리, 오늘날 감자칩 포장지는 감자칩을 튀긴 기름부터 감자나 곡물이 수확된 국가까지 모든 것을 소비자에게 알려줄 수 있다.

따라서 맛도 문화적으로 코딩돼 있다는 것은 놀라운 일이 아니다. 이노바의 연구와 일치하게, 이는 라틴 아메리카에서 칠리와 할라페뇨 칠리가 일관되게 인기 있는 음식 맛인 반면, 북미에서는 바다소금, 체다, 바비큐가 지배적인 이유를 보여준다.

더욱 흥미로운 것은 외국 맛이 다른 시장에 도입되는 방식이다. 외국 맛들은 사회적 트렌드에 의존하고 함께 작용해 대형 식품 회사들이 어느 방향으로 갈지를 좌우한다.

미역 맛은 20년 전 미국에서 거의 들어본 적이 없었지만, 이제 북미에서 상위 10위 안에 드는 판매 맛 중 하나가 됐다. 만화책, 애니메이션, 스시를 포함한 일본 문화에 대한 관심 증가가 그 맛을 서구 소비자들에게 더 흥미롭게 만들었다. 그리고 감자칩 제조업체들이 이를 주목해, 소비자 트렌드가 다시 바뀌기 전에 그 변화를 활용했다.

이제 사람들은 한국 음식, 한국 전자제품, 한국 대중문화에 정말로 관심이 있어서, 김치가 새로운 감자칩 맛으로 좋은 아이디어일 수 있다. 20년 전이라면 사람들이 그 아이디어를 비웃었을 것이다.

097

하위내용영역	배점	예상정답률
일반영어 A형 서술형	4점	45%

모범답안 The reason is that people in Latin America are culturally-coded to enjoy it. Next, the meaning of the underlined words is that twenty years earlier, when Korean culture was not held in interest among Americans, kimchi would have been perceived as a ridiculous idea for potato chip flavoring.

채점기준

+ 2점 : 칠리가 라틴아메리카에서 계속 인기 있는 이유를 "people in Latin America are culturally-coded to enjoy it"이라 서술하였거나 유사하였다.
+ 2점 : 밑줄 친 부분의 의미를 "twenty years earlier, when Korean culture was not held in interest among Americans(1점), kimchi would have been perceived as a ridiculous idea for potato chip flavoring(1점)"이라 서술하였거나 유사하였다.

098

하위내용영역	배점	예상정답률
일반영어 B형 서술형	4점	50%

모범답안 The main idea of the passage is that society has ignored one lesson of the Icarus myth : not to fly too low. Next, the word that corresponds to the underlined words is "hubris".

유희태 | 일반영어 ❹-1

채점 기준

+ 2점: 글의 요지를 "society has ignored one lesson of the Icarus myth: not to fly too low"라 서술하였거나 유사하였다.

☞ 다음과 같이 답하였어도 2점을 준다.
- The original full teaching of the Icarus myth not to soar(fly) too low (as well as too high) has been ignored in order to discourage disobedience (by industrialists).
- Society has ignored the original lesson of the Icarus myth not to soar(fly) too low as well as too high (to discourage disobedience).

+ 2점: 밑줄 친 부분과 상응하는 단어가 "hubris"라 서술하였다. 이외에는 답이 될 수 없다.

한글번역

[1] 그리스 사모스 섬 바로 남쪽에 이카리아해가 있다. 전설에 따르면 이곳이 이카루스가 죽은 곳이다—오만함의 희생자로서. 그의 아버지 다이달로스는 뛰어난 장인이었다. 미노스 왕(미노타우루스의 포획자)의 작업을 방해한 죄로 감옥에 유배된 다이달로스는 우리가 어린 시절 들었던 신화에 묘사된 훌륭한 탈출 계획을 세웠다. 그는 자신과 아들을 위한 날개 한 쌍을 만들었다. 밀랍으로 날개를 붙인 후, 그들은 탈출을 시작했다. 다이달로스는 이카루스에게 태양에 너무 가까이 날지 말라고 경고했다. 마법 같은 비행 능력에 매혹된 이카루스는 불복종하고 너무 높이 날았다. 다음에 무슨 일이 일어났는지 우리 모두 안다: 밀랍이 녹았고, 사랑하는 아들 이카루스는 날개를 잃고 바다로 추락해 죽었다.

[2] 이 신화의 교훈: 왕에게 불복종하지 마라. 아버지에게 불복종하지 마라. 자신이 실제보다 더 낫다고 상상하지 마라. 그리고 무엇보다도 신이 할 수 있는 일을 자신이 할 수 있는 능력이 있다고 믿지 마라. 당신이 듣지 못한 신화의 부분: 이카루스에게 너무 높이 날지 말라고 말하는 것 외에도, 다이달로스는 아들에게 너무 낮게, 바다에 너무 가까이 날지도 말라고 지시했다. 물이 날개의 양력을 망칠 것이기 때문이었다. 사회는 신화를 변형시켜 우리가 바다에 관한 부분을 잊도록 부추기고, 일어서고, 두드러지고, 소동을 일으키는 위험에 대해 서로 끊임없이 상기시키는 문화를 만들었다. 산업가들은 교만을 대죄로 만들었지만 훨씬 더 흔한 결함은 편리하게 무시했다: 너무 적은 것에 만족하는 것을. 너무 높이 나는 것보다 너무 낮게 나는 것이 훨씬 더 위험하다. 낮게 나는 것이 안전하게 느껴지기 때문이다.

099

하위내용영역	배점	예상정답률
일반영어 A형 기입형	2점	45%

모범답안 war

채점 기준
- 2점: 모범답안과 같다. 이외에는 답이 될 수 없다.
- 0점: 모범답안과 다르다.

한글번역

전쟁의 가능성은 사회의 합리화와 문화 전반에 걸친 통일된 사회 구조 창출을 위한 강력한 힘이다. 정치적 자율성을 유지하고자 하는 모든 국가는 적과 경쟁국의 기술을 채택하도록 강요받는다. 하지만 그것보다 더 나아가, 전쟁의 위협은 국가들로 하여금 기술을 생산하고 배치하는 데 가장 도움이 되는 방향으로 사회 체계를 재구성하도록 강요한다. 예를 들어, 국가들은 이웃국과 경쟁하기 위해 특정 규모가 돼야 하며, 이는 국민 통합을 위한 강력한 동기를 만들어낸다. 국가 차원에서 자원을 동원할 수 있어야 하는데, 이는 과세와 규제의 권력을 가진 강력한 중앙집권적 국가 권위의 창설을 요구한다. 국민 통합을 잠재적으로 방해하는 다양한 형태의 지역적, 종교적, 혈연적 유대를 해체해야 한다. 기술을 다룰 수 있는 엘리트를 양성하기 위해 교육 수준을 높여야 한다. 국경 너머에서 일어나는 발전과의 접촉과 인식을 유지해야 한다. 그리고 나폴레옹 전쟁 중 대중 군대의 도입과 함께, 총동원이 가능하려면 적어도 사회의 빈곤층 계급의 참정권 부여의 문을 열어야 한다. 이 모든 발전들은 다른 동기—예를 들어 경제적 동기—때문에 일어날 수 있지만, 전쟁은 사회 근대화의 필요성을 특히 절실한 방식으로 규정하고 그 성공에 대한 명확한 시험을 제공한다.

100

하위내용영역	배점	예상정답률
일반영어 A형 서술형	4점	35%

모범답안 The meaning of the underlined words is that he felt like a celebrity entering a popular event past waiting *(trendy)* young people. Second, the writer mentions "public schools" to show how capitalism, exemplified by the tax break, is making lives for the average people more difficult.

채점 기준

+ 2점 : 밑줄 친 부분의 의미를 "the narrator*(he)* felt <u>like a celebrity</u>(1점) entering <u>a popular event</u>(1점) past waiting young people"이라 서술하였거나 유사하였다.
  ☞ 첫 번째에 special; famous; prideful 등이 들어가는 내용을 서술했어도 2점을 준다.

+ 2점 : 공립학교를 언급한 이유를 "to show <u>how capitalism, exemplified*(shown; indicated; proved)* by the tax break</u>(1점), is <u>making lives for the average people*(or millennials) more difficult*</u>(1점)"라 서술했거나 유사하였다.
  ☞ capitalism 없이 the tax bill (or the tax break)만 서술했어도 맞는 것으로 한다.

한글번역

지난달 금요일 밤, 나는 자본주의를 폐기해야 하는지에 대한 맨해튼에서의 토론을 사회했다. 이는 잡지 《야코빈》이 주최한 것이었고, 자본주의를 옹호하는 쪽은 자유주의 출판물 《리즌》의 편집자들이었다. 이용 가능한 450석 모든 티켓이 하루 만에 매진됐다. 그래서 《야코빈》은 두 배 정도 많은 인원을 수용할 수 있는 장소로 옮겼다. 추가 티켓들은 8시간 만에 매진됐다.

내가 도착했을 때, 사람들이 몇 블록에 걸쳐 줄을 서 있었다. 문으로 걸어가면서 나는 마치 지하 나이트클럽의 게스트 리스트에 있는 것 같은 기분이었다. 참석자 대부분은 20대와 30대로 보였는데, 대부분의 기성세대가 당연하게 여기는 체제인 자본주의를 유독 의심하는 세대의 일부였다.

반공주의 공산주의 희생자 추모 재단은 최근 조사에서 밀레니얼 세대의 44%가 사회주의 국가에서 살기를 선호한다는 것을 발견하고 놀랐다. 자본주의 하에서 살고 싶어 하는 42%와 비교되는 수치였다. 나이 든 미국인들에게는 공산주의의 붕괴가 자본주의에 대한 대안이 전혀 없는 것처럼 보이게 만들었다. 하지만 우리 경제의 점점 더 과두적인 성격을 고려할 때, 많은 젊은이들에게 자본주의가 실패한 신처럼 보이는 것은 놀라운 일이 아니다.

그것이 토요일 새벽 상원에서 통과된 형편없는 세법 개정안보다 더 명확한 곳은 없는데, 이는 부자를 더 부유하게 하고 가난한 사람을 더 가난하게 만들 것이다. 초당파 조세 정책 센터에 따르면, 이 법안은 소득 대비 최대 세금 감면을 납세자 상위 5%에게 집중시킨다. 2027년까지 최저 소득자들의 세금은 오를 것이다.

권리의식 강한 투덜이들로 비난받는 세대인 밀레니얼들이 특히 큰 타격을 받을 것이다. 하원과 상원에서 통과된 조치들로 혜택을 받을 부유한 사람은 전체 인구보다 더 나이 들고 더 백인인 경향이 있다. 젊은 사람들이 더 높은 세금이나 공공 서비스 축소, 또는 둘 모두를 통해 그 비용을 부담하게 될 것이다. 그들은 자신들이 태어난 사회보다 더욱 계층화된 사회를 물려받을 처지에 있다.

한 가지 예를 들어보자. 상원 법안은 자녀가 사립 학교에 다니는 부모들에게 세금 감면을 제공한다. 하지만 주정부와 지방정부 세금에 대한 공제를 삭감해, 밀레니얼 세대 대다수가 자녀들을 보낼 공립학교에 자금을 지원하기 더 어렵게 만들 수 있다.

101

하위내용영역	배점	예상정답률
일반영어 B형 서술형	4점	45%

모범답안 The meaning of the underlined words is that the timing is suspicious because the inclusion of male cheerleaders appears as a shallow*(token)* way to counter accusations of sexism by the Saints. Next, all advantages offered by male cheerleaders can be illuminating sexist rules, improving treatment of cheerleaders, diversifying role modeling for boys, and broadening viewers' conception of maleness.

유희태 | 일반영어 ❹-1

채점 기준

+ 2점: 밑줄 친 부분의 의미를 "the timing is suspicious because the inclusion of male cheerleaders appears as a shallow(token) way to counter accusations of sexism by the Saints"라 서술하였거나 유사하였다.
+ 2점: 남성 치어리더가 가져올 모든 긍정적 변화를 "① illuminating sexist rules, ② improving treatment of cheerleaders, ③ diversifying role modeling for boys, and ④ broadening viewers' conception of maleness"라 서술하였거나 유사하였다.
  ☞ 4개 중 3개를 서술한 경우 1점, 2개를 서술한 경우 0.5점, 1개 또는 서술하지 못한 경우 0점을 준다.

한글번역

앞으로 며칠 안에, 두 NFL 치어리딩 팀이 리그 최초의 남성 댄서들을 선보일 예정이다. 나폴레옹 지니스와 퀸턴 페론이 로스앤젤레스 램스의 치어리더에 합류했고, 제시 에르난데스가 뉴올리언스 세인츠의 세인테이션즈 멤버로 공연할 것이다. 세인츠를 포함한 NFL 팀들이 신체적 스턴트를 위한 보조 치어리더로 남성을 포함시킨 적은 있지만, 주요 댄스 루틴의 일부가 된 적은 결코 없었다.

프로 풋볼 치어리딩 팀에 남성을 추가하는 것은 성별 구성에서 작은 변화를 만들어낼 것이지만 큰 영향을 미칠 수 있다. 올해 초, 한 쌍의 치어리더가 NFL을 상대로 성차별 고발을 제기했고, 다른 여러 NFL 치어리더들도 자신들의 형편없는 급여, 외모와 사생활에 가해지는 극도의 제약, 그리고 팬들로부터 견뎌야 하는 성희롱에 대해 공개적으로 말했다. 이런 상황을 고려할 때, 이 특별한 유리 천장이 깨지는 시기는 의심스럽다. 세인츠가 성차별적 직장 환경 때문에 공개적 감시를 받은 지 몇 달 만에 첫 남성 치어리더를 고용한 것은 우연의 일치가 아닐 가능성이 높다. 이 팀들의 남성들이 아무리 그 자리에 합당하다고 해도, 팀들이 여성 직원들에 대한 지속적인 신체적, 재정적 착취를 가능하게 하는 겉치레로 남성 치어리더들을 이용할지 숙고해볼 만하다.

그렇다고 해서 약간의 성별 다양성에서 좋은 것이 나올 수 없다는 뜻은 아니다. 남성을 들여오는 것은 치어리딩 팀의 제한적 규칙들의 성차별적 성격을 드러내거나, 심지어 팀 리더십이 치어리더들을 대하는 방식을 개선하도록 강요할 수도 있다. 그리고 지니스와 페론은 이미 또 다른 가능한 긍정적 효과를 보여줬다: 풋볼을 보는 소년들과 젊은 남성들이 자신들의 미래에 무엇이 가능한지에 대한 새로운 아이디어를 얻을 수 있다는 것이다. 에르난데스는 어머니가 지니스와 페론이 램스 치어리딩 팀에 합류한다는 기사 링크를 보내준 후 세인테이션즈 오디션을 보기로 결정했다고 말했다. 남성 치어리더들의 존재는 또한 시청자들로 하여금 에르난데스와 동료들이 옆에 있는 여성들과 같은 섹시한 댄스 동작을 수행하는 것을 보면서 남성성과 남성다움에 대한 개인적 개념을 확장하도록 강요할 수도 있다. 남성들이 NFL 팬의 대다수를 차지한다―은밀한 남성성 재교육 캠페인을 위한 사로잡힌, 준비된 관객인 셈이다.

102

하위내용영역	배점	예상정답률
일반영어 A형 기입형	2점	50%

모범 답안 ⓐ life span ⓑ premature

채점 기준

• 2점: 모범답안과 같다. 이외에는 답이 될 수 없다.
• 1점: 둘 중 하나만 맞았다.
• 0점: 모범답안과 다르다.

한글번역

지난 100년간 평균 수명이 두 배가 됐지만, 다음 세기에 다시 두 배로 늘려 150세까지 만들 수 있다고 추정하고 결론내리는 것은 정당하지 않다. 1900년 전 세계 평균 수명이 40세를 넘지 못했던 것은 많은 사람들이 영양실조, 감염성 질병, 폭력으로 젊은 나이에 죽었기 때문이다. 하지만 기근, 전염병, 전쟁을 피한 사람들은 70대와 80대까지 충분히 살 수 있었는데, 이것이 호모 사피엔스의 자연 수명이다. 일반적인 통념과 달리, 70세 노인들은 이전 세기에 자연의 희귀한 괴물로 여겨지지 않았다. 갈릴레오 갈릴레이는 77세에, 아이작 뉴턴은 84세에 죽었고, 미켈란젤로는 항생제, 백신, 장기 이식의 도움 없이도 88세의 고령까지 살았다. 실제로 정글의 침팬지들도 때로는 60대까지 산다.

사실 지금까지 현대 의학은 우리의 자연 수명을 1년도 연장하지 못했다. 현대 의학의 위대한 성취는 우리를 조기 사망에서 구하고 우리 삶의 온전한 기간을 누릴 수 있게 해준 것이다. 이제 암, 당뇨병,

그리고 다른 주요 살인자들을 극복한다고 해도, 그것은 단지 거의 모든 사람이 90세까지 살게 된다는 뜻일 뿐이다―하지만 150세는 말할 것도 없고 500세에 도달하기에는 충분하지 않을 것이다. 그러려면 의학이 인체의 가장 기본적인 구조와 과정을 재설계하고 장기와 조직을 재생하는 방법을 발견해야 할 것이다. 우리가 2100년까지 그것을 할 수 있다는 것은 결코 분명하지 않다.

의미 기억은 일반적으로 삽화 기억에서 파생되는데, 우리가 경험으로부터 새로운 사실이나 개념을 배우기 때문이며, 삽화 기억이 의미 기억을 지지하고 뒷받침하는 것으로 여겨진다. 삽화 기억에서 의미 기억으로의 점진적 전환이 일어날 수 있는데, 여기서 삽화 기억은 특정 사건들에 대한 민감성과 연관성을 줄여서 정보가 의미 기억으로 일반화될 수 있도록 한다.

103

하위내용영역	배점	예상정답률
일반영어 A형 기입형	2점	55%

모범 답안 ⓐ episodic ⓑ semantic

채점 기준

- 2점: 모범답안과 같다. 이외에는 답이 될 수 없다.
- 1점: 둘 중 하나만 맞았다.
- 0점: 모범답안과 다르다.

한글번역

삽화 기억(에피소드 기억)은 우리의 경험과 시간 속 특정 사건들에 대한 기억을 연속적 형태로 나타내며, 이로부터 우리는 삶의 어느 시점에서든 실제로 일어났던 사건들을 재구성할 수 있다. 이는 명시적으로 진술될 수 있는 자서전적 사건들 (시간, 장소, 관련 감정, 기타 맥락적 지식)의 기억이다. 개인들은 이런 사건들에서 자신을 행위자로 보는 경향이 있으며, 감정적 충격과 사건을 둘러싼 전체 맥락이 보통 기억의 일부가 된다. 사건 자체의 단순한 사실만이 아니라.

반면 의미 기억은 우리가 습득한 외부 세계에 대한 사실, 의미, 개념, 지식에 대한 더 구조화된 기록이다. 이는 개인적 경험과 그것이 습득된 공간적/시간적 맥락과는 독립적이며 다른 사람들과 공유되는 일반적 사실적 지식을 의미한다. 의미 기억은 한때 개인적 맥락을 가졌을 수도 있지만, 이제는 단순한 지식으로서 독립적으로 존재한다. 따라서 음식의 종류, 수도, 사회적 관습, 사물의 기능, 어휘, 수학에 대한 이해 등을 포함한다. 의미 기억의 상당 부분은 추상적이고 관계적이며 언어적 기호의 의미와 연관이 있다.

104

하위내용영역	배점	예상정답률
일반영어 A형 서술형	4점	40%

모범 답안 Being honest is not a solution to the author's problem because her and her husband were being honest in their own mutually intelligible ways. Second, the justification from her background she provides is that in her family, explanations were offered as a matter of course unlike her husband's family, in which explanations were not offered.

채점 기준

- 2점: 솔직한 것이 해결책이 되지 못하는 이유를 "because her and her husband were being honest"라 서술하였거나 유사하였다.
- 2점: 남편과 다른 자신의 관점이 어떻게 형성되었는지를 자신의 (성장) 배경을 근거로 어떻게 정당화하는지에 대한 질문에 "in her family, explanations were offered as a matter of course unlike her husband's family"라 서술하였거나 유사하였다.

105

하위내용영역	배점	예상정답률
일반영어 B형 서술형	4점	45%

모범 답안 The study differs from the previous ones in that it includes a much larger set of data taken from 42 countries. Next, the writer uses "intriguingly" because the handling of friend and loved ones differs from patterns with other types of groups in the case of Romanians.

채점 기준

+ 2점 : 이전의 연구와 다른 점을 "it includes a much larger set of data"라 서술하였거나 유사하였다.
+ 2점 : 저자가 "(정말) 놀랍게도"란 말을 한 이유를 "because the handling of friend and loved ones differs from patterns with other groups in the case of Romanians"라 서술하였거나 유사하였다.

한글번역

한글번역 (좌측)

우리 결혼에서 가장 큰 골칫거리 중 하나는 겉보기에 무해해 보이는 작은 질문 "왜?"였다. 설명이 당연히 제공되는 가정에서 자란 나는 항상 남편에게 "왜?"라고 물었다. 그는 설명이 제공되지도 요구되지도 않는 가정에서 자랐기 때문에, 내가 "왜?"라고 물으면 숨겨진 의미를 찾았고—내가 그의 결정과 심지어 그것을 내릴 권리까지 의심하고 있다고 결론지었다. 내가 계속해서 왜냐고 묻는 것이 그에게는 그를 무능하다고 보여주려는 노력처럼 보였다. 게다가 사람들이 일을 하는 이유를 설명하는 것을 듣는 데 익숙하지 않았고, 과거에 자신의 이유를 설명해달라는 요청을 받은 적이 없었기 때문에, 그는 본능에 따라 행동하는 경향이 있었다. 그래서 원했다고 해도 정말로 자신의 이유를 설명할 수 없었다.

결과적으로, 우리는 종종 이런 대화를 나눴다:

"오늘 밤 앤서니 집에 들러보자"
"왜?"
"알았어, 갈 필요 없어."

그러면 그는 자신을 위한 이 작은 일을 기꺼이 하지 않는다고 나에게 화를 냈고, 나는 그가 즉석에서 마음을 바꾸고, 왜 가고 싶었는지 또는 왜 가기 싫은지 설명을 거부하고, 알 수 없이 토라지는 것에 대해 그에게 화가 났다.

이런 오해들을 바로잡기 어려운 이유는 우리의 소통 방식이 우리에게는 자명하게 자연스러워 보이기 때문이다. 그는 자신이 암시를 주고 있다고 느끼지 않았다. 소통하고 있다고 느꼈다. 그는 내게서 암시를 받아들이고 있다고 느끼지 않았다. 내가 소통하는 것을 듣고 있다고 느꼈다.

그래서 자주 듣는 "솔직하게 하라"는 조언이 별로 도움이 되지 않는다. 우리는 솔직했다. 하지만 우리의 솔직함의 방식이 달랐고—서로 이해할 수 없었다. 내가 그의 암시를 놓쳤을 때, 그는 내가 그의 뜻을 알고 있으면서 그것을 존중하기를 거부한다고 생각했다. 내가 그가 내 말에서 들은 것(또는 내가 암시했다고 들은 것—같은 말이다)을 의도했다는 것을 부인했을 때, 그는 내가 변덕스럽거나 부정직하다고 생각했다. 나는 그가 내 말에서 들은 것을 의도하지 않았고, 그가 자신이 의미했다고 알고 있던 것을 듣지 못했기 때문에, 문제를 해결하려는 우리의 시도는 실패할 운명이었다. 우리가 알고 있던 유일한 치료 방법이 바로 그 병을 일으키는 것이었다—대화하기.

한글번역 (우측)

사람들과 이야기할 때 가까이 서는 것을 좋아한다면, 아르헨티나를 사랑하게 될 것이다. 이 남미 국가는 "가까이서 말하는 사람들"로 가득하다—낯선 사람과 대화할 때 2.5피트(0.76미터) 떨어져 서는 사람들을. 만약 더 많은 개인 공간을 선호한다면, 대신 루마니아로 가라. 그곳 주민들은 낯선 사람으로부터 4.5피트(1.4미터)라는 널찍한 거리를 두고 서는 것을 좋아한다.

개인적 "버블"에 대한 이 정보는 최근 《문화 간 심리학 저널》에 발표된 선호하는 대인 거리에 관한 연구에서 나온 것이다. 다른 국가들의 개인 공간 문제는 이전에도 조사된 적이 있지만, 이 연구의 저자들은 이전 연구들에서 사용된 것보다 훨씬 큰 데이터 세트(42개국에 거주하는 거의 9,000명)를 사용했다. 참가자들은 두 사람을 나타내는 두 인물과 그들 사이에 표시된 몇 가지 거리가 있는 선이 그려진 그림을 봤다. 피험자들은 만약 두 인물이 낯선 사람 대 가까운 친구 대 동료(지인)라면 얼마나 가까이 서야 하는지 묻는 질문을 받았다. 피험자들은 자신이 두 인물 중 하나라고 가정해야 했다.

과학자들은 아르헨티나, 페루, 불가리아 주민들이 낯선 사람에게 가장 가까이 서는 반면, 루마니아, 헝가리, 사우디아라비아 출신들은 가장 많은 공간을 원한다는 것을 발견했다. 미국인들은 중간 어디쯤에 있었다.

연구자들은 또한 우리가 가족과 친구들 사이에 그은 개인적 버블도 연구했다. 우리는 모두 가족과 친구들이 낯선 사람보다 우리에게 더 가까이 서는 것을 괜찮아한다—거기에는 놀라움이 없다. 그리고 친구들과의 일반적인 버블 크기는 일관성을 유지한다. 즉, 더 많은 개인 공간을 좋아한다면, 적은 개인 공간이 괜찮은 사람들보다 친구들을 더 멀리 두게 될 것이다.

하지만 흥미롭게도, 가까운 친구나 사랑하는 사람들에게 올 때는 상황이 바뀐다. 자신과 낯선 사람, 동료 모두 사이에 많은 개인 공간을 좋아하는 루마니아인들은 친밀한 관계는 자신에게 상당히 가까이 있기를 좋아한다—약 1.5피트(0.45미터). 이는 연구된 거의 다른 어떤 집단보다도 더 가깝다.

에 사용할 수 있도록 그것을 저장한다. 당연히, 강력한 사와로는 사막 생활의 중요한 부분이다. 사실, 이 거인은 딱따구리, 올빼미, 비둘기, 박쥐, 곤충 등 많은 동물이 서식처가 될 수 있다. 또한, 사와로가 50 정도의 나이가 된 후, 1년에 한 번씩 식물의 꼭대기에 강건한 꽃이 나타난다. 이 꽃들은 검은 색 씨앗을 가진 맛있는 꽃과 꿀을 얻기 위해 오는 새, 박쥐, 꿀벌을 유혹한다. 리갈 사와로들은 남서부 지역에 풍부하지만, 불행히도 위험에 처해 있다. 이 거대한 선인장은 조경 원예에서 큰 가치가 있으며, 밀렵꾼은 그들을 뿌리 뽑고 종묘원에 팔아 수천 달러를 벌 수 있다.

106

하위내용영역	배점	예상정답률
일반영어 A형 기입형	2점	70%

모범 답안 regal saguaros

채점 기준

- 2점 : 모범답안과 같다. 이외에는 답이 될 수 없다.
- 0점 : 모범답안과 다르다.

한글번역

애리조나 남부와 멕시코 북부의 메마른 소노란 사막을 방문하는 사람들은 경관에 독특한 모습을 선사하는 많은 팔들을 가진 거인에게 경탄한다. 이것들은 거대한 사와로 선인장들이다. 건조하고 울퉁불퉁한 사막에서 선인장은 200년 이상 살고 60피트 높이로 자라며 50개의 팔이 있다. 놀랍게도, 이 사와로 선인장들은 가혹하고 힘든 사막 기후에도 불구하고 살아남아 존속한다. 성장해 노령이 된 것들은 모종들을 먹어치우는 쥐 떼들은 물론이고 가뭄, 얼어붙은 돌발, 홍수, 관목 화재들을 이겨내고 살아남는다. 모든 사막 식물과 마찬가지로, 사와로들은 물을 저장한다. 이 잎이 없는 식물들은 긴 뿌리를 통해 물을 흡수하여 사막의 긴 건조한 기간들

107

하위내용영역	배점	예상정답률
일반영어 B형 서술형	4점	35%

모범 답안 The corresponding sentence is "The eight-hour group also had significantly decreased appetite, that is, they weren't starving." Second, the importance of "lower insulin levels" is that they lose their weight because their fat cells can release their stored sugar to be used as energy.

채점 기준

+ 2점 : 상응하는 문장을 "they weren't starving" 또는 "(The eight-hour group also) had significantly decreased appetite"라 서술하였거나 유사하였다.
+ 2점 : 낮은 인슐린 수치가 갖는 중요성을 "they lose their weight (because their fat cells can release their stored sugar to be used as energy)"이라 서술하였거나 유사하였다.

한글번역

간헐적 단식은 체중을 줄이길 원하면, 일리가 있다. 우리가 먹는 음식은 내장에서 효소에 의해 분해돼 혈관을 통해 신체 곳곳으로 전달된다. 탄수화물, 특히 설탕과 정제된 곡물(밀가루와 백미)은 우리 세포의 에너지원이 되는 당분으로 쉽게 분해된다. 세포가 이를 사용하지 않을 때는 지방 세포에 지방으로 저장된다. 하지만 당분이 세포에 들어오기 위해서는 췌장이 만드는 호르몬인 인슐린이 필요하다. 인슐린은 당분이 지방 세포로 들어가 저장될 수 있게 만들어준다.

식사 사이에 간식을 먹지 않을 경우 우리의 인슐린 수치는 떨어지고 지방세포는 저장했던 당분을 에너지로 사용할 수 있게 내어놓는다. 곧, 인슐린 수치가 낮아져야만 우리는 체중을 낮출 수 있다. 간헐적 단식은 바로 이 인슐린 수치를 충분한 시간 동안 충분히 낮춰 지방을 태우는 방법을 말한다.

모든 간헐적 단식이 다 같은 효과를 내는 것은 아니며, 어떤 단식은 (다른 단식보다) 더 효과적이고 지속 가능하다. 그 비밀은 밤과 낮을 따라 신체가 바뀌는 생체주기에 있다. 우리의 신진대사 또한 낮에는 음식을 섭취하고 밤에는 수면을 취하도록 만들어져 있다. 야식 습관은 비만과 관련이 높으며, 당뇨의 위험 또한 있다.

이걸 기반으로, 연구진은 초기 당뇨의 위험이 있는 비만 환자들을 두 그룹으로 나눠 한 그룹은 이른 8시간 동안에만(아침 7시에서 3시 사이) 음식을 주는 "조기 시간 제한 식이요법"을 하게 했고, 다른 그룹은 12시간(아침 7시부터 저녁 7시 사이)에 걸쳐 음식을 골고루 먹게 했다. 처음엔 두 그룹 모두 체중이 변하지는 않았다. 하지만 5주 후엔 8시간 그룹은 인슐린 수치가 크게 떨어졌고, 인슐린 민감성 또한 높아졌으며, 혈압 역시 크게 낮아졌다. 특히, 이 그룹은 식탐이 크게 줄었는데, 이는 식사량이 줄었음에도 자신이 전혀 굶었다고 생각하지 않았다는 것이다.

108

하위내용영역	배점	예상정답률
일반영어 B형 서술형	4점	45%

모범답안 "To win the game" refers to completely stop death. Second, the underlined words mean that not everyone has to face death because only some very rich people are able to purchase immortality as opposed to the poor who cannot.

채점 기준

+ 2점: "게임에서 이기는 것"이 가리키는 것을 "completely stop death"라 서술하였거나 유사하였다.
  ☞ "find a cure for death" 또는 "achieve immortality"라 했어도 맞는 것으로 한다.

+ 2점: 밑줄 친 "평등 끝, 불멸 시작"이라는 말이 의미하는 것이 "(not everyone has to face death) because only some very rich people are able to purchase immortality as opposed to the poor who cannot."이라 서술하였거나 유사하였다.

한글번역

요즘 들어 자신의 생각을 서슴없이 드러내는 과학자와 사상가가 조금씩 늘고 있다. 그들은 현대 과학의 주력 사업이 죽음을 격파하고 인간에게 영원한 젊음을 제공하는 것이라고 말한다. 그 대표 주자가 노년학자 오브리 드 그레이와 석학이자 발명가인 레이 커즈와일이다. 그는 2012년에 구글 엔지니어링 이사로 임명됐고, 1년 뒤 구글은 죽음 해결하기가 창립 목표임을 밝히는 칼리코라는 자회사를 설립했다. 2009년 구글은 불멸을 믿는 또 한 명의 신고인 빌 마리스를 영입해 구글의 벤처투자사 구글벤처스를 맡겼다. 2015년 1월 한 인터뷰에서 마리스는 이렇게 말했다. "오늘 나에게 500살까지 사는 것이 가능하냐고 묻는다면 내 답은 '그렇다'이다." 마리스는 자신의 용감한 발언을 현금으로 뒷받침한다. 구글벤처는 보유 자산 20억 달러 중 36%를 원대한 생명 연장 프로젝트와 생명 과학 벤처기업들에 투자하고 있다. 마리스는 죽음과의 싸움을 미식축구에 빗대어 설명했다. "몇 야드 얻는 것이 목표가 아니다. 게임에서 이기는 것이 목표이다."

실리콘밸리의 여러 유명인사들이 이런 꿈을 공유한다. 페이팔의 공동창립자 피터 틸은 최근 영원히 사는 것이 자신의 목표라고 고백했다. 그는 이렇게 설명한다. "죽음에 접근하는 방식에는 크게 세 가지가 있다고 생각한다. 수용하거나 부정하거나 싸우는 것이다. 수용하거나 부정하는 사람이 대부분이겠지만 나는 싸우는 쪽을 택한다." 많은 사람들이 이 발언을 철없는 몽상으로 치부할 것이다. 하지만 틸의 말이라면 진지하게 받아들일 필요는 있다. 그는 실리콘밸리에서 가장 성공했고 가장 영향력 있는 기업가 중 한 명으로, 개인 자산이 22억 달러에 이른다. 조만간 "평등 끝, 불멸 시작"이라는 광고(경)가 내걸릴 듯한 조짐이 보인다.

109

하위내용영역	배점	예상정답률
일반영어 A형 기입형	2점	50%

모범 답안 culture

채점 기준

- 2점: 모범답안과 같다. 이외에는 답이 될 수 없다.
- 0점: 모범답안과 다르다.

한글번역

탈냉전 시대의 세계에서 인류를 구분하는 가장 중요한 기준은 이념, 정치, 혹은 경제가 아니다. 그것은 문화이다.

인류 역사 대부분의 기간 동안 문명 간의 접촉은 간헐적이거나 거의 존재하지 않았다. 그러나 서기 1500년경 근대가 시작되면서 세계 정치에는 두 가지 차원이 생겨났다. 400여 년 동안 서방 문명에 속한 여러 국가들—영국, 프랑스, 스페인, 오스트리아, 프로이센, 독일, 미국 등—은 서구 내부의 다극적 국제 체계를 형성하며 서로 교류하고 경쟁하며 전쟁을 벌였다. 동시에 서방 국가들은 다른 모든 문명에 대해 팽창하고, 정복하며, 식민지화하거나, 결정적인 영향을 미쳤다. 냉전 시기에 세계 정치는 양극 체제가 됐고, 세계는 세 부분으로 나뉘었다. 미국이 주도한, 대부분 부유하고 민주적인 사회들은 소련이 주도한, 상대적으로 가난한 공산주의 사회들과 사상적·정치적·경제적, 그리고 때로는 군사적인 전면 경쟁을 벌였다. 이러한 갈등의 상당 부분은 두 진영에 속하지 않은 제3세계에서 벌어졌는데, 그곳의 국가들은 대체로 가난하고 정치적 불안정에 시달렸으며, 최근에 독립했고, 비동맹을 주장했다.

1980년대 후반 공산권이 붕괴하면서 냉전 체제는 역사가 됐다. 사람들과 국가들은 인간이 직면할 수 있는 가장 근본적인 질문, 즉 "우리는 누구인가?"에 답하려 하고 있다. 그리고 그들은 인간이 전통적으로 그래왔듯, 자신들에게 가장 의미 있는 것들을 통해 이 질문에 답하고 있다. 사람들은 혈통, 종교, 언어, 역사, 가치, 관습, 제도 등을 기준으로 자신을 정의한다.

110

하위내용영역	배점	예상정답률
일반영어 A형 기입형	2점	45%

모범 답안 evolutionary

채점 기준

- 2점: 모범답안과 같다. 이외에는 답이 될 수 없다.
- 0점: 모범답안과 다르다.

한글번역

사회생물학은 사회적 행동이 진화의 결과라는 가설에 기반한 과학 연구 분야이며 이런 맥락에서 사회적 행동을 조사하고 설명하려 한다. 그것은 사회적 행동을 다루는 생물학의 한 분과이며, 또한 (동물)행동학, 인류학, 진화, 동물학, 고고학, 집단 유전학 및 다른 분야에서 이론을 끌어낸다. 그들 중에서 가장 잘 알려진 사람은 에드워드 윌슨이지만, 사회생물학자들은 동물의 사회적 행동을 위한 생물학적 기초가 있다고 주장하며, 또 그들은 각종 상황들에서 동물 관찰을 통해 가설을 검증한다. 연구된 종은 흰개미와 히말라야 원숭이(가장 잘 알려진 구세계 원숭이 종 중 하나)를 모두 포괄할 정도로 다양하다. 사회생물학자들은 나아가 인간 행동을 연구하는 학생들이 단지 문화, 민족, 환경과 같은 전통적 변수를 통해서만 인간 본성의 대단함을 설명할 수는 없고, 오히려 진화 과정을 포함시켜야만 한다고 주장한다. 그러나 많은 과학자들, 특히 스티븐 제이 굴드와 리차드 루웡틴은 인간에 대한 이 연구의 접근 방식을 비판해 왔다. 예를 들어, 그것은 유럽 중심적인 개념을 기반으로 하고 또 그것은 방법론적 문제로 어려움을 겪고 있다고 비판해 왔다. 이 비방자들은 사회 생물학적 이론이 거짓됨이 증명될 수 없기 때문에 그것을 의사(사이비) 과학이라고 칭하고 있고, 따라서 이러한 점에서 보면 연금술이나 점성술과 유사하다.

111

하위내용영역	배점	예상정답률
일반영어 B형 서술형	4점	50%

모범답안 The main commonality between Pavlov and Wendell is the abusive use of orphans in both of their experiments. Second, the difficulty Pavlov had was the orphans' unwillingness to accept food from strangers.

채점 기준

+ 2점: 둘의 주요한 공통점을 "the abusive use of orphans"라 서술하였거나 유사하였다.
  ☞ "abusive"의 의미가 없다면 0.5점 감점한다.

+ 2점: 파블로프가 직면한 어려움이 "the orphans' unwillingness to accept food from strangers"라 서술하였거나 유사하였다.

한글번역

　대부분의 사람들은 파블로프가 개들이 음식을 보거나 냄새를 맡을 수 없을 때도 음식을 예상하도록 조건화될 수 있다는 것을 증명한 유명한 개 실험에 대해 안다. 그것은 심리학의 초석이 되는 실험이었고 상당히 무해하게 들린다. 하지만 파블로프는 개 애호가와는 거리가 멀었다. 그의 실험 중 많은 것들이 긍정적 강화가 아닌 개들의 우리에 물을 채워 익사할 것이라고 믿게 만들거나, 계단 한두 층에서 반복적으로 밀어내 계단을 두려워하도록 조건화하는 것과 같은 부정적 강화로 이뤄졌다. 개에 대한 파블로프의 실험은 잔혹했을지 모르지만, 그는 개에만 관심이 있던 것이 아니었다. 이상적으로 그는 인간의 정신이 어떻게 작동하는지 알고 싶어 했고, 그래서 지역 고아원에서 아이들을 구했다―아시다시피, 대신 나서줄 부모가 없는 감수성이 강한 정신들을. 그는 개들에게 했던 것과 같은 타액 분비 실험을 고아들에게 실시했는데, 유일한 함정은 고아들이 개들만큼 기꺼이 낯선 사람으로부터 음식을 받으려 하지 않는다는 것이었다. 그래서 그는 그들을 의자에 묶고, 입을 테이프로 벌려놓고, 타액을 측정하는 장치를 삽입한 다음, 단것과 나쁜 맛의 것들을 강제로 먹였다.

　파블로프만이 아니었다. 웬델 존슨은 1939년에 말더듬에 관한 작은 실험을 실시했다. 그는 22명의 고아를 데려왔다. 고아들의 절반에게는 긍정적인 언어 치료를 제공했고, 나머지 절반은 그들의 언어 능력이 끔찍하고 말더듬이라고 말해서 (이는 완전히 거짓이었다) 정신적으로 고문했다. 놀랍지 않게도 부정적 강화 집단의 아이들은 위축됐다. 많은 아이들이 연구가 끝날 때까지 전혀 말하기를 거부했고, 말을 한 아이들 중 일부는 이전에는 존재하지 않던 영구적인 말더듬을 갖게 됐다. 이런 피해를 되돌리려는 노력은 전혀 이뤄지지 않았고, 이 실험은 그를 도와 실시한 학부생들에 의해 "괴물 실험"이라는 별명이 붙었다.

112

하위내용영역	배점	예상정답률
일반영어 B형 서술형	4점	45%

모범답안 The two words for the blank are "self repair". Next, biology can handle heavy loads reliably due to constant self repair and recycling.

채점 기준

+ 2점: 빈칸에 "self repair"라 서술하였다. 이외에는 답이 될 수 없다.
+ 2점: (우리 몸의) 생명 작용이 매우 무거운 짐을 감당할 수 있는 이유를 "constant (self) repair and recycling" 때문이라 서술하였다.

한글번역

　우리 몸에 있는 뼈와 힘줄(건)은 우리 몸을 구성하는 물질이 버틸 수 있는 한계를 넘어 압축되거나 늘어난다. 하지만 우리 몸은 그 구성요소의 한계보다 훨씬 높은 '신뢰성'을 가지고 있다. 예를 들어, 가벼운 달리기만으로도 아킬레스건에는 자신이 버틸 수 있는 장력 한계의 75%가 가해진다. 역도 선수들이 수백 킬로그램의 바벨을 들 때 허리에는 한계의 90%에 가까운 힘이 걸린다.

그럼 어떻게 생명 작용(우리 몸)은 이런 부담을 해결하는 것일까? 그 답은 바로 우리의 몸은 자신의 구성요소를 끊임없이 수리하고 재건한다는 것이다. 손상을 입은 힘줄은 콜라겐 섬유를 교체함으로써 전체 힘줄이 여전히 안전한 수준에 머무르게 한다. 일상적인 자가 수리는 저렴하고 효율적이며, 특히 주어진 부담에 맞춰 대응이 가능한 방법이다. 사실 인체의 모든 구성요소는 이러한 자가 수리의 힘을 가지고 있다. 인체를 구성하는 원자의 98%가 매년 바뀌는 것으로 알려져 있다.

  우리는 최근 이러한 자가 수리 개념을 이용해 현존하는 물질만으로도 안전한 우주 엘리베이터를 만들 수 있다는 것을 보였다. 이는 적도에서 우주로 뻗은 91,000km 길이의 테더라는 이름의 케이블 형태의 구조이다. 테더는 마치 콜라겐 섬유가 힘줄을 구성하고 골원(osteon)이 뼈를 구성하는 것처럼 평행섬유로 만들어진 케이블들로 이뤄져 있다.

  우리를 물러서게 했던 울타리가 더 이상 없음에도 우리는 여전히 그 오래전 경계들에 편안함을 느낀다. 혁명이 오고, 경제판도가 뒤집히고, 규칙들이 이제 바뀌었기 때문에, 우리는 이제 명확한 진실을 마주해야만 한다. 즉, 안전지대가 바뀌었으나 안락지대는 바뀌지 않았다. 안전하다고 느끼는 지역들—즉, 고급 사무실(회사의 최고위급 간부가 사용함), 유명 대학, 안정적인 직장 등—은 이제 안전하지 않다. 우리는 머뭇거리며, 정상으로 돌아갈 거라 생각하지만, 이 뉴노멀(시대 변화에 따라 새롭게 떠오르는 기준)시대에서는, 우리의 변화에 대한 저항은 더 이상 소용이 없다.

  우린 실수를 했다. 우리는 충분히 대담하지 못한 안전지대에 안주했다. 그 안전지대는 권위와 복종을 받아들이는 곳이었다. 우리는 순종적이고 눈에 띄지 않는 태도를 중심으로 편안한 영역을 세웠고, 그 결과 파도에 너무 가까워져 버렸다. 아무리 많은 회의에 가고, 아무리 많은 책을 읽고, 아무리 많은 세미나에 참석한다 해도, 당신의 안락지대를 오늘날의 새로운 안전지대와 다시 맞추는 법을 알아내지 못한다면, 세상의 그 어떤 전략도 도움이 되지 않을 것이다.

113

하위내용영역	배점	예상정답률
일반영어 A형 기입형	2점	45%

모범답안 ⓐ safe ⓑ comfort zone

채점기준

- 2점 : 모범답안과 같다. 이외에는 답이 될 수 없다.
- 1점 : 둘 중 하나만 맞았다.
- 0점 : 모범답안과 다르다.

한글번역

  오랫동안 이 둘은 하나였다. 언제 자신이 안전지대 밖에 있는지를 아는 산악인은 그것에 대해 불편하여 멈춘다. 그리고 다음 날 오르기 위해 살아간다. 우리의 전체 생애는 안락지대와 안전지대를 조율해가는 과정이라고 할 수 있다. 언제 나아가고 언제 물러설지를 배우며, 내가 지금 위험지대에 들어섰을 때 어떤 느낌인지를 이해하는 것 등이다. 여우처럼, 우리는 울타리 안에 가만히 있도록 훈련받았다. 울타리 안에 있는 것이 안전하기 때문이다. 적어도 최근까지는 그랬다.

  우리에겐 의사결정을 할 때마다 안전지대 안에 있는지 확인할 여유가 없다. 그러다 보니 안전지대는 차츰 잊어버리고 안전지대의 쌍둥이인 안락지대(심리적으로 안전하다는 느낌)에만 주목하기 시작했다. 우리를 안락하게 하는 것이 또한 우리를 안전하게 한다고 생각했다.

114

하위내용영역	배점	예상정답률
일반영어 A형 기입형	2점	50%

모범답안 spaghetti breaking

채점기준

- 2점 : 모범답안과 같다. 이외에는 답이 될 수 없다.
- 0점 : 모범답안과 다르다.

한글번역

  인터넷에 현대 물리학의 난제들을 검색해보면 보기만 해도 주눅 드는 어려운 내용이 끝도 없이 나온다. 암흑물질이란 무엇인가? 왜 시간은 한 방향으로만 흐르는가? 블랙홀 안에서는 무슨 일이 일어날까? 이런 질문들이다.

  그러나 천재 물리학자들도 풀지 못한 난제라고 나오는 수수께끼 가운데는 도대체 왜 난제가 됐는지 의아하기까지 한 문제들도 있다. 노벨상까지 받은 미국의 물리학자 리처드 파인만이 수십 년 전에 씨름했던 '마른 스파게티 면 부러뜨리기' 문제도 그 가운데 하나다.

어느 저녁 파인만은 슈퍼컴퓨터 연구의 선구자인 대니 힐리스와 집에서 자신이 평소 즐겨 먹는 스파게티를 같이 먹으려고 요리하다가 스파게티 면의 특이한 점을 발견한다. 삶기 전의 마른 면을 절반으로 부러뜨리려 하면 좀처럼 의도한 대로 두 동강이 나지 않고, 대신 거의 예외 없이 서너 조각 이상으로 잘게 부서지는 것이었다. 조각이 부서지는 방향도 제각이어서 온 부엌에 금세 스파게티 면 조각이 난무했다.

"도대체 왜 이런 일이 일어날까? 왜 두 조각이 아니라 세 조각으로 부러질까? 우리는 이상한 이론들을 만들어 내면서 2시간을 보냈죠." 힐리스는 파인만 전기에서 회상했다. 그러나 천재 과학자 두 명이 두 시간 동안 머리를 싸매고 고민했지만, 신통한 결론은 나지 않았고, 파인만의 부엌 곳곳에 널브러진 스파게티 면 조각만이 남겨졌다.

그로부터 수십 년이 지난 2015년 봄 어느 날, MIT 대학원생 로널드 헤이저와 에드가 그리델로는 우연히 같은 문제에 봉착한다. 파인만, 힐리스처럼 왜 스파게티 면을 둘로 쪼갤 수 없을지 궁금한 나머지 이 문제를 붙잡고 씨름하게 된 건 같았지만, 헤이저와 그리델로는 두 시간보다 훨씬 더 긴 시간을 이 문제를 푸는 데 할애했다. 다만 헤이저와 그리델로가 씨름한 질문은 왜 마른 스파게티 면이 정확히 둘로 쪼개지지 않는지가 아니었다. 헤이저와 그리델로는 좀 더 심오한 질문에 도전했다. 처음부터 스파게티 면을 절반으로 쪼개는 게 가능한가? 그렇게 할 수 있는 방법이 있다면 정확히 어떻게 하면 될까? 가능했다. 스파게티 면을 한 바퀴 꼬아서 부러뜨리면 됐다. 문자 그대로.

115

하위내용영역	배점	예상정답률
일반영어 A형 서술형	4점	40%

모범답안 The musician can deliver emotions without words by selecting scales, tempos, instruments, and body movements. Next, our musical language develops as we are influenced by the tastes of our parents, siblings, and people we hang out with, as early as in our mother's womb.

채점기준

+ 2점: 뮤지션이 언어를 사용하지 않고 감정을 전달하는 방법을 "selecting ① scales, ② tempos, ③ instruments, and ④ body movements"라 서술하였거나 유사하였다.
  ☞ 4개 중 2개 또는 3개만 서술한 경우 1점, 1개 또는 서술하지 못한 경우 0점을 준다.

+ 2점: 우리 개개인의 음악언어가 어떻게 발전되는가라는 질문에 "as we are influenced by ① the tastes of our parents or siblings, ② mother's womb, and ③ the people we get along with"라 서술하였거나 유사하였다.
  ☞ 3개 중 2개만 서술한 경우 1점, 1개 또는 서술하지 못한 경우 0점을 준다.

한글번역

장조 음계는 행복한 감정과 연관되고, 단조 음계는 슬픈 감정과 연관되는 경향이 있다. 하나의 높은 음은 흥분을 전달할 수 있고, 낮은 음은 임박한 파멸을 전달한다. 느린 템포는 성찰적인 감정을 더 나타내는 반면, 빠른 비트는 재미와 흥분을 의미한다. 악기의 종류도 중요하다. 헤비메탈 뮤지션들은 분노한 소리를 만들어내기 위해 일그러진 기타를 사용한다. 만약 이런 뮤지션들이 플루트와 피콜로를 사용한다면 같은 효과를 내지 못할 것이다.

우리 뇌의 일부는 다른 사람들에게서 보는 감정을 반향하도록—공감을 느끼도록 진화했다. 많은 심리학자들은 우리가 뮤지션들의 연주를 볼 때도 뇌의 같은 부분이 활성화된다고 믿는다. 소리를 끈 상태에서도 사람들은 연주자의 몸짓만 보고도 그가 표현하려는 감정을 정확하게 판단할 수 있었다. 최고의 록 스타들은 몸짓으로도 노래의 감정을 우리에게 전달한다.

하지만 우리 모두가 같은 음악을 좋아하지는 않는다. 나에게 슬픈 것이 당신에게는 기분을 좋게 하는 것일 수 있다. 그 이유는 부분적으로 우리가 자라면서 접하는 음악적 언어와 관련이 있다. 예를 들어, 부모나 형제자매가 리듬 앤 블루스 듣기를 좋아했다면, 당신도 그것을 좋아하게 될 가능성이 높다. 하지만 그보다 훨씬 더 복잡하다. 우리의 선호도는 아직 어머니 자궁에 있을 때부터 형성되고 있다. 나이가 들수록, 특히 십대가 되면서, 우리의 취향은 종종 어울리는 사람들에 의해 결정된다.

철학자 쇼펜하우어는 "음악의 형언할 수 없는 깊이는 그것이 우리 내면 존재의 모든 감정을 재현한다는 사실 때문이다"라고 썼다. 음악은 우리 자신의 가장 깊은 부분에 말을 걸고 인간이 된다는 것이 무엇을 의미하는지 탐구할 수 있게 해준다: 우리 감정적 삶의 혼란, 복잡성, 기쁨의 메아리를 듣는 것을.

116

하위내용영역	배점	예상정답률
일반영어 B형 서술형	4점	45%

모범 답안 The writer thinks these specific "net neutrality" regulations are being exploited by large companies to avoid paying their fair share. Second, the word that fits the blank is "costs".

채점 기준

+ 2점: 망 중립성 규정에 대해 저자의 생각을 "net neutrality regulations <u>are being exploited by large companies to avoid paying their fair share</u>"라 서술하였다.
+ 2점: 빈칸에 들어갈 단어를 "<u>costs</u>"라 답하였다. 이외에는 답이 될 수 없다.

한글번역

특수 이익 집단들이 인터넷에 공공 유틸리티 규제를 적용할 것을 요구하고 있다. 이 사람들은 우리 시대의 가장 혁신적이고 사회를 변화시키는 규제 완화 성공 사례인 인터넷을 "망 중립성" 규제를 통해 통제하려고 시도하고 있는데, 이는 아마도 소수의 거대한 인터넷 회사들과 상위 1%의 인터넷 사용자들에게만 혜택을 줄 것이다.

망 중립성은 인터넷 사용자들이 원하는 모든 합법적 콘텐츠를 자유롭게 볼 수 있도록 보장하기 위해 개발됐다. 하지만 최근에는 초점이 바뀌었다 : 일부 대형 인터넷 회사들이 주로 자신들에게 혜택을 주는 특정 특권을 확립하기 위한 이유로 "망 중립성"을 인용하고 있다.

이런 콘텐츠 회사들이 의도한 대로 된다면, 미국인들은 넷플릭스와 같은 대용량 인터넷 트래픽 생성자들을 지원하는 데 필요한 고속 네트워크와 인프라 업그레이드 비용을 떠안게 될 것이다. 계산은 간단하다. 네트워크가 더 많은 트래픽을 처리하면, 확장하거나 혼잡해질 것이다. 네트워크를 확장하려면 상당한 투자와 비용이 필요하다—인터넷 서비스 제공업체(ISP)의 경우 연간 수백억 달러.

이런 비용은 두 가지 방법으로 회수될 수 있다. 모든 소비자에게 동일하게 청구하거나 네트워크 자원을 훨씬 더 많이 사용하는 대기업들이 공정한 몫을 지불하게 하는 것이다. 현실 세계에서는 다른 사람들보다 더 많이 사용하는 자원에 대해 더 많이 지불하는 것이 합리적이고 심지어 당연하다. 하지만 망 중립성이라는 미명 하에, 대기업들은 자원의 대부분을 소비하는 자신들과 사용자들이 지불하지 않아도 되도록 모든 사람이 더 많이 지불하기를 원한다.

117

하위내용영역	배점	예상정답률
일반영어 A형 기입형	2점	55%

모범 답안 employment

채점 기준

- 2점: 모범답안과 같다. 이외에는 답이 될 수 없다.
- 0점: 모범답안과 다르다.

한글번역

요즘 정치인이나 전문가의 말을 듣다 보면 미국이 더 가난한 나라들에게 일자리를 잃고 있다는 말을 듣지 않기 어렵다—제조업 일자리는 중국에게, 백오피스 업무는 인도에게, 거의 모든 일자리는 라틴 아메리카에게. 이런 한탄은 더 나은 일자리를 위해 더 많은 미국인들을 준비시키는 더 큰 과제로부터 우리의 관심을 분산시킨다.

미국 제조업 고용이 수년간 감소해온 것은 사실이지만, 그것이 주로 외국인들이 이런 일자리를 빼앗았기 때문은 아니다. 공장 일자리는 전 세계적으로 사라지고 있다. 나는 최근에 2명의 직원과 400대의 컴퓨터화된 로봇이 있는 미국 공장을 견학했다. 두 명의 사람은 컴퓨터 화면 앞에 앉아서 로봇들에게 지시를 내렸다. 몇 년 후에는 이 공장에 로봇을 수리하고 업그레이드하는 가스 검침원처럼 가끔 방문하는 기술자를 제외하고는 현장에 직원이 한 명도 없을 것이다.

제조업은 농업과 같은 추세를 따르고 있다. 생산성이 높아지면서 더 적은 사람이 필요하기 때문에 고용이 줄어든다. 1910년에는 미국인의 3분의 1이 농장에서 일했다. 지금은 3% 미만이다. 1995년 이후, 전 세계적으로 제조업 고용이 감소했음에도 불구하고 전 세계 생산량은 30% 이상 증가했다. 무언가를 탓하고 싶은가? 이제 거의 모든 일상적 업무를 할 수 있는 전자 기기와 소프트웨어를 만들어낸 새로운 지식을 탓하라. 이는 공장 현장을 훨씬 넘어선다.

118

하위내용영역	배점	예상정답률
일반영어 A형 기입형	2점	40%

모범답안 prison slavery

채점기준

- 2점: 모범답안과 같다. 이외에는 답이 될 수 없다.
  ☞ "prison jobs"이나 "involuntary servitude"는 답이 될 수 없다.
- 0점: 모범답안과 다르다.

한글번역

　미국 각지의 교도소 수감자들이 최근 파업에 돌입했다. 수감자들이 파업이라는 수단을 선택한 이유는 자신들의 어려움을 표출할 다른 방법이 없기 때문이다. 당국의 승인 없이는 어떠한 조직도 만들 수 없다. 일부 교도소에서는 청원마저 금지한다. 메인주와 버몬트주를 제외한 주에서는 유죄 판결을 받고 나면 투표권을 박탈당한다. 형을 살고 나서도 투표권을 되찾지 못하는 경우도 있다. 이번 파업의 요구사항 중 하나가 바로 투표권이기도 하다. 교도소 환경 개선과 사회 복귀 활동 강화 역시 요구사항에 포함돼 있다. 하지만 목록에서 가장 눈길을 끄는 것은 파업을 조직한 사람들이 말하는 소위 "교도소 내 노예 노동"의 중단이다.
　미국은 수정헌법 제13조에 따라 노예제와 강제 노역을 폐지했지만, "당사자가 정식으로 유죄 판결을 받은 범죄에 대한 처벌"에는 해당되지 않는다고 명시했다. 이에 따라 죄수들은 매우 적은 보수를 받거나, 전혀 보수를 받지 못한 채 일을 해왔고, 노동을 거부하면 처벌을 받을 수 있다. 내 경험에 비춰 보면, 수감자들은 대부분 일을 하고 싶어 한다. 뭔가 생산적인 일을 하면서 시간을 보내길 원한다. 교도소 내에서 할 수 있는 일들은 세탁부터 정원 관리, 감방 청소부터 요리까지 다양하다. 노동에는 매우 긍정적인 효과가 있다. 수감자들은 노동을 통해 기술을 익히고 자존감을 얻을 수 있으며, 지루한 수감 생활에 필요한 활력을 얻기도 한다. 하지만 수감자와 고용주 사이의 엄청난 권력 차이로 인해 착취나 학대가 발생할 가능성도 매우 높다.

119

하위내용영역	배점	예상정답률
일반영어 A형 서술형	4점	35%

모범답안 The writer mentions "sickle cell anemia" as an example of a simple trait influenced by a single gene. Next, the large GWAS study mentioned included more than a million people.

채점기준

+ 2점: 저자가 겸상 빈혈증을 언급한 이유를 "as an example of a simple trait influenced by a single gene"이라 서술하였거나 유사하였다.
+ 2점: 연구에 필요한 사람의 규모에 대한 질문에 "more than a million people"이라 서술하였다.

한글번역

　유전학에서 가장 중요한 문제는 겉으로 드러나는 어떤 인간의 특정한 형질이 유전자와 구체적으로 어떤 관계를 가지느냐는 것이다. 어떤 이는 붉은 머리카락을 가지고 있고, 다른 어떤 이는 금발을 가지고 있다. 어떤 이는 30세에 헌팅턴 병으로 세상을 떠나지만 또 어떤 이는 천수를 누려 102번째 생일 파티를 맞이한다. 방대한 유전자코드에서 하나의 형질이 어떤 유전자에 의한 것인지를 알게 된다면, 우리는 치료법을 찾고, 위험을 예측할 수 있으며, 생물학과 진화가 이루어지는 방식에 대해 더 깊은 이해를 가질 수 있다. 어떤 형질들은 유전자와의 관계가 명확하다. 예를 들어, 겸상 빈혈증은 특정한 유전자 하나의 돌연변이에 의해 일어나는 질병이다.
　하지만 이렇게 간단한 것을 좋아하는 사람들에게는 안타깝게도, 이런 것들은 예외에 불과하다는 것이다. 한 사람의 키나 조현병과 같은 대부분의 형질은 그 형질에 영향을 미치는 유전자의 수가 훨씬 많다. 사실 그 수는 너무나 많아, 지난 해 발표된 한 논문은 사실상 모든 유전자가 어떤 방식으로든 그런 복잡한 형질에 영향을 미친다는 주장을 펼쳤다.
　약 15년 전, 유전학자들은 동일한 형질을 가진 수천 명의 사람들로부터 그들의 유전자에서 공통점을 찾기 위해 유전자를 수집하기 시작했다. 이는 전장 유전체 연관 분석(GWAS)이라 불리는 방법이다. 그들이 발견한 것은 첫째, 통계적으로 유의미한 결과를 얻기 위해서는 엄청난 수의 데이터가 있어야 한다는 것이다. 예를 들어, 최근 발표된 불면증과 유전자의 관계를 본 한 연구는 100만 명 이상의 유전자 데이터를 수집했다. 둘째, 각 연구에서 가장 영향을 크게 미치는 유전자의 영향력은 극히 적었다. 이는 모든 형질은 그 형질에 조금씩 관여하는 다수의 유전자 위치가 있다는 다유전자 가설(polygenic hypothesis)로 발전했다.

120

하위내용영역	배점	예상정답률
일반영어 B형 서술형	4점	50%

모범 답안 Gravity transformed the atoms into galaxies. Second, hydrogen an helium atoms were formed by nuclear reactions.

채점 기준

+ 2점 : 원자들을 은하계로 이동시키는 것을 "gravity(중력)"라 정확히 서술하였다. 이외에는 답이 될 수 없다.
+ 2점 : 수소원자와 헬륨원자가 "nuclear reactions"에 의해 생성된다고 서술하였다. 이외에는 답이 될 수 없다.

한글번역

현재의 우주를 상상하는 것도 충분히 어렵고, 모든 것이 어떻게 시작됐는지에 대한 이론을 만드는 것은 더욱 어렵다. 1940년대에 조지 가모프가 그런 이론을 개발하기 시작했다. 또 다른 과학자인 조르주 르메트르도 이 문제를 연구하고 있었고, 가모프는 르메트르의 아이디어 중 일부를 사용해서 자신의 이론을 발전시켰다.

가모프는 다음과 같은 이론을 제시했다 : 100억 년에서 210억 년 전 어느 시점에 우주에서 거대한 폭발이 있었다. 폭발 이전에 우주는 원자핵 크기였으며, 온도는 약 100억도였다. 폭발이 우주의 팽창을 시작시켰다. 쿼크나 기본 입자들이 엄청난 수로 존재했다.

1밀리 초 안에 우주는 자몽 크기로 팽창했다. 온도는 10억도로 냉각됐다. 쿼크들이 양성자와 중성자로 뭉치기 시작했다. 몇 분 후, 우주는 여전히 전자와 양성자가 원자를 형성하기에는 너무 뜨거웠다 : 초고온의 안개 같은 환경이었다.

시간이 지나고 온도가 냉각되면서 핵반응이 일어났고, 30만 년 안에 수소와 헬륨 원자들이 나타나기 시작했다. 원자들이 형성되면서 빛이 비치기 시작했다. 우주가 모습을 갖춰가고 있었다.

중력이 원자들에 작용하기 시작해서 그들을 은하로 변화시켰다. 그 첫 번째 대폭발 후 10억 년 안에 은하와 별들이 형성되기 시작했다. 150억 년 안에 별들의 죽음으로 방출된 무거운 원소들로부터 행성들이 나타나기 시작했다. 이 이론에 따르면 우주는 빅뱅으로 시작돼 계속해서 성장하고 변화하고 있다.

121

하위내용영역	배점	예상정답률
일반영어 A형 기입형	2점	50%

모범 답안 uncertainties

채점 기준

- 2점 : 모범답안과 같다. 이외에는 답이 될 수 없다.
- 0점 : 모범답안과 다르다.

한글번역

인류는 전례 없는 변화를 경험하고 있다. 모든 과거의 이론이 붕괴하고 있으며 어떤 새로운 이론도 이를 대체하지 못하고 있다. 이런 유례없는 불확실성의 시대에 우리와 우리 아이들은 어떻게 대처해야 할까? 지금 태어나는 아이들은 2050년에 겨우 30대 초반일 것이다. 이들 중 대부분은 2100년, 곧 22세기에도 여전히 활발하게 살아갈 것이다. 오늘날 태어나는 아이들을 어떻게 가르쳐야 이들이 2050년 또는 22세기를 제대로 살아갈 수 있을까? 그 시대에도 직장을 얻고 세상을 이해하고 인생의 미로를 헤쳐나가기 위해서는 어떤 종류의 기술을 가져야 할까?

안타깝게도 오늘날 누구도 2100년, 아니 2050년의 세상조차도 어떤 모습일지 알지 못하며, 따라서 누구도 이 질문의 답을 말할 수 없다. 물론 지금까지 인류가 미래를 정확하게 예측했던 적은 없다. 하지만 기술이 신체와 뇌, 마음을 제어할 수 있게 된 오늘날, 과거에는 고정됐고 영원할 것이라 여겼던 모든 사실들을 이제 확신할 수 없게 됐고, 따라서 미래를 예측하는 것은 그 어느 때보다도 더 어려운 일이 됐다.

유희대 | 일반영어 ❹-1

지금으로부터 천 년 전인 1018년에도 사람들은 여전히 미래를 알지 못했다. 하지만 그들은 사회의 기본적인 요소가 크게 바뀌지 않으리라는 것은 알았다. 만약 당신이 1018년의 중국에 살고 있다면, 당신은 1050년 쯤 송 제국이 멸망하고 거란족이 침입하며, 또 역병이 돌아 수백 만 명이 죽는 것을 겪게될 것이다. 하지만 적어도 1050년에도 대부분의 사람들은 농부와 베 짜는 직공으로 일하고, 정부는 사람들로 이루어진 군대와 관료를 가질 것이며, 가부장제가 유지될 것이며, 평균수명은 여전히 40세 언저리일 것이고, 인간의 육체적 특징 또한 전혀 변하지 않을 것임을 알았을 것이다. 1018년, 가난한 이들은 아이들에게 어떻게 쌀을 파종하고 비단을 짜야할 것인지를 가르쳤다. 부유한 이들은 아들에게는 공자의 가르침과 서예, 말을 타고 싸우는 법을 가르쳤고, 딸에게는 검소하고 성실한 부인이 되는 법을 가르쳤다. 그들은 1050년에도 이런 기술이 유용하리라는 데 의심의 여지가 없었다.

하지만 오늘날, 우리는 중국뿐 아니라 다른 세계 역시 2050년에 어떤 특징을 가질지를 전혀 예측할 수 없다. 사람들이 무엇으로 생계를 꾸릴지, 군대와 관료들은 어떤 역할을 하게 될지, 그리고 남자와 여자가 어떤 관계를 가지게 될지를 알지 못한다.

기울이고, 백신의 위험성에 대한 트윗을 30차례 이상 올린다. 하지만 백신 반대론자와 "비주류" 정치인들의 만남은 여기서 끝이 아니다.

유럽의 포퓰리스트 정치인들 역시 백신 회의론자들을 들먹이곤 한다. 인구의 20%가 백신에 반대한다는 프랑스에서는 극우 정치인 마린 르펜이 백신의 안전성에 의문을 제기하면서 의무 접종 반대에 나섰다. 올해 선거를 치른 이탈리아에서도 백신은 논란의 대상이었는데, 당시 백신 접종률 감소에 따라 홍역이 유행했기 때문이다. 포퓰리스트 정당 "오성운동"은 의무 백신의 개수를 늘이고 의무 접종을 거부하는 부모들에게 벌금을 부과하는 정책에 반대했다. 유럽 전역에서 백신 접종률이 떨어지고, 홍역 발생은 늘어나는 중이다.—작년에 300% 증가했다. 이렇게 질병이 늘어남에도 불구하고, 혹은 백신과 싸우려는 노력에 대한 대응으로, 백신 회의론자들의 목소리는 잦아들지 않고 있다. 6월에는 백신 반대론자들이 "백신 위험 인식의 날"을 맞아 이탈리아와 프랑스에서 수 천 명 단위로 백신 의무 접종에 반대하는 시위를 열기도 했다.

122

하위내용영역	배점	예상정답률
일반영어 A형 기입형	2점	50%

모범 답안 vaccine doubters

채점 기준

- 2점: 모범답안과 같다. 이외에는 답이 될 수 없다.
- 0점: 모범답안과 다르다.

한글번역

1998년 의학저널 "란셋"에는 이후 계속해서 공공 토론의 장을 오염시킨 주장을 담은 논문이 실렸다. 백신이 자폐를 유발한다는 내용의 논문이었다. 이후 해당 논문의 제1저자 앤드루 웨이크필드는 의사 면허증을 잃었고 논문 게재는 철회됐다. 그러나 웨이크필드는 2016년에 이르러 미국에서 귀빈 대접을 받기 시작한다. 대통령 선거 후보와의 만남에 이어, 워싱턴DC에서 열린 대통령 취임식 파티에도 초청을 받게 된다. 도널드 트럼프는 그의 말에 귀를

123

하위내용영역	배점	예상정답률
일반영어 A형 서술형	4점	35%

모범 답안 The commonality of those species is that they are microorganisms that cannot be seen with the naked eye. Next, the cultivation method had the problems that most microorganisms are hard to grow, and also might perform similar functions without being easily identifiable.

채점 기준

- +2점: 관찰 가능성의 관점에서 미생물들의 공통점을 "they are microorganisms that cannot be seen with the naked eye"라 서술하였거나 유사하였다.
- +2점: 미생물 배양방법의 결점을 "most microorganisms are hard to grow(1점), and also might perform similar functions without being easily identifiable(1점)"이라 서술하였거나 유사하였다.

☞ 다음과 같이 서술하였어도 맞는 것으로 한다.
- "It is difficult to grow the vast majority of microorganisms(1점), and unrelated microbial species can perform similar functions and are unlikely to be distinguished by their appearance(1점)."

한글번역

인간은 지난 수백 년간 지구상의 다양한 생물을 발견하고 이해하기 위해 끊임없이 노력해왔다. 과학자와 동식물 연구자들은 오대양 육대주를 누비며 수많은 생물을 찾아냈다. 땅 속 깊은 곳부터 높은 산꼭대기까지, 또 사람의 발길이 좀처럼 닿지 않는 정글부터 수많은 사람이 모여 사는 대도시에 이르기까지 빠트리지 않고 탐사를 거듭한 끝에 진화의 산물이라 할 수 있는 수많은 생물종을 발견하고 생명체를 이해하는 토대를 닦을 수 있었다. 최근까지 지구상에 사는 생물종은 약 1천만 개 정도일 것으로 추정된다. 이것만 해도 절대 작은 숫자가 아니지만, 이는 육안으로 확인할 수 있는 종의 숫자만 말한 것이다.

그렇다면 박테리아나 고세균류, 원생생물, 균류 등 (맨눈으로는 볼 수 없는) 작은 생물들까지 더하면 어떨까? 이런 미생물들은 지구상에서 가장 오랫동안 진화를 거듭하며 성공적으로 퍼진 생물종이기도 하다. 그렇다면 이것들(박테리아, 고세균류, 원생생물, 균류 등)은 전 지구적 생물다양성에 어떤 기여를 하고 있을까? 여러 미생물을 모두 포함해 계산하면 지구상에 사는 생물종은 무려 1조 개로 늘어난다. (맨눈으로 볼 수 있는 생물의 10만 배, 0을 다섯 개 더 붙인 어마어마한 숫자이다.) 이 추정치가 사실일 경우 우리 눈에 보이는 생물종을 아무리 열심히 연구해도 지구상에 사는 생물의 10만분의 1, 그러니까 0.0001%를 연구하는 데 불과하다.

사실 아무리 평범한 곳을 살펴보더라도 그 안에 얼마나 다양한 미생물이 있는지 관찰하고 측정하는 일은 대단히 어려운 일이다. 과학자들이 미생물종을 판별하는 방법은 20세기 내내 크게 달라지지 않았다. 어떤 미생물종을 실험실의 넓적한 페트리(Petri) 접시에 배양한 뒤 세포의 특징을 관찰하거나 온도에 대한 반응, 어떤 물질을 섭취하고 어떤 효소를 생성하는지 등 생리적 특징을 관찰하는 것이다. 그런데 이런 방법은 사실 미생물종의 다양성을 정확히 측정하기엔 턱없이 부족한 방법이다. 미생물을 충분히 관찰할 수 있을 만큼 많이 배양하는 것도 쉽지 않을뿐더러 실은 서로 전혀 다른 미생물종도 얼마든지 비슷한 기능을 할 수 있기 때문이다. 게다가 생김새로 미생물을 구분한다는 건 불가능에 가까운 일이다.

그러다 1990년대 중반에 들어 일군의 미생물학자들이 실험실에서 미생물을 배양하던 기존의 방식을 버리고 직접 자연에서 미생물의 핵산 염기 순서(DNA)를 분석하기 시작한다. 자연을 분석한다는 건 바닷물, 나뭇잎 표면, 습지 바닥의 침전물, 심지어 샤워꼭지 안의 생물막(biofilms)에서 직접 어떤 미생물이 있는지 살펴보고 조사하는 것이다.

124

하위내용영역	배점	예상정답률
일반영어 B형 서술형	4점	45%

모범답안 The writer mentions the developmental stage because it is a better guide for understanding a dog's age than counting years. Second, the factors affecting dogs' lifespans are breed, associated size, as well as nutrition and associated weight.

채점 기준

+ 2점: 발달단계를 언급한 이유를 "because it is a better guide for understanding a dog's age than counting years"라 서술하였거나 유사하였다.
  ☞ 다음과 같이 서술하였어도 2점을 준다.
  - "Because it is a better guide for understanding a dog's age than assigning a single number."

+ 2점: 개의 기대 수명에 기여하는 요소들이 "breed, size, nutrition, and weight"라 서술하였거나 유사하였다.
  ☞ 4개 중 3개만 서술한 경우 1점, 2개만 서술한 경우 0.5점, 1개 또는 서술하지 못한 경우 0점을 준다.

125

하위내용영역	배점	예상정답률
일반영어 A형 기입형	2점	45%

모범답안 mental retardation

채점기준

- 2점 : 모범답안과 같다. 이외에는 답이 될 수 없다.
- 0점 : 모범답안과 다르다.

한글번역

"우리 강아지를 개 나이로 환산하면 몇 살쯤 될까요?" 내가 정기적으로 듣는 질문이다. 사람들은 인간의 성격을 동물에서 찾고 반려동물을 의인화하기를 상당히 좋아한다. 그리고 많은 사람은 반려동물이 오래오래 건강하게 살기를 바란다.

반려동물에 대한 보호자들의 사랑과 인간-동물 간의 유대감을 고려할 때 이런 생각은 바보 같아 보일 수도 있다. 그러나 반려동물의 "실제 나이"를 생각해보는 일은 사실 중요한 일이다. 나와 같은 수의사가 삶의 단계에 맞는 건강관리를 동물 환자에게 추천하는 데 도움이 되기 때문이다.

사람의 1년은 개와 고양이의 7년과 같다는 통설이 있다. 이것에는 약간의 논리가 있다. 보통 체격을 가진 중형 개가 최적의 건강관리를 받았을 때 평균적으로 보호자 수명의 약 1/7을 산다는 관찰 기록이 쌓여, 인간의 1년은 개의 7년과 같다는 것이 어느덧 정설이 됐다.

하지만 모든 개의 체격이 보통 체격이 아니며 소위 7년의 법칙은 처음부터 지나치게 단순화됐다. 개와 고양이는 사람과 나이를 다르게 먹을 뿐 아니라 개와 고양이 사이에도 부분적으로 품종의 특징과 크기에 따라 나이를 다르게 먹는다. 더 큰 동물일수록 작은 동물보다 수명이 대개 더 짧다. 고양이는 크기 면에서 그다지 다르지 않지만, 개의 크기와 기대 수명은 상당히 다를 수 있다. 그레이트데인과 치와와의 차이를 생각하면 쉽게 이해가 될 것이다.

인간의 기대 수명은 몇 년간 변화했다. 수의사들은 10년 전에 제공할 수 있었던 의료 서비스보다 더 나은 서비스로 건강을 관리해 줄 수 있다. 따라서 이제는 1년을 '동물 나이' 7년으로 계산하는 오래된 방법보다 더 나은 방법으로 동물의 나이를 정의할 수 있다.

미국 동물병원협회가 마련한 개의 삶의 단계 가이드라인에 따라 오늘날 수의사들은 개의 삶의 단계를 강아지, 청년견, 성견, 원숙견, 노견, 고령견과 같이 6개의 범주로 나눈다. 삶의 단계는 숫자를 부여하는 것보다 나이를 생각하는 더 실용적인 방법이다. 인간 건강에 대한 권장 사항도 사람이 정확하게 몇 살인지보다 성장 단계를 바탕으로 한다. '신체 나이'라는 말이 그래서 있는 것이다.

개의 기대 수명에 가장 큰 영향을 주는 것은 견종과 (그에 따른) 크기이고, 영양 상태와 체중은 다음으로 중요한 요소이다.

한글번역

아기들은 많은 것을 배운다. 얼굴, 목소리, 색깔, 모양, 단어를 인식하는 법을 배운다. 음식이 무엇이고 바닥에 놓인 단순히 반짝이는 것이 무엇인지를 배운다. 촉각, 냄새, 소리를 배우지만 가장 중요하게는 세상에서 자신의 위치를 배운다. 건강한 환경에서 아기는 돌봄 제공자를 인식하는 법을 배우고 자연스럽게 그들이 자신을 안전하게 지키고 필요를 돌봐줄 것이라고 신뢰하기 시작할 것이다. 사랑받는다는 것이 무엇인지 배울 것이다. 하지만 방치된 환경의 아기들은 울 것이고, 충분히 많은 횟수의 무반응을 겪으면 그 반대를 배울 것이다. 돌봄 제공자의 안정성을 불신하게 될 것이다. 스스로를 돌보는 법을 배우기 시작할 것이고 더 나쁘게는 지속적인 투쟁 또는 도피 상태에서 살기 시작할 것이다. 아무도 의존할 수 없고 누구와의 애착도 극도로 어려워질 것이다.

포옹 받지 못하는 아기들은 다른 인간과 안정적인 유대를 형성하는 법을 배우지 못할 것이다. 울도록 방치된 아기들은 아무도 의지할 수 없고 세상이 무섭고 비참한 곳이라는 것을 배울 것이다. 말을 걸어주지 않는 아기들은 말에 필요한 소리를 배우지 못할 것이다. 이런 아이들의 정신 지체율은 적절하고 긍정적인 환경에서 사는 아이들보다 훨씬 높다. 정신 지체만이 문제가 아니라 신체적 발달 지연도 문제가 될 수 있으며, 아이가 말 그대로 성장해야 할 만큼 자라지 않는다. 이는 항상 영양실조 때문은 아니지만, 그런 경우라면 확실히 도움이 되지 않는다. 이런 아이들은 일반 아이들보다 훨씬 더 자주 두려워하며 그들의 뇌는 아드레날린과 스트레스 호르몬인 코르티솔에 절여진다. 지속적으로 스트레스를 받으면 더 많은 칼로리를 태우고 식욕이 부족해질 것이다. 이런 경우 뇌는 종종 물리적으로 기형이 된다.

126

하위내용영역	배점	예상정답률
일반영어 A형 기입형	2점	40%

모범답안 soil microbial communities

채점기준

- 2점: 모범답안과 같다. "soil microbial community"라 해도 맞는 것으로 한다. 이외에는 답이 될 수 없다.
- 0점: 모범답안과 다르다.

한글번역

　기후 온난화, 영구동토층 해빙, 산불, 가뭄과 같은 지구적 변화 현상들이 육상 생태계 생지화학에 영향을 미치고 있는데, 특히 북위 지역뿐만 아니라 미국 본토에서도 그렇다. 토양 미생물 군집은 생태계의 탄소 생지화학에 중요한데, 식물이 연간 광합성으로 생산하는 만큼 탄소를 분해하기 때문이다. 토양 미생물 군집의 구성 변화가 생태계 기능 방식에 영향을 미치며, 이는 지역에서 전 지구적 생지화학에 영향을 줄 수 있다는 강력한 증거가 있다. 분해 곰팡이와 같은 특정 기능 집단의 미생물들은 원소 순환에 비례하지 않는 큰 영향을 미친다. 예를 들어, 북위 지역 토양에서 기후 온난화는 영구동토층 해빙과 산불 강도를 가속화해 토양 분해자들의 풍부도를 변화시키며, 이는 생지화학적 과정의 속도에 직접적인 영향을 미친다. 이것과 다른 유형의 미생물 군집 정보는 차세대 기계론적 미생물 기반 탄소 순환 모델에 사용될 수 있다. 다음 단계는 생물정보학과 지리정보학을 융합해 환경 및 과정 데이터와 연결된 미생물 생물지리학의 공간적으로 명시적인 지도를 구축하는 데 사용할 수 있도록 하는 것이다. 그런 지도는 군집 구성과 다양성을 구조화하는 생태학적 원리를 이해하는 것 외에도 많은 용도가 있다. 그런 공간적으로 명시적인 정보는 잠재적으로 지구적 변화가 특정 지역 내의 미생물 군집과 생지화학적 과정에 어떤 영향을 미칠지 평가하는 데 사용될 수 있다.

127

하위내용영역	배점	예상정답률
일반영어 A형 서술형	4점	35%

모범답안 The writer mentions Mary Anderson to show how there was opposition to women taking up more power in the US, similar to the way Fascist nations suppressed them. Second, the policy in which the US came closest to performing fascism was Executive Order 9066, in which Japanese-American families were arrested and held in camps.

채점기준

+ 2점: 글쓴이가 매리 앤더슨을 언급한 이유를 "to show how there was opposition to women taking up more power in the US, *(similar to the way Fascist nations suppressed them)*."라 서술하였거나 유사하였다.
+ 2점: 미국의 정책 중 파시즘과 유사한 것을 "Executive Order 9066, in which Japanese-American families were arrested and held in camps"라 서술하였거나 유사하였다.
  ☞ "Executive Order 9066"이라고 했거나 "Japanese-American families were arrested and held in camps"라고만 했어도 맞는 것으로 한다.

한글번역

　파시스트 국가들은 여성의 자리가 가정에 있다고 주장하는 것으로 악명 높았다. 하지만 파시즘에 맞선 전쟁은 절실히 필요했던 국방 산업에 여성을 활용했음에도 불구하고, 여성의 종속적 역할을 바꾸기 위한 특별한 조치를 취하지 않았다. 전시 인력 위원회는 전쟁 업무에 종사하는 여성의 수가 많았음에도 불구하고 정책 결정 기구에서 여성을 배제했다. 노동부 여성국 국장인 메리 앤더슨의 보고서는 전시 인력 위원회가 "여성 지도자들 편에서 발전하는 투쟁적 태도나 십자군적 정신으로 당시 여겨진 것"에 대해 "의구심과 불안감"을 가지고 있었다고 말했다.

미국은 정책 중 하나로 파시즘을 직접적으로 모방하는 데 가까웠다. 이는 서부 해안에 거주하는 일본계 미국인들에 대한 처우였다. 진주만 공격 후, 반일 히스테리가 정부에 퍼졌다. 한 하원의원은 이렇게 말했다: "나는 지금 미국, 알래스카, 하와이에 있는 모든 일본인을 잡아서 강제 수용소에 넣는 것에 찬성한다. 젠장! 그들을 없애버리자!"

프랭클린 D. 루스벨트는 이런 광란을 공유하지 않았지만, 1942년 2월 침착하게 행정명령 9066호에 서명했다. 이는 군대에 영장이나 기소장, 청문회 없이 서부 해안의 모든 일본계 미국인—11만 명의 남녀노소—을 체포해 집에서 데려가 내륙 깊숙한 수용소로 이송하고 감옥 같은 조건에서 구금할 권력을 부여했다. 이들 중 4분의 3은 일본인 부모에게서 미국에서 태어난 니세이로, 따라서 미국 시민이었다. 나머지 4분의 1인 일본에서 태어난 이세이는 법에 의해 시민이 되는 것이 금지돼 있었다. 1944년 대법원은 군사적 필요성을 근거로 강제 소개를 지지했다. 일본인들은 3년 넘게 그 수용소에 남아있었다.

한글번역

"학계를 떠나는 것이 '실패'가 아닌 이유"; "학계를 떠나는 것은 부끄러운 일이 아니다"—이런 것들은 최근 논평 풍경을 흩뿌리고 있는 기사들의 연발 중 일부이다. 이런 기사들은 전염병 수준의 우울증과 불안을 경험하고 있는 학계 인력을 위로하려는 고귀한 시도이지만, 본질적으로 잘못된 방향으로 인도하고 있다. 이런 방식으로 진로 전환에 대한 대화의 틀을 짜는 것으로, 저자들은 무의식적으로 근본적인 전제를 확인하고 있다: 학계를 떠나는 것이 실제로 다뤄져야 할 실패라는 것을.

아이러니하게도, 학계 과학을 떠나는 것이 실패라는 개념 자체가 비과학적이다. 일관된 경험적 기초가 부족하다. 학계의 과학자들이 영리, 비영리, 정부 부문의 과학자들보다 더 성공적이거나, 더 자아실현을 했거나, 심지어 지적으로 더 자유롭다고 제안하는 증거는 없다. 이 비경험적 개념이 학계의 불안감—지적, 실존적, 그리고 아마도 가장 중요하게는 재정적(평균적으로 조교수는 연간 87,000달러를 번다)—의 직접적 발현일 가능성이 있다.

실패는 종종 개인적 열망과 목표와 얽혀 있는 주관적 경험이지만, 학계에서의 전환을 논의할 때는 종종 비개인화된다. 학계 서사 안에서 학계는 모든 사람이 추구하고 있거나 추구해야 하는 궁극적인 상이다. 이 뒤에 있는 이유는 두 가지 주요 전제에 기반한다.

첫 번째는 학계가 과학자들을 해방시킨다는 것—호기심이 어디로 이끌든 따라갈 지적 자유를 부여한다는 것이다. 두 번째는 학자들이 지식과 진리를 고귀하게 추구하면서 충만하고 목적 있는 삶을 산다는 개념에 의존한다. 두 경우 모두, 이런 특성들이 학계 추구에 고유한 것이라고 제안된다.

학계는 관례적 통념과 달리 절대적 지적 자유를 제공하지 않는다. 대학원생과 박사후 연구원들은 토론의 여지없이 직접적으로 주어진 실험 설계가 아니라면, 지도 교수의 연구와 관련된 질문들만 추구하도록 제한된다. 멘티들이 발전하면서, 명확하고 정의된 제한 내에서지만 자신만의 질문을 할 수 있도록 허용된 만큼 운이 좋을 수도 있다.

128

하위내용영역	배점	예상정답률
일반영어 B형 서술형	4점	50%

모범답안 The main idea is that leaving academia should not be considered as a failure. Second, the conventional wisdom is that academia provides absolute intellectual freedom.

채점 기준

+ 2점: 글의 요지를 "leaving academia should not be considered as a failure" 또는 "leaving academia is not a failure"이라 서술하였거나 유사하였다.
+ 2점: 관례적 통념을 "academia provides absolute intellectual freedom"이라 서술하였거나 유사하였다.

129

하위내용영역	배점	예상정답률
일반영어 A형 서술형	4점	50%

모범답안 The word is "imitated". Second, the main point is that play can be more of a learning experience than direct teaching, which prompts students only to directly imitate.

채점기준

+ 2점: 빈칸에 들어갈 단어를 "imitated"라 정확히 기입하였다.
+ 2점: Stahl의 연구의 핵심 주장을 "play can be more of a learning experience than direct teaching, which prompts students only to directly imitate"라 서술하였거나 유사하였다.

한글번역

우리는 어린아이들이 "모든 것에 열중"하는 것을 당연하게 여긴다. 하지만 "적극적인 학습"에 대한 새로운 연구는 아이들이 장난감을 가지고 놀 때 그 아이들이 상당히 실험을 진행하는 과학자들과 같이 행동한다는 것을 보여준다. 미취학 아동들은 그들에게 가장 많은 것을 가르쳐 줄 장난감을 가지고 노는 것을 선호하고, 세상이 어떻게 돌아가는지에 대한 가장 많은 정보를 줄 수 있는 바로 그 방식으로 그 장난감들을 가지고 노는 것을 좋아한다.

예를 들어, 최근의 한 실험에서, Aimee E. Stahl 교수는 11개월 된 아기들에게 일종의 마술을 보여줬다. 공이 단단한 벽을 통과하는 것처럼 보이거나, 장난감 자동차가 선반 끝에서 굴러 떨어져 허공에 매달려 있는 것처럼 보이는. 그 아기들은 분명히 이러한 이상한 사건들에 놀랄 만큼 일상의 물리학에 대해 충분히 알고 있었기에, 이 사건들에 많은 관심을 기울였다.

그러고 나서 연구원들은 아기들에게 가지고 놀 장난감을 줬다. 벽을 통해 공이 사라지는 것을 본 아기들은 벽을 쾅하고 쳤고, 공중에서 맴도는 차를 본 아이들은 계속해서 차를 떨어뜨렸다. 그것은 마치 그 아이들이 공이 정말로 고체인지 아니면 장난감 차가 정말로 중력을 거스르는지 알아보기 위해 시험하는 것 같았다.

그것은 단지 어린아이들이 배우기 위해 가르침을 받을 필요가 없다는 것을 말하는 것이 아니다. 실제로 연구들이 보여주는 것은 명시적인 가르침—즉 학교나 "육아"와 어울리는 종류의 가르침—은 제한적일 수 있다는 것이다. 아이들은 자신들이 가르침을 받고 있다고 생각할 때, 새로운 것을 창조하는 대신에 단순히 어른이 하는 것을 모방할 가능성이 훨씬 많다.

내 실험실은 복잡한 장난감을 가지고 여러 다른 종류의 실험을 했었다. 하지만 이번에는 실험자가 선생님처럼 행동했다. 그녀는 "이 장난감이 어떻게 작동하는지 궁금해" 대신 "내 장난감이 어떻게 작동하는지 보여줄게"라고 말했다. 아이들은 그녀가 한 것을 정확히 모방했고, 그들 자신의 해결책을 생각해내지 못했다.

130

하위내용영역	배점	예상정답률
일반영어 A형 서술형	4점	50%

모범답안 The word is "recidivism". Second, it is implied that society will see more criminals returning to crime if halfway houses aren't well organized.

채점기준

+ 2점: 빈칸에 들어갈 단어를 "recidivism"이라 정확히 기입하였다.
+ 2점: 정책 입안자들이 사회복귀훈련시설이 얼마나 중요한지 인식하지 못할 때, 사회에 어떤 일이 일어날 가능성이 있냐는 질문에 "society will see more criminals returning to crime (if halfway houses aren't well organized)"이라 서술하였거나 유사하였다.

한글번역

비록 일부 사회복귀훈련시설들은 적절하게 관리되고 유능한 전문가들로 구성돼 있지만, 다른 곳들은 범죄자들이 성공적으로 사회에 복귀하도록 돕는 것에 대한 관심보다는 이윤을 위해 운영된다. 제대로 감독되지 않은 사회복귀훈련시설 거주자들이나 무관심하거나 심지어 범죄적인 직원들의 행동을 포함해 너무 많은 사건들이 연방 교도소 시스템뿐만 아니라 거의 모든 주의 교도소에서 발생하고 있다.

잘 관리된 사회복귀훈련시설은 곧 석방될 죄수들에게 안전한 환경을 제공한다; 어떤 사람들은 비교적 짧은 기간 동안 감옥에 있었을 수도 있고, 다른 사람들은 몇 년 또는 심지어 수십 년 동안 갇혀 있었을 수도 있다. 사회로의 원활한 이행을 제공한다는 사회복귀훈련시설의 주요 목표는 재범을 막는 첫 번째 방어선을 제공한다는 것이다. 사회복귀훈련시설 거주자들은 종종 그들이 풀려난 지역 사회와 현재 거의 관련이 없으며, 설사 있다 하더라도 그들을 도울 가족이나 친구가 없을 수 있다. 그들은 취업 알선 및 주거 지원을 포함한 실행 가능한 재진입 서비스가 필요하며, 종종 약물 남용 프로그램이 필요하다. 그러나 사회복귀훈련시설은 시설의 소유자나 운영자가 돈을 벌 수 있는 수익원으로만 보는 경우가 너무 많다.

효과적인 서비스와 프로그램을 제공하는 데 있어 아무리 형편없는 사회복귀훈련시설이라도, 많은 경우 그것이 이용 가능한 유일한 선택이다. 몇몇 주에서는 출소 직전인 수감자들에게 사회복귀훈련시설을 배치하는 것이 의무적인 데 반해, 다른 주에서는 재입소 시설에서 보내는 시간을 요구하지 않는다. 초당파적인 퓨 자선 신탁에 따르면, 8개 주의 죄수들은 지역 사회로의 원활한 복귀를 위한 재입국 프로그램 없이 형량을 "최대"로 늘릴 수 있다. 그 주들에서 약 40%의 죄수들이 과도기적 서비스(사회복귀훈련시설) 없이 석방된다.

법무부 통계국의 2014년 4월 재범 보고서에 따르면 범죄자의 49.7%가 출소 후 3년 이내에, 55.1%가 5년 이내에 다시 감옥으로 돌아가는 것으로 나타났다. 분명히 대부분의 주 및 연방 교정 시설은 죄수들을 '교정'하고, 그들의 석방을 준비하는 데 형편없는 일을 하고 있는데, 이것이 재진입 서비스를 제공하는 사회복귀훈련시설에 훨씬 더 큰 부담을 주고 있다.

양쪽 정당 모두의 정책 입안자들은 공공 안전에 대해 진지하게 생각한다면, 더 효과적인 전략이 필요하다는 것을 깨닫기 시작해야 한다.

131

하위내용영역	배점	예상정답률
일반영어 A형 서술형	4점	40%

모범답안) The word is "comparisons". Second, a movie review would be a qualitative scale.

채점기준

+ 2점: 빈칸에 들어갈 단어를 "comparisons"라 정확히 기입하였다.

+ 2점: 영화 비평이 "a qualitative scale"에 속한다고 정확하게 서술하였다.

한글번역

스카치 보넷 고추(아주 맵기로 유명)는 복수초보다 얼마나 더 매운가? 다이아몬드는 수정보다 얼마나 더 단단한가? 저울은 우리가 물리적 세계를 측정하는 데 도움을 준다. 수량을 비교하기 위해, 우리는 대부분 빈도와 수량에 대해 알려주는 수치 측정인 정량적 척도에 의존한다. 인치, 피트, 야드, 마일; 온스, 쿼트, 리터, 갤런; 초, 분, 세기 등 이 모든 것이 정량적 척도이다. 하지만 질적 척도(정성적 척도)는 어떨까? 이는 관측 가능한—하지만 반드시 수치적일 필요는 없는—특성들을 측정하는 척도이며, 우리는 이러한 척도를 항상 사용한다. 질적 척도는 때때로 유머러스하고 종종 완전히 기괴하지만, 속성 간의 관계를 상상하고 아이디어를 표준화하는 데 있어 양적 척도만큼이나 가치가 있다. 질적 척도의 범위는 고추의 열에서부터 광물질의 경도, 그리고 바닷바람에 이르기까지 다양하다. 질적 척도를 사용하면 정량적 정보가 거의 없거나 전혀 없는 변수에 꼬리표(이름)를 붙일 수 있도록 해준다. 이러한 특이한 측정 단위(즉, 질적 척도)는 종종 일상에서 사용하는 구어체이다 : 어림짐작이나 "까마귀 날기" 경험법칙 따위가 그 예인데, 이것들은 빠른 평가와 비교를 하는 데 유용하다. 하지만 질적 척도는 그 유용성을 계속해서 증명한다. 만일 질적 척도가 없다면, 우리는 고통에 대한 생각을 개념화하거나 (의사가 환자에게 그의 증상의 순위를 매기도록 요청할 수도 있다), 기상 조건의 심각성을 (뷰포트 척도가 하는 것처럼) 등급화하는 데 어려움을 겪을 것이다.

날짜가 BC나 AD와 같은 자의적인 시대를 통해 측정될 때, 우리가 시간을 이해하는 데 도움을 준다. 다른 한편으로, 진북(지구의 자전축이 지나는 진짜 북극을 말함) 또는 자북(나침반이 가리키는 북쪽을 말함)으로부터 측정된 방향은 우리로 하여금 물리적 공간 속에서 방향을 제대로 잡을 수 있도록 해준다.

정량적 척도는 평가하기가 (질적 척도 보다) 훨씬 쉬운데, 그 이유는 정량적 척도는 사실상 알려진 표준과 비교하기 때문이다. 1평방킬로미터, 티스푼 한 개의 설탕 또는 한 시간의 강의는 기본적으로 변하지 않는 척도이다. 질적 척도는 (정량적 척도보다) 더 주관적이다. 그러나 양적 척도나 질적 척도 모두 100% 정확하지는 않다. 그 둘은 서로 각자가, 단위 자체를 정의할 때 내재된 불확실성에 의해 한계가 있을 수밖에 없다.

132

하위내용영역	배점	예상정답률
일반영어 B형 서술형	4점	50%

모범답안 The word is "peripheral vision". Second, the complete stillness of a dead person can upset a person.

채점기준

+ 2점: 빈칸에 들어갈 단어를 "peripheral vision"이라 정확히 기입하였다.
+ 2점: 시체를 봤을 때 즉각적으로 당황하게 만드는 불안 요인을 "the complete stillness of a dead person"이라 서술하였거나 유사하였다.

한글번역

생명력의 경험은 움직임의 행위 속에 내재돼 있다. 운동과 그 운동의 고유 감각은 생명체가 살아있다는 것을 보여주는 가장 기본적인 표현이며, 살아 있음에 대한 제 일차적 감각이다. 우리는 육체적으로나 정신적으로나 항상 움직인다. 만약 우리의 마음과 몸이 깨어있을 때 끊임없이 변화하는 과정에 있지 않다면, 우리는 살아있고 활력이 있다고 느끼지 못할 것이다. 나는 끊임없이 발생하는 역동적 변화에 대해 쓰고 있다. 우리의 호흡은 3, 4초마다 반복되는 주기에 따라 오르내린다. 우리의 몸은 거의 일정한 움직임을 하고 있다: 우리는 입을 움직이고, 경련하고, 얼굴을 만지고, 머리 위치와 방향을 약간 조절하고, 얼굴 표정을 바꾸고, 시선의 방향을 바꾸고, 신체 위치의 근육긴장을 조절한다. 서있든, 앉아있든, 누워있든(만일 깨어있다면) 관계없이. 이러한 과정은 외부에서 보이지 않을 때에도 계속된다. 몸짓과 더 큰 행동들은 시간이 흐르면서 전개된다. 그것들(몸짓과 더 큰 행동들)은 일단 행동이 시작되면 유동적으로 변한다. 우리는 이것들 가운데 어떤 것을 의식할 수도 있고, 아니면 주변적 인식에 머물 수도 있다. 게다가, 모든 움직임에는 의식적이든 의식적이지 않든, 고유 감각이 있다. 육체가 움직이는 것과 동시에, 생각도 마음속에서 (가상적으로) 움직이는데, 때로는 방황하고, 때로는 속도를 내거나, 폭발하거나, 이리저리 뒤척이거나, 사라져 버린다. 비슷하게, 감정도, 가볍게 또는 극적으로, 밀려왔다 밀려간다. 감각은, 음악적 흐름이나 춤, 또는 자극이 그러하듯이, 시간이 지나면서 강도와 지속 시간에 영향을 주고, 더 강해지고, 압도한다. 게다가, 종종 무시되지만, 우리의 자극 수준은 미세한 변화를 겪는다. 지나가는 사건에 대한 경계, 관심, 관여도 변화한다. 죽은 사람을 보는 것은 그 죽은 시체가 움직이지 않고, 아무것도 움직이지 않으며, 심지어 거의 알지 못하는 사이에 영향을 미치는 (근육의) 탄력성의 떨림마저 멈추기 때문에 즉시 충격을 준다. 우리는 이것을 주변 시야를 통해 한 번에 파악한다. 움직임 없이는, 우리는 얼굴 표정 밑에 숨겨져있는 정신적 활동, 마음속의 생각, 감정, 또는 "의지"를 인식하거나 상상할 수 없다. 그것이 바로 우리가 필수적 존재가 없다는 것(즉, 죽었다는 것)을 아는 방법이다. 마찬가지로, 엄마가 아기를 마주한 채 "정지된 얼굴"을 하면—즉, 심지어 아주 작은 표정조차 짓지 않은 채, 얼굴을 전혀 움직이지 않으면—, 태어난 지 얼마 안 되는 신생아조차 몇 초 안 돼서 당황하게 된다. 신생아들은 이미 주변부에서 움직임을 감지하도록 설계된 주변 시야를 가지고 있다. 따라서, 움직임 없음은, 신생아의 초점 시력이 엄마 얼굴의 어디를 바라보고 있든 관계없이, 감지된다.

133

하위내용영역	배점	예상정답률
일반영어 A형 서술형	4점	50%

모범답안 The word is "occupational". Second, "black" is included in the word "blacksmith" because "black" is the color iron turns after it is exposed to heat.

채점기준

+ 2점: 빈칸에 들어갈 단어가 "occupational"임을 정확히 기입하였다. 이외에는 답이 될 수 없다.
+ 2점: "블랙스미스"에서 "블랙"의 어원학적 기원을 "because "black" is the color iron turns after it is exposed to heat"이라 서술하였거나 유사하였다.

한글번역

대장장이업은 수천 년 동안 인류 역사에서 중요한 기술이었다. 대장장이들은 금속을 단조로 가열하고 가열된 금속을 끝없는 모양으로 망치로 두들기는데—일단 식으면—편리한 도구로 사용하거나 아름다운 예술품으로 감탄 받을 수 있다. 대장장이들은 전통적으로 말굽, 농기구, 무기, 갑옷, 그리고 생활용품들을 만들었다.

오늘날 살아서 일하고 있는 대장장이들은 똑같이 많은 제품들을 만들지만, 또한 예술품들과 장식품들을 벼려서 만든다. 시대나 만들어진 물건에 상관없이 대장장이는 사회에서 중요한 존재임이 증명됐다. 사실 너무 중요해서, "대장장이"라는 단어와 "smith대장장이"와 같은 다른 변종들은 몇몇 주요 언어들에서 풍부한 어원을 가지고 있다.

"대장장이blacksmith"라는 단어는 대장장이smith의 작업에서 두 가지 구별되는 요소를 결합한다: (하나는) 열이 가해졌을 때 철의 색과 (다른 하나는) 도구로 그 금속(철)을 두드리는 행위. 대부분의 학자들은 "검은색"은 철이 화염에 접하게 될 때 겪는 산화를 의미한다고 믿는다. 철의 표면에 검은 코팅이 형성되는데, 이것 때문에 대장장이의 작업과 그가 사용하는 재료에 대한 독특한 묘사적 특징이 발생한다. 이것은 대장장이 같은 철공인과 금세공이나 은세공 같은 유사한 일을 하는 장인들을 구별하게 해준다.

"Smith"는 "때리다"의 의미를 가지고 있는 고대영어인 "smythe", 또는 "망치"를 의미하는 "smitan"에서 유래됐다. 오늘날 그 단어는 일반적으로 "금속의 노동자"로 정의된다. "smith"라는 단어는 서기 900년 이전에 영어로 들어왔는데, 이것은 그 단어를 아주 오래된 단어이고, 직업으로서의 스미싱이 영국의 전통에서 중요한 것이라는 것을 시사해준다.

"스미스"는 영어권 국가에서 가장 흔한 성 중 하나이며, 조상이 금속으로 일했던 사람들에게 붙여진 직업형 성이다. "스미스"라는 단어는 여러 유럽 언어에서 같은 의미를 지니고 있는 다른 단어들과 관련이 있다. 스페인어로 대장장이blacksmith에 해당되는 용어는 "헤레로"이다. 이 단어는 "철을 다루는 노동자" 또는 "스미스"를 의미하며, 헤레로의 영어 상응물(즉, blacksmith)처럼 때때로 성으로 사용된다. "헤레로"는 라틴어 "페라리우스"에서 유래됐는데, 번역을 하면 "철로 만든 것"이란 의미이다.

134

하위내용영역	배점	예상정답률
일반영어 A형 서술형	4점	35%

모범답안 The word is "class". Second, it can be inferred that America was portrayed as favorable to create confidence in wary investors and state officials.

채점기준

+ 2점: 빈칸에 들어갈 단어가 "<u>class</u>"임을 정확히 기입하였다. 이외에는 답이 될 수 없다.
+ 2점: 초창기 영국에서 식민지 건설을 홍보한 이들이 아메리카를 멋진 장소라 묘사한 주요한 이유를 "<u>to create confidence in wary investors and state officials</u>"라 서술하였거나 유사하였다.

한글번역

미국의 계급을 둘러싼 언어와 사고방식은 영국 식민지 건설이 남긴 강력한 흔적에서 시작됐다. 영국이 아메리카의 자연환경을 폭넓게 활용하는 쪽에 무게를 뒀던 1500년대와 1600년대 세대들은 이런 목적의식이 반영된 묘사와 날것 그대로의 심상이 혼합된 하나의 어휘를 사용했다. 그들은 고운 말에 탐닉하지 않았다. 식민지라는 개념이 조심성 많은 투자자들에게 먹혀야 했다. 신세계 아메리카 식민지 건설이 구세계의 목적 달성에 기여해야 했다. 전반적으로 식민지 건설 기획자들은 아메리카를 기회가 넘치는 에덴동산이 아니라 생산적인 공간으로 바꿀 수 있는 거대한 쓰레기 더미로 생각했다. 소모품, 즉 폐기물 같은 사람들이 영국을 떠나 그곳으로 갈 것이다. 그들의 노동이 머나먼 황무지에 싹을 틔울 것이다. 가혹하다 싶을지 모르지만 이들 게으른 가난뱅이, 사회의 찌꺼기들을 저쪽으로 보내 황무지에 거름을 뿌리고 흙먼지 속에 죽게 할 수밖에 없다. 성서에 나오는 기독교 이상향인 '언덕 위의 도시'로 그럴듯하게 포장되기 전의 아메리카는 16세기 모험가들의 눈에는 지저분한 잡초투성이 황야, 무지렁이 서민에게 어울리는 하수구 같은 곳이었다. 신세계에 대한 이런 암울한 이미지는 그보다 매혹적인 이미지와 함께 제시됐다. 초기 영국에서 식민지 건설을 주도하고 홍보한 이들은 북아메리카를 풍요롭고 비옥한 땅으로 그릴 때면 엄청나게 과장을 했다(아마도 자신도 과장이라는 것을 인식하고 있었을 것이다). 물론, 그들 대부분은 한 번도 직접 본 적이 없는 땅에 대해 떠들고 있었다. 경계심 많은 투자자와 공무원들이 위험한 해외로 나가는 모험에 뛰어들게 확신을 줘야 했기 때문이다. 그러나 가장 중요한 것은 역시 그곳이 내부의 소외계층들을 내보낼 수 있는 좋은 장소라는 점이었다.

'세계 최고의 희망'으로서 아메리카라는 개념은 훨씬 나중에 나타났다. 역사적 기억은 그동안 '자유의 땅과 용자들의 고향'(*미국국가 성조기여 영원하라The Star-Spingled Banner*」의 후렴구)의 고상하지 못한 기원을 가리고 위장해왔다. 오늘날 애국자들이 자신들의 나라가 과거에도 지금도 항상 '특별한' 곳이라는 확증을 찾을 때 머릿속에 떠오르는 심상이 무엇인지 우리 모두 잘 알고 있다. 그것은 바로 인심 좋은 아메리카 원주민에게 씨 뿌리기를 배우는 겸손한 필그림 파더스(*1620년 메이플라워호를 타고 건너가 북아메리카에 플리머스 식민지를 건설한 청교도들*), 제임스강을 따라 늘어선 세련된 주택에서 손님을 접대하는 버지니아 왕당파의 모습이다. 나아가 역사를 가르치는 방식 때문에 미국인들은 최초 식민지인 플리머스와 제임스타운을 계급이 나뉜 사회보다는 계급이 없는 협력적인 사회를 떠올리는 경향이 있다.

역사적 기억은 점점 감상적으로 미화된다. 무질서와 불협화음을 이야기하는 것은 국민적 자부심을 키운다는 긍정적인 목표에 도움이 되지 않기 때문이다. 흔히들 간과하지만, 초기 아메리카 식민지에 대한 여러 가정에서 사실 계급은 가장 두드러지는 요소다. 심지어 지금도 완충지대 역할을 하는 광범위하고 온순한 중산계급이라는 개념이 강한 진통제겸 연막 기능을 하고 있다. 우리는 하층 없는 중산층도 있을 수 없다는 사실을 망각하고, 중산층이라는 위안에 매달리고 있다. 이런 생각은 가끔 흔들린다. 최근 월스트리트 점령 시위(*2011년 9월부터 11월까지 빈부 격차 심화와 금융기관의 부도덕성에 반발하면서 미국 월가를 비판하며 일어난 시위*)에서 금융 부문, 그리고 1%와 99% 사이의 기묘한 분리라는 당혹스러운 현실이 부각됐을 때가 대표적이다. 그러나 공룡 언론들이 다른 새로운 위기들을 찾아내 지면을 장식하면, 대대로 내려오는 미국국민의 계급 무시 전통이 다시 고개를 들고, 관련 주제들은 스르르 관심의 뒷전으로 물러난다.

135

하위내용영역	배점	예상정답률
일반영어 B형 기입형	2점	45%

모범답안 reason

채점기준

- 2점: 빈칸에 들어갈 단어가 "reason"임을 정확히 기입하였다. 이외에는 답이 될 수 없다.
- 0점: 모범답안과 다르다.

한글번역

낭만주의는 개인의 발달에 있어서 자유주의적 가치를 추구했다. 낭만주의는 초기 단계에서는 매우 해방적이었다. 하지만, 부분적으로는 상응하는 사회 이론의 불충분함과 개인주의가 주관주의로 결과적으로 쇠퇴해버렸기 때문에, 낭만주의는 자신의 가장 깊은 충동을 부정하고 심지어 그 충동들을 뒤집는 것으로 끝났다. 거의 모든 우리의 혁명적인 언어는 사실 낭만주의에서 비롯됐는데, 이 사실은 부수적인 당혹감뿐만 아니라 실질적인 장애물이 돼왔다. 낭만주의는 현대 문학에서 혁명의 첫 번째 충동에 대한 가장 중요한 표현이다 : 새롭고도 절대적인 인간의 이미지. 낭만주의는 그 특유의 성격대로 이상적인 세계로의 초월과 이상적인 인간 사회를 연관시킨다. 인간이 처음으로 자기 자신을 만들어내는 존재로 보여진 것은 바로 이 낭만주의에서였다. 그러나 물론 이것이 사회비판이나 사회구성으로 구체화될 때는, 낭만주의는 근본적인 장애물을 만나게 된다. 이국적이거나 전설적인 공동체(또는 이러한 요소들에 의해 변형된 역사적 공동체)에서 이상을 시각화하는 것이 더 쉽다. (기득권이 지배하는) 기존의 사회세계는 가장 깊은 곳에 있는 인간적인 것에 대해 너무나 적대적인 것으로 간주돼, 사회 비판으로 시작한 것조차도 결국 허무주의로 빠져버리는 경향이 있다.

여기서 결정적인 요소는 다름 아닌 이성에 대한 낭만주의의 태도였다. 형식에 있어서, 낭만주의는 계몽주의에 대한 부정적인 반응으로 보일 수 있다 : 즉, 낭만주의의 비합리적이고 이상한 것에 대한 강조는 이성에 대한 강조의 절대적인 반대로 보인다. 하지만, 여기에, 흥미로운 변증법이 있다. 낭만주의는 계몽주의가 반대했던 것을 제안하는 것이 아니었다; 인간에 대한 하나의 버전은 인간에 대한 또 다른 버전만큼 새로운 것이었다. 하지만, 이런 사실이

(앞 문장내용) 보이지 않았기 때문에, 인간 해방을 위한 프로그램으로서의 이 운동들(계몽주의와 낭만주의)의 본질적인 통합은 비참하게 협소해지고 혼란스러웠다. 낭만주의자들이 이성이라고 비판한 것은 논리적 활동이 아니라, 이 논리적 활동을 추상화시킨 뒤 궁극적으로 소외시킨 것일 따름이었는데, 이것은 이른바 합리적 체계라 불렸지만, 실제로는 기계적 체계일 따름이었다.

136

하위내용영역	배점	예상정답률
일반영어 B형 서술형	4점	40%

모범답안 The word is "pleasure". Second, Mozart's advice seems hypocritical in that Mozart tells the student to only compose duets on the grounds that the student is young, though Mozart is also young himself and composing more complicated works.

채점기준

+ 2점: 빈칸에 들어갈 단어가 "pleasure"임을 정확히 기입하였다. 이외에는 답이 될 수 없다.
+ 2점: 모차르트의 충고가 학생에게 처음에는 위선적으로 들렸을 수도 있는 이유를 "in that Mozart tells the student to only compose duets on the grounds that the student is young, though Mozart is also young himself and composing more complicated works"라 서술하였거나 유사하였다.

한글번역

한 음악학도가 모차르트에게 다가가 정말 좋은 것을 만들기 위해 어떤 곡을 작곡해야 하는지 그리고 어떻게 작곡해야 하는지에 대한 조언을 구한 적이 있었다고 한다. 모차르트는 그를 찬찬히 바라보더니 (바꾸어 표현해보면) 다음과 같이 말했다고 한다. "당신은 아직 젊어요. 우선 이중주곡부터 작곡하는 게 좋을 것 같아요." 이 젊은이는 화가 나서 모차르트에게 (모차르트) 본인 역시 아직 어린데도, 이중주곡보다 더 진지한 음악을 작곡했는데, 왜 자기는 그러지 말아야 하냐며 (항의하듯) 말했다고 한다. 모차르트는 그의 주장에 (바꾸어 표현해보면) 다음과 같이 대답했다고 한다. "그것은 사실이지만, 나는 사람들에게 무엇을 작곡해야 할지 물어보고 다니지 않았답니다. 나는 무엇을 해야 할지 알고 있답니다." 여기서 말하고자 하는 핵심은 많은 사람들이 위대한 예술을 창조하려고 시도했지만, 아주 극소수만이 진정한 대가가 됐다는 것이다.

그렇긴 하지만, 여기에 또 다른 중요한 요소가 있는데, 이것은, 가수들만이, 어떤 악기도 할 수 없는, 그런 상황에 가져올 수 있는 것인 바로 구어가 있다. 노래에서 가사를 이해 못하는 것은 그 음악으로부터 거의 아무것도 빼앗지 않는다는 것을 위에서 언급했지만, 이것의 의미는 가사들이 완전히 (노래와) 무관하다고 주장하기 위한 것이 아니라, 단지 가사들이 너무 과대평가됐다는 것을 지적하는 것일 뿐이다. 사람들은 이탈리아어로 된 좋은 오페라를 즐길 수 있는데, 비록 (오페라 가수들이) 말하는 것을 한마디도 이해하지 못하더라도 말이다. 노래에서, 본질적으로는 시인 가사의 올바른 위치를 이해하는 것은 자세히 설명할 가치가 있다.

핵심은 음악이 음표의 율동적 구성에 불과하듯이 시는 단어의 율동적 구성에 지나지 않는다는 것이다. 음악이 우리에게 율동적으로 작곡된 마음을 진정시켜주는 소리를 전달하는 반면, 시는 청중에게 느낌이나 개념을 전달하는 율동적으로 작곡된 일련의 단어들을 전달한다. 가수들이 가사를 노래할 때, 가수들은 시와 음악을 조화롭게 융합하고, 그렇게 함으로써 그들은 전체적인 믹스에 또 하나의 리듬적 구성을 추가한다. 음악의 즐거움이 주로 리듬의 본능을 만족시키는 데서 비롯된다면, 시에 리듬의 층이 더해져 그 효과와 즐거움이 높아진다.

비록 노래에 있는 음악에 비해 가사의 소리와 의미는 정량화할 수 있는 요소는 아니지만, 완성된 작품에 대한 각각의 가치와 기여에 대해 경험에서 우러난 추측을 해볼 수 있다. 그중 얼마나 많은 즐거움이 음악 속에 있는 리듬 덕분인지, 또 즐거움 가운데 얼마나 많은 부분이 시 속에 있는 리듬에 귀속될 수 있는지, 또한 얼마나 많은 즐거움이 가사가 지니고 있는 생각이나 의미에 귀속될 수 있는지 궁금하다. 앞서 언급했듯이, 난 노래의 진정한 가치는, 가사나 시 전체가 담고 있는 의미가 아니라, 가수들이 만들어내는 음악과 아름다운 음에 주로 있다고 주장한다.

137

하위내용영역	배점	예상정답률
일반영어 A형 기입형	2점	55%

모범답안 personally

채점기준
- 2점: 모범답안과 같다.
- 0점: 모범답안과 다르다.

한글번역

준사회관계는 한쪽은 상대방에 대해 많이 알고 있지만 다른 한쪽은 상대방에 대해 아무것도 모르는 사회적 상호작용의 한 형태이다. 이 관계는 어떠한 사람이 방송인과 개인적으로 친구로서 교류할 때 종종 발생한다. 방송에 나오는 인물은 리얼리티 TV에 나오는 유명인, 비디오 게임 탤런트, 소셜 미디어 인플루언서를 포함할 수 있다. 이러한 관계의 정도는 다양하다. 어떤 팬들은 단순히 자신들의 '친구'의 행동에 관심이 있는 반면, 다른 팬들은 그들과 관계를 맺는 것을 상상할 정도로 그들에게 집착하게 된다. 준사회관계는 그런 관계가 존재하는지조차 인플루언서가 모르는 상황에서도 발생한다. 일단 아이돌을 숭배하는 어떤 사람이 그 아이돌에 집착하면, 준사회관계는 독이 되고 그들의 정신 건강에 해로울 수 있다. 이러한 관계는 외로움을 줄이고 사회적 상호작용의 공백을 메울 수 있지만, 현실의 상호작용만큼 효과적이고 만족스러운 것은 결코 아니다. 게다가, 이러한 관계는 스토킹과 괴롭힘의 우려로 확대될 수 있다.

준사회관계는 책과 그 이후의 텔레비전이 발명된 이래로 계속 존재해 왔다. 이러한 유형의 상호작용의 가장 초기 형태는 독자와 작가들 사이였다. 그러나 텔레비전이 나오고 나서야 비로소 준사회관계가 각광을 받게 됐다. 초창기 텔레비전 시대에는, 리얼리티 쇼도 소셜 미디어 인플루언서도, 비디오 게임도 없었다. 대신에, 이런 종류의 관계를 형성하는 유일한 방법은 TV나 영화를 보는 것을 통해서였다. 예를 들어, 사람들은 똑같은 배우들을 계속해서 반복적으로 보곤 했다. 그 결과, 그들은 이 등장인물들에 대한 애착을 쌓고, 자신들이 그 배우들을 개인적으로 안다고 느끼곤 했다. 오늘날, 그 관계는 TV 스타들과 관계를 맺는 것으로부터 소셜 미디어 인플루언서, 트위치 스트리머, 유튜버, 그리고 온라인 유명인들로 서서히 바뀌고 있다.

138

하위내용영역	배점	예상정답률
일반영어 A형 서술형	4점	45%

모범답안 The word is "extremism". Second, his ideas did not fit well because he was moderate and his era was one of fanaticism.

채점기준
- +2점: 빈칸에 들어갈 단어를 "extremism"이라 정확히 기입하였다.
- +2점: 에라스무스의 사상이 그가 살던 시대정신과 얼마나 잘 들어맞았는가라는 질문과 이유에 대해 "his ideas did not fit well(1점) because he was moderate and his era was one of fanaticism(1점)"이라 서술하였거나 유사하였다.

한글번역

데시데리우스 에라스무스는 통일된 기독교 유럽의 마지막 위대한 지식인이었다. 보편적으로 알려진 학자이자, 왕들의 친구이자 왕자들의 가정교사였고, 스스로 "세계 시민"이라 생각한 사람이었다. 그는 기독교인들이 그들의 신앙에 대해 생각하는 방식을 바꾼 신약성서의 번역본을 제작했다. 그는 또한 대중문화를 형성했다. 그의 사전은 "서먹서먹한 분위기를 깨다", "늙은 개에게 새로운 재주를 가르치다", "온갖 수를 다 쓰다"와 같은 문구를 어둠 속에서 구해냈다. 그의 《우신예찬》(1511)은 유머러스한 걸작으로 환영받았다.

출생이 일반적으로 운명이었던 시대에, 그는 자수성가한 사람이었다. 1466년 로테르담이라는 작은 지방 마을에서 성직자의 사생아로 태어난 그는, 기회가 닿는 대로 최대한 일찍, 지역 수도원에 버려졌다. 그는 당시 르네상스의 중심이었던 북부 이탈리아에서 멀리 떨어져서 자랐다. 이후 그의 스타덤은 순전히 그의 비범한 지적 재능의 결과였다.

에라스무스는 그의 시대뿐 아니라 그 이후 시대에 있던, 다른 많은 위대한 사상가들과는 달리, 결코 극단주의의 희생양이 되지 않았다. 그는 절제와 이성의 치유력을 믿었고, 동시에 와인과 대화의 교화시키는 힘을 믿었다. 이것은 부분적으로 개인적인 스타일의 문제였다. 그는, 역사학자 휴 트레버 로퍼가 말했듯이, "서재에서 살다가 침대에서 죽는" 학문적으로 안락한 삶을 갈망했다. 왕이나 잠재적인 후원자와 정면으로 부딪히게 될 땐 그는 무릎을 꿇었고, 불한당에게 도전받을 땐, 주제를 바꿨다.

그것은 또한 확신의 문제였다. 에라스무스는 이 데올로기의 확실성을 싫어했고 극단주의가 서로를 더 광신적인 행동으로 이끄는 경향에 대해 걱정했다. 그는 혁명의 확실성 대신, 중도를 설교했다. 그는 기득권층을 개혁하는 최선의 방법은 내부에서 나온다고 주장했다. 카톨릭 교회는 원래 목적대로 되돌림으로써 다시 활기를 불어넣어야 하고, 사회는 통치기술을 왕자들에게 교육함으로써 개혁돼야 한다.

하지만 이 온건한 옹호자는 열정적인 시대에 살기에는 엄청난 불운을 겪을 수밖에 없었다. 유럽의 지적, 사회적 정점에 오른 직후, 에라스무스는 내동댕이쳐져 비난을 받았다. 오직 죽어서야, 그는 마땅히 받아야 할 것을 받았다. 그의 이야기는 현대의 온건파에 대한 경고이기도 하지만 영감이 되기도 한다.

139

하위내용영역	배점	예상정답률
일반영어 A형 서술형	4점	60%

모범답안 The word is "endangered". Second, it is because cloning does not address the root causes for endangered species and the techniques are not effective enough to make a difference.

채점기준

+ 2점 : 빈칸에 들어갈 단어를 "endangered"라 정확히 기입하였다.
+ 2점 : 복제가 효과적인 전략이 되지 못하는 이유를 "because cloning does not address the root causes for endangered species(1점) and the techniques are not effective enough to make a difference(=to have an impact)(1점)"라 서술하였거나 유사하였다.

한글번역

2009년 브라질 농업 연구 회사(엠브라파)와 브라질리아 동물원은 로드킬과 주로 세라도 사바나에서 죽은 다른 야생동물들로부터 혈액, 정자, 탯줄 세포를 수집해서 냉동하기 시작했다. 세라도 사바나에는 적어도 10,000종이나 되는 식물 종들과 800종 이상의 새와 포유동물들이 살고 있는데, 그것들 중 몇몇은 세계 어디에도 살지 않는다. 그리고 나서 표본들은 덤불개, 목걸이 개미핥기, 들소, 그리고 다른 종들 중에서 수집됐다.

이 아이디어는 멸종 위기에 처한 브라질의 야생동물의 유전 정보를 보존하는 것이었다. 그 단체들은 다음과 같이 추론했다. 언젠가 수집된 DNA를 멸종 위기에 처한 이 동물들을 복제해서 줄어드는 개체수를 지원하기 위해(늘리기 위해) 사용할 수 있을지도 모른다고. 지금까지 두 기관이 최소 420개의 조직 샘플을 수집했다. 현재 그들은 번식 및 복제 기술을 향상시키기 위해 이것들의 DNA를 사용할 관련 프로젝트에 협력하고 있다. 현재의 복제 기술은 친숙한 종을 가지고 작업을 할 때에도 평균 5% 미만의 성공률을 가지고 있다; 야생동물을 복제하는 것은 보통 1% 미만이다.

엠브라파 연구원인 카를로스 마틴스는 브라질의 새로운 사업 기간 동안 태어난 모든 동물들은 브라질리아 동물원에서 살 것이라고 말한다. 그와 그의 팀은 야생동물의 포획 개체수를 늘리는 것이 동물원과 연구원들이 그 동물들의 서식지에서 더 많은 야생동물을 빼내는 것을 단념시킬 것이라 보고 있다. 마틴스와 그의 동료들은 아직 어떤 종들을 복제하려고 시도할지 결정하지 않았지만 갈기 있는 늑대와 재규어는 강력한 후보이다. 국제 자연 보전 연맹(IUCN)은 두 종을 멸종위기종 목록에서 준위협 단계로 분류하는데, 이 등급은 멸종위기종보다는 두 단계 아래 등급이다.

많은 연구자들은 현재 복제가 실현 가능하거나 효과적인 보존 전략이 아니라는 데 동의한다. 무엇보다도, 일부 환경 보호론자들은 복제는 많은 동물들이 애초에 멸종 위기에 처하게 되는 이유, 즉 사냥과 서식지 파괴를 다루지 않는다고 지적한다. 이론적으로 복제가 정말 절박한 상황에서 도움이 될 수 있다고 해도, 현재의 복제 기술은 큰 차이를 만들어 내기에는 너무나 비효율적이다.

140

하위내용영역	배점	예상정답률
일반영어 A형 서술형	4점	40%

모범답안 The word is "humbug". Second, those characters, Mr. Gradgrind and the Barnacle family, are more representative of 2020 living than other Dickens characters.

채점기준

+ 2점: 빈칸에 들어갈 단어를 "humbug"라 정확히 기입하였다.
+ 2점: 밑줄 친 부분의 의미를 "those characters, Mr. Gradgrind and the Barnacle family, are more representative of 2020 living than other Dickens characters"라 서술하였거나 유사하였다.

한글번역

영국의 크리스마스는 빨간 양복을 입은 유쾌한 뚱뚱한 남자뿐만 아니라 심술궂고, 마르고, "쥐어짜고, 비틀고, 꽉 쥐고, 긁어대고, 와락 움켜쥐고, 탐욕스러운 늙은 죄인"과도 떼려야 뗄 수 없다. 찰스 디킨스의 소설 《크리스마스 캐롤》은 (책이 나오자마자) 즉각적인 히트를 쳤다. 1843년 출간된 지 두 달도 안 돼 런던에 있는 극장에서는 (그 원작을) 각색한 것이 12개나 공연됐다. 거의 2세기 동안, 그 작품의 반영웅(일반인과 다를 바 없거나 도덕적으로 나빠 전통적인 영웅답지 않은 소설 속 주인공)은 대중적 상상력을 여전히 계속 유지하고 있다.

이 계절에는 반드시 "크리스마스 캐롤"을 즐겨라 —영화보다는 빅토리아풍으로 아이들에게 큰 소리로 읽어주는 것이 좋다. 디킨스의 동시대인이자 라이벌이었던 윌리엄 새커리는 이 책을 "국가적 이익이며, 이 작품을 읽는 모든 남성이나 여성에게는 개인적 친절"이라고 묘사했다. 그는, 셰익스피어 다음으로, 영국에서 창조적인 등장인물을 가장 많이 만들어 낸 사람이었는데, 그 숫자가 위키피디아에 천 명 이상이나 등재됐다. 그 등장인물들이 그의 시대만큼이나 오늘날에도 여전히 의미가 있다는 것은 인간의 본질적인 특성을 포착하는 그의 능력뿐만 아니라 빅토리아 시대와 우리 시대 사이에 유사성이 있다는 것을 보여준다.

너무나 많은 디킨스의 등장인물들이 2020년의 독특한 정신을 환기시키기 때문에, 이것들 중 하나를 선택하기란 어렵다. 《어려운 시절》에서 그래드그라인드는—목표와 알고리즘에 대한 현대 관료집단의 강박관념을 깔끔하게 압축해 보여주는—"인간 본성의 어떤 꾸러미든 저울질하고 측정"하려고 노력한다. 《리틀 도릿》에서 바너클 가문은 번문 욕례청(수속만 번거롭고 사무능률은 조금도 오르지 않는 관청)의 사업을 통제하는데, 이것은 연줄이 든든한 토리당이 요즘에 정부 아웃소싱(자체 인력·설비·부품 등을 이용해 하던 일을 비용 절감과 효율성 증대를 목적으로 외부 용역이나 부품으로 대체하는 것)의 혜택을 누리는 것과 유사하다. 하지만 그 캐릭터들은 2020년의 구현으로서 그들의 라이벌(즉, 디킨스의 다른 등장인물들)보다 우위에 있다.

《우리의 상호 친구》에 나오는 존 포드스냅은 브렉시트 영국이 육체화된 존재이다. 가장 편협한 부류의 젠체하는 속물인, "대부분의 것에, 그리고 무엇보다도, 자기 자신에 대해 특히 만족하는" 그는 다른 나라들을 "실수"라고 생각하고, 외국인들은 "불행하게 태어났다"고 생각하며, 영국 헌법은 "신의 섭리가 우리에게 주신" 세계 최고의 것이다. 요약하면, "우리나라만큼 사랑을 받는 다른 나라는 없다"는 것이다.

세계가 사기꾼에 중독됐다는 것은 불행한 일이다. 오늘날 거의 모든 것이 그것이 가장하는 것과는 정반대이다. 회사들은 동성애자들의 권리를 증진시키고, 다문화주의를 장려하거나, 쿰바야 노래를 같이 부르면서 세상을 통합하는 데 전념하고 있다고 주장하는데, 사실 그들은 오로지 이익을 극대화하는 데 관심이 있을 뿐이다. 최고 경영자들은 자신들이 언제나 겸손한 "팀장들"이라고 주장하지만, 실제로 그들은 전례가 없는 규모로 회사로부터 돈을 받아가고 있다. 이튼 같은 사립학교들은 "다양성"과 "포용성"을 촉진하는 일을 진행하고 있다고 주장하는데, 현실은 그 학교에 다니려면 1년에 4만 2천 파운드나 되는 엄청난 수업료를 내야한다. 미래의 역사학자들이 만일 우리가 살고 있는 이 시대를 요약한다면, 그들은 아마도 "사기꾼의 시대"라고 부를 것 같다.

141

하위내용영역	배점	예상정답률
일반영어 B형 서술형	4점	45%

모범답안 The word is "intelligence". Second, it is an awareness of death.

채점기준

+ 2점: 빈칸에 들어갈 단어를 "intelligence"라 정확히 기입하였다.
+ 2점: 니체와 그레그가 공통으로 언급하는 인간 불행의 핵심적 원인을 "awareness of death"라 서술하였거나 유사하였다.

한글번역

만약 우리가, 하나의 종으로서, 다른 동물들과 더 같다면 우리는 더 나아질까? 저스틴 그레그가 테리 프래쳇의 책 《피라미드》—이 책은 내가 가장 좋아하는 공상과학 소설 가운데 하나인데—에서 나오는 한 구절로 시작할 때 그가 제기한 이 질문을 읽는 것을 난 즐겼다고 생각했다. "단순한 동물들은 이런 행동을 할 수 없을 것입니다. 정말 멍청해지려면 사람이 돼야 해요."

동물 인식 전문가인 그레그는 철학자 프리드리히 니체를 원용하면서, 인간의 허점이 동물 지능에 대해 드러내는 것을 탐구한다. 동물 인식 전문가인 그레그는 철학자 프리드리히 니체를 원용하면서, 인간의 허점이 동물 지능에 대해 드러내는 것을 탐구한다. 그레그가 보는 니체의 딜레마는 그가 소를 부러워하면서 동시에 같은 이유로 소를 불쌍히 여겼다는 것이다: 즉, 소는 자신이 죽을 것이라는 인식을 갖고 있지 않다는 것이다. 니체는 지적 천재이자 동시에 정신적으로 문제가 있는 사람이었고, 후자(정신적 붕괴)가 전자(지적 천재)를 압도해 버렸는데, 그 이유는 이탈리아 토리노에서 말이 채찍을 맞는 것을 목격한 뒤에, 그 후 정신분열증을 겪었기 때문이라고 한다. 여기서 전제는, 불행은 우리 종이 지능을 위해 지불하는 대가라는 것이다. 하지만 다른 동물들이 실제로 더 행복한지 아닌지 어떻게 알 수 있을까?

그레그는 인공지능을 만드는 데 경력을 바치는 과학자(일반적으로 똑똑한 인간으로 여겨지는)도 지능이 무엇인지에 대해서는 동의할 수 없다고 맹랑하게 지적한다. 인간은 기본적으로 어떤 것을 볼 때 그것에 대해 알게 되고, 지능에 대해 긍정적인 특성이라 간주한다. 우리는 종종 먼 행성에서 오는 메시지나 신호를 찾아 외계 지성의 징후를 찾는다. 우리가 우리 행성(지구)에서 이 탐색을 잘 하지 못하는 점은 특이한 일이다.

거짓말을 예로 들어보자. 거짓말은 이익을 위해 자주 사용되는 과도하게 발달된 인간의 특성이다. 그레그는 거짓말의 주요 특징은 의도라고 주장한다. 비록 동물의 왕국 도처에 속임수를 쓰는 증거가 분명히 있지만, 우리 종은 언어와 "정신의 이론"이라는 이른바 최고의 능력을 가지고 있다. 하지만 그것들이 우리에게 잘 봉사할까? 우리가 더 나은가? 그레그는, 제인 오스틴("우리는 매일 증거를 가지고 있다")부터 현대의 허위 정보의 맹공격에 이르기까지 덜 긍정적인 것에 대한 매혹적인 토론 속으로 뛰어들었다. 여기로부터 그는 "죽음의 지혜와 사망률의 관점에서 우리 종과 다른 종을 비교한 뒤, 나중에 꿀벌의 행복과 미래를 예측하는 것이 무엇을 의미하는지에 대해 숙고한다.

142

하위내용영역	배점	예상정답률
일반영어 A형 서술형	4점	40%

모범답안 The word is "ranks". Second, the writer cites Israel.

채점기준

+ 2점: 빈칸에 들어갈 단어가 "ranks"임을 정확히 기입하였다. 이외에는 답이 될 수 없다.
+ 2점: 디지털 전쟁 능력을 은폐할 능력이 있는 나라를 "Israel"이라 정확히 서술하였다.

한글번역

중국은 세계에서 가장 큰 군대를 가지고 있다. 러시아는 가장 많은 탱크를 휘두른다. 미국은 가장 화려한 인공위성을 소유하고 있다. 하지만 누가 가장 강력한 사이버 파워를 가지고 있을까? 새로운 <국가 사이버 전력 지수>는 각 국가들의 야망과 능력에 따라 30개국의 순위를 매긴다. 컴퓨터 네트워크 안에서 또는 컴퓨터 네트워크를 통해서 해를 끼칠 수 있는 능력인 공격적인 사이버 파워가 하나의 척도이다. 하지만 한 국가의 국방력, 사이버 보안 산업의 정교함, 그리고 (자국에 유리한) 선전선동을 퍼뜨리는 능력과 (다른 나라의) 선전선동에 대응하는 능력도 마찬가지로 중요한 척도이다.

미국이 그 목록의 맨 위에 있다는 것은 놀랍지 않다. 2020년 회계연도의 사이버 보안 예산은 170억 달러 이상이었고, 미국의 신호 지능기관인 국가안보국은 아마도 100억 달러를 훨씬 넘게 쓸 것이다. 2위인 중국은 해외에서 상업적인 사이버 스파이 활동에 대한 열렬한 욕구와 국내에서의 강력한 인터넷 장악력을 보여줬다. 영국은 3위이다. 영국은 현재 스파이들과 군인들이 합동으로 일하는 공격형 국가 사이버군을 창설하고 있다. 러시아가 4위인데, 러시아의 첩자들이 미국의 지난 선거에 개입했다. 매우 놀라운 일은 네덜란드가 프랑스, 독일, 캐나다를 제치고 5위에 올랐다는 점이다. 많은 전문가들은 이스라엘이 뛰어난 해킹 능력에도 불구하고 벨퍼 지수에서 상대적으로 낮은 순위에 머무르는 것에 대해 어리둥절해하고 있다. 아마도 이스라엘의 비밀 엄수가 이런 낮은 랭킹의 한 가지 이유일 수 있다.

영국의 신호 지능기관인 GCHQ의 전 부국장인 마커스 윌렛은 사이버 파워를 측정하는 것이 어렵다고 충고한다. "남극의 군함은 쉽게 볼 수 있지만, 발전소에 삽입된 코드 조각은 탐지하기 어렵다"고 윌렛은 말한다. 몇몇 국가들은 자기들의 공격 능력을 인정하지만—(예를 들어) 미국과 영국은 이라크와 시리아에 있는 이슬라믹 스테이트 네트워크를 파괴한 것을 자랑하는데, 이렇게 하는 것은 부분적으로 러시아와 중국에 대해(함부로 까불지 말라는) 경고를 하기 위한 것이다—, 대다수의 국가들은 그렇게 하는 것을 피한다.

많은 국가들은 극도로 더러운 일을 "핵티비스트"나 범죄자들과 같은 부인 가능한 대리인들(문제가 발각됐을 때 자국은 관계가 없다고 부인할 수 있는)에게 외부 위탁한다. 그리고 군함이나 미사일을 조달하는 것은 비용이 많이 들고 시간도 많이 걸리는 반면, 강력한 악성코드는 도난당하거나 온라인으로 구입할 수 있다. 2017년에 북한에 의해 사용된 랜섬웨어(컴퓨터의 작동이 중단되게 만든 뒤 재가동을 조건으로 금품을 요구하는 데 이용되는 악성 프로그램의 일종) 공격인 워나크라이는 (미국의) 국가안보국에서 유출된 해킹 도구인 이터널블루를 사용했다.

싱크탱크인 국제전략문제연구소에서 일하는 윌렛과 그의 동료들에 의한 사이버 파워에 대한 연구는 다음과 같이 결론을 내린다. 물건을 훔치고 네트워크를 교란시키는 것도 중요하지만, 장기적으로 가장 중요한 것은 이동통신과 핵심 앱들을 운영하는 하드웨어와 같은 디지털 인프라를 통제하는 것이다. 거기서의 지배력은 경제력과 국가 안보에 매우 중요할 것이라고 국제전략문제연구소는 말한다. 그 기준으로 평가해보면, "현재 오직 중국만이 1위에 있는 미국에 합류할 수 있는 위치에 있다"고 밝혔다.

143

하위내용영역	배점	예상정답률
일반영어 A형 서술형	4점	45%

모범답안 The word is "algorithm". Second, the previous surveys had less resolution in the images produced.

채점기준

+ 2점: 빈칸에 들어갈 단어가 "algorithm"임을 정확히 기입하였다. 이외에는 답이 될 수 없다.
+ 2점: 이전의 조사들이 현재의 조사보다 어떤 측면에서 덜 적절한 것인가에 대해 "the previous surveys had less resolution in the images produced(=used/available)"라 서술하였다.

한글번역

나무는 환경과학과 더 광범위한 사회적, 정치적 환경보호주의 운동 모두에서 크게 다가온다. 환경보호주의자들이 때때로 "트리 허거"라고 불리는 것은 다 충분한 이유가 있다. 일반적으로 나무와 관련된 뉴스는 넓은 숲이 개간되거나 불에 타거나 제재소로 편도 여행을 떠나는 등 우울한 것들이다. 하지만 NASA의 마틴 브란트가 네이처에 발표한 논문은 반가운 좋은 소식을 전한다. 이전에 나무가 없다고 여겨졌던 세계의 어떤 지역에서 거의 20억 그루의 나무가 실제로 살고 있는 것으로 나타났다.

문제의 지역은 사하라 사막의 서쪽 끝과 그 남쪽에 있는 준사막 사헬 지역을 포함한다. 과거 조사에서는 여기에 나무가 거의 보이지 않았는데, 그 이유는 그런 조사는 각각의 나무들의 캐노피(숲의 나뭇가지들이 지붕 모양으로 우거진 것)를 발견하기 위해 해상도가 충분하지 않은 위성사진을 사용했기 때문이었다. 대신에, 그들은 (작은 규모의) 숲과 (큰 규모의) 숲을 상징하는 인접한 녹색 부분을 찾으려 했다.

브란트 박사와 터커 박사는 이런 방식이 구닥다리 방식이라고 생각했다. 이제는 지구 표면을 아주 고해상도로 찍을 수 있는 위성들이 존재한다. 군대와 정보기관의 손에 있는 일부는 비밀이다. 그러나 민간 지구관측 회사가 소유한 다른 것들은 상당히 비싼 가격으로 접근할 수 있다. 때마침, 그 비용은 이미 미국 정부에 의해 적절한 이미지에 대해선 지불됐다. 이를 통해 연구진은 과거에 사용됐던 10~30m가 아닌 50cm 정도의 작은 해상도로 촬영된 것에 접근할 수 있게 됐다.

그러나 적절한 해상력을 갖는다는 것과 그 해상력을 사용할 수 있는 능력은 별개의 것이다. 그것을 사용하기 위해서, 브란트 박사와 터커 박사는 그 문제에 인공지능을 적용해야만 했다. 여기에는 일련의 훈련용 이미지들에 있는 89,899개의 각각의 나무에 일일이 손으로 이름을 붙이는 것이 포함됐는데, 이렇게 하는 이유는 검색 알고리즘이 하루 중 서로 다른 시간—구름에 덮여 있을 때 또는 먼지로 덮여 있을 때, 또는 서로 다른 각도에서 보여질 때—에 나무가 어떻게 보이는지 알 수 있도록 하기 위해서였다. 그리고 물론, 각각의 나무들 자체도 서로서로 다르게 보인다. 일단 이 이미지들을 소화한 후, 알고리즘은 사하라사막과 사헬의 백삼십만 평방킬로미터나 되는 지역을 커버하는 고해상도 사진을 자유롭게 사용했다. 이전의 부정적인 결과와 대조적으로, 그 지역에 18억 그루의 나무가 있다고 보고했다.

144

하위내용영역	배점	예상정답률
일반영어 A형 서술형	4점	40%

모범답안) The word is "deception". Second, the two words are "Second Coming".

채점 기준

+ 2점 : 빈칸에 들어갈 단어가 "<u>deception</u>"임을 정확히 기입하였다. 이외에는 답이 될 수 없다.
+ 2점 : 밑줄 친 부분과 가장 잘 상응하는 두 단어를 "<u>Second Coming</u>"이라 정확히 서술하였다.

한글번역

초기 기독교 사상가들이, 세상의 악이 (예수 그리스도의) 재림시기에 결정적으로 패배하기 위해서는 그 악에 초점, 프로젝트, 이름이 필요하다고 결정한 이후, 적그리스도가 형태를 바꾸어 끊임없이 우리 주위를 맴돌았다.

적그리스도의 등장은 종말의 시대—묵시론적 사건들이 세상에 풀리고, 그리스도가 돌아와서 모든 것을 정리하는—를 의미하기 때문에, 산불, 전염병, 기후 변화가 모두 수렴되는 지금이 바로 적그리스도의 순간이라고 하는 것이 그럴듯하게 들린다. 어느 쪽이든 아는 것이 좋을지도 모른다.

하지만 필립 아몬드가 설명하듯이, 그것은 단지 문제일 뿐이다. 그 또는 그것을 딱 꼬집어서 찾아내는 것은 매우 어렵다. (적그리스도를) 영속적으로 감시해야만 한다는 의무감을 느끼고 사는 기독교인들—그리고 이런 기독교인들 가운데는 아이작 뉴턴도 있었다. 적그리스도의 이름을 언급하지 않은 《요한계시록》은 바빌론의 창녀에서부터 바다에서 떠오르는 용의 일곱 번째 머리까지 모든 가명과 단서를 제공했다.

이런 가운데, 교황이 적그리스도였다는 마틴 루터의 분명한 확신은 신선한 공기의 질풍으로 다가온다. 이런 주장은 놀랍게도 아주 오래된 것이었는데, 1190년 피오레의 요아힘이 처음 주장했고, 가톨릭교회가 성직매매와 성적 일탈, 면죄부 판매에 휘말리면서 점점 더 열정적으로 받아들여졌다. 그 뒤에 있는 이론은 적그리스도가 기독교 밖에서 기독교인들을 파멸시키며 은밀히 활동하는 폭군이 아니라, 그(기독교) 안에서, 심지어 기독교의 바로 그 핵심과 최고위층에서까지 작용하는 악의적 영향력이라는 것이었다.

잠복해 있는 적그리스도의 본질은 기만, 특히 신자들을 기만하는 것이었다. 중세 그림들이 종종 멸망의 아들(적그리스도)을 왕관을 쓰고 예복을 입고 있는 자비로운 왕자로, 또는 심지어 수염을 기른 사려 깊고 기적을 행하는 예수를 꼭 닮은 사람으로 묘사하는 이유가 여기에 있다. 악은 언제나 기만하면서, 기꺼이 따르는 사람들을 많이 끌어들였다. 그것에 대한 대안—적그리스도를 완전히 흉악하고 극도로 불쾌한 존재로 만드는 것, 예를 들어 윌리엄 블레이크가 적그리스도를 뿔 달린 사체로 묘사하는 것과 같은—은 그 적(적그리스도)을 사람들이 쉽게 알아볼 수 있도록 만들므로, 기독교인들로 하여금 너무 쉽게 자신들의 행동에 대해 조사하는 것에서 벗어나게 해준다.

적그리스도를 찾는 것은 아몬드 씨를 많은 애매모호한 길로 인도한다. 적그리스도를 발명해서라도 해결해야 할 문제점은 그리스도가 이 세상으로 다시 돌아와 자신의 왕국을 세우겠다고 약속했지만, 아직 그렇게 하지 않았다는 것이다. 그럼에도 불구하고 기독교인들은 선과 악의 마지막 대결이 다가오고 있다고 믿을 필요가 있었다. 사탄 자신은 이미 지옥으로 보내졌지만, 철저하게 악마처럼 묘사된 그의 새끼들은 이 세상에서 일하고 있다. 신자들은 주변의 어두운 속임수에 대해 경각심을 가져야 했다.

145

하위내용영역	배점	예상정답률
일반영어 B형 서술형	4점	45%

모범답안 The word is "speed of sound". The lightness of hydrogen makes it ideal.

채점기준

+ 2점: 빈칸에 들어갈 단어가 "speed of sound"임을 정확히 기입하였다. 이외에는 답이 될 수 없다.
+ 2점: "수소의 어떤 측면이 트라첸코 박사의 실험을 위한 가장 이상적인 상황이 되는지"에 대한 질문에 "the lightness of hydrogen"이라 서술하였거나 유사하였다.

한글번역

우주 속도 제한에 관해서는 빛이 모든 관심을 받는다. 진공에서의 빛의 속도—초속 3억 미터보다 약간 낮은—는 우주에 존재하는 어떤 물체가 얼마나 빨리 움직일 수 있는지에 대한 절대적인 상한(선)이다. 물리학자들에 의해 "c"라고 불리는 이 값은 기본 상수로 알려진 것으로 현실의 구조에 내재적으로 자리 잡고 있다.

대조적으로, 소리의 속도는 그 자체의 분명한 상한선을 가지고 있지 않다. 다음과 같은 가정이 항상 있어 왔다. 즉, 올바른 재료를 찾으면 (빛의 속도를 깨지 않는 한) 당신은 소리의 이동을 임의적으로 빠르게 할 수 있다라고.

그러나 런던에 있는 퀸 메리 대학의 코스탸 트라첸코는, 적어도 문제의 소리가 고체나 액체를 통해 이동할 때 이런 주장에 대해 이의를 제기한다. 그는 이러한 상황(고체나 액체를 통해 이동할 때)에서는 소리도 또한 최대로 낼 수 있는 속도에 있어서 한계가 있다고 주장한다. 아주 흥미롭게도, 그는 이것도 또한 오직 보편 상수로만 구성됨으로써 현실의 구조에 내재적으로 자리 잡고 있다고 제안한다. 그는 한 논문에서 그 이유를 설명한다.

소리는 사물을 진동시킴으로써 이동한다. 고체와 액체—물리학자들에게 물질의 응축상으로 알려진—에서 분자는 서로서로가 단단히 결합된다. 하나가 움직이면 그것의 옆에 있는 것들도 앞이 한 것을 그대로 따라 함으로써 소리의 파장이 전달된다. 밀도와 원자간 결합 강도와 같은 성질의 차이를 감안해, 트렌체코 박사와 그의 동료들은 다음과 같은 추정을 했다. 즉, 응축된 물질에서 소리의 속도는 단순한 추세에 따른다고. 진동을 하는 입자가 가벼울수록, 그 입자는 소리를 더 빨리 전달한다. 그렇기에 그 학자들은 그와 같은 물질에서 소리의 가장 빠른 속도는 가장 가벼운 원자로 만들어진 고체를 통해서일 것이라고 예측한다.

안타깝게도 일반적으로 기체로 존재하는 수소는 고체 형태로 짜내기 어렵기로 악명이 높다. 따라서 고체 상태 내에서 소리의 속도를 측정하는 것은 매우 까다롭다. 하지만 트라첸코 박사의 분석은, 만약 이것이 이루어진다면, 그 결과는 초속 약 3만 6천 미터일 것이라고 예측한다. 그가 제시한 이론의 검증 가능한 예측은 현재 다이아몬드와 같은 결정화된 탄소가 보유하고 있는 응축 물질 음파를 측정한 기록의 두 배이다.

146

하위내용영역	배점	예상정답률
일반영어 A형 서술형	4점	50%

모범답안 The word is "artistic". Second, the condition is that quilts should not be intimately related to the daily lives of people.

채점기준

+ 2점: 빈칸에 들어갈 단어가 "artistic"임을 정확히 기입하였다. 이외에는 답이 될 수 없다.
+ 2점: 퀼트에 대한 역사적 기록이 남으려 할 때 필요한 조건이 "the condition is that quilts should not be intimately related to the daily lives of people"이라 서술하였거나 유사하였다.

☞ 다음과 같이 서술하였어도 2점을 준다.
- It can be inferred that less usage is required for the quilts to be preserved for the record.

147

하위내용영역	배점	예상정답률
일반영어 A형 서술형	4점	45%

모범답안) The word is "wrong". Second, though people at the beginning resist any kind of currency change, if the change occurs, they will gladly accept such new currency(standard) and consider it as the sole valuable currency.

채점기준

+ 2점 : 빈칸에 들어갈 단어가 "wrong"임을 정확히 기입하였다. 이외에는 답이 될 수 없다.
+ 2점 : 밑줄 친 부분에서 저자가 주요하게 말하려 하는 바를 "though people at the beginning resist any kind of currency change, if the change occurs, they will gladly accept such new currency(standard) and consider it as the sole valuable currency"라 서술하였거나 유사하였다.

☞ 다음과 같이 서술하였어도 2점을 준다.
- People became adjusted to the new status quo and resistant to changes suggested against it.

한글번역

퀼트의 역사는 유럽 정착민들이 신대륙에 도착하기 훨씬 전에 시작됐다. 세계의 거의 모든 지역의 사람들은 옷, 침구, 그리고 심지어 갑옷에 패딩 천을 사용했다. 북아메리카에 영국과 네덜란드 정착민들의 도착으로, 퀼팅은 더욱 생기를 띄게 되고 번창했다.

퀼트는 천으로 만든 샌드위치로, 보통 장식된 부분인 윗부분과 뒷부분, 그리고 중간의 충전재로 구성돼 있다. 패치워크의 일반적인 용어에는 세 가지 다른 유형의 퀼트가 있다 : 평범한 또는 원단 퀼트, 아플리케(천 조각을 덧대거나 꿰맨 장식) 퀼트, 조각 또는 패치워크(여러 조각들로 이뤄진) 퀼트.

우리가 미국에서 알고 있는 퀼트는 원래 침대를 따뜻하게 덮을 필요성에서 탄생한 엄격한 실용주의적인 물품이었다. 퀼트는 또한 추위를 막아줄 만큼 잘 밀봉되지 않은 문과 창문을 걸기 위한 걸이로 사용됐다. 영국과 네덜란드 정착민들에 의해 만들어진 최초의 미국 퀼트는 초기 식민지 개척자들의 일상생활과 매우 밀접하게 연결돼 있어서 그들에 대한 어떠한 기록도 존재하지 않는다.

미국 식민지의 초창기 동안, 대부분의 식민지 여성들은 그들의 가족을 위해 옷을 돌리고, 짜고, 바느질하느라 바빴기 때문에 예술적인 퀼트를 할 시간이 거의 없었다. 상업적인 담요나 직조된 침대보는 더 많이 사용될 가능성이 있었지만, 돈이 부족하거나 수입 직물이 제한된 어려운 시기에는 많은 식민지 여성들은 추운 계절에 가족을 따뜻하게 유지하기 위해 수중에 있는 재료를 사용하는 데 창의적이 돼야만 했다.

그 초기 정착민들은 물건들이 닳아 없어졌을 때 그냥 그 물건들을 버릴 여유가 없었다; 필요는 그들이 자원을 조심스럽게 사용할 것을 요구했다. 따라서 이불이 닳으면 덧대거나, 다른 이불과 붙이거나, 다른 이불 사이에 들어갈 충전재로 사용했다. 이것들은 정성스럽게 만들어진 집안의 가보가 아니었다. 오히려 오직 사람들을 따뜻하게 만들기 위해 사용된 기능적인 물건들이었을 따름이다. 미국에서 직물이 제조되고 더 저렴해져서, 여성들이 자신의 실과 직물을 만드는 노동으로부터 해방됐던 훗날이 돼서야, 더 예술적인 형태의 퀼팅이 더 널리 퍼지게 됐다.

한글번역

프랭클린 루스벨트 대통령이 그의 경제 고문들에게 금본위제에서 미국을 떼어내려고 한다고 말했을 때, 그들은 기겁했다. 그중 한 명은 대통령이 나라를 "통제되지 않는 인플레이션과 완전한 혼란"으로 이끌고 있다고 말했다. 또 다른 고문은 그것(금본위제에서 미국을 떼어내는 것)이 "서구 문명의 끝"이라고 말했다. 루스벨트의 참모들이 과격한 반동주의자들은 아니었다. 그들의 견해는 일반적 통념이었다.

거의 모든 사람들이 금본위제가 화폐를 운용하는 자연스러운 방법이라는 사실에 동의했다. 금본위제의 규칙에 따르면, 누구든지 고정된 양의 금과 지폐를 교환할 수 있었다. 미국에서는 20달러 67센트로 언제나 1온스의 금을 얻을 수 있었다. 그 변하지 않는 가치가 금본위제의 핵심이었다. 금에서 떠나가면, 돈은 가치 없는 종이일 뿐이란 것은 자명했다.

이런 세계관은 완전히 터무니없는 것으로 드러났다. 금본위제를 고수했던 것이 애초에 대공황이 일어나게 하는 데 있어서 일정 부분 역할을 했다. 1933년에 금본위제에서 벗어나는 것은 경제 회복을 위한 필수적인 단계였다. 그렇다면 왜 루스벨트의 고문들과 그 시대의 대부분의 명망 있는 경제학자들은 금에 대한 헌신에 눈이 멀었을까?
　　우리는 거의 항상 돈에 대해 가지고 있는 이러한 생각의 오류가 있다. 그것은 그 어떠한 주어진 순간에 돈이 작동하는 방식을 자연 질서의 일부분처럼 느끼는 것인데, 마치 물이나 중력이 그런 것처럼 말이다. (그렇기에) 돈이 돌아가는 방식에 대한 그 어떤 대안도 모두 터무니없는 게임처럼 보인다. 어떤 것에 의해서 뒷받침되지 않는 종이 돈? 그것은 물이 오르막으로 흐르기를 기대하는 것과 같다!
　　그러다가 정치적, 기술적, 재정적 충격이 생기게 되니, 갑자기 새로운 것이 존재하게 된다. 즉, 금속이 뒷받침해주는 종이 돈, 또는 아무것도 뒷받침되지 않거나, 단지 컴퓨터 화면에 표시된 숫자에 의해서 뒷받침되는 종이 돈. 곧, 우리는 새로운 돈에 익숙해지게 된다. 그 새로운 돈은 자연스러운 상황처럼 보이게 되고, 그 밖에 모든 다른 것들은 어리석어 보이게 된다.
　　우리가 지금 그런 변화들 가운데 하나의 지점에 있을지도 모른다. 상황이 어떻게 전개될지 확실히 말하는 것은 불가능하지만, 역사는 무엇이 우리를 돈의 미래에 대해 희망을 갖게 해야 하는지, 무엇이 우리를 두렵게 하는지에 대한 깊은 통찰을 제공한다.

148

하위내용영역	배점	예상정답률
일반영어 A형 서술형	4점	55%

모범답안 The word is "plastic". Second, these cups made of bagasse can be gladly dumped because people know that they will biodegrade, unlike their plastic counterparts.

채점 기준

+2점: 빈칸에 들어갈 단어가 "plastic"임을 정확히 기입하였다. 이외에는 답이 될 수 없다.

+2점: 밑줄 친 부분의 의미를 "these cups made of bagasse can be gladly dumped because people know that they will biodegrade, (unlike their plastic counterparts)"라 서술하였거나 유사하였다.

☞ 다음과 같이 서술하였어도 2점을 준다.

- These cups can be dumped knowing that they will biodegrade, (unlike their plastic counterparts).

한글번역

　　사탕수수는 약 10%의 설탕을 함유하고 있다. 그러나 그것은 사탕수수가 약 90%의 비당분을 함유하고 있다는 것을 의미하는데, 사탕수수가 분쇄되고 설탕이 함유된 주스가 짜낸 후에 남는 바게스라고 알려진 물질이다. 2017년 세계 사탕수수 설탕 생산량은 1억 8천 5백만 톤이었다. 그것은 결과적으로 많은 바게스를 만들어낸다.
　　현재, 이것의 대부분은 태워진다. 종종, 그것은 제분소에 동력을 공급하는 지역 발전기에 연료를 공급하기 때문에 낭비되지 않는다. 그러나 기계공학자인 주 훌리는 그것이 더 잘 사용될 수 있다고 생각한다. 그녀와 그녀의 동료들이 이번 주 학술지 *Matter*에서 묘사했듯이, 약간만 바꾸면 바게스는 커피 컵과 같은 일회용 식품 용기에 사용되는 플라스틱에 대한 아주 훌륭하고 생분해성 있는(박테리아에 의해 무해 물질로 분해돼 환경에 해가 되지 않는) 대체물이 될 수 있다.
　　이런 생각을 한 사람은 주 박사가 처음이 아니다. 하지만 이전의 시도들은 액체와의 접촉에서 살아남지 못하는 경향이 있었다. 그녀는 사탕수수 과육에 다른 생분해성 물질을 첨가함으로써 그것을 극복할 수 있다고 생각했다. 그녀는 과거의 노력이 산산조각이 나는 주된 이유는 바게스가 완제품에 복원력을 부여할 수 있을 만큼 충분히 겹쳐지 않는 짧은 섬유로 구성돼 있기 때문이라는 것을 이전 연구를 통해 알고 있었다. 따라서 그녀는 적절한 장섬유 물질을 삽입하려고 노력했다.
　　대나무가 딱 필요한 것을 공급시켜주는 것 같았다. 대나무는 빨리 자라고, 쉽게 분해되며, 적절하게 긴 섬유를 가지고 있다. 그리고 그것은 효과가 있었다. 연구원들이 소량의 대나무 펄프를 바게스에 섞었을 때, 그 결과가 짧은 섬유와 긴 섬유의 강한 상호 직조라는 것을 그 연구원들은 발견했다. 덤으로, 그들은 또한 그 과정의 일부로 사용된 뜨거운 압착이 섬유에 있는 리그닌을 동원했고, 이 뻣뻣하고 발수성이 있는 물질(리그닌)이 이제 섬유들을 서로 묶는 접착제의 역할을 한다는 것을 발견했다.
　　이 새로운 재료의 기량을 시험하기 위해, 주 박사와 그녀의 동료들은 먼저 뜨거운 기름을 그 재료 위에 부었고, 그 기름이 이전의 바게스 제품들이 그랬듯 재료 속으로 침투하는 것이 아니라 그들의 발명품(새로운 재료)에 의해 거부되는 것을 발견했다.

게다가, 이 새로운 물질은 컵을 만드는 데 사용되는 플라스틱보다 두 배나 더 강하고, 확실히 생분해성이 있다. 주 박사가 그 재료로 만든 컵을 땅에 묻었을 때, 반절이 두 달 안에 썩어 없어졌고, 그녀 생각엔, 6개월이면 완전히 없어질 것이라 봤다.

전반적으로, 주 박사는 바게스가 커피 컵을 만들기 위한 명백한 선택이라고 주장한다. 일단 사용되면, 이것들은 깨끗한 양심을 가지고 쓰레기 매립지에 버려질 수 있다.

149

하위내용영역	배점	예상정답률
일반영어 B형 서술형	4점	50%

모범 답안) The word is "revolutionaries". It can be inferred that borders were easy to pass through in the 1910s.

채점 기준

+ **2점**: 빈칸에 들어갈 단어가 "revolutionaries"임을 정확히 기입하였다.
  ☞ "radicals"라 했으면 1점을 준다.

+ **2점**: 1910년대 국경이 "borders were easy to pass through in the 1910s"라 서술하였거나 유사하였다.
  ☞ 다음과 같이 서술하였어도 2점을 준다.
  − Borders were porous in the 1910s.

한글번역

1917년 러시아의 니콜라이 2세가 퇴위하자, "외부의 세계의 폭풍은 수라바야와 세마랑의 가정에 직접 불어 닥쳤다." 권력을 장악한 블라디미르 레닌은 더 광범위한 혁명을 촉진하기 위해 유럽의 노동계급에 관심을 기울였다. 그 희망이 흐지부지됐을 때,—레닌이 식민주의자들과 마찬가지로 지금까지 낙후되었다고 여겼던—아시아 농민들의 혁명적 잠재력이 재평가됐다. 아시아의 급진주의자들이 모스크바로 소환됐다. 호치민(Nguyen Ai Quoc), 마나벤드라 나트 로이(인도의 독립 운동가이자 혁명가), 탄 말라카(인도네시아의 독립 운동가이자 혁명가)는 16세기 예수회가 중국, 인도, 일본을 개종하기 시작한 이래 하퍼 씨가 아시아에서 가장 위대한 선교 활동이라고 부르는 것의 중심에 있었다.

아시아, 그리고 심지어 제국주의의 본국에서도, 행동은 때때로 폭력적인 형태를 띠었다. 영국령 인도 총독과 프랑스령 인도차이나 총독에 대한 암살 시도가 있었다. 1925년 초, 상하이와 도쿄에서 파리나 뉴욕보다 먼저 유행한 "모던 걸"의 단발머리를 한 젊은 중국 여성이 쿠알라룸푸르 복지사무소에 들어가 두 명의 영국 공무원을 폭파시키려 했다.

그러한 폭력은 "황화"(황색 인종이 서양 문명을 압도한다는 백색 인종의 공포심; Wilhelm II가 주장한 말)에 대한 야단스런 두려움을 불러일으켰다. 실제로는, 식민지 주체가 생산자이자 소비자일 것을 요구하는 경제를 겨냥한 파업과 불매운동이 더 큰 효과가 있었다. 그러나 1920년대 후반까지 (식민지) 당국이 우위를 점했다. 특히, 국경은 더 이상 구멍이 뚫리지 않았고, 세레테(치안 유지)와 그와 상응 관계에 있는 조직들은 신분증을 만들고, 지문 채취, 엄격한 기록 보관을 했다. 그들은 혁명가들이 거주하는 부둣가와 사창가에서 경찰 끄나풀이나 파수꾼을 고용했다. 국제 협력은 1923년 인터폴이 설립됐을 때 정규화됐다.

식민지 그물망에 걸린 급진분자들은 체포돼 강제 수용소로 보내졌고, 인도네시아인의 경우 말라리아가 만연한 뉴기니의 강 상류인 보벤 디고엘로 보내졌다. 제2차 세계대전에서 승리한 강대국들조차 겪은 대대적인 파괴 이후, 아시아의 혁명가들은 새로운 기회를 봤다. 어떤 이들은 그 순간을 포착하고 권좌에 올랐다. 오늘날 호찌민에는 그의 이름을 딴 아시아에서 가장 붐비는 대도시 중 하나가 있다. 이와는 대조적으로 탄 말라카는 그가 확산을 도운 혁명에 의해 삼켜졌다. 즉, 그는 네덜란드와 영국이 싸우는 동안 자기 쪽 사람에게 죽임을 당했다.

하지만 이 두 사람의 삶은 인간 미래의 최전선에 놓여있던 아시아가—제국주의의 강력한 후원을 요구하는 후진성의 수렁이 결코 아니라—지니고 있던 초기의 전조의 증거다. 그래서 비록 많은 혁명가들이 이제 잊혀졌지만,—혹은 일부 아시아 국가들에게는 기억하기 너무 불편하지만—,그들의 지하운동의 이야기는 여전히 시간을 거슬러 울려 퍼지고 있다.

150

하위내용영역	배점	예상정답률
일반영어 A형 서술형	4점	55%

모범 답안 The word is "hotels". Second, they appeared in the Middle Ages.

채점 기준

+ 2점: 빈칸에 들어갈 단어를 "hotels"라 정확하게 기입하였다. 이외에는 답이 될 수 없다.
+ 2점: 유럽에서 여관이 등장한 시기를 "in the Middle Ages"라 정확하게 서술하였다.

한글번역

호텔의 역사는 문명의 역사와 밀접하게 연관 있다. 오히려, 호텔의 역사는 문명의 역사의 한 부분이다. 손님에게 환대를 제공하는 시설들은 초기 성서의 시대 이래로 증거로 남아 있다. 그리스인들은 휴식과 회복을 위해 설계된 마을에 온탕을 개발했다. 훗날, 로마인들은 공무로 출장중인 사람들이 머물 숙소를 제공하기 위해 대저택을 지었다. 로마인들은 영국, 스위스, 중동에서 최초로 온탕을 개발했다.

한참 후 카라반세라이(과거 아시아·북부 아프리카 사막에 있던 여행자 쉼터)가 나타나 중동 루트를 따라 여행하는 대상들에게 휴식처를 제공했다. 중세 시대에는 수도원과 수녀원이 정기적으로 여행하는 사람들에게 피난처를 제공한 최초의 시설이었다. 수도회는 이동 중인 사람들의 요구를 만족시키기 위해 여관, 호스피스, 병원을 지었다. 여관은 크게 증가했지만, 아직 식사를 제공하지는 않았다. 공무를 위한 수송과 휴게소로서 정기 기착지가 설치됐다. 정기 기착지들은 쉴 곳을 제공했고 말이 더 쉽게 바뀔 수 있도록 했다. 성지로 향하는 순례자들과 십자군들을 위해 수많은 쉼터가 생겨났다. 그 후 여행은 점점 더 위험해졌다. 동시에 유럽 대부분에서 점차적으로 여관들이 생겨났다. 그들 중 일부는 여전히 유명세를 떨치고 있는데, 중세 시대에 설립된 스위스 바젤의 오베르주 데 트로이 로이스가 그런 예이다.

15세기 초에 프랑스에서는, 법률로 호텔들이 등록부를 작성하도록 요구했다. 또한 그 당시에 영국법은 여관에 대한 규칙을 도입했다. 동시에 칼스바드(체코슬로바키아 서부의 온천 휴양 도시)와 마리엔바드(체코슬로바키아 서부 온천·휴양 도시)에서 약 1500개의 온천이 개발됐다. 이 시기 동안 영국에는 600개 이상의 여관이 등록됐다. 그 여관들의 건축은 종종 아치형 현관을 통해 접근할 수 있는 포장된 내부 마당으로 구성됐다. 침실은 안뜰의 양쪽에, 부엌과 공용실은 앞쪽에, 마구간과 창고는 뒤쪽에 있었다. 여행자들을 위한 최초의 가이드북은 이 시기에 프랑스에서 출판됐다.

초기 호텔 산업은 유럽에서 발전하기 시작했다. 세련된 요리로 유명한 업소 밖에는 독특한 간판이 걸려 있었다. 1600년대 말에, 정규 시간표에 따른 역마차가 처음으로 영국에서 운행되기 시작했다. 반세기 후, 영국 신사 클럽과 프리메이슨 집회소와 비슷한 클럽들이 미국에 등장하기 시작했다.

151

하위내용영역	배점	예상정답률
일반영어 A형 서술형	4점	55%

모범 답안 The word is "economic". Second, it is the habits of agricultural life.

채점 기준

+ 2점: 빈칸에 들어갈 단어를 "economic"이라 정확하게 기입하였다. 이외에는 답이 될 수 없다.
+ 2점: 초기 공장 노동자들이 (공장에서) 낮잠을 자는 습관이 "the habits of agricultural life"에서 기인한다고 정확하게 서술하였다.

한글번역

철도 시대가 시작되자 정치철학자 칼 마르크스는 철도 기술을 세계관으로 비유하는 은유를 사용했다. 오늘날 누군가가 정신을 컴퓨터에 비유하는 것을 듣는 것이 놀랍지 않듯, 19세기 중반의 유럽인이 철도 은유를 사용하는 것도 놀랍지 않았다. 아주 많은 영향력을 끼치게 된 용어로, 마르크스는 인간 사회와 의식을 상부구조라 불렀는데, 이 상부구조는 경제적 하부구조—공장이나 광산, 그리고 다른 생산양식들—에 의존한다고 주장했다. 이것들은 철도에서 직접 가져온 용어들이었다. 하부구조(기반시설)는 선로와 관련 시스템을 의미했고 상부구조는 열차였다. 한마디로 말해서, 마르크스에게 인간의 정신은 일련의 경제적 궤도 위를 달리는 기차였다.

철도는 사람들의 삶의 방식을 바꿔 놓았고, 자신(철도)만의 시간과 공간을 만들었다. 오늘날에도 여전히 사용되고 있는 현대의 표준시간대(세계적으로 24개로 나눠져 있음)는 정확한 철도 시간표를 만들기 위해 처음 고안됐다. 그때까지는, 현지 시간은 장소마다 달랐다. 영국 철도는 런던 시간을 표준으로 삼았다. 1855년이 돼서야, 대부분의 국가 시계에서 그리니치 표준시를 채택했지만, 법조계에서는 1880년까지 현지 시간을 계속 사용했다. 비슷한 패턴이 미국에서도 나타났다. 1883년, 미국 철도 회사들은 표준화된 시간대를 만들었지만, 1918년이 돼서야 의회에 의해 합법화됐다. 시간이 과거엔 매우 국지적이었던 반면, 이제 넓은 지역에서 획일적으로 됐다가, 그런 다음엔 임의의 지점에서 갑자기 바뀌었다. 이것(시간이 매우 국지적이었던 것)을 묘사하는 또 다른 방법은 아마도 다음과 같은 것일 것이다. 즉, 기차가 등장하기 전의 시간은 아날로그라는 것인데, 이 말은 시간이 각각의 지역에서 태양과의 관계에 따라 고르게 보정됐다는 것을 의미한다. 그 후, 그것은 디지털이 됐고, 이는 (컴퓨터의 1 또는 0과 같은) 자의적인 시간 단위로 바뀌었다는 것을 의미한다.

공장들은 이러한 변화를 새로운 산업 노동자들에게는 현실이 되도록 만들었다. 산업화 초기엔, 노동자들은 마음이 내키면 낮에 떠돌거나, 피곤하면 낮잠을 자곤 했다. 그들은 농경 생활의 습관을 산업적 상황에 그대로 가져왔다. 그러나 곧 근무시간대가 있다는 것과 가능한 한 많은 시간을 노동에 바쳐야 한다는 것이 "자연스러운" 느낌으로 다가오게 됐다. 고용주들과 직원들은 노동 시간을 연장하거나 단축하기 위해 그때나 지금이나 똑같이 싸웠다. 철도망의 형성은 사람들이 도심 밖에서 살 수 있게 했고, 도심에 있는 일터로 가는 것을 가능하도록 했다. 1910년까지, 전체 프랑스인의 3분의 1은 기차 정기권을 소지하고 매일매일 도시 중심가를 드나들었다. 한 세기 후, 프랑스는 여전히 철도 수송에 있어서 선두적인 유럽 국가인데, 연간 540억 마일 이상의 승객 수송을 한다.

152

하위내용영역	배점	예상정답률
일반영어 A형 서술형	4점	55%

모범답안 They are pain and pleasure. Second, the word is "pain".

채점기준

+2점: 두 가지 힘이 가리키는 것을 "pain and pleasure" 또는 "pleasure and pain"이라 정확하게 서술하였다. 이외에는 답이 될 수 없다.
+2점: 빈칸에 들어갈 단어를 "pain"이라 정확하게 기입하였다. 이외에는 답이 될 수 없다.

한글번역

종종 우리를 움직이는 두 가지 힘에 대한 토론에서 흥미로운 질문이 나온다. 도대체 왜 사람들은 고통을 경험하면서도 변하지 못하는가? 아마도 아직 충분한 고통을 겪지 않아서일 것이다. 즉, 내가 정서적 한계치라고 부르는 것에 도달하지 못했기 때문일 것이다. 만약 당신이 파괴적인 관계에 있었던 적이 있고 마침내 당신의 개인적인 힘을 사용하고, 행동을 취하고, 삶을 바꾸기로 결심했다면, 그것은 아마도 당신이 더 이상 기꺼이 받아들이고 싶지 않은 수준의 고통에 부딪혔기 때문일 것이다. 우리 모두는 인생에서 그런 시기를 겪게 되는데, 우리가 다음과 같이 말할 때("더 이상 못 참겠어. 겪을 만큼 겪었어—다시는 절대로 겪지 않을 거야—이것은 반드시 바뀌어야 해 당장") 바로 그런 시기이다. 고통이 우리의 친구가 되는 마법의 순간이다.

이 과정이 관계에만 국한되지 않는다는 것은 확실하다. 아마도 여러분은 신체 상태에 대한 한계치를 경험해 본 적이 있을 것이다: 비행기 좌석에 비집고 들어갈 수 없어서, 또는 옷에 몸이 맞지 않아서, 그리고 계단을 오를 때 숨이 턱턱 막혀서, 마침내 짜증을 잔뜩 내게 된 경험을. 드디어 당신은 "더 이상 못 참겠어!"라고 말한 뒤 결심을 한다. 무엇이 그 결심을 하도록 만들었을까? 그것은 삶에서 고통을 제거하고 다시 한 번 즐거움을 확립하려는 욕망이었다: 자부심의 즐거움, 안락의 즐거움, 자존감의 즐거움, 당신이 설계한 대로 삶을 사는 즐거움.

물론, 고통과 즐거움에는 많은 단계가 있다. 예를 들어, 굴욕감을 느끼는 것은 정서적 고통의 다소 강한 형태이다. 불편함을 느끼는 것도 고통이다. 지루함도 마찬가지다. 이것들 가운데 어떤 것은 강도가 덜하다는 것은 분명하지만, 여전히 그런 것들도 의사 결정의 방정식에서 하나의 요인으로 작동한다. 마찬가지로, 즐거움도 이 과정에 영향을 미친다. 인생에서 추진력의 대부분은 우리의 (지금의) 행동이 더 강렬한 미래로 이끌 것이고, 오늘의 노력에 대한 대가가 확실할 것이고, 기쁨의 보상이 가까이에 있을 것이라는 기대에서 비롯된다. 하지만 즐거움도 또한 다양한 수준이 있다. 예를 들어, 황홀경의 쾌락은—비록 대부분의 사람들은 이것이 강렬하다고 동의할 것이지만—때로는 편안함의 쾌락보다 강도가 작을 수도 있다. 이것은 모두 개인의 관점에 달려 있다.

당신이 점심시간에 베토벤 교향곡이 연주되고 있는 공원을 지나가고 있다고 가정해보자. 멈춰서 음악을 들을 것인가? 그것은 당신이 클래식 음악에 연상시키는 의미에 달려있다. 어떤 사람들은 영웅 교향곡의 강력한 곡조를 듣기 위해 어떤 것이든 놓쳐버릴 것이다. 그들에게 베토벤은 순수한 즐거움과 같은 것이다. 하지만, 다른 사람들에게, 그 어떠한 것이든 클래식 음악을 듣는 것은 물감이 마르는 것을 보는 것만큼 흥미진진한 것이다. 음악을 견뎌야 한다는 것은 꽤 많은 고통을 준다.

153

하위내용영역	배점	예상정답률
일반영어 B형 서술형	4점	45%

모범답안 The word is "market system". Second, it means the allotment of TARP.

채점기준

+ 2점: 빈칸에 들어갈 단어를 "market system"이라 정확하게 기입하였다. 이외에는 답이 될 수 없다.
+ 2점: 밑줄 친 "재분배"가 의미하는 바를 "the allotment of TARP" 또는 "the allotment of largest welfare program for companies and their investors"라 서술하였거나 유사하였다.

한글번역

　주택 버블과 2008년 금융 위기는 시장의 도덕적 부당성에 큰 역할을 했다. 천문학적으로 높은 부동산 가격의 압력으로 지어진 플로리다와 애리조나에서 새로운 개발(주택들)이 텅 비어있을 때, 사람들은 시장 가격의 효율성에 의문을 갖기 시작한다. 편안한 은퇴와 가난한 은퇴의 차이가 열심히 노력한 것이나 검소한 생활방식이 아니라 집을 사고파는 타이밍이라는 운에 의해 결정될 때, 사람들은 시장 제도의 공정성에 의문을 갖기 시작한다. 부동산 버블이 10년도 되지 않아 터진 두 번째 대형 버블이라는 사실은 자원을 어디에 투자할지를 보여주는 좋은 지표로서 시장에 대한 신뢰를 더욱 약화시켰다.

　하지만 규칙이 모든 사람에게 동등하게 적용되지 않는다는 인식만큼 사람들을 화나게 하는 것은 없다. 내 아이들이 어렸을 때, 아이들은 때로는 모노폴리 게임을 하려고 했다. 이러한 시도는 필연적으로 논쟁으로 전락했다. 아들보다 두 살 어린 딸은 아들이 속임수를 쓰고 있다고 주장하곤 했다. 아들은 공식 지침을 손에 쥔 채 자신의 결백을 주장하곤 했다. 그리고 아들은 옳았다: 그는 어떤 규칙도 날조해 지어내지 않았다. 그럼에도 불구하고, 딸도 또한 옳았다: 아들은 딸의 무지를 믿고 자신에게 유리한 규칙만 꺼내면서 규칙을 선택적으로 사용하고 있었다. 비록 어렸지만, 딸아이는 무언가가 공정하지 않다는 것을 이해했고, 그래서 자신이 할 수 있는 유일한 대응인 포기를 사용했다.

　내 딸의 좌절감은 2008년 (월가)금융 시스템에 대한 구제 금융을 지원한 후에 많은 사람들이 느꼈던 것과 비슷했다. 시장제도는 확실히 위험에 처해 있었고, 일부 정부의 개입은 확실히 필요했다. 그러나 벤 버냉키 연방준비제도 의장과 헨리 폴슨 재무장관이 반복적으로 말했던 것처럼, (지금 할 수 있는) 선택은 부실자산구제프로그램(TARP)과 금융위기 둘 사이에 있다고 말하는 것은 거짓이었다. 실현 가능한 그리고 사실, 더 뛰어난 대안이 있었기 때문이다. 부실자산구제프로그램이 지금까지 인류 역사에서 만들어진 것 가운데, 기업들과 그 기업들에 투자한 투자자들을 위한 가장 큰 복지 프로그램이라는 것을, 대부분의 미국인들은 알고 있었다. 그것들 가운데 일부 빵 부스러기가 자동차 노동조합에 갔다고 해서 상황이 개선되지는 않았다. 사실, 그것은 상황을 더욱 악화시켰는데, 그 재분배가 우연히 이뤄진 것이 아니라, 강력한 로비에 의한 무방비상태에 있는 납세자에 대한 계획적인 약탈이었다는 것을 보여줬기 때문이다. 부실자산구제프로그램은 메인 스트리트(대다수 미국인들이 경제생활을 하는 공간)에 대한 월가(금융자본)의 승리일 뿐 아니라, 나머지 미국 전 지역(미국국민)에 대한 워싱턴 로비스트의 승리였다.

154

하위내용영역	배점	예상정답률
일반영어 A형 서술형	4점	45%

모범 답안) The word is "represent". Second, it is representational drift.

채점 기준

+ 2점: 빈칸에 들어갈 단어가 "represent"임을 정확히 기입하였다. 이외에는 답이 될 수 없다.
+ 2점: 다른 과학자들이 인정한 현상을 "representational drift"라 정확히 서술하였다.

한글번역

칼 스쿠노버와 앤드류 핑크는 혼란스럽다. 신경과학자로서, 그들은 뇌가 유연해야 하지만 너무 유연해서는 안 된다는 것을 알고 있다. 뇌는 새로운 경험에 직면해 스스로를 갈아 끼워야 하지만, 또한 외부 세계의 특징들을 일관되게 드러내야 한다. 어떻게? 신경과학 교과서에서 발견되는 비교적 간단한 설명은 다음과 같다. 어떤 한 사람이 장미 향기를 맡거나 일몰을 보거나 종소리를 들을 때, 특정 뉴런 그룹이 안정적으로 발화한다는 것이다. 이러한 표상들—즉 신경 발화 패턴—은 한 순간에서 다음 순간으로 넘어가도 동일하게 유지될 거라 짐작된다. 하지만 스쿠노버와 핑크가 발견했듯이, 그 표상들은 때때로 그렇지 않은 경우가 있다. 그것들은 변화하는데, 심지어 혼란스럽고 예상치 못한 정도로 변하기도 한다.

스쿠노버와 핑크는 쥐들이 몇 날 몇 주 동안 똑같은 냄새들을 맡도록 한 다음, 그 설치류(쥐)의 조롱박피질(냄새를 식별하는 데 관여하는 뇌 영역)의 신경활동을 기록했다. 주어진 순간에, 각각의 냄새는 이 영역(조롱박피질)에 있는 한 그룹의 독특한 뉴런들이 발화하도록 만들었다. 하지만 시간이 지나면서, 이 그룹들의 구성이 서서히 바뀌었다. 어떤 뉴런들은 냄새에 반응하는 것을 멈췄고, 다른 뉴런들은 반응하기 시작했다. 한 달 후, 각 그룹은 거의 완전히 달라졌다. 다르게 표현해보면 이렇다. 5월에 사과 냄새를 나타냈던 뉴런들과 6월에 같은 냄새를 나타내는 뉴런들은 서로가 매우 달랐는데, 이것은 마치 어떤 같은 특정 시기에, 사과의 냄새와 풀의 냄새가 서로서로 다른 것만큼이나 달랐다.

물론, 이것은 쥐를 대상으로 한 어떤 한 특정 뇌 영역에 대한 하나의 연구일 뿐이다. 그러나 다른 과학자들도 표상적 표류라고 불리는 똑같은 현상이 조롱박피질 외에도 다양한 뇌 영역에서 발생한다는 것을 보여주고 있다. 표상적 표류가 존재한다는 것은 명확하다, 하지만 그 밖의 다른 모든 것은 여전히 미스터리다. 스쿠노버와 핑크는 왜 이런 일이 일어나는지, 그것이 의미하는 것이 뭔지, 어떻게 뇌가 대처하는지, 또는 뇌의 어느 정도가 이런 식으로 행동하는지 알지는 못한다고 나에게 말했다. 만일 동물들이 세상에 대한 자기들의 신경 반응이 끊임없이 유동(변화)하는 것이라면, 어떻게 동물들은 세상을 지속적(안정적)으로 이해할 수 있을까? 스쿠노버는 이런 유동성이 흔한 것이라면, "뇌에는 아직 발견되지 않고, 심지어 (이제까지) 상상조차 하지 못한 메커니즘—이런 유동성이 지속되는 것을 가능하게 만드는—이 있음이 틀림없다. 과학자들은 무슨 일이 일어나고 있는지 알고 싶어 하지만, 이와 같은 특별한 경우에, 우리는 정말 혼란스럽다. 이 문제를 해결하는 데 많은 시간이 걸릴 것으로 예상한다."고 말했다.

155

하위내용영역	배점	예상정답률
일반영어 A형 서술형	4점	45%

모범 답안) The word is "technologies". Second, the writer thinks the metaverse is not fully innovative currently and has to offer something new to fulfill its aims.

채점 기준

+ 2점: 빈칸에 들어갈 단어를 "technologies"라 정확히 기입하였다. 이외에는 답이 될 수 없다.
+ 2점: 메타버스에 대한 저자의 입장을 "the writer thinks the metaverse is not fully innovative currently and has to offer something new to fulfill its aims"라 서술하였거나 유사하였다.

한글번역

어느 정도까지는, "메타버스"가 무엇을 의미하는지에 대해 말하는 것이, 1970년대에 "인터넷"이 무엇을 의미했는지에 대해 토론을 하는 것과 비슷한 점이 다소간 있다. 새로운 형식의 의사소통의 구성요소들이 만들어지고 있었지만, 아무도 그 현실이 어떤 모습을 띄게 될지는 실제로는 알 수 없었다. 그래서 그 당시에 "인터넷"이 다가오고 있는 것이 사실이었음에도 불구하고, 그것이 어떤 모습일 것인가에 대한 생각들 모두가 사실인 것은 아니었다.

다른 한편, 메타버스라는 아이디어로 포장된 수많은 마케팅 (과장)광고도 있다. 특히 페이스북과 애플이 추적광고를 제한하려는 움직임이 자신의 회사의 이익을 강탈한 이후 특히나 취약한 위치에 있다. 모든 사람이 쓸 수 있는 디지털 옷장을 가진 미래에 대한 페이스북의 비전을 페이스북이 실제로는 가상 옷을 팔아서 돈을 벌기를 원한다는 사실과 분리하는 것은 불가능하다.

"메타버스"라는 용어가 얼마나 모호하고 복잡한 것인지를 이해하는 것을 돕기 위해, 여기 주어진 연습을 한번 해보자 : 머릿속으로, "사이버스페이스"란 단어가 있는 문장에서 그 단어를 "메타버스"라는 단어로 대체해보라. 십중팔구, 그 문장의 의미는 실질적으로 변하지 않을 것이다. 그 이유는 이 메타버스라는 용어가 실제로 특정 유형의 기술을 지칭하는 것이 아니라, 우리 인간이 기술과 상호작용하는 방식에 있어서의 광범위한 변화를 의미하는 것이기 때문이다. 그리고 이 메타버스란 용어 자체도, 그것이 묘사했던 특정한 기술이 흔해지는 바로 그 순간에, 결국 한물가버릴 가능성이 아주 높다.

넓게 말해서, 메타버스를 구성하는 기술에는 가상현실(우리가 플레이 하지 않을 때조차 계속 존재하는 지속적인 가상세계가 특징인)과 증강현실(디지털세계와 물리적 세계의 특징들을 결합한)이 포함될 수 있다. 그러나 이러한 공간에 VR이나 AR을 통해 배타적으로 액세스할 필요는 없다. PC, 게임기, 심지어 전화를 통해 접근할 수 있는 포트나이트와 같은 가상 세계도 메타버스가 될 수 있다.

메타버스를 정의하는 것의 역설은, 메타버스가 미래가 되기 위해서는 현재를 정의해야 한다는 것이다. 우리는 이미 본질적으로 전적으로 가상세계인 MMO(대규모 멀티플레이어 온라인 게임)를 가지고 있고, 디지털 콘서트, 전 세계 사람들과의 화상통화, 온라인 아바타 및 커머스 플랫폼을 가지고 있다. 그렇기에, 이러한 것들을 세상에 대한 새로운 비전으로 팔기 위해서는, (진정) 새로운 요소가 반드시 있어야만 한다.

156

하위내용영역	배점	예상정답률
일반영어 A형 서술형	4점	40%

모범답안 The word is "weirdness". Second, this means that Old English is almost unrecognizable to modern English speakers, seeming like a completely different language like Turkish.

채점기준

+ 2점 : 빈칸에 들어갈 단어를 "weirdness"라 정확히 기입하였다. 이외에는 답이 될 수 없다.
+ 2점 : 밑줄 친 부분의 의미를 "Old English is almost unrecognizable to modern English speakers, seeming like a completely different language like Turkish"라 서술하였거나 유사하였다.

한글번역

영어는 왜 이렇게 별난가? 우리가 지금 말하고 있는 이것은 무엇이고, 무엇이 이 언어(영어)를 이런 식으로 만들었을까? 영어는 본질적으로 독일어의 한 갈래로 시작됐다. 고대 영어는 현대 영어와는 너무 달라서 아예 같은 언어라고 생각하는 것이 지나친 것처럼 느껴진다. "Hwæt, we gardena in geardagum þeodcyninga þrym gefrunon"—이 표현이 "그럼, 우리 스피어-데인 사람들은 옛날 부족 왕들의 영광에 대해 들어본 적이 있다"는 것을 정말로 의미하나? 아이슬란드 사람들은 여전히 1,000년 전에 그들의 언어의 조상인 고대 노르웨이어로 쓰여진 비슷한 이야기들을 읽을 수 있겠지만, (이 분야에서) 훈련을 받지 않은 사람들에게는 베오울프는 터키어로 쓰여진 것이나 다름없다.

우리를 거기서 여기로 데려온 첫 번째는 앵글족, 색슨족, 주트족이 그들의 언어를 영국으로 가져왔을 때, 그 섬에는 이미 매우 다른 언어를 사용하는 사람들이 살고 있었다는 사실이다. 그들의 언어는 켈트어였는데, 오늘날 웨일즈인, 아일랜드인, 그리고 해협을 가로질러 프랑스 땅에 있는 브르타뉴인들에 의해 표현된다. 켈트인들은 지배됐지만 살아남았고, 게르만족 침입자의 수가 기껏 약 250,000명 밖에 되지 않았기 때문에—(뉴저지 주의) 저지 시티 같은 소도시 정도의 인구—, 매우 신속하게도 고대 영어를 사용하는 대부분의 사람들은 켈트족이었다.

유희대 | 일반영어 ❹-1

결정적으로, 그들의 언어는 영어와 매우 달랐다. 우선 동사가 먼저 왔다. 또한 동사 do가 있는 이상한 구조를 가지고 있었다. 그들은 질문을 만들고, 문장을 부정문으로 만들고, 그리고 심지어 모든 동사 앞에 일종의 양념처럼 do를 사용하기도 했다. 당신은 걷나? 나는 걷지 않는다. 나는 걷는다. 이제 이런 것은 익숙해 보이는데, 켈트족들이 영어를 실생활에서 옮길 때 그렇게 했기 때문이다. 하지만 그 이전에는, 그러한 문장들은 영어 사용자들에게는 이상하게 느껴졌을 것인데, 마치 그런 문장들이 오늘날 우리 자신의 언어(영어)와 살아남은 켈트어를 제외한 거의 모든 언어에서 이상하게 보였을 것처럼 말이다. 이런 이상한 do의 사용법을 곰곰이 생각해보면 이것이 얼마나 괴이한 것인지를 갑자기 깨닫게 된다. 마치 우리 입속에 혀가 항상 있다는 것을 갑자기 알게 됐을 때처럼 말이다.

현재 지구상에는 켈트어와 영어 외에 이런 식으로 do를 사용하는 (서류로) 입증된 언어는 없다. 그러므로 영어의 이상함은 매우 다른 혀(언어)를 가진 사람들의 입속에서 편안하게 (영어가) 변형됨으로써 발생했다. 우리는 여전히 그들처럼 말하고 있는데, (사실 이것은) 우리가 결코 생각하지 못했던 방식이었다.

한글번역

물론 악은 전통적인 이름이지만, 다른 이름들처럼, 악은 스스로를 비극적 전통으로 제공하는 특정 이데올로기에 의해 이용됐다. 특히 최근 몇 년 동안 우리는 소위 초월적 악이라는 실재에 의해 끊임없이 질책을 받아왔으며, 우리 세기의 거대한 사회적 위기는 이 빛이나 어둠 속에서 구체적으로 해석되고 있다. 문명과 진보에 대한 이전 시대의 모든 환상과는 반대로 인간 본성은 이제 극적으로 드러난다고 주장되고 있다. 특히 강제수용소는 인간이, 같은 인간에 의해, 사물로 전락하는 절대적인 조건에 대한 하나의 이미지로 사용된다. 수용소의 기록은 실제로 충분히 어둡고, 다른 많은 사례들이 추가될 수 있다. 하지만 수용소를 절대적인 조건의 이미지로 사용하는 것은, 결국, 신성모독일 따름이다. 왜냐하면, 사람들이 수용소를 건설하는 동안, 다른 사람들은 의식적으로 위험을 무릅쓰고 그 수용소를 파괴하기 위해 죽었기 때문이다. 비록 어떤 사람들은 (다른 사람들을) 투옥했지만, 다른 사람들은 해방시켰다. 인간이 만들어 낸 악—그것이 어떠한 종류이든 간에—가운데 다른 인간들이 투쟁해서 끝장내지 못하는 악은 존재하지 않는다. 이런 행동 가운데 어떤 한 부분만을 취해서 그것을 절대적이라느니 초월적이라느니 부르는 것은, 결국 인간 삶의 다른 부분들에 대한 억압이 될 수 있는데, 이 억압은 너무나 방대해서 악에 대한 무관심은 이데올로기 안에서의 악의 역할로만 설명될 수 있다.

문화적으로 볼 때, 악은 현실적 삶을 부식시키거나 파괴하는 많은 종류의 무질서를 나타내는 이름이다. 악은 비극에서 흔히 볼 수 있는데, 복수, 야망, 자부심, 냉혹함, 정욕, 질투, 반항, 반란과 같은 많은 구체적이고 가변적인 형태로 말이다. 모든 경우에 악은 어떤 한 특정 문화나 전통의 가치체계 속에서만 완전히 이해될 수 있다. 어떤 특정 이데올로기에서는 악을 일반화하는 것이 가능할 수도 있는데, 이것은 악이 절대적이고 심지어 특이한 힘으로 나타날 때까지만 그렇다. 또한, 보통명사로서, 악은 일반적인 성격을 띠는 것으로 보인다. 하지만 그렇다면 우리는 비극이 초월적인 악을 인식하는 것이라고 말할 수는 없다. 일반적으로 비극은 많은 특정한 형태로 악을 극화한다. 우리가 매우 다양하게 극화된 바로 그 구체적 힘을 추상화하고 일반화할 때, 우리는 (우리가 살아가고 있는) 실제 삶에서의 비극들을 향해 가는 것이 아니라, 오히려 현실의 비극으로부터 멀어져 간다. 우리가 비극을 악을 극화해서 인식하는 것만으로 해석한다면, 우리는, 훨씬 더 결정적으로, 일상의 비극적 행위들로부터 멀어진다.

157

하위내용영역	배점	예상정답률
일반영어 B형 서술형	4점	35%

모범답안 The word is "ideology". Second it is because there were good people behind their destruction.

채점기준

+ 2점: 빈칸에 들어갈 단어가 "ideology"임을 정확히 기입하였다. 이외에는 답이 될 수 없다.
+ 2점: 수용소가 절대 악의 상징이 아닌 이유를 "it is because there were good people behind their destruction"이라 서술하였거나 유사하였다.

158

하위내용영역	배점	예상정답률
일반영어 A형 서술형	4점	50%

모범답안 The word is "origins". Second, it is the mythical account of the first Japanese Emperor being descended from gods and goddesses.

채점기준

+ 2점: 빈칸에 들어갈 단어가 "origins"임을 정확히 기입하였다. 이외에는 답이 될 수 없다.
+ 2점: 밑줄 친 "연대기적 설명"이 가리키는 것을 "the mythical account of the first Japanese Emperor being descended from gods and goddesses"라 서술하였거나 유사하였다.

한글번역

일본인의 기원을 파헤치는 것은 당신이 추측하는 것보다 훨씬 어려운 작업이다. 일본의 부상하는 지배력과 이웃 국가들과의 민감한 관계는 신화를 걷어내고 답을 찾는 것을 그 어느 때보다 중요하게 만든다.

답을 찾는 것은 증거가 너무 상충되기 때문에 어렵다. 한편으로는, 일본인들은 생물학적으로 특별하지 않으며, 다른 동아시아인들, 특히 한국인들과 외모와 유전자에서 매우 유사하다. 종합해보면, 많은 사실들이 일본인들이 아시아 대륙에서 최근에야 일본에 도착했고, 대륙의 사촌들과 차이를 진화시키기에는 너무 최근이었으며, 원주민을 대표하는 아이누족을 대체했다는 것을 시사한다. 하지만 그것이 사실이라면, 앵글로색슨족이 대륙에서 6세기에 영국을 정복했기 때문에 영어가 다른 게르만어와 명백히 밀접한 관련이 있는 것처럼, 일본어가 어떤 대륙 언어와 밀접한 유사성을 보일 것으로 예상할 수 있다. 일본의 추정되는 고대 언어와 최근 기원에 대한 증거 사이의 이 모순을 어떻게 해결할 수 있을까?

고고학자들은 네 가지 상충되는 이론을 제시했다. 일본에서 가장 인기 있는 견해는 일본인이 기원전 20,000년 훨씬 이전에 일본을 점령했던 고대 빙하시대 사람들로부터 점진적으로 진화했다는 것이다. 일본에서 또한 널리 퍼진 이론은 일본인이 4세기에 한국을 거쳐 일본을 정복한 기마 아시아 유목민의 후손이지만, 그들 자신은—강조하건대—한국인이 아니었다는 것이다. 많은 서구 고고학자들과 한국인들이 선호하고, 일본의 일부 집단에서는 인기가 없는 이론은 일본인이 기원전 400년경 논농사와 함께 도착한 한국에서 온 이민자들의 후손이라는 것이다. 마지막으로, 다른 세 이론에서 언급된 민족들이 섞여서 현대 일본인을 형성했을 수도 있다.

다른 민족들의 기원에 대한 유사한 질문이 제기될 때, 그것들은 냉정하게 논의될 수 있다. 일본인의 경우는 그렇지 않다. 1946년까지, 일본 학교들은 8세기에 기록된 가장 초기의 일본 연대기에 기반한 신화적 역사를 가르쳤다. 그것들은 창조신 이자나기의 왼쪽 눈에서 태어난 태양신 아마테라스가 어떻게 지상의 신과 결혼하기 위해 손자 니니기를 일본의 규슈 섬으로 보냈는지를 묘사한다. 니니기의 증손자 진무는 적들을 무력화시키는 눈부신 신성한 새의 도움을 받아 기원전 660년에 일본의 첫 번째 천황이 됐다. 기원전 660년과 역사적으로 문서화된 가장 초기의 일본 군주 사이의 공백을 메우기 위해, 연대기는 똑같이 허구적인 13명의 다른 천황들을 발명했다. 히로히토 천황이 마침내 자신이 신의 후손이 아니라고 발표한 제2차 세계대전 종료 이전에는, 일본의 고고학자들과 역사학자들은 그들의 해석을 이 연대기 기록에 부합하도록 만들어야 했다.

159

하위내용영역	배점	예상정답률
일반영어 A형 서술형	4점	45%

모범답안 The word is "pagan". Second, both Cromwell and the pilgrims opposed the celebrating of Christmas.

채점기준

+ 2점: 빈칸에 들어갈 단어가 "pagan"임을 정확히 기입하였다. 이외에는 답이 될 수 없다.
+ 2점: 크롬웰과 필그림들의 공통점을 "both Cromwell and the pilgrims opposed the celebrating of Christmas"라 서술하였거나 유사하였다.

한글번역

기독교 초기에는 부활절이 주요 휴일이었고, 예수의 탄생은 기념되지 않았다. 4세기에 교회 관리들은 예수의 탄생을 휴일로 제정하기로 결정했다. 불행히도 성경은 그의 탄생 날짜를 언급하지 않는다(이 사실을 청교도들이 나중에 지적해 그 기념의 정당성을 부인했다). 그의 탄생이 봄에 일어났을 수도 있다는 일부 증거가 있지만 (목자들이 한겨울 중에 양을 치고 있었겠는가?), 교황 율리우스 1세는 12월 25일을 선택했다. 교회가 이교도 사투르날리아 축제의 전통을 받아들이고 흡수하려는 노력으로 이 날짜를 선택했다고 일반적으로 믿어진다. 처음에는 성탄 축제라고 불렸던 이 관습은 432년까지 이집트로, 6세기 말까지 영국으로 퍼졌다.

전통적인 동지 축제와 같은 시기에 크리스마스를 개최함으로써, 교회 지도자들은 크리스마스가 대중적으로 받아들여질 가능성을 높였지만, 그것이 어떻게 기념되는지를 지시할 수 있는 능력을 포기했다. 중세까지 기독교는 대부분 이교도종교를 대체했다. 크리스마스에 신자들은 교회에 참석한 다음, 오늘날의 마르디 그라와 유사한 술에 취한 카니발 같은 분위기에서 떠들썩하게 축하했다. 매년 거지나 학생이 "무질서의 왕"으로 왕관을 썼고 열성적인 축하객들은 그의 신하 역할을 했다. 가난한 사람들은 부자들의 집에 가서 그들의 최고의 음식과 음료를 요구했다. 주인들이 응하지 않으면, 방문객들은 십중팔구 장난으로 그들을 괴롭혔다. 크리스마스는 상류층이 덜 운 좋은 시민들을 대접함으로써 사회에 대한 실제적이거나 상상적인 "빚"을 갚을 수 있는 한 해의 시기가 됐다.

17세기 초, 종교 개혁의 물결이 유럽에서 크리스마스가 기념되는 방식을 바꿨다. 올리버 크롬웰과 그의 청교도 세력이 1645년 영국을 장악했을 때, 그들은 영국에서 타락을 없애겠다고 맹세했고, 그들의 노력의 일환으로 크리스마스를 취소했다. 대중의 요구에 의해 찰스 2세가 왕좌에 복귀했고, 그와 함께 인기 있는 휴일의 복귀가 왔다.

1620년 아메리카에 온 영국 분리주의자들인 순례자들은 크롬웰보다도 그들의 청교도 신념에서 더욱 정통적이었다. 그 결과 크리스마스는 초기 아메리카에서 휴일이 아니었다. 1659년부터 1681년까지 크리스마스 기념은 실제로 보스턴에서 불법이었다. 크리스마스 정신이 보이는 누구나 5실링의 벌금을 물었다. 대조적으로 제임스타운 정착지에서는 존 스미스 선장이 크리스마스가 모든 사람에 의해 즐겨졌고 사건 없이 지나갔다고 보고했다. 미국 혁명 후, 크리스마스를 포함한 영국 관습들이 인기를 잃었다. 사실 크리스마스는 1870년 6월 26일까지 연방 휴일로 선언되지 않았다.

160

하위내용영역	배점	예상정답률
일반영어 A형 서술형	4점	45%

모범답안 The word is "chaotic". Second, Communism is given as a negative example of philosophy.

채점기준

+ 2점 : 빈칸에 들어갈 단어가 "chaotic"임을 정확히 기입하였다. 이외에는 답이 될 수 없다.
+ 2점 : 대중화된 이데올로기(철학)의 부정적 예로서 언급된 철학을 "Communism"이라 정확하게 서술하였다.

한글번역

만약 당신이 백 명의 사람들에게 "철학"이라는 용어에 대한 그들의 이해를 설명해달라고 요청한다면, 아마도 백 가지 다른 답변을 얻을 것이다. 이 현상에 대한 통일된 이해가 없기 때문에, 각 철학자가 철학에 대한 자신의 인식이 무엇인지 묘사하는 것이 가치 있다. 실제 삶에서 우리는 종종 특정 사상 체계들이 광범위한 수용을 얻고, 많은 수의 사람들을 특정 방향으로 흔드는 의견들을 만들어내는 것을 관찰한다. 이는 올바르다면 좋고 건설적인 경향을, 잘못됐다면 매우 파괴적인 경향을 시작할 수 있다. 공산주의의 전 세계적 확산이 이러한 현실의 한 예이다.

내 관점에서 좋은 철학은 여러 필요를 충족시켜야 한다. 한 차원에서 철학적 접근법은 그 시점까지 주목받지 못했던 특정 중요한 요소들을 드러낼 수 있다. 그러한 현상들을 탐지하는 것은 중요한 것들에 대한 가치 있는 현실을 드러낼 수 있다. 알 수 있는 것을 모르는 것은 과실이라고 가장 잘 설명될 수 있으며, 이는 제때 탐지되지 않으면 중대하고 예방 가능한 해를 일으킬 수 있다. 다른 차원에서, 그것은 복잡하고 겉보기에 설명할 수 없는 현상들에 대한 중요한 이해를 드러낼 수 있으며, 그렇지 않다면 세상은 이를 박탈당했을 것이다. 예를 들어, 초기 단계에서 중력의 개념과 지구가 태양 주위를 돈다는 사실은 철학적 발견이었다. 따라서 궁극적으로 과학으로 발전하는 철학적 연구를 통해 그러한 숨겨진 현상들을 탐지하는 것은 인류와 전체 세계에 유익하다.

게다가 그러한 사실들이 철학을 통해 탐지되고 설명됨에 따라, 우리는 혼돈스러운 우리 세계가 점점 더 질서정연함을 발견한다. 철학을 통해 우리는 한때 이해하기 불가능해 보였던 질문들에 대한 답을 찾는다. 예를 들어, 아이작 뉴턴 경이 중력을 발견하기 직전에, 당시의 탐구하는 마음들은 물체들이 지구와 관련해 행동하는 다양한 방식들을 관찰하면서 완전히 혼란스러워했다. 예를 들어, 높은 곳에 있던 물체가 놓였을 때, 그것은 완벽하게 지구 쪽으로 이동했다. 그러나 기체 형태의 물과 같은 다른 물체는 상승했다. 그리고 동일한 물체인 유체 형태의 물이나 눈이나 우박과 같은 단단한 물체는 지구로 다시 떨어졌다. 게다가 먼지 조각들과 같은 일부 물체들은 공중에 떠 있었다.

다양한 물체들 사이의 그러한 다양한 행동은 당시에 완전히 혼돈스러워보였다. 그러나 중력이 모든 물체를 자신에게 끌어당기는 힘으로 확인됐을 때, 왜 일부 물체들이 떨어지는지 이해하기가 쉬워졌다.

161

하위내용영역	배점	예상정답률
일반영어 B형 서술형	4점	35%

모범 답안 The word is "identified". Second, it is because the time between occurrences was so great that authors of historical records were unaware it was a repeating phenomenon.

채점 기준

+ 2점 : 빈칸에 들어갈 단어가 "identified"임을 정확히 기입하였다. 이외에는 답이 될 수 없다.
+ 2점 : 핼리 혜성을 보는 것이 단일한 사건으로 간주됐던 이유를 "because the time between occurrences was so great that authors of historical records were unaware it was a repeating phenomenon"이라 서술하였거나 유사하였다.

한글번역

사람들은 역사를 통틀어 항상 하늘을 관찰했고, 때때로 특이한 광경을 봤다 : 혜성, 밝은 유성, 육안으로 쉽게 볼 수 있는 다섯 개의 행성 중 하나 또는 그 이상, 행성 연결, 그리고 부등변과 렌즈 구름과 같은 대기 광학 현상들을. 특히 유명한 하나의 예로는 핼리 혜성이 있는데, 이것은 기원전 240년 중국 천문학자에 의해 처음 기록됐으며, 기원전 467년경에 기록됐을 가능성도 있다. 핼리 혜성은 매 76년마다 태양계 내에 도달하기 때문에, 그것이 반복되는 현상이라는 것을 몰랐던 고대 역사 문헌에서 종종 독특한 고립된 사건으로 식별됐다. 역사상 그러한 기록들은 종종 초자연적인 징조, 천사, 또는 다른 종교적 (불길한) 징조로 취급됐다. UFO 애호가들은 때때로 중세 회화의 특정 종교적 상징과 UFO 보고서 사이의 서사적 유사성에 대해 언급했지만, 이러한 그림들의 규범적이고 상징적인 성격은 예술사가들에 의해 그러한 이미지에 더 전통적인 종교적 해석을 부여하고 있다.

제2차 세계대전 당시 태평양과 유럽에선 "푸 파이터"로 알려진 둥글고 빛나는 불덩어리가 연합군과 추축국의 조종사들에 의해 보고됐다. 당시 연합군이 제안한 설명 중에는 성 엘모의 불(폭풍우 치는 밤에 마스트나 비행기의 날개 따위에 나타나는 방전(放電) 현상으로 죽음의 징조라고 여겨짐), 금성, 산소 결핍으로 인한 환각, 또는 독일의 비밀 무기 따위가 포함돼 있었다. 1946년, 스웨덴 군대에 의해, 스칸디나비아 국가들 상공에 떠있는 미확인 비행물체에 대한 2,000건이 넘는 보고가 수집됐고, 프랑스, 포르투갈, 이탈리아, 그리스로부터도 각각 독립적인 보고서가 작성됐다. 이 물체들은 러시아가 나포한 독일 V1 로켓이나 V2 로켓에 대한 시험일 것이라 생각됐기 때문에 "러시아의 우박"(나중에 "유령 로켓")이라고 불렸다. 대부분은 유성과 같은 자연 현상으로 판명됐다.

162

하위내용영역	배점	예상정답률
일반영어 A형 기입형	2점	60%

모범답안 daylight

채점기준

- 2점: 모범답안과 같다.
- 0점: 모범답안과 다르다.

한글번역

　대영제국은 지구 전체에 걸쳐 있었다. 이로 인해 제국 어딘가에서는 항상 낮이었기 때문에 해가 결코 지지 않는다는 말이 생겨났다.
　이 긴 낮이 언제 시작됐는지 정확히 알아내기는 어렵다. (이미 다른 사람들이 점령하고 있던 땅에) 식민지를 주장하는 전체 과정은 애초에 몹시 자의적이다. 본질적으로 영국인들은 항해하며 무작위하게 해변에 깃발을 꽂는 것으로 그들의 제국을 건설했다. 이는 한 나라의 특정 지점이 언제 제국에 "공식적으로" 추가됐는지 결정하기 어렵게 만든다.
　제국에서 해가 지는 것이 멈춘 정확한 날은 아마도 최초의 호주 영토들이 추가된 1700년대 후반이나 1800년대 초반 어느 때였을 것이다. 제국은 20세기 초에 대부분 해체됐지만, 놀랍게도—기술적으로는 해가 다시 지기 시작하지는 않았다.
　영국은 제국의 직접적인 잔재인 14개의 해외 영토를 가지고 있다. 새로 독립한 많은 영국 식민지들이 영연방에 가입했다. 캐나다와 호주 같은 일부는 엘리자베스 여왕을 그들의 군주로 한다. 그러나 그들은 우연히 같은 여왕을 가진 독립 국가들이다; 그들은 어떤 제국의 일부가 아니다.
　해는 14개 영국 영토 모두에서 동시에 지지 않는다. 그러나 영국이 하나의 작은 영토를 잃는다면, 2세기 넘게 처음으로 제국 전체의 일몰을 경험할 것이다. 매일 밤 GMT 자정 무렵, 케이맨 제도에서 해가 지고, 영국령 인도양 영토에서는 오전 1시 이후까지 해가 뜨지 않는다. 그 한 시간 동안, 남태평양의 작은 핏케언 제도가 햇빛 아래 있는 유일한 영국 영토이다.
　핏케언 제도는 HMS 바운티호의 반란자들의 후손인 수십 명의 인구를 가지고 있다. 이 섬들은 시장을 포함한 성인 남성 인구의 3분의 1이 아동 성학대로 유죄 판결을 받았을 때 악명이 높아졌다. 이 섬들이 아무리 끔찍할지라도, 그들은 대영제국의 일부로 남아 있으며, 그들이 쫓겨나지 않는 한 2세기에 걸친 영국의 낮이 계속될 것이다.

163

하위내용영역	배점	예상정답률
일반영어 A형 서술형	4점	50%

모범답안 The words are "infant perceptual abilities". Second, they refer to an infant's state prior to a stimulus and during or immediately after a stimulus.

채점기준

- +2점: 빈칸에 들어갈 단어가 "infant perceptual abilities"임을 정확히 기입하였다. 이외에는 답이 될 수 없다.
- +2점: 밑줄 친 부분이 가리키는 것을 "an infant's state prior to a stimulus and during or immediately following(immediately after/immediately subsequent to) a stimulus"라 서술하였거나 유사하였다.

한글번역

　유아 지각 능력 연구에서, 다양한 자극에 대한 유아들의 반응을 결정하기 위해 여러 기법들이 사용된다. 그들은 언어로 표현하거나 설문지를 작성할 수 없기 때문에, 유아들이 무엇을 보고, 듣고, 느낄 수 있는지 등을 결정하는 주요 수단으로 자연주의적 관찰의 간접적 기법들이 사용된다. 이러한 방법들 각각은 자극의 도입 전 유아의 상태를 자극 도중이나 직후의 상태와 비교한다. 두 측정치 사이의 차이는 연구자에게 자극에 대한 반응의 수준과 지속 시간의 지표를 제공한다. 예를 들어, 어떤 종류의 균일하게 움직이는 패턴이 신생아의 시야를 가로질러 지나간다면, 눈의 반복적인 추적 움직임이 일어난다. 이러한 눈 움직임의 발생은 움직이는 패턴이 신생아에 의해 어떤 수준에서 지각된다는 증거를 제공한다. 마찬가지로, 유아의 전반적인 운동 활동 수준의 변화—머리 돌리기, 눈 깜빡이기, 울기 등—가 연구자들에 의해 유아의 지각 능력의 시각적 지표로 사용돼왔다.
　그러나 그러한 기법들은 한계가 있다. 첫째, 두 명 이상의 관찰자들이 특정 반응이 일어났는지, 또는 어느 정도로 일어났는지에 대해 동의하지 않을 수 있다는 점에서 관찰이 신뢰할 수 없을 수 있다. 둘째, 반응들을 정량화하기 어렵다. 종종 유아의 빠르고 분산된 움직임들이 반응 횟수의 정확한 기록을 얻기 어렵게 만든다. 셋째, 그리고 가장 강력한 한계는 유아의 반응이 제시된 자극 때문인지 또는 자극이 없는 상태에서 자극이 있는 상태로의 변화 때문인지 확실하게 알 수 없다는 것이다. 유아는 조사자가 확인한 것과는 다른 자극의 측면들에 반응하고 있을 수도 있다. 따라서 관찰 평가가 유아 지각 능력 연구의 기법으로 사용될 때, 데이터로부터 과도하게 일반화하거나 하나 또는 두 개의 연구를 유아의 특정 지각 능력에 대한 결정적 증거로 의존하지 않도록 주의해야 한다.

164

하위내용영역	배점	예상정답률
일반영어 A형 서술형	4점	50%

모범 답안) The word is "rhythm". Second, the musical piece had an unusual or striking rhythm that did not reflect the human instinct.

채점 기준

+ 2점: 빈칸에 들어갈 단어가 "rhythm"임을 정확히 기입하였다. 이외에는 답이 될 수 없다.
+ 2점: 스트라빈스키의 음악작품이 관객을 화나게 한 이유를 "the musical piece had an unusual or striking rhythm that did not reflect the human instinct"라 서술하였거나 유사하였다.

한글번역

스트라빈스키의 음악작품 중 하나에 대한 강한 반응을 기억해볼 가치가 있을 것이다. 다른 어떤 예술 형태도 이 특정한 음악작품이 그랬던 것처럼 그러한 자발적인 반응을 일으킬 수 없었을 것이다.
이제, 리듬의 본능은 모든 인간 본능 중 가장 깊은 것 중 하나이다. 그것은 우리의 물질세계로부터 리듬을 끊임없이 요구하며, 연결이 적절하게 이루어질 때 큰 쾌락과 기쁨을 경험한다. 이는 대부분의 사람들이 이 쾌락과 기쁨의 근원을 확인하기 위해 의식적으로 연결을 만들 수 없다는 사실에도 불구하고 그렇다. 게다가, 리듬은 인간 본능 안에만 존재하는 것이 아니라, 모든 자연이 그것으로 스며들어 있다. 리듬적 예술을 이해하기 위해서는 먼저 리듬과 세상에서의 그것의 더 큰 역할을 이해해야 한다.

리듬은 자연에서 편재하며 자연적이고 인공적인 무수한 방식으로 나타난다. 리듬은 우리가 그것에 너무 익숙해졌다는 사실에도 불구하고 가장 깊은 방식으로 우리를 둘러싼다. 사실, 우리가 숨 쉴 필요를 느끼지 못하는 것과 같은 방식으로, 우리는 종종 그것을 알아차리지도 못한다.

예를 들어, 가장 명백한 것부터 시작하면, 태양은 매일 아침 동쪽에서 떠서 매일 저녁 서쪽으로 진다. 이 주기는 24시간마다 리듬적으로 낮에서 밤으로, 빛에서 어둠으로, 그리고 다시 그 역으로의 교환을 촉진한다. 달이 체계적으로 나타나고, 모양을 바꾸고, 사라져서 매달 다시 나타나는 방식도 마찬가지이다. 조석파는 많은 해양 동물들이 그것을 중심으로 삶을 구조화할 정도로 리듬적으로 일어난다.

다른 영역에서 또 다른 예를 들면, 각 언어는 고유한 리듬을 가지고 있다. 몇 문장만 써보고 그 다음 이 쓰인 줄들을 다른 언어들로 번역해보라. 그런 다음 각 문장을 그들의 모국어와 억양으로 읽어줄 사람들을 찾아보라. 각 모국어가 고유한 독특한 선율적 소리를 가지고 있다는 것을 들을 것이다. 각 언어가—어휘, 문법, 그리고 무수한 다른 미묘함에서 다른 것들과 다른 것 외에도—나머지로부터 각각을 쉽게 구별되게 만드는 고유한 리듬을 가지고 있다는 것을 알아차릴 것이다.

165

하위내용영역	배점	예상정답률
일반영어 B형 서술형	4점	45%

모범 답안) The word is "manipulated." Second, the study reveals that crowds are more herdlike than wise, following the path of others even when randomly prompted.

채점 기준

+ 2점: 빈칸에 들어갈 단어가 "manipulated"임을 정확히 기입하였다. 이외에는 답이 될 수 없다.
+ 2점: 쉬난 애럴의 연구가 드러내는 것을 "crowds are more herdlike than wise, following the path of others even when randomly prompted"라 서술하였거나 유사하였다.

한글번역

"군중의 지혜"는 인터넷 시대의 주문이 됐다. 새로운 진공청소기를 선택해야 하는가? 온라인 상점 아마존의 리뷰들을 확인해보라. 하지만 새로운 연구는 그러한 온라인 점수들이 항상 최선의 선택을 드러내는 것은 아니라고 시사한다. 웹 사용자들을 대상으로 한 대규모 통제 실험은 그러한 평가들이 비합리적인 "군중 행동"에 매우 취약하며—그리고 군중이 조작될 수 있다는 것을 발견한다.

때때로 군중은 정말로 당신보다 현명하다. 고전적인 예들은 황소의 무게나 항아리 안의 껌볼 개수를 추측하는 것이다. 당신의 추측은 아마도 정답에서 멀 것이지만, 많은 사람들의 선택의 평균은 놀랍도록 실제 숫자에 가깝다. 하지만 목표가 제품의 품질이나 가치와 같이 덜 구체적인 것을 판단하는 것일 때는 어떻게 될까?

한 이론에 따르면, 군중의 지혜는 여전히 유효하다—사람들의 의견의 총합을 측정하는 것은 안정적이고 신뢰할 만한 값을 만들어낸다. 그러나 회의론자들은 사람들의 의견이 다른 사람들의 의견에 의해 쉽게 조작된다고 주장한다. 따라서 반대 의견들을 제시함으로써—예를 들어, 그들을 매우 좋거나 매우 나쁜 태도에 노출시킴으로써—초기에 군중을 살짝 밀어주는 것이 군중을 다른 방향으로 이끌 것이다. 어느 가설이 맞는지 검증하려면, 엄청난 수의 사람들을 조작하고, 그들을 거짓 정보에 노출시키고, 그것이 그들의 의견에 어떻게 영향을 미치는지 결정해야 할 것이다.

매사추세츠 공과대학의 네트워크 과학자 쉬난 애럴이 이끄는 팀이 정확히 그것을 했다. 애럴은 뉴스 기사들을 모으는 인기 웹사이트와 비밀리에 작업해 오고 있었다. 그 웹사이트는 사용자들이 뉴스 기사에 대해 댓글을 달고 서로의 댓글에 찬성이나 반대 투표를 할 수 있게 한다. 투표 집계는 각 댓글 옆에 숫자로 보이며 댓글들의 위치는 시간 순이다. 이는 개별 사람들이 온라인에서 서로에게 얼마나 영향을 미치는지 측정하기 위해 사람들의 영화 평점을 사용한 그의 실험의 후속이다 (답: 많이). 이번에는 군중이 개인에게 얼마나 영향을 미치는지, 그리고 그것이 외부에서 통제될 수 있는지 알고 싶었다.

5개월 동안, 사용자가 제출한 모든 댓글은 무작위로 "찬성" 투표(긍정적), "반대" 투표(부정적)를 받았거나, 통제군으로서 아예 투표를 받지 않았다. 그런 다음 팀은 사용자들이 그 댓글들을 어떻게 평가하는지 관찰했다. 사용자들은 1,000만 번 이상 조회되고 다른 사용자들에 의해 30만 번 이상 평가된 10만 개 이상의 댓글을 생성했다.

적어도 뉴스 사이트의 댓글에 관해서는, 군중이 현명하기보다는 더 양떼 같다. 연구자들로부터 가짜 긍정 투표를 받은 댓글들은 통제군과 비교해 더 많은 긍정 투표를 받을 가능성이 32% 더 높았다.

166

하위내용영역	배점	예상정답률
일반영어 A형 서술형	4점	40%

모범답안 The words are "sun's atmosphere". Second, it is where solar winds can break free of the sun's atmosphere and affect electrical grids and communication networks on earth.

채점기준

+ 2점: 빈칸에 들어갈 단어가 "sun's atmosphere" 또는 "solar atmosphere"이라 답하였다.
+ 2점: 지구 생명체와 연관해서 알벤 지점은 어떠한 의미를 지니고 있는지에 대한 질문에 "it(the Alfvén point) is where solar winds can break free of the sun's atmosphere and affect electrical grids and communication networks on earth"라 서술하였거나 유사하였다.

한글번역

NASA의 우주 (무인) 탐사선이 태양과학 사상 처음으로 태양의 대기에 진입해 맹렬히 타오르는 코로나를 건드렸다. 2018년에 발사된 파커 태양 탐사선은 7번의 태양 근접 비행을 수행한 뒤, 2021년 4월 28일 8번째 근접 비행을 하는 동안에 코로나 속으로 들어갔다. 그것은 태양의 대기로 세 번 여행을 했고, 그중 하나는 5시간 동안 지속됐다.

평균 기온이 화씨 약 200만 도(섭씨 1백만 도)인 태양 대기의 상류에서—화씨 1만 도(섭씨 5500도)인 발광하는 태양 표면보다 더 뜨거운—그 우주선은 태양 탐사선 컵이라고 불리는 특수한 기구로 대기 입자들을 수집했다. 파커 태양탐사선은 태양 대기에 진입해 표본을 추출함으로써 달에 착륙하는 것과 유사한 과학적 업적을 이뤘다.

흘러나오는 플라즈마와 고에너지 입자로 만들어진 강력한 태양풍은 코로나에서 태어나지만, 대부분 태양의 자기장에 의해 억제되며, 이 자기장은 또한 태양 표면에서 분출되는 플라즈마의 폭발을 억제하기도 한다. 태양풍이 일정한 속도를 초과해 태양의 대기를 막 지나면 (이 막 지난 지점은 알벤 지점이라 불린다), 태양풍은 자기장의 구속으로부터 벗어날 수 있다. 하지만, 과학자들은 그 지점(알벤 지점)이 정확히 어디에 있는지 알지 못했다.

이제, 파커 태양 탐사선은 그 질문에 답했다. 코로나의 원격 사진을 근거로 한 이전의 추정치는 알벤 지점이 태양 표면으로부터 약 430만~860만 마일 떨어진 곳에서 발견될 것이라고 예측했다. 파커는 4월 28일 태양위쪽으로 약 810만 마일 떨어진 곳에서 이러한 상태를 탐지해 연구자들에게 처음으로 태양 대기권에 진입했다고 말했다.

태양풍과 태양 플레어—태양광의 빠른 폭발—는 전력망에 영향을 주고 지구의 통신망을 교란시킬 수 있으며, 탐사선으로부터 얻은 새로운 데이터는 그 이전에는 전혀 하지 못했던 이러한 태양의 이벤트들에 대해 이해할 수 있는 가능성을 제공해준다.

167

하위내용영역	배점	예상정답률
일반영어 A형 서술형	4점	35%

모범 답안) The word is "comparisons". Second, it is that citizens of the Roman Republic allowed political violence and obstruction and thus they can lose their political institutions, leading to conversion to the perceived stability of an Emperor.

채점 기준

+ 2점: 빈칸에 들어갈 단어가 "comparisons"임을 정확히 기입하였다. 이외에는 답이 될 수 없다.
+ 2점: 에드워드 와츠가 암시하는 로마 공화정의 몰락을 야기한 가장 중요한 요소를 "citizens of the Roman Republic allowed political violence and obstruction and thus they can lose their political institutions, leading to conversion to the perceived stability of an Emperor"라 서술하였거나 유사하였다.

한글번역

미국 헌법은 고대 로마에게 막대한 빚을 지고 있다. 건국의 아버지들은 그리스와 로마 역사에 정통했다. 토마스 제퍼슨과 제임스 매디슨 같은 지도자들은 역사가 폴리비우스를 읽었는데, 폴리비우스는 다양한 파벌과 사회 계층의 대표들이 엘리트들의 권력과 군중들의 권력을 견제하는 로마 공화국의 헌법에 대한 가장 명확한 설명 중 하나를 제시했다. 미국의 초창기에, 고대 로마와 비교하는 것이 일반적이었다는 것은 놀라운 일이 아니다. 그리고 로마는 482년이나 되는 긴 세월 동안 공화국—수백 년의 군주제와 1,500년의 제국 통치에 의해 종지부를 찍었지만—을 유지했는데, 이것은 현재까지도 여전히 인류 역사상 가장 긴 공화국으로 남아있다.

현대 정치의 양상은 샌디에이고 캘리포니아 대학의 역사학자 에드워드 왓츠로 하여금 기원전 130년에서 기원전 27년의 로마 공화국의 마지막 세기를 떠올리도록 만들었다. 그것이 왓츠가 자신의 새 책 《치명적 공화국 : 로마는 어떻게 폭정에 빠졌는가》에서 그 시기를 새롭게 살펴본 이유이다. 왓츠는 한때 국가에 대한 봉사와 개인의 명예에 헌신했던 인구가 점점 커지는 부의 불평등, 당파적 교착상태, 정치적 폭력, 그리고 영합주의적 정치인들에 의해 갈기갈기 찢겨져버리는 방식을 연대기적으로 기록한 뒤에, 로마 시민들이 결국 자신들의 정치 제도를 보호하지 않음으로써 그들의 민주주의를 죽게 놔두고 불안정하고 타락한 공화국의 지속적인 폭력에 맞서는 대신에, 이른바 황제가 제공한다고 알려진 안정을 향해 돌아서는 선택을 했다고 주장한다.

왓츠는 로마를 미국과 직접 비교하고 대조하지는 않지만, 로마에서 일어난 일은 모든 현대 공화국에 대한 교훈이라고 말한다. 그는 "그 무엇보다도 로마 공화국은 현대의 공화국에 사는 시민들에게, 정치적 방해를 묵인하고 정치적 폭력을 구애하는 것이 야기하는 믿을 수 없는 정도로 큰 위험에 대해 가르친다"고 썼다. "로마 역사는 지도자들의 이러한 좀먹는 행위에 관여하는 것을 시민들이 외면할 때, 그들의 공화국이 치명적인 위험에 처할 수 있다는 것을 가장 명확하게 보여준다."

로마 공화정의 많은 부분이 꽤 익숙하게 느껴진다. 로마인들의 강한 애국심은 지중해 세계에서 독특했다. 제2차 세계대전 이후 미국과 마찬가지로 로마도 기원전 201년 제2차 포에니 전쟁에서 승리한 뒤 세계의 패권국이 되면서, 군사비 지출이 대폭 증가했고, 베이비붐이 일었고, 자신의 돈으로 정치에 영향력을 행사하고 자신이 원하는 의제를 추진할 수 있는 초부자 엘리트 계층을 낳았다. 이러한 유사성들이 비록 토가(고대 로마 시민이 입던 헐렁한 겉옷)나, 검투사 싸움, 그리고 동면쥐들에 대한 식욕은 완전히 낯선 것이지만 두 나라 사이의 비교를 가치 있는 것으로 만든다.

168

하위내용영역	배점	예상정답률
일반영어 A형 서술형	4점	35%

모범답안 The word is "enlightenment". Second, it is because naturalism no longer included the aim of changing the human condition.

채점기준

+ 2점: 빈칸에 들어갈 단어가 "enlightenment"임을 정확히 기입하였다. 이외에는 답이 될 수 없다.
+ 2점: 자연주의가 체제의 기괴한 형태가 된 핵심적 이유를 "because naturalism no longer included the aim of changing the human condition"이라 서술하였거나 유사하였다.

한글번역

자연주의 문학이 가장 명백한 예이다. 자연주의 문학은 운명이나 절대적 질서 그리고 인간의 힘을 초월한 설계라는 전통적인 관념이, 이성에 대한 확신과 설명과 통제의 능력이 지속적으로 확장될 가능성에 대한 확신으로 대체됐던 자유주의 계몽의 진정한 자녀인 것 같다. 정치에서는 이것은 인간 운명에 대한 새로운 사회적 의식을 만들어 냈고; 철학에서는 종교와 사회적 관습의 이데올로기에 대한 분석을 합리적 설명의 새로운 체계와 함께 만들어 냈다. 문학에서는 현대 사회 세계에 대한 정확한 관찰과 묘사에 대한 새로운 강조를 낳았다.

그러나 자연주의 문학은 결국 계몽주의의 사생아다. 자연주의 문학은 특유의 성격대로 관찰과 기술의 기법을 그것들이 봉사하고자 하는 목적에서 분리했다. 자연주의가 된 것, 그리고 자연주의가 더 중요한 (문학)운동인 사실주의와 구별되는 지점은 (자연주의가) 인간 자신을 둘러싼 환경에 의해 만들어지는 피조물로 기계적으로 묘사한 것이었는데, 마치 인간과 사물이 같은 본성을 가진 것처럼 기록한 문학이었다는 점이었다.

자연주의의 비극은 수동적인 고통의 비극이다. 그 고통이 수동적인 이유는 인간은 (자기가 살고 있는 세상을) 참아내야만 하는 것일 뿐, 결코 진정으로 그 세상을 바꿀 수 없기 때문이다. 견뎌내는 것은 도덕적으로나 종교적으로나 가치가 주어지지 않는다; 견뎌내는 것은 전적으로 기계적이다. 왜냐하면 인간과 세상은, 현재 이성적인 설명으로 이해되고 있는 것에서는, 시간이 지남에 따라 변화하지만 어떤 목적도 없는 비인격적이고 물질적인 과정의 산물이기 때문이다. 인간의 상황을 묘사하고 그런 뒤에 변화시키려는 충동은 신이나 인간의 개입이 있을 수 없는 상태를 묘사하는 단순한 충동으로 협소해졌고, 인간의 의지 행위는 인간의 운명을 단번에 결정짓고 그 운명에 무관심한—우주적인 것이든 사회적인 것이든 간에—거대한 물질적 과정 속에서 작고 하찮은 것일 따름이다.

우리 문학의 가장 일반적인 이론이자 가장 일반적인 실천인 이 자연주의는 자유주의에서 시작됐지만, 아이러니하게도 무신론이 신앙의 괴상한 버전으로 끝나는 것처럼 자유주의가 원래 도전했던 체제의 괴상한 버전으로 끝난다. 살아있는 기획은 기계적인 운명이 됐고, 후자는 전자보다 인간으로부터 훨씬 더 멀리 떨어져 있다; 인간 자신의 그 어떤 이미지로부터도 더 결정적으로 소외돼 있다. 하지만 (자연주의가) 이런 식으로 진행된 데에는 진짜 원인이 있다. 그것은 본질적으로, 비판적 참여를 하려하던 바로 그 시점에 계몽의 과정을 의도적으로 저지하는 것이다.

169

하위내용영역	배점	예상정답률
일반영어 A형 서술형	4점	40%

모범답안 The words are "historical evidence". Second, it is implied that he was President at that time.

채점기준

+ 2점: 빈칸에 들어갈 단어가 "historical evidence"임을 정확히 기입하였다. 이외에는 답이 될 수 없다.
+ 2점: 밴 뷰런이 1839년에 어떤 직업을 가지고 있었는지 추론하는 문제에 "he was President at that time"이라 서술하였다.

한글번역

'OK'라는 단어의 기원은 무엇인가? 19세기 중반 미국에서 대중적으로 사용되기 시작한 이 기묘한 구어 표현의 출현을 설명하려는 수많은 시도들이 있었다. 그것들 대부분은 의심할 여지 없이 순전한 추측이다. 역사적 증거로 볼 때 그것이 스코틀랜드 표현 och aye, 그리스어 ola kala (좋다), 촉토족 인디언어 oke 또는 okeh (그렇다), 프랑스어 aux Cayes (좋은 럼으로 명성이 있는 아이티의 항구 케예스에서), au quai (프랑스어를 말하는 부두 노동자들이 사용했다고 여겨지는 부두로), 또는 자신이 확인한 선하증권에 그것들을 썼다고 전해지는 오베다이아 켈리라는 철도 화물 담당자의 이니셜에서 유래했을 가능성은 전혀 없어 보인다.

'OK'에 대한 가장 오래된 문서상 언급들은 1840년 미국 대통령 선거 동안 민주당이 그것을 슬로건으로 채택한 것에서 비롯된다. 그들의 후보인 마틴 밴 뷰런은 (뉴욕주에 있는 그의 출생지를 따라) 올드 킨더훅이라는 별명을 가졌고 그의 지지자들은 OK 클럽을 만들었다. 이는 의심할 여지없이 이 용어의 대중화에 도움이 됐다 (비록 밴 뷰런의 재선에는 도움이 되지 않았지만). 1830년대 후반 미국에서는 유머러스한 철자법 틀리기에 대한 짧지만 광범위한 유행이 있었고, 그중 하나인 'orl korrekt'라는 형태가 'OK'라는 이니셜을 설명할 수 있을 것이다. 그러한 이론은 한 명 이상의 저명한 미국 학자들에 의해 지지받아 왔고 옥스퍼드 사전을 포함한 많은 사전에 실려 있다. 적어도 어느 정도 그럴 듯한 유일한 다른 이론은 이 용어가 서아프리카 출신의 흑인 노예들 사이에서 기원했으며 다양한 서아프리카 언어에서 괜찮은, 정말 그렇다를 의미하는 단어를 나타낸다는 것이다.

불행히도, 이 표현의 기원이 최종적이고 확고하게 확립될 수 있게 하는 역사적 증거를 발굴하는 것은 어렵다.

170

하위내용영역	배점	예상정답률
일반영어 A형 서술형	4점	40%

모범답안 It means that Paul is only acknowledging one aspect of the whole of empathy. Second, the word is "reason".

채점 기준

+ 2점: "Paul is only acknowledging one aspect of the whole of empathy"라 서술하였거나 유사하였다.
+ 2점: 빈칸에 들어갈 단어가 "reason"임을 정확히 기입하였다. 이외에는 답이 될 수 없다.

한글번역

폴, 당신은 공감에 의존하는 것의 위험을 적절히 지적한다. 하지만 당신은 또한 그 문제점들을 과장하고 그 중요성을 과소평가한다.

우선, 당신은 "공감"의 허수아비 버전과 싸우고 있다. 화난 친구를 마주했을 때, 누군가는 그의 감정을 대리적으로 공유하고, 그 감정들이 어디서 오는지 이해하고, 그가 기분이 나아지기를 바랄 수 있다. 이 모든 경험들이 공감의 조각이지만, 당신은 그 정의를 감정 공유 요소만 포함하도록 축소했다. 이는 유럽 음식이 맛있지 않다고 주장하면서, 먼저 "유럽 음식"을 엄격히 해기스로만 정의하는 것과 같다.

당신은 또한 감정을 변덕스럽고 비합리적인 것으로 묘사한다. 이 관점은 구식이며, 사람들이 야생마 위의 기수처럼 이성을 통해 열정을 억제해야 한다는 그리스적 개념을 연상시킨다. 하지만 실제로 사람들은 자신의 감정에 맞서는 것이 아니라 함께 작업하며, 자신의 필요에 맞게 감정을 높이거나 낮춘다. 공감도 다르지 않다. 그렇다, 그것은 감정적 스포트라이트이지만, 사람들은 이 스포트라이트를 자신이 적절하다고 보는 곳에 비출 수 있는 능력을 가지고 있다. 내 자신의 연구는 사람들이 단순히 공감이 자신의 통제 하에 있다고 믿을 때, 그들이 그것을 더 열심히 시도하도록 영감을 받는다는 것을 보여준다—예를 들어, 윤리적으로나 정치적으로 자신과 다른 사람들의 감정에 주의를 기울이는 것에서.

당신이 주장하듯이 우리가 원칙만으로 자신을 개선할 수 있다면 왜 공감과 함께 일하는 수고를 해야 하는가? 공감이 차이를 만들어내기 때문이다—항상은 아니지만, 당신이 시사하는 것보다는 더 자주. 공감을 받는 것이 도움이 된다. 예를 들어, 암 환자들은 의사들이 공감을 표현할 때 우울증을 덜 경험하고 더 많은 권한을 느낀다. 그것을 주는 것도 도움이 된다: 친절하게 행동하는 사람들은 더 행복하고 건강해지며, 특히 공감에서 우러나와 행동할 때 그렇다. 공감을 선택하는 사람들은 더 넓고 풍부한 감정적 삶을 키운다.

물론, 폴, 당신이 사람들이 게으르게 공감을 배분한다는 것—자신과 비슷하게 생기거나 생각하는 다른 사람들에게—은 옳다. 하지만 도덕성을 인도하기 위해 순수한 이성을 신성시하는 것은 순진하다. 사람들이 객관적이려고 노력할 때조차, 그들은 종종 자신이 믿고 싶어 하는 것을 확인한다. 우리의 탈 진실 세계에서, 사람들은 이성을 방패처럼 사용할 수 있으며, 편안한 가정들 속에 웅크리고, 자신의 편견을 증폭시키는 다른 사람들로 자신을 둘러싼다. 사람들이 자신의 공감을 넓히고 싶어 하지 않는다면, 그들은 아마도 이성도 좁게 사용할 것이다.

171

하위내용영역	배점	예상정답률
일반영어 B형 서술형	4점	50%

모범 답안 The word is "cinema". Second, it is depicted as a closed world (undead or similar to the afterlife).

채점 기준

+ 2점: 빈칸에 들어갈 단어가 "cinema"임을 정확히 기입하였다.
  ☞ "film"이라 했으면 1점을 준다.

+ 2점: 영화 2046에서 '마지막 남은 공산주의 국가'가 "a closed world (undead or similar to the afterlife)"라 묘사되었다고 서술하였거나 유사하였다.

한글번역

'소피의 선택'(1982)부터 '쉰들러 리스트'(1993), '더 리더 : 책 읽어주는 남자'(2008) 그리고 더 많은 영화들에 이르기까지 30년간의 홀로코스트 영화에서는 기차가 핵심적인 역할을 한다. 지금 현재, 현대 유럽의 폭력과 기차를 연결시키는 것은, 진보의 아이콘으로서 기차를 개념 짓는 것보다 훨씬 더 눈에 띈다.

대조적으로, 세계 디지털 경제가 값싼 노동력과 값싼 제품 때문에 의존하는 중국의 1억 5천만 이주 노동자들은 특별 경제 구역에 있는 공장으로 갔다가 기차를 타고 집으로 돌아온다. 2014년 1월 중국 춘절 당시 신문 보도에 따르면, 명절에 고향을 방문하기 위해 36억 번의 기차 여행이 이주 노동자들에 의해 행해졌다고 추정했다. 이것은 (실제로는) 인류 역사에서 가장 큰 이주라 할 만하다. 이 노동자들은 서양인들이 실제적인 것의 종말과 기차의 죽음을 대수롭지 않은 듯 쉽게 써대는 컴퓨터, 전화기, 태블릿의 대부분을 만든다. 아시아에서 기차 여행의 엄청난 역할을 고려할 때, 기차 여행이 계속해서 아시아 영화에 나타나는 것은 놀라운 일이 아니다. 중국과 일본의 시속 268마일의 자기부상열차는 모든 유럽과 미국의 동급열차를 앞지르는 등 동아시아에서 열차는 매우 선진적이다.

홍콩 감독 왕가위의 스타일리시하고 영감을 주는 영화 '2046'에서 첨단 열차는 핵심 역할을 한다. 이 영화는 히치콕과 고다르의 영향을 받아 서양 누아르 영화(세상을 사람들의 탐욕이나 잔인성이 가득한 암울한 곳으로 묘사하는 영화 기법)와 아방가르드 스타일을 중국 폐쇄적인 세계로 흡수했다. 마치 히치콕 영화에서처럼 남자 주인공 주모완(토니렁: 양조위)은 가까이에 있는 구멍을 통해 여자들을 염탐하곤 한다. 기차는 2046으로 향해 가거나—그곳은 어디나 될 수 있다—또는 기차 자체가 2046일 수도 있다. 영화에서, 2046은 1966년 홍콩을 배경으로 한 장면들에서 차우가 호텔에서 세 들어 사는 방의 번호이다. 2046은 또한 그 영국 식민지(즉, 홍콩)가 공식적으로 (중국에) 반환된 지 50년 후로, 홍콩이 운영되는 방식을 변화시킬 수 있도록 허용된 해이기도 하다. 1997년 (홍콩이 영국에서) 중국으로 양도될 때 제공된 민주주의를 요구하는 시위는, 2046년보다 수십 년 전인 2014년 점거운동으로 이어졌다. 기차는 이 모든 의미의 층들이 연결되는 닫힌 "차량"이며, 또한 기억이 발생하거나 회복되는 장소이기도 하다. 이 양식화된 일련의 연결고리는 마지막 남은 공산주의 국가의 닫힌 세계의 사후 세계를 묘사하는데, 이것은 죽은 것이 아니라 죽음과 살아있음이 동시에 같이 존재하는 언데드한 상태이다.

172

하위내용영역	배점	예상정답률
일반영어 A형 서술형	4점	50%

모범답안 It is because he wishes to find which oarsmen average higher numbers of wins. Second, the words are "adverse wind".

채점기준

+ 2점 : 코치가 선수들끼리 경쟁을 하게 한 이유를 "because he wishes to find which oarsmen average higher numbers of wins" 또는 "because he wishes to find which oarsmen achieve the greater average numbers of wins"라 서술하였거나 유사하였다.
+ 2점 : 빈칸에 들어갈 단어가 "adverse wind"임을 정확히 기입하였다. 이외에는 답이 될 수 없다.

한글번역

한 명의 조정 선수가 혼자 힘으로 옥스퍼드대학과 케임브리지대학 대항의 조정 경기를 이길 수는 없다. 그에게는 8명의 동료가 필요하다. 각각의 선수는 항상 보트의 특정 부분에 앉는 전문가이다. 즉 뱃머리에서 노를 젓든 조정수든 키잡이든 그들은 각각 어떤 역할을 맡고 있다. 보트를 젓는 것은 협력 작업이지만, 그중에는 다른 사람보다 실력이 더 나은 사람이 있을 수 있다. 코치는 뱃머리에서 노를 젓는 전문 선수, 키잡이 전문 선수 등 한 그룹의 후보 중에서 이상적인 조정 팀(크루)을 뽑아야 한다. 그가 다음과 같이 뽑았다고 가정해 보자.

그는 매일 각 위치의 후보자를 무작위로 조합해 세 조로 짠 뒤 그 세 조의 크루를 서로 경쟁시킨다. 이것을 몇 주간 계속하면 이긴 보트에는 종종 동일 인물이 타고 있음을 알 수 있다. 이들은 우수 선수로 기록된다. 또 그중에는 항상 뒤처지는 크루에 있는 선수도 있다. 이들은 결국 탈락된다. 그러나 뛰어난 선수라도 때로는 뒤처지는 크루에 있는 경우가 있다. 다른 멤버가 열등한 탓이거나 운이 나빠서 —역풍 따위—이다. 가장 뛰어난 선수들이 이긴 보트에 있다는 것은 단지 '평균'을 나타낼 뿐이다.

이 선수들에 해당하는 것이 바로 유전자이다. 보트의 각 위치를 점하려는 경쟁자는 염색체상의 동일 위치를 점할 가능성이 있는 대립 유전자이다. 노를 빨리 젓는 것은 생존에 필요한 성공적인 몸을 만드는 것과 같다. 이때의 역풍은 외부 환경에 해당된다. 교체 요원의 집단은 유전자 풀이다. 하나의 몸은 그 몸의 유전자 전부가 한 보트에 타고 있는 것이라고 보면 된다. 좋은 유전자가 나쁜 동료 속으로 들어가 치사 유전자와 한 몸 속에서 동거하는 일도 흔히 있다. 이 경우 치사 유전자는 그 몸을 어릴 때 죽이는 데 좋은 유전자는 다른 유전자와 함께 파괴된다. 그러나 이것이 유일한 몸은 아니다. 좋은 유전자의 복제물은 치사 유전자를 갖지 않는 다른 몸 속에서 살고 있다.

173

하위내용영역	배점	예상정답률
일반영어 A형 서술형	4점	35%

모범답안 The word is "universal". Second, the words are "acknowledging historical specificity".

채점기준

+ 2점 : 빈칸에 들어갈 단어가 "universal"임을 정확히 기입하였다. 이외에는 답이 될 수 없다.
+ 2점 : 밑줄 친 부분과 상응하는 세 단어를 "acknowledging historical specificity"라 정확하게 서술하였다.

한글번역

많은 교사들이 자신의 지식 수준에 편안함을 느끼지 못하고 자신이 완전히 숙달하지 못했을 수도 있는 것을 학생들에게 소개하는 것을 꺼리기 때문에 교육에서 현대 미술을 사용하는 것을 피한다. 이러한 반응은 교육자들에게만 국한된 것이 아니다. 미술 비평가이자 역사학자인 루시 리퍼드가 지적했듯이, 현대 미술 분야는 "많은 사람들이 자신의 반응을 의심하고 심지어 부끄러워할 정도로 신비화됐다." 설상가상으로, 교육 자료는 부족하다. 현대 미술에 대한 교육과정 자료의 부재는 유일하게 가치 있는 미술은 "시간의 시험을 견뎌낸" 것이라는 태도를 반영한다. 이 태도는 결국 고정되고 영구적으로 유지되는 보편적 문화 기준을 확립하는 것이 가능하다는 믿음을 반영한다.

다문화 교육에 대한 현대 미술의 관련성은 아무리 강조해도 지나치지 않다. 지난 20년 동안, 예술가들과 비평가들의 감성과 관점에 상당한 변화가 나타났으며, 철학자이자 신학자이자 활동가인 코넬 웨스트가 차이의 정치학이라고 언급한 것을 만들어냈다. 이 새로운 차이의 문화 정치학의 특징들은 다양하고, 다중적이고, 이질적인 관점의 이름으로 역사의 단일하고 동질적인 관점들에 도전하는 것; 구체적이고, 특수하고, 특정한 현실들에 비추어 보편적 선언들을 거부하는 것; 그리고 역사적 특수성을 인정하는 것을 포함한다. 이 새로운 미술에서, 차이를 구성하는 것이 무엇이고 그것이 어떻게 결정되는지의 문제들은 새로운 비중과 중요성을 부여받았다.

그러한 미술의 연구는 학생들이 역사에서 자신의 위치에 대한 이해를 구축하는 것을 돕고 문화적으로 비하되고, 정치적으로 억압되고, 경제적으로 착취당한 사람들을 포함해 모든 인간의 능력과 역량을 강조함으로써 다문화적이고 사회적으로 활동적인 교육을 향상시킬 수 있다. 우리는 사회적이고 역사적인 분석의 틀 안에서 학교 안팎의 학생들 삶 사이의 중요한 연결을 강조하는 접근법을 옹호한다. 이 접근법은 학생들이 자신의 관점에서 말하도록 격려할 뿐만 아니라, 미술 연구와 종합된 방식으로 자신의 환경을 비판하고 사회 문제들에 맞서도록 격려한다.

174

하위내용영역	배점	예상정답률
일반영어 B형 서술형	4점	45%

모범답안 The words are "human condition". Second, it is because they have ignored the mental force of instinct.

채점기준

+ 2점: 빈칸에 들어갈 단어가 "human condition"임을 정확히 기입하였다. 이외에는 답이 될 수 없다.
+ 2점: 많은 사상가들이 인간의 본질이 무엇인지 파악하지 못한 이유를 "because they have ignored the mental force of instinct"라 서술하였거나 유사하였다.

한글번역

모든 방면에서 진보가 증가하고 있는데도 인간 개체 자체가 여전히 미스터리로 남아 있는 이유를 궁금해 본 적이 있는가? 지난 2,400년 동안 위대한 지성들이 인간을 해명하려고 열심히 노력해왔지만, 인간의 많은 측면들이 여전히 답이 없다.

이러한 답변 실패의 일부는 위대한 사상가들이 종종 인간의 특정 정신적 능력에 매혹돼 이 단일한 정신적 요소만으로 전체 존재를 이해하려고 했다는 사실에서 비롯된다. 물론 그 요소는 인간의 지성이다. 이것에 매혹돼, 많은 사람들이 지성보다 모든 수준에서 우리의 행동을 훨씬 더 강력하게 이끄는 또 다른 정신적 힘을 계속 무시하고 있다.

이 강력한 힘을 무시하는 것은 그들의 작업 대부분에 빠진 고리를 만들어냈고, 그것들을 오해의 소지가 없다면 결론이 없는 것으로 만든다. 따라서 인간의 수수께끼는 인간사의 많은 측면에서 계속 나타나고 있다. 하지만 이 빠진 고리를 정당한 위치에 복원하면 인간이 적나라하게 명확하고 이해하기 쉬워진다. 본능이 빠진 고리이고, 세 가지 유형(성적, 공격적, 모성 본능)이 보편적으로 인정되고 받아들여진다. 이러한 본능들의 올바른 취급은 인류를 정확히 이해하는 데 필수적이다.

우리가 이러한 정신적 힘의 특성과 임무를 배울 때, 이러한 힘들이 처음부터 어떻게 인간 조건을 만들어냈는지를 명확히 본다. 그리고 불변하는 이러한 정신적 요소들은 이 인간 조건을 영구적으로 굳어지게 했고, 인간이 지속적인 갈등을 겪는 이 기본적인 행동 양식에서 벗어날 수 없게 만들었다. 이것이 시간 속에 얼어붙은 많은 다른 인간 조건들 중 하나일 뿐이지만, 그것은 가장 심오한 방식으로 인간사의 다른 주요 측면들에 영향을 미친다. 예를 들어, 전쟁은 영구적이고 엄청나게 비용이 드는 인간 조건이 됨으로써 세계의 전체 경제를 형태로 만든다. 또한 경쟁의 궁극적 형태인 전쟁은 최첨단 과학과 기술을 요구한다. 이는 결국 인간의 두뇌력의 큰 측면을 이끌고 과학과 기술 진보의 거대한 부분에 방향을 크게 제시한다. 게다가 전쟁은 극도로 파괴적이어서, 많은 사람들의 사랑하는 이들의 생명을 폭력적으로 앗아가는 그러한 갈등에 노출된 사람들을 심리적으로 괴롭힌다. 그리고 인류를 이 바람직하지 않은 조건에 영구적으로 가둔 이러한 정신적 힘들을 인식하고 그것들을 보상하기 위한 필요한 조치를 취하는 것에서만 우리는 이 영구적인 순환에서 벗어나기를 희망할 수 있다.

2S2R

유희태 일반영어 ④-1 문제은행
● 모범답안 및 번역

초판 1쇄	2014년 4월 14일	
2판 1쇄	2016년 6월 15일	
3판 1쇄	2019년 2월 20일	
2쇄	2019년 5월 10일	
3쇄	2019년 7월 10일	
4판 1쇄	2020년 10월 23일	
2쇄	2021년 7월 30일	
3쇄	2022년 4월 15일	
5판 1쇄	2023년 1월 10일	
6판 1쇄	2026년 1월 15일	

저자와의
협의하에
인지생략

저자 유희태 **발행인** 박 용 **발행처** (주)박문각출판
표지디자인 박문각 디자인팀
등록 2015. 4. 29. 제2019-000137호
주소 06654 서울시 서초구 효령로 283 서경 B/D
팩스 (02) 584-2927
전화 교재 문의 (02) 6466-7202 동영상 문의 (02) 6466-7201

이 책의 무단 전재 또는 복제 행위는 저작권법 제136조에 의거, 5년 이하의 징역 또는 5,000만원 이하의 벌금에 처하거나 이를 병과할 수 있습니다.

정 가 25,000원(분권 포함)
ISBN 979-11-7519-526-4
ISBN 979-11-7519-524-0(세트)